Time has failed to erase the courage
and bravery, the terror and
torment endured by early
Protestant martyrs. Their stories
continue to inspire and inform.
Their faith has stood, and will
forever stand, as a beacon to
courageous action for the
generations who follow.

FOXE'S
BOOK OF MARTYRS

Edited by
MARIE GENTERT KING

SPIRE BOOKS

Fleming H. Revell Company • Old Tappan, N.J.

FOXE'S BOOK OF MARTYRS

A SPIRE BOOK
Published by Pyramid Publications for
Fleming H. Revell Company

Spire Books edition published February, 1968
    Ninth printing August, 1974

Printed in the United States of America

SPIRE BOOKS are published by Fleming H. Revell Company
Old Tappan, New Jersey 07675, U.S.A.

INTRODUCTION

HUMAN LIFE is a record of experience and of principles in action; but surely if we look to the past for its legacies of experimental wisdom, we cannot discover more practical lessons on truth and holiness than are to be found in the lives and deaths of those who have formed the noble army of Martyrs. The heathen philosopher thought that there was no sublimer sight for heaven or earth than a great man struggling with adversity; but there is a greater emphasis in this reflection if we apply it to the noble victory of the Christian Martyr over the assaults of the world, the flesh, and the devil. In him we behold a spirit upheld, not by the motives of vanity, self-sufficiency, or indifference, but by the simple power of truth; we witness a soul so under the influence of good, that evil, even in its most cruel form, cannot dim its beauty, but serves as a contrast to heighten its lustre. Here is self-sacrifice, springing not from pride, but from humility; founded not upon ignorant prejudice, but upon a faith based upon conviction; arising not from hatred or contempt for man, but from the love of God. Truly theirs was the victory that overcame the world, even their faith—a faith which, accepting the future as a true inheritance, enabled them to give up for Christ's sake houses and lands, children and relationships, yea, and their own lives also, rather than be false to their conscience and their God. The history of Christian Martyrdom is, in fact, the history of Christianity itself; for it is in the arena, at the stake, and in the dungeon that the religion of Christ has won its most glorious triumphs.

It only remains to be said that the greatest prominence will be given in this edition to those familiar names which are luminous in the roll of English Martyrology.

CONTENTS

THE LIFE OF THE
REV. JOHN FOXE,

Original Author of the "History of the Christian Martyrs."

JOHN FOXE was born at Boston, in Lincolnshire, of respectable parents, A.D. 1517. His father died soon after, and his mother married again. He lived under the paternal roof until the age of sixteen, when he was entered at Brasenose College, Oxford. In 1538 he took his degree of Bachelor of Arts, and that of Master in 1543. The same year he was elected Fellow of Magdalen College. While at the University, and for some time after, he was a zealous Papist, and led a life of strict morality. His researches into ecclesiastical writings, and those of the Fathers, and, above all, his study of the Holy Scriptures, at length convinced him of the errors of the Romish Church. With such zeal did he apply himself in prosecuting his inquiries, that before he was thirty years of age he had read over all the Greek and Latin Fathers, together with the acts of all the councils and the scholastic writings; and, besides, made himself master of Hebrew. He openly professed the Gospel, was publicly accused of heresy, and, being convicted, was soon after expelled from the University. His friends, and even his step-father, were afraid to countenance him. Oppressed and forsaken, he was in great need, when a patron was raised up for him in Sir Thomas Lucy, of Warwickshire. He became a tutor to his family, married a lady of Coventry, and continued in his service until the pupils were grown up. After some stay at Coventry he removed to London a few years before the death of Henry VIII. Being for some time in the capital without friends or money, he was reduced to extreme want. From this he was relieved in the following extraordinary manner:—Sitting one day in St. Paul's Church, and looking like a spectre, being almost starved to death, a stranger, whom he never remembered to have seen, sat down by him, and, putting a large sum of money into his hands, exhorted him to be of good courage, for God would in a few days give him more

certain means of subsistence. Foxe in vain endeavoured to
discover the name of this messenger of mercy; it remained
a mystery. However, the prophecy was fulfilled, for within
three days after the above remarkable occurrence he was
appointed by the Duchess of Richmond tutor to her
nephew, the Earl of Surrey's children—the earl being then
a prisoner in the Tower. He lived with them at Reigate, in
Surrey, during the latter part of Henry VIII's reign, the
reign of Edward VI, and part of Mary's. Gardiner's malice
was soon directed towards him, and Foxe would not have
escaped a violent end but for the protection of one of his
pupils, the then Duke of Norfolk. Finally, however, he felt
obliged to leave England, so bitter did Gardiner's persecution become. The Duke of Norfolk, failing to shake his
resolution, provided him with every comfort for his
voyage, and he set sail from Ipswich, with his wife and
several other refugees. The vessel had to put back on
account of a violent storm, and with great difficulty and
danger the passengers were landed. Foxe received information that Gardiner was seeking his life, and though the
tempest still raged, he persuaded the captain of the ship
once more to set sail. They arrived in two days at Nieu-
port, in Flanders; whence Foxe and his party travelled to
Antwerp and Frankfort, and at last reached Basle, in
Switzerland, where they found great numbers of Englishmen, who had been driven there by persecution. It was in
this city, famous for printing, that Foxe began his inestimable work on Martyrology. On Elizabeth's accession he
returned to England, and was hospitably entertained by the
Duke of Norfolk at the Manor, Christ Church, London,
until the duke's death, when he inherited a pension from
his noble benefactor. Nor did his good fortune end here.
Cecil recommended him to Elizabeth, who forced him to
accept the prebendary of Shipton, in the cathedral of
Salisbury. On his settlement at Salisbury he set himself to
revise and enlarge his admirable Martyrology. With prodigious pains and constant study he finished that celebrated
work in eleven years. For the sake of greater accuracy, he
never employed any amanuensis, but wrote every line of
this vast book with his own hand, and searched and
transcribed all the records and papers himself. But by such
excessive toil, leaving no part of his time free from study,
nor affording himself either the repose or recreation which
nature required, his health was so reduced, and his person
became so emaciated and altered, that such of his friends

and relations as only conversed with him occasionally could not recollect him at sight. Yet, though he grew daily more lean, withered, and exhausted, his hard studies went on as briskly as ever, nor would he be persuaded to lessen his accustomed labours. The papists, foreseeing how extremely detrimental his history of their errors and cruelties would prove to their cause, exerted their whole art and strength to lessen the reputation of his work. This malice of theirs was of signal service, both to Mr. Foxe himself and to the Church of God at large, as it eventually made his book more intrinsically valuable, by inducing him to weigh with the most scrupulous attention the certainty of the facts he recorded, and the validity of the authorities from whence he drew his information.

After a long life of usefulness and holiness, he resigned his soul to Christ on the 18th April, 1587. He had a forewarning of his approaching end, and was so fully persuaded it was near, that he sent his two sons from home to avoid causing them grief. Before they returned, as he had foreseen, his spirit had flown to heaven. He was interred in the chancel of St. Giles's, Cripplegate, of which parish he had been vicar for some time, in the reign of Elizabeth.

HISTORY

OF

CHRISTIAN MARTYRDOM

CHRIST, in the Gospel of St. Matthew (chap xvi.), hearing the confession of Simon Peter, who first openly acknowledged him to be the Son of God, and perceiving the secret hand of his Father therein, answered again; and alluding to his name, called him a rock, upon which rock he would build his Church so strong, that the gates of hell should not prevail against it. In these words three things are to be noted:—first, that Christ will have a Church in this world; secondly, that the same Church should be mightily impugned, not only by the world, but also by the powers of hell; and, thirdly, that the same Church, notwithstanding the efforts of the devil, should continue.

Account of the Lives, Sufferings, and Martyrdom of the Apostles and Evangelists.

ST. STEPHEN.—This early martyr was elected, with six others, as a deacon of the first Christian Church. He was also an able and successful preacher. The principal persons belonging to five Jewish synagogues entered into dispute with him; but he, by the soundness of his doctrine and the strength of his arguments, overcame them all, which so much irritated them, that they bribed false witnesses to accuse him of blaspheming God and Moses. On being carried before the council, he made a noble defence; but this so much exasperated his judges, that they resolved to condemn him. At the instant Stephen saw a vision from heaven, representing Jesus, in his glorified state, sitting at the right hand of God. This vision so enraptued him, that he exclaimed, "Behold, I see the heavens open, and the Son of Man standing on the right hand of God." This caused him to be condemned, and, having dragged him out of the city, they stoned him to death.

ST. ANDREW.—This apostle and martyr was the brother of St. Peter, and preached the Gospel to many Asiatic nations. On arriving at Edessa, the governor of the country, named Egeas, threatened him for preaching against the idols they worshipped. St. Andrew, persisting in the propagation of his doctrines, was ordered to be crucified, two ends of the cross being fixed transversely in the ground. He boldly told his accusers that he would not have preached the glory of the cross had he feared to die on it. And again, when they came to crucify him, he said that he coveted the cross, and longed to embrace it. He was fastened to the cross, not with nails, but cords, that his death might be more slow. In this situation he continued two days, preaching the greatest part of the time to the people, and expired on the 30th of November.

ST. PETER.—When Herod Agrippa caused St. James the Great to be put to death, and found that it pleased the Jews, he resolved, in order to ingratiate himself with the people, that Peter should be the next sacrifice. He was accordingly apprehended and thrown into prison; but an angel of the Lord released him, which so enraged Herod, that he ordered the sentinels who guarded the dungeon in which he had been confined to be put to death. St. Peter, after various miracles, retired to Rome, where he defeated the artifices and confounded the magic of Simon Magus, a great favourite of the Emperor Nero: he likewise converted to Christianity one of the minions of that monarch, which so exasperated the tyrant, that he ordered both St. Peter and St. Paul to be apprehended. During the time of their confinement, they converted two of the captains of the guard and forty-seven other persons to Christianity. Having been nine months in prison, Peter was brought from thence for execution, when, after being severely scourged, he was crucified with his head downwards; which position, however, was at his own request.

ST. PAUL.—This apostle and martyr was a Jew of the tribe of Benjamin, born at Tarsus in Cilicia. He was at first a great enemy to and persecutor of the Christians; but, after his miraculous conversion, he became a strenuous supporter of Christianity. At Iconium, St. Paul and St. Barnabas were near being stoned to death by the enraged Jews; on which they fled to Lycaonia. At Lystra, St. Paul was stoned, dragged out of the city, and left for dead. He, however, happily revived, and escaped to Derbe. At Philippi, Paul and Silas were imprisoned and whipped; and both were again persecuted at Thessalonica. Being afterwards taken at Jerusalem, he was sent to Caesarea, but appealed to Caesar at Rome. Here he continued a prisoner at large for two years; and at length, being released, he visited the churches of Greece and Rome, and preached in France and Spain. Returning to Rome, he was again apprehended, and, by the order of Nero, martyred, by beheading.

About the same time Saints James, Philip, Matthew, Mark, Matthias, Jude, Bartholomew, Thomas, and Luke the Evangelist also suffered martyrdom for the cause of Christ.

ST. JOHN.—He was distinguished as a prophet, an apostle, a divine, an evangelist, and a martyr. He is called the beloved disciple, and was brother to James the Great. He was previously a disciple of John the Baptist, and afterwards not only one of the twelve apostles, but one of the three to whom Christ communicated the most secret passages of His life. He founded churches at Smyrna, Pergamos, Sardis, Philadelphia, Laodicea, and Thyatira, to which he directs his Book of Revelation. Being at Ephesus, he was ordered by the Emperor Domitian to be sent bound to Rome, where he was condemned to be cast into a caldron of boiling oil. But here a miracle was wrought in his favour; the oil did him no injury, and Domitian, not being able to put him to death, banished him to Patmos, to labour in the mines, A.D. 73. He was, however, recalled by Nerva, who succeeded Domitian, but was deemed a martyr on account of his having undergone an execution, though it did not take effect. He was the only apostle who escaped a violent death, and lived the longest of any, he being nearly 100 years of age at the time of his death.

Account of the First Primitive Persecution
Beginning in the year 67, under the reign
of the Emperor Nero

The first persecution in the primitive ages of the Church was under Nero Domitius, the sixth Emperor of Rome, A.D. 67. This monarch reigned for the space of five years with tolerable credit to himself; but then gave way to the greatest extravagance of temper, and to the most atrocious barbarities. The barbarities inflicted on the Christians, during the first persecution, were such as excited the sympathy of even the Romans themselves. Nero nicely refined upon cruelty, and contrived all manner of punishments for his victims. He had some sewed up in the skins of wild beasts, and then worried by dogs till they expired; and others dressed in shirts made stiff with wax, fixed to axle-trees, and set on fire in his garden. This persecution was general throughout the Roman Empire; but it increased rather than diminished the spirit of Christianity. Besides St. Paul and St. Peter, many others, whose names have not been transmitted to posterity, and who were mostly their converts and followers, suffered.

Among other diabolical outrages, he ordered that the city of Rome should be set on fire, which was done by his officers. While the city was in flames, he went up to the tower of Maecenas, played upon his harp, sung the song of the burning of Troy, and declared that he wished the ruin of all things before his death. Among the noble buildings burnt was the Circus, the place appropriated to civic sports: it was half a mile in length, of an oval form, with rows of seats rising above each other, and capable of receiving with ease upwards of 100,000 spectators. This dreadful conflagration continued nine days.

Nero, finding that a severe odium was cast upon him, determined to charge the whole upon the Christians, at once to excuse himself and have an opportunity of fresh persecutions. But the savagery of this inhuman monster, so far from crushing out the faith which he hated, only tended, in God's good providence, to its extension. The charred ruins of the noble Circus, the bleeding bodies of the slaughtered Christians, the desolated city, when contrasted with the meek, inoffensive lives of those who suffered such tortures, and to whose account the tyrant dared to lay the destruction of that city, exercised an influence amongst the people in favour of Christianity.

Erastus, the chamberlain of Corinth; Aristarchus, the Macedonian; Trophimus, an Ephesian by birth, and a Gentile by religion, converted by St. Paul; Joseph, commonly called Barsabas, and usually deemed one of the seventy; and Ananias, Bishop of Damascus, are among those who perished during this persecution.

Account of the Second Primitive Persecution,
Under the Emperor Domitian.

The Emperor Domitian was naturally of a cruel disposition; he first slew his brother, and then raised a second persecution against the Christians. His rage was such, that he even put to death several Roman senators; some through malice, and others to confiscate their estates. He then commanded all the lineage of David to be sacrificed. Two Christians were brought before the emperor, and accused of being of the tribe of Judah, and line of David;

but from their answers, he despised them as idiots, and dismissed them accordingly. He, however, was determined to be more secure upon other occasions; and on this plea he took away the property of many Christians, put several to death, and banished others.

Among the numerous martyrs that suffered during this persecution was Simeon, Bishop of Jerusalem, who was crucified; and St. John, who was boiled in oil, and afterwards banished to Patmos. Flavia, the daughter of a Roman senator, was likewise banished to Pontus; and a cruel law was made, that no Christian, once brought before the tribunal, should be exempted from punishment without renouncing his religion.

During this reign there were various tales published in order to injure the Christians. Among other falsehoods, they were accused of indecent nightly meetings, of a rebellious spirit, of murdering their children, and even of being cannibals; and at this time, such was the infatuation of the pagans, that if famine, pestilence, or earthquakes afflicted any of the Roman provinces, it was charged on the Christians. These persecutions naturally multiplied the number of informers; and many, for the sake of gain, swore away the lives of the innocent. When any Christians were brought before the magistrates, a test was proposed, when, if they refused to take the oath, death was pronounced against them; and if they confessed themselves Christians, the sentence was the same. The various kinds of punishments and inflicted cruelties were, during this persecution, imprisonment, racking, searing, broiling, burning, scourging, stoning and hanging. Many were lacerated with red-hot pincers, and others were thrown upon the horns of wild bulls. After having suffered these cruelties, the friends of the deceased Christians were refused the privilege of burying their remains.

Amongst the most distinguished of the martyrs of this period was Timothy, the celebrated disciple of St. Paul, and Bishop of Ephesus.

St. Paul sent to Timothy to come to him in his last confinement at Rome; and after that great apostle's martyrdom, he returned to Ephesus, where he governed the church till nearly the close of the century. At this period the pagans were about to celebrate a feast, the principal ceremonies of which were, that the people should carry sticks in their hands, go masked, and bear about the streets the images of their gods. When Timothy met the procession, he severely reproved them for their idolatry, which so exasperated them, that they fell upon him with their clubs, and beat him in so dreadful a manner, that he expired two days after.

Account of the Third Primitive Persecution,
Under the Roman Emperors.

Only one year elapsed between the second and third Roman persecutions. Upon Nerva succeeding Domitian, he gave a respite to the Christians; but reigning only thirteen months, his successor, Trajan, in the tenth year of his reign, and in the year 108, began the third persecution against them. While this persecution raged, Plinius Secundus, a heathen philosopher, wrote to the emperor in favour of the Christians, to whose epistle Trajan returned this indecisive answer:—"That Christians ought not to be sought after, but when brought before the magistracy they should be punished." Provoked by this reply, Tertullian exclaimed in the following words: "Oh, confused sentence! he would not have them sought for as innocent men, and yet would have them punished as guilty." His officers were uncertain how to interpret the meaning of his decree. Trajan, however, soon after wrote to Jerusalem, and gave orders to exterminate the stock of David; in consequence of which, all that could be found of that race were put to death.

Trajan likewise commanded the martyrdom of Ignatius, Bishop of Antioch. This holy man received the Gospel from St. John the Evangelist, and was exceedingly zealous in his mission and ministry. He boldly vindicated the faith of Christ before the emperor, for which he was cast into prison, and was cruelly tormented; for, after being dreadfully scourged, he was compelled to hold fire in his hands, and, at the same time, papers dipped in oil were put to his sides and lighted. His flesh was then torn with hot pincers, and at last he was dispatched by the fury of wild beasts.

Ignatius had either presentiment or information of his fate; for writing to Polycarp, at Smyrna, he thus described his adventures: "From Syria, even till I came to Rome, had I battle with beasts, as well by sea as land, both day and night, being bound in the midst of a cruel legion of soldiers who, the more benefits they received at my hands, behaved so much the worse unto me. *And would to God I were once come to the beasts which are prepared for me;* which also I wish with gaping mouths were ready to come upon me, whom also I will provoke that they, without delay, may devour me. And if they will not, unless they be provoked, I will then enforce them against myself. Now begin I to be a scholar; I esteem no visible things, nor yet invisible things, so that I may get or obtain Christ Jesus. Let the fire, the gallows, the wild beasts, the breaking of bones, the pulling asunder of members, the bruising of my whole body, and the torments of the devil and hell itself come upon me, so that I may win Christ Jesus!"

Trajan was succeeded by Adrian, who continued the persecutions with the greatest rigour.

Account of the Fourth Primitive Persecution,
Under the Roman Emperors, which commenced A.D. *162*

Antoninus Pius was succeeded by Marcus Aurelius Antoninus Verus, who began the fourth persecution, in which many Christians were martyred, particularly in several parts of Asia and France. Such were the cruelties used in this persecution, that many of the spectators shuddered with horror at the sight, and were astonished at the intrepidity of the sufferers. Some of the martyrs were obliged to pass, with their already wounded feet, over thorns, nails and sharp shells, others were scourged till their sinews and veins lay bare; and after suffering most excruciating tortures, they were destroyed by the most terrible deaths.

Germanicus, a young Christian, being delivered to the beasts on account of his faith, behaved with such courage, that several pagans became converts to the faith which inspired such fortitude. This so enraged others, that they cried he merited death, as they did also of Polycarp, the venerable Bishop of Smyrna.

Polycarp, hearing that persons were seeking to apprehend him, escaped, but was discovered by a child. From this circumstance, and having dreamed that his bed suddenly became on fire, and was consumed in a moment, he concluded that it was God's will he should suffer martyrdom. He therefore did not attempt to make a second escape. Those who apprehended him were amazed at his serene countenance and gravity. After feasting them, he desired an hour for prayer, which being allowed, he prayed with such fervency, that his guards repented that they had been instrumental in taking him. He was, however, carried

before the pro-consul, condemned, and conducted to the
market-place. Wood being provided, the holy man earnestly prayed to Heaven, after being bound to the stake; and as
the flames grew vehement, the executioners gave way on
each side, the heat becoming intolerable. In the meantime
the bishop sang praises to God in the midst of the flames,
but remained unconsumed. Determined, however, to put
an end to his life, the guards struck spears into his body,
when the quantity of blood that issued from the wounds
extinguished the flames. After considerable attempts, they
put him to death, and burnt his body. Twelve other
Christians who had been intimate with Polycarp were soon
after martyred.

Justin, the celebrated philosopher, fell a martyr in this
persecution. He was a native of Neapolis, in Samaria, and
was born A.D. 103. About the year 133, when he was thirty
years of age, he became a convert to Christianity. Justin
wrote an elegant epistle to the Gentiles, to convert them to
the faith he had newly acquired, and lived in so pure and
innocent a manner, that he well deserved the title of a
Christian philosopher. He likewise employed his talents in
convincing the Jews of the truth of the Christian rites, and
spent much time in travelling, till he took up his abode in
Rome. He kept a public school, taught many who afterwards became great men, and wrote a treatise to confute
heresies of all kinds. As the pagans began to treat the
Christians with great severity, Justin wrote his first apology in their favour, and addressed it to the Emperor. This
piece, which occasioned the emperor to publish an edict in
favour of the Christians, displays great learning and genius.

A short time after, he entered into contests with Crescens, a celebrated cynic philosopher; and his arguments
appeared so powerful, yet disgusting, to the cynic, that he
resolved on his destruction. Justin's second apology upon
fresh severities gave Crescens an opportunity of prejudicing
the emperor against the writer of it; upon which Justin and
six of his companions were apprehended. Being commanded to deny their faith, and sacrifice to the pagan idols,
they refused to do either; they were, therefore, condemned
to be scourged and beheaded.

During this period the terrors of persecution raged in
France, particularly at Lyons, where the torture to which
many Christians were put almost exceeds description. Even
the servants and slaves of opulent Christians were racked

and tortured, to make them accuse their masters and employers.

At Lyons some of the martyrs were sewn up in nets, and thrown on the horns of wild bulls. Indeed, so far did the malice of the pagans proceed, that they set guards over the bodies, lest the friends of the deceased should get them by stealth.

Account of the Fifth General Persecution,
Under the Roman Emperors.

Severus became emperor, in the year 192. When he had been recovered from a severe fit of sickness by a Christian, he became a great favourer of Christians generally. But the prejudice and fury of the ignorant multitude again prevailed against them.

The pagans were alarmed at the progress of Christianity, and revived the calumny of placing incidental misfortunes to the account of its professors. Fire, sword, wild beasts, and imprisonments were resorted to, and even the dead bodies of Christians were torn from their graves, and submitted to every insult: yet the Gospel withstood the attacks of its barbarous enemies. Tertullian, who lived in this age, informs us, that if the Christians had collectively withdrawn themselves from the Roman territories, the empire would have been greatly depopulated.

Irenaeus, Bishop of Lyons, was born in Greece, and received a Christian education. It is generally supposed that the account of the persecution at Lyons was written by him. He succeeded the martyr Pothinus as Bishop of Lyons, and ruled his diocese with great propriety; he was a zealous opposer of heresies in general, and wrote a celebrated tract against heresy, which had great influence at the time. This zeal in favour of Christianity pointed him out as an object of resentment to the emperor; and he was accordingly beheaded in A.D. 202.

The persecutions about this time extended to Africa, and many were martyred in that part of the globe; the principal of whom was Perpetua, a married lady of about twenty-six years of age, with an infant child. She was seized for being a Christian. Her father, who tenderly loved her, went to console her during her confinement, and attempted to persuade her to renounce Christianity. Perpetua, however, resisted every entreaty. This resolution so much incensed her father, that he beat her severely, and did not visit her

for some days after; and, in the meantime, she and some
others who were confined were baptised, as they were
before only catechumens. On being carried before the
pro-consul Minutius, she was commanded to sacrifice to
the idols: refusing, she was ordered to a dark dungeon, and
deprived of her child. Her father at length paid her a
second visit, and again entreated her to renounce Christianity. His behaviour was now all tenderness and humanity;
but inflexible to all human influence, she knew she must
leave everything for Christ's sake; and she only said to
him, "God's will must be done."

Perpetua gave the strongest proof of fortitude and
strength of mind on her trial. The judge entreated her to
consider her father's tears, her infant's helplessness, and
her own life; but triumphing over all the sentiments of
nature, she forgot the thought of both mental and corporeal pain, and determined to sacrifice all the feelings of
human sensibility to that immortality offered by Christ. In
vain did they attempt to persuade her that their offers were
gentle, and her own religion otherwise. Being conducted
back to prison, she waited for execution, when several
other persons were to be executed with her; of these were
Felicitas, a married Christian lady.

Revocatus was a catechumen of Carthage, and a slave.
The names of the other prisoners who were to suffer upon
this occasion were Satur, Saturninus, and Secundulus.
When the day of execution arrived, they were led to the
amphitheatre. Satur, Saturninus, and Revocatus were ordered to run the gauntlet between the hunters, such as had
the care of the wild beasts. The hunters being drawn up in
two ranks, they ran between, and as they passed were
severely lashed. Felicitas and Perpetua were thrown to a
beast. The beast made his first attack upon Perpetua, and
stunned her; he then attacked Felicitas, and wounded her
much; but not killing them, the executioner did that office
with a sword. Revocatus and Satur were destroyed in the
same manner; Saturninus was beheaded; and Secundulus
died in prison. These executions took place in the month of
March, A.D. 205.

Account of the Sixth General Persecution,
Under the Roman Emperors.

About two hundred years had now passed since the
death of the founder of Christianity, and the same sublime-

ly moral spectacles continued to be exhibited. with that constancy and frequency to lead us to ascribe them to the power of God.

Maximus, who was emperor in A.D. 235, raised a persecution against the Christians; and in Cappadocia, the president Semiramus made great efforts to exterminate the Christians from the kingdom.

While this persecution continued, numerous Christians were slain without trial, and buried in indiscriminate heaps: sometimes fifty or sixty being cast into a pit together. Maximus died in A.D. 238; he was succeeded by Gordian, during whose reign, and that of his successor Philip, the Church was free from persecution for the space of more than ten years; but in the year 249 a violent persecution broke out in Alexandria. It is, however, worthy of remark, that this was done at the instigation of a pagan priest, without the emperor's knowledge. At this time the fury of the people being great against the Christians, they broke open their houses, stole the best of their property, destroyed the rest, and murdered the owners.

Account of the Seventh General Persecution,
Under the Roman Emperors.

In the year 249, Decius being Emperor of Rome, a dreadful persecution was begun against the Christians. This was occasioned partly by the hatred he bore to his predecessor Philip, who was deemed a Christian, and partly by his jealousy concerning the amazing progress of Christianity; for the heathen temples were almost forsaken, and the Christian churches crowded with proselytes. Decius, provoked at this, attempted, as he said, to extirpate the name of Christian; and, unfortunately for the cause of the Gospel, many errors had about this time crept into the Church: the Christians were at variance with each other, and a variety of contentions ensued among them. The heathens in general were ambitious to enforce the imperial decrees upon this occasion, and looked upon the murder of a Christian as a merit to be coveted. The martyrs were, therefore, innumerable.

Julian, a native of Cilicia, as we are informed by St. Chrysostom, was seized for being a Christian. He was tortured, but remained inflexible.

When all endeavours to make him recant his religion were found ineffectual, he was brought before a judge and whipped. He was then put into a leathern bag, with a number of serpents and scorpions, and in that condition thrown into the sea.

Origen, the celebrated presbyter and catechist of Alexandria, at the age of sixty-four was seized, thrown into a loathsome prison, loaded with chains, and his feet placed in the stocks for several days. He was threatened with fire, and tormented by every means. But his Christian fortitude sustained him. Such was the rigour of the judge, that his tortures were ordered to be as lingering as possible, that death might not too soon put a period to his miseries. During this cruel interval, the Emperor Decius died, and Gallus, who succeeded him, engaging in a war with the Goths, the Christians met with a respite. Thus Origen obtained his enlargement, and retiring to Tyre, he remained there till his death, which happened when he was in the sixty-ninth year of his age. Many interesting particulars have been preserved concerning this truly great and laborious man. We are informed by Eusebius that when his father Leonidas was martyred, Origen, then seventeen years old, would have suffered with his father, had not his mother, in the night, taken away his clothes. From this circumstance, and from shame rather than from fear, he was obliged to remain at home, but sent a message to his father, encouraging him in these words: "Take heed to yourself, that you turn not your thought and purpose for our sake."

After the death of Leonidas, the property of the family was confiscated to the emperor, and Origen was reduced to a state of abject poverty; his energy and piety, however, shone more brightly in adversity, and he supported himself, his mother, and six brothers, by keeping a school.

Account of the Eighth General Persecution,
Under the Roman Emperors.

After the death of Gallus, Aemilian, the general, having many enemies in the army, was slain, and Valerian elected to the empire. This emperor, for the space of four years, governed with moderation, and treated the Christians with peculiar lenity and respect; but in the year 257, an Egyptian magician, named Macriamus, gained a great ascendancy over him, and persuaded him to persecute the Christians. Edicts were accordingly published, and the

persecution, which began in the month of April, continued
for three years and six months.

Laurentius, generally called St. Laurence, the principal
of the deacons, who taught and preached under Sextus,
Bishop of Rome, followed him to the place of execution;
when Sextus predicted that he should meet him in heaven
three days after. Laurentius considered this as a certain in-
dication of his own approaching martyrdom, at his return
collected all the Christian poor, and distributed amongst
them the treasures of the Church which had been committed to his care. His conduct alarmed the persecutors,
who seized on him, and commanded him to give an immediate account to the emperor of the Church treasures.

Laurentius promised to satisfy them. Then with great
diligence he collected together a great number of aged,
helpless, and impotent poor, and repaired to the magistrate,
presenting them to him saying, "These are the true treasures of the Church."

Fancying the matter meant in ridicule, the governor
ordered him to be immediately scourged. He was beaten
with iron rods, set upon a wooden horse, and had his limbs
dislocated. He endured these tortures with such fortitude
and perseverance, that he was ordered to be fastened to a
large gridiron, with a slow fire under it, that his death
might be more tedious. But his astonishing constancy
during these trials, and his serenity of countenance under
such excruciating torments, gave the spectators so exalted
an idea of the dignity and truth of the Christian religion,
that many immediately became converts.

Having lain for some time upon the gridiron, the martyr
cheerfully lifted up his eyes to heaven, and with calmness
yielded his spirit to the Almighty. This happened August
10, A.D. 258.

Fourteen years before this period persecution raged in
Africa, and thousands received the crown of martyrdom,
among whom was Cyprian, Bishop of Carthage. He was
educated in his youth in the maxims of the heathen, and
having a considerable fortune, he lived in great splendour.
About the year 246, Coecilius, a Christian minister of
Carthage, became the instrument of Cyprian's conversion.

Before his baptism Cyprian studied the Scriptures with
care, and being struck with the excellence of the truths
they contained, he determined to practise the virtues they
recommended. After baptism he sold his estate, distributed
the money among the poor, dressed himself in plain attire,

and commenced a life of austerity and solitude. Soon after
he was made a presbyter; and being greatly admired for his
virtues and his works, on the death of Donatus, in A.D. 248,
he was elected Bishop of Carthage.

In the year 250 Cyprian was proscribed by the Emperor
Decius, and the cry of the pagans was, "Cyprian to the
lions!" The bishop, however, withdrew from the rage of the
populace, and his effects were confiscated. The rigour of
the persecution abating, he returned to Carthage, and did
everything in his power to expel false doctrines. A plague
breaking out at Carthage, was laid to the charge of the
Christians: and the magistrates began to persecute them
accordingly; this occasioned an epistle from them to Cyprian, in answer to which he vindicated the cause of
Christianity.

Cyprian was brought before the pro-consul Aspasius
Paternus, A.D. 257, when being commanded to conform to
the religion of the empire, he boldly made a confession of
his faith. This did not occasion his death, but an order was
made for his banishment to a little city on the Libyan Sea.
On the death of the pro-consul who banished him, he
returned to Carthage, but was soon after seized, and
carried before the new governor, who condemned him to
be beheaded; and on the 14th of September, A.D. 258, this
sentence was executed.

Perhaps one of the most dreadful events in the history of
martyrdom was that which took place at Utica, where 300
Christians were, by the orders of the pro-consul, placed
around a burning lime-kiln. They were commanded either
to sacrifice to Jupiter or to be thrown into the kiln.
Unanimously refusing, they bravely jumped into the pit,
and were suffocated immediately.

Account of the Ninth General Persecution,
Under the Roman Emperors.

In the year 274 the Emperor Aurelian commenced a
persecution against the Christians, but it was soon put a
stop to, by the emperor being murdered by his own
domestics, at Byzantium.

Diocletian mounting the imperial throne, A.D. 284, at
first showed great favour to the Christians. In the year 286
he associated Maximian with him in the empire; when Fe-
lician and Primus, two Christian brothers, were put to
death before any general persecution broke out.

A remarkable affair occurred in A.D. 286. A legion of soldiers, consisting of 6,666 men, contained none but Christians. This was called the Theban Legion, because the men had been raised in Thebais. About this time Maximian ordered a general sacrifice, at which the whole army were to assist; and he commanded that they should take oaths of allegiance, and swear, at the same time, to assist him in the extirpation of Christianity in Gaul. Terrified at these orders, each individual of the Theban Legion absolutely refused either to sacrifice or take the oaths prescribed. This so enraged Maximian, that he ordered every tenth man to be selected from the rest, and put to the sword. This cruel order having been put into execution, those who remained alive were still inflexible, when a second decimation took place, and every tenth man of those living were again put to the sword.

This second severity made no more impression than the first; the soldiers preserved their fortitude and their principles; but, by the advice of their officers, drew up a remonstrance to the emperor, in which they told him that they were his subjects and his soldiers, but could not, at the same time, forget the Almighty; that they received their pay from him, and their existence from God.

Such a declaration, it might be presumed, would have prevailed with the emperor, but it had a contrary effect; for, enraged at their perseverance and unanimity, he commanded that the whole legion should be put to death, which was accordingly executed by the other troops, who cut them to pieces with their swords. This barbarous transaction occurred on the 22nd of September, A.D. 286.

Alban was the first British martyr. This man was a pagan, but being of a humane disposition, he sheltered a Christian ecclesiastic, named Amphibalus, whom some officers were in pursuit of on account of his religion. The example and discourses of the refugee made a great impression on the mind of Alban; he longed to become a member of a religion which charmed him; the fugitive minister, happy in the opportunity, took great pains to instruct him, and, before his discovery, perfected Alban's conversion.

Alban now took a firm resolution to preserve the sentiments of a Christian, or to die the death of a martyr. The enemies of Amphibalus having intelligence of the place where he was secreted, came to the house of Alban to apprehend him. The noble host, desirous of protecting his

guest, changed clothes with him; and when the soldiers
came, offered himself up as the person for whom they were
seeking. Being carried before the governor, the deceit was
immediately discovered. The officer determined to wreak
his vengeance upon Alban and with this view he commanded him to sacrifice to the pagan deities. Alban declared that he would not comply and professed himself to
be a Christian. The governor ordered him to be scourged,
but he bore the punishment with great fortitude, and
seemed to acquire new resolution from his sufferings: he
was then beheaded. The venerable Bede states that upon
this occasion the executioner suddenly became a convert to
Christianity, and entreated permission either to die for
Alban or with him. Obtaining the latter request, they were
beheaded by a soldier, who voluntarily undertook the task.
This happened on the 22nd of June, A.D. 287, at Verulam.

Account of the Tenth General Persecution,
Under the Roman Emperors.

Galerius, the adopted son of Diocletian, stimulated by
his mother, a bigoted pagan, persuaded the emperor to
commence the persecution. It began on the 23rd of February, A.D. 303.

Among the most distinguished persons who forfeited
their lives during this persecution, was Sebastian, born at
Narbonne, in Gaul, instructed in Christianity at Milan, and
afterwards an officer of the Imperial Guard at Rome. He
remained a Christian in the midst of idolatry, unallured by
the splendour of a court, and untainted by evil examples
around him. He was informed against and betrayed.

On hearing the accusation, the emperor sent for Sebastian, and charged him with ingratitude in betraying the
confidence reposed in him, and being an enemy to the gods
of the empire. To this he answered that the greatest proof
he could give of his fidelity was praying to the only true
God for the health and prosperity of his person and
government. Incensed at this reply, the emperor ordered
him to be shot to death with arrows. A few Christians
attending the execution, in order to give his body burial,
perceived signs of life in him, and removing him, in a short
time effected his recovery. So soon as he was able to walk,
he placed himself in the emperor's way as he was going to
the temple. The appearance of a person supposed to be
dead astonished the emperor, nor did the words of the

martyr less surprise him, for he began to reprehend him for his prejudices against Christianity. Having overcome his surprise, he ordered Sebastian to be seized and beaten to death.

While Maximus, Governor of Cilicia, was at Tarsus, three Christians were brought before him. Tarachus, the eldest, was asked by Maximus what he was. The prisoner replied, "A Christian." This reply offending the governor, he again made the demand, and was answered in a similar manner. The governor then told him that he ought to sacrifice to the gods, as the only way to promotion, riches, and honours; and that the emperors themselves did what he recommended him to perform. Tarachus answered that avarice was a sin, and gold itself an idol as abominable as any other. As for promotion, he desired it not, as he could not in conscience accept of any place which would subject him to pay adoration to idols; and with regard to honours, he desired none greater than the honourable title of Christian. As to the emperors themselves, he added, that they were deceived in adoring idols, and misled by the devil himself. For this speech his jaws were broken. He was then scourged, loaded with chains, and thrown into a dungeon, to remain there till the trials of the other two prisoners.

Probus was then brought before Maximus, who asked his name. The prisoner answered, the most valuable name that he could boast of was that of a Christian. To this Maximus replied in the following words: "Your name of Christian will be of little service to you; be therefore guided by me; sacrifice to the gods, engage my friendship, and the favour of the emperor. Probus answered, that as he had relinquished a considerable fortune to become a soldier of Christ, it might appear evident that he neither cared for his friendship nor the favour of the emperor. Probus was then scourged; and Demetrius, the officer, observing to him how his blood flowed, advised him to comply; but his only answer was, that those severities were agreeable to him. After being scourged, suffering with as much intrepidity as before, and still repeating, "The more my body suffers and loses blood, the more my soul will grow vigorous, and be a gainer," he was committed to gaol, and his hands and feet were stretched on the stocks.

Andronicus was next brought up, when being asked the usual questions, he said, "I am a Christian, a native of Ephesus, and descended from one of the first families in that city." He was ordered to undergo punishments similar

to those of Tarachus and Probus, and then was remanded
to prison. Having been confined some days, the three
prisoners were brought before Maximus, who began to
reason with Tarachus, saying, that he was in hopes that
what had already passed must have caused a change in his
sentiments. Finding himself mistaken, he ordered him to be
tortured by various means: fire was placed in the palms of
his hands; he was hung up by his feet; a mixture of salt and
vinegar was poured into his nostrils: and in this state he
was remanded to his dungeon. Probus being called, and
asked if he would sacrifice, replied, "I come better prepared to die than before; for what I have already suffered
has only confirmed me in my resolution." Provoked at this
speech, the governor ordered him to be struck upon the
mouth for uttering blasphemy: his body was then seared
with hot irons; he was put to the rack, and scourged; his
head was shaved, and red-hot coals placed upon the crown;
and after all these tortures, he was remanded to prison.

When Andronicus was again brought before Maximus,
the latter attempted to deceive him, by pretending that
Tarachus and Probus had repented of their obstinacy, and
owned the gods of the empire. To this the prisoner answered, "I cannot believe that they have renounced their
hopes in our God, nor will I fall short of them in faith in
our common Saviour. Thus armed, I neither know your
gods nor your authority; fulfil your threats, employ every
cruel art in your power; I am prepared to bear it for the
sake of Christ." For this answer he was scourged, and his
wounds rubbed with salt.

These intrepid Christians were brought to a third examination, when they retained their constancy, were again
tortured, and at length ordered for execution. Being
brought to the amphitheatre, several beasts were let loose
upon them; but none of the animals, though hungry, would
touch them. The keeper then brought out a large bear that
had that day destroyed three men; but this creature, and a
fierce lioness, also refused to touch the Christians. Finding
the design of destroying them by the means of wild beasts
ineffectual, Maximus ordered them to be slain by a sword,
which was done on the 11th of October, A.D. 303.

The Emperor Diocletian becoming ill, in the year 304,
the persecution was carried on by Galerius, and the governors of the several provinces, when many fell victims to the
zeal or malice of the persecutors.

Theodotus, a Dalmatian, kept an inn at Ancyra. Being a

Christian, he devoted a great part of his time to visit the afflicted, and a great part of his property to relieve the poor. Theotecnus, governor of these parts, received the mandate for persecuting the Christians, and wrote the emperor word that he would root out Christianity from every place under his jurisdiction. Encouraged by the governor, the pagans began to inform against the Christians. Numbers were imprisoned, and their estates confiscated. Many fled to the woods or caves, where some supported themselves by roots, and others perished by famine. It was in these dreadful times Theodotus did all that he could to comfort the imprisoned. He assisted many with food; for having laid in a stock of food, he sold it at a low price, and often gave it away.

Polychronicus, a Christian, being seized, in order to preserve his life, informed against his friend Theodotus, who, hearing of this treachery, surrendered himself to the governor. When placed at the bar, the governor informed him that it was still in his power to save himself by sacrificing to the gods. Theodotus refused to renounce his faith, and treated their idols with contempt. The pagans on this were clamorous against him, and demanded that he should be punished. Theodotus was then scourged, torn with hooks, and then placed upon the rack. After this, vinegar was poured into his wounds, his flesh was seared with burning torches, and his teeth were knocked out. He was then remanded to prison; and as he went, he said to the people, "It is but just that Christians should suffer for Him who suffered for us all." Five days afterwards he was brought from prison, tortured, and then beheaded.

Timothy, a deacon of Mauritania, and Maura his wife, had not been married above three weeks, when they were separated from each other by the persecution. Timothy was carried before Arrianus, the governor of Thebais, who did all in his power to induce him to embrace the pagan superstition. Perceiving his endeavours vain, and knowing that Timothy had the keeping of the Scriptures, the governor commanded him to deliver them up, that they might be burnt: to which Timothy answered, "Had I children, I would sooner deliver them up to be sacrificed, than part from the Word of God." The governor, incensed at this reply, ordered his eyes to be put out with hot irons, saying, "The books shall at least be useless to you, for you shall not see to read them." He endured the punishment with such patience, that the governor was the more exasperated, and ordered him to be hung up by the feet, with a weight tied about his neck, and a gag in his mouth. This treatment he bore with the greatest courage, when some person acquainted the governor that he had been but newly married to a wife of whom he was extremely fond. Arrianus accordingly ordered Maura to be sent for, and promised a handsome reward, with the life of her husband, if she could prevail upon him to sacrifice to the idols. Maura, wavering in her faith, and impelled by affection for her husband, undertook the impious affair.

When conducted to him, she assailed his constancy with all the language of affection. When the gag was taken out of his mouth, he blamed her mistaken love, and declared his resolution of dying for the faith. Maura repeated her importunities, till her husband reproved her so strongly, that she returned to his way of thinking. The governor ordered her to be tortured, which was executed with great severity; and after this Timothy and Maura were crucified near each other, A.D. 304.

It now happened that, weary of the farce of state and public business, the Emperors Diocletian and Maximian resigned the imperial diadem, and were succeeded by Constantius and Galerius—the former a prince of the most humane disposition, and the latter remarkable for his tyranny and cruelty. These divided the empire into two equal governments, Galerius ruling in the east, and Constantius in the west.

As Galerius bore an implacable hatred to Christians, we are informed that "he not only condemned them to tortures, but to be burnt in slow fires."

Constantine the Great at length determined to redress the grievances of the Christians, for which purpose he raised an army of thirty thousand foot and eight thousand horse, with which he marched towards Rome, against Maxentius, the emperor. He therefore rejected the adoration of idols, and implored the assistance of the Almighty, who heard his prayers, and answered them in a manner so miraculous, that Eusebius acknowledges it could not have been credible, had he not received it from the emperor's own mouth. The narrative is as follows:—"The army arriving near Rome, the emperor was employed in devout ejaculations on the 27th of October, about three o'clock in the afternoon, when, the sun declining, there suddenly appeared to him a pillar of light in the heavens, in the form of a cross, with this plain inscription, (In this sign thou shalt conquer). Constantine was greatly surprised at the sight, which was visible to the whole army. At length Christ appeared to him in a vision, with the cross in his hand, commanding him to make it a royal standard, and cause it to be carried before his army, as an ensign both of victory and safety."

In the subsequent engagement with Maxentius, he defeated him, and entered the city of Rome in triumph. A law was now published in favour of the Christians.

After these events, the Romans were not only plagued by their emperors, but also by civil wars, three of which happened in two years at Rome, after the death of Nero.

The Persecution of the Christians in Persia.

The Gospel having spread itself into Persia, the priests became alarmed, and dreaded the loss of their influence over the public mind. They complained to the emperor that Christians were enemies to the State, and held a treasonable correspondence with the Romans, the great enemies of Persia. The emperor, being averse to Christianity, believed what was said against its disciples, and gave orders to persecute them throughout his empire.

Simeon, Archbishop of Seleucia, with many other ecclesiastics, to the number of 128, were apprehended and accused of having betrayed the affairs of Persia to the Romans. The emperor being exasperated, ordered Simeon to be brought before him. The archbishop in his presence boldly defended the cause of Christianity. The emperor, offended at his freedom, ordered him to kneel before him, as he had done in former interviews. To this Simeon answered, that being now brought before him a prisoner, for the truth of his religion, and the sake of his God, it was not lawful for him to kneel.

The emperor then ordered him to prison. A short time after, Simeon and his fellow-prisoners were commanded to worship the sun, agreeable to the Persian custom; but this they unanimously refused. The emperor then sentenced them to be beheaded, and the sentence was executed without delay.

An aged eunuch, named Usthazares, who had been tutor to the emperor, and was in great estimation at court, on observing Simeon proceeding to prison, saluted him. Simeon, however (as Usthazares had formerly been a Christian, and since apostatised to oblige the emperor), would not return his salute, but reproved him for his apostacy. This so affected the eunuch, that he burst into tears.

The emperor, learning that his ancient tutor was afflicted, asked him whether he desired anything which could be procured for him; to which the eunuch replied, that there was nothing that he wanted which this earth could afford; but that his grief was of another kind, and for which he justly mourned, namely, that to oblige him he had denied his God.

The emperor, offended at this explanation, ordered Usthazares to be beheaded. While going to execution, he desired that a messenger might be sent to the emperor, to request that it might be proclaimed that Usthazares did not die for any crime against the king or state, but only that, being a Christian, he would not deny his God. This petition was granted, and was a great satisfaction to Usthazares, whose chief reason for desiring it was, because his apostacy from Christ had caused many to follow his example; but now, hearing that he died for no crime but his religion, they might return to Christ.

On the Good Friday after his execution, an edict was published to put to death all who confessed themselves Christians, which caused the destruction of multitudes.

Acepsimus, and many other clergymen, were seized upon, and ordered to adore the sun; which refusing, they were scourged, and then tortured to death, or kept in prison till they expired. In short, by this edict, above 16,000 either suffered by torture or were barbarously executed.

Persecutions Under the Arian Ascendancy.

The Arian heresy had its origin from Arius, a native of Lybia, and a priest of Alexandria, who in A.D. 318, began to publish his errors. He was condemned by a council of the Lybian and Egyptian bishops, and the sentence was confirmed by the Council of Nice in A.D. 325. After the death of Constantine the Great, the Arians found means to ingratiate themselves into the favour of Constantius, his successor in the East; and hence a persecution was raised against the orthodox clergy. Athanasius, and other bishops, were banished, and their sees filled with Arians.

In Egypt and Lybia, thirty bishops were martyred. George, the first Arian Bishop of Alexandria, began a persecution in that city, which was continued some time with the utmost severity. If a man accused of being an orthodox Christian made his escape, his family were massacred, and his effects forfeited. By this means, being deprived of all places of public worship in Alexandria, the persecuted used to perform their devotions in a desert at some distance from it. On a Trinity Sunday, when they had met, Sebastian, a general, fell upon them with his soldiers, while they were at prayers; and several fell a sacrifice to the fury of the troops. The modes of cruelty were various, and the degrees equally diversified; for they were beaten on their faces till their features were disfigured, or were lashed with twigs of palm-trees with such violence, that they expired under the blows or by the mortification of the wounds.

At this time, being dissatisfied with the cruelties exercised upon the orthodox Christians in Alexandria, the persecutors applied to the emperor for an order to banish them from Egypt and Lybia, and to put their churches into possession of the Arians. A great number of the clergy were imprisoned for examination; when, it appearing that they adopted the opinions of Athanasius, an order was signed for their banishment. While the clergy were thus used, many of the laity were condemned to work in the quarries.

The Persecution Under Julian the Apostate.

Julian the Apostate was the son of Julius Constantius, and the nephew of Constantine the Great. His father sent him to Nicomedia, to be instructed in the Christian religion by Bishop Eusebius; but his principles were corrupted by the doctrines of Maximus, the magician, and Ecebolius, a professor of rhetoric.

Constantius died in the year 361, when Julian succeeded him; but he had no sooner attained the imperial dignity, than he renounced Christianity and embraced paganism. He recalled all banished pagans, allowed the free exercise of religion to every sect; but deprived all Christians of office at court, in the magistracy, or in the army. He was chaste, temperate, vigilant, laborious, and apparently pious; so that by his hypocrisy and pretended virtues he for a time did more mischief to Christianity than the most profligate of his predecessors; especially as he deprived the Christian clergy of the privileges which had been granted them by Constantine the Great.

Julian ordered that Christians might be treated coldly upon all occasions and in all parts of the empire, and employed persons to turn them and their principles into ridicule. Many were likewise martyred in his reign: for though he did not publicly persecute them himself, he connived at their being murdered by his governors and officers.

By his opposition to Arianism, Basil made himself famous, which brought upon him the vengeance of the Arian Bishop of Constantinople, who issued an order to prevent him from preaching. He continued, however, to perform his duty at Ancyra, till his enemies accused him of being a disturber of the public peace. The monarch, however, was too intent on an expedition to Persia to take notice of the accusation. Basil therefore continued to preach against paganism on the one hand, and Arianism on the other; and exhorted the people to serve Christ in the purity of faith and fervency of truth. By this conduct both heathens and Arians were exasperated against him.

One day meeting with a number of pagans going in procession to a sacrifice, he boldly expressed his abhorrence of the idolatrous proceedings. This liberty caused the people to seize him, and carry him before Saturninus, the governor, when they brought three accusations against him. Saturninus desired to know the sentiments of Basil from his own mouth and when, finding him a strenuous Christian, he ordered him to be put to the rack. The governor wrote an account of his proceedings to the emperor. Julian, on receiving the letter, sent Pagosus and Elipidius, two apostates, to Basil, to employ both promises and threatenings to constrain him to renounce his faith; and in case of their failure, they had orders to surrender him to the governor. The emperor's agents tampered with Basil in vain by means of promises, threatenings, and the rack: he was firm in his faith, and remained in prison when the emperor by accident came to Ancyra. The two agents then gave the emperor an account of what Basil had suffered, and of his resistance. Julian on this determined to examine the sufferer himself, when that holy man being brought before him, the emperor did everything in his power to dissuade him from the faith. Basil, however, not only continued firm, but with a prophetic spirit foretold the death of the emperor, and that he might be tormented in the other world. Julian then lost his usual clemency, and told Basil, in anger, that though he had an inclination to pardon him, he had put it out of his power by the insolence of his behaviour. He then commanded that the body of Basil should be torn every day in seven different parts, till his skin and flesh were entirely mangled. The inhuman sentence was executed with rigour, and the martyr expired on the 28th of June, A.D. 362.

Cassian, a schoolmaster of Imola, in the province of Romagno, for refusing to sacrifice to the idols, was taken before a judge; who, being apprised of his profession, and informed that many of the boys had an aversion to him on account of the strictness with which he kept them to their studies, determined they should have permission to murder him. He was accordingly delivered to the boys, with his hands tied behind him, who fell upon him with rods, whips, and steel pencils, which were then used in writing, and at length murdered him. This singular martyrdom happened on the 13th of August, A.D. 362.

About the end of the year 363 the persecution raged with more than usual violence. In Palestine many were burnt alive, others were dragged by their feet through the streets till they expired; some were scalded to death, many stoned, and great numbers had their brains beaten out with clubs. In Alexandria innumerable martyrs suffered by the sword, burning, crucifixion, and stoning.

Theodorus, for singing the praises of God, was apprehended and put to the rack, though not to death. After being taken down, he was asked how he could so patiently endure such tortures; to which he returned this remarkable reply: "At first I felt some pain, but afterwards there appeared to stand by me a young man, who wiped the sweat from my face, and frequently refreshed me with cold water, which so delighted me, that I regretted being let down."

When Julian formed an expedition against the Persians, he imposed a large fine upon every one who refused to sacrifice to the idols, and by that means gained a great sum from the Christians towards defraying the expense. Many of the officers, in collecting these fines, exacted more than was due, and some of them tortured the Christians to make them pay what they demanded, telling them in derision, that when they were injured they ought to take it patiently, for so their God commanded them.

Julian died of a wound which he received in his Persian expedition, A.D. 363, and even while expiring he uttered the most horrid blasphemies. He was succeeded by Jovian, who restored peace to the Church. After the decease of Jovian, Valentinian succeeded to the empire, and associated with himself Valens, who had the command in the East. The latter was a great favourer of Arianism, and so incensed against the Christians, that on a certain day he ordered all in Edessa to be slain while they were at their devotions in the churches. The officers, however, being more compassionate than the emperor, privately gave notice to the Christians not to assemble on the day appointed, so that they might escape death.

The Christians thanked the officers for their advice, but disregarded both that and the emperor's menaces, rather than neglect their duty.

Upon this the officers returned to the emperor, and telling him that the Christians were prepared to die in defence of their faith, represented to him the rashness of murdering so great a multitude, and entreated him to abandon the design at least for the present. He reluctantly complied with the humane advice.

Urbanus, Menidemus, and Theodorus, with eighty other orthodox clergymen in the neighbourhood of Constantinople, petitioned the emperor to relieve them from the oppressions and cruelties of the Arians. But the tyrant, instead of redressing their grievances, ordered them all to be embarked in a ship, and the vessel to be set on fire. This infernal order being executed, they perished in the flames.

The Persecutions of the Christians Under the Arian Vandals.

The pagan hordes which had poured from the north of Europe had become converts to Christianity, but, unhappily, to a spurious form, refusing to acknowledge the real Divinity of Jesus, the Messiah of the Old Testament prophecies. Intolerance was speedily proved to be the handmaid of error.

The Arian Vandals, commanded by Genseric, proceeded from Spain to Africa in the fifth century, and committed many cruelties. They persecuted the Christians wherever they went, and laid waste the country as they passed, in order that those who had escaped might perish from hunger. They plundered the churches, and murdered the bishops and ministers by a variety of cruel devices. They also wreaked their vengeance on several of the nobility, whom they loaded with heavy burdens, and obliged them to carry their baggage; and if they did not travel fast enough, they goaded them with sharp weapons, so that several died under their burdens. Stately buildings were burned or destroyed, and the chief churches in Carthage were perverted to heretical worship, or put to profane uses; and where any castles held out against them, they brought great numbers of Christians and slew them, leaving their bodies under the walls, that the besieged might be forced to surrender by means of the offensive stench which arose from them. When they had seized and plundered the city of Carthage, they put the bishop and all the clergy into a leaky ship, and committed it to the mercy of the waves, thinking that they must all perish; but the vessel, through Divine Providence, arrived safe at Naples.

Genseric, after having made an expedition into Italy, and plundered the city of Rome, returned to Africa, flushed with the success of his arms; and the Arians took this occasion to persuade him to persecute the orthodox Christians.

Cyrilla, the Arian Bishop of Carthage, was a furious persecutor and a determined enemy to those Christians who professed the faith in its purity. He persuaded the king that he could never prosper in his undertakings, or enjoy his kingdom in peace, while he suffered any of the orthodox Christians to practise their principles; and the monarch, believing the prediction, sent for several of the most eminent Christians. He at first attempted to draw them from their faith by flattery, and to bribe them by the promise of immediate worldly rewards; but they were firm and constant, declaring resolutely, "We acknowledge but one Lord and one faith; you may therefore do whatever you please with our bodies, for it is better that we should suffer a few temporary pains than to endure everlasting misery." The king, being greatly exasperated at this remark, sent them to a dungeon, and ordered them to be put in irons. The keeper, however, suffered their friends to have access to them, by which they became daily more confirmed in their resolution of dying for the sake of their Redeemer.

The king hearing of the indulgence they received, was exceedingly angry, and ordered these Christians to be put on board a vessel filled with combustible materials, and set on fire. The names of those who suffered by this cruel expedient were Rusticus, Severus, Liberatus, Rogatus, Servus, Septimus, and Boniface.

The Persecution from the Middle of the Fifth to the
Conclusion of the Seventh Century.

Hermengildus, a Gothic prince, was the eldest son of
Leovigildus, King of the Goths, in Spain. This prince, who
was originally an Arian, became a convert to the faith by
means of his wife Ingonda. The king, on hearing that his
son had changed his religion, deprived him of the command at Seville, where he was governor, and threatened to
put him to death unless he renounced the new faith. On
this the prince, in order to prevent the execution of his
father's menaces, began to prepare for defence, and many
of the orthodox persuasion in Spain declared on his side.
Exasperated at this act of rebellion, the king began to
punish all the orthodox Christians who could be seized,
and thus originated a severe persecution. He marched
against his son, who, knowing that he could not oppose the
force that his father was bringing against him, implored the
assistance of the Roman troops left to garrison those parts
of Spain which the emperor still possessed.

The Roman commander undertook to assist Hermengildus; but, being bribed by the king, he broke his promise.
Finding himself forsaken by those in whom he confided,
the prince was obliged to retreat towards Seville. The king
proceeded to Seville and laid siege to it. The prince
defended the place with great bravery, and held out for
twelve months; but finding that it must be taken, he made
his escape, and fled to Asseto, which he fortified for his
defence. The king pursued his son, laid siege to Asseto, and
soon obliged it to surrender. The king took his son, loaded
him with chains and carried him to Seville, where he
endeavoured, by promises and menaces, to make him
renounce the Christian faith. Nevertheless, the prince remained true, and at Easter, when the king sent an Arian
bishop to him to administer the eucharist, Hermengildus
refused to receive it, which so enraged the king, that he
ordered his guards to cut him to pieces.

John, Bishop of Bergamo, in Lombardy, did his utmost
to clear the Church from the errors of Arianism, and
joining with John, Bishop of Milan, he was very successful
against the heretics. He exerted himself strenuously to
prevent the heresy from spreading, on which account he
was assassinated on the 11th of July, A.D. 683.

A name remarkable in the roll of martyrs is now
brought before our notice; it is that of Kilien. He was born
in Ireland, and received from his parents a pious and

Christian education. In the course of time he crossed the
sea, with eleven other persons, in order to make converts
on the Continent. On landing, they directed their route to
the circle of Franconia, in Germany. Although upon arriving at the city of Wurtzburg, they found the people in
general, with their governor Gozbert, to be pagans, the
greater part of them became Christians in less than two
years.

Gozbert had married his brother's widow; but Kilien,
though he held the sinfulness of the thing, did not consider
it wise to rebuke him till he was confirmed in his faith.
When he deemed him established in the truth, he entreated
him, as the proof of his sincerity, to quit the person whom
he had looked upon as a wife, as he could not retain with
her without sin. Gozbert, surprised at the proposal, told the
bishop this was the hardest test he had ever exacted from
him. "But," said he, "since I have renounced my own
inclinations and pleasures in so many particulars for the
love of God, I will make the work complete by complying
with your advice in this too." His wife, however, determined to be revenged on those who had persuaded Gozbert
to adopt such a resolution. She accordingly sent to the
place where they assembled, and had them all beheaded.
Kilien and his companions submitted without resistance,
the former telling them that they need not fear those who
had no power over the soul. This happened A.D. 689, and
the martyrs were privately buried in the night, together
with their books, clothes, and all that they had.

The Persecutions of the Waldenses in France.

Before this time the Church of Christ was more than
tainted with the errors of popery, and superstition began to
predominate; but a few, who perceived the pernicious
tendency of such errors, determined to preserve the light of
the Gospel in its purity and splendour. The principal of
these worthies was Berengarius, who, about the year 1000,
boldly preached evangelical truth according to its primitive
simplicity. Many from conviction embraced his doctrine,
and were on that account termed Berengarians. Berengarius was succeeded by Peter Bruis, who preached at Toulouse, under the protection of the Earl Hildephonsus; and
the tenets of the reformers, with the reasons of their
separation from the Church of Rome, were published in a
book written by Bruis, under the title of "Antichrist."

In the year 1140 the number of the reformed was so

great, that the probability of their increasing alarmed the
pope, who wrote to several princes to banish them from
their dominions, and employed learned men to write
against them. In 1147, Henry of Toulouse became their
most eminent preacher and because of this they were called
Henricians; and as they would not admit of any proofs
relative to religion but what could be deduced from the
Scriptures, the popish party gave them the name of Apos-
tolics. Peter Waldo, a native of Lyons, at this time became
a strenuous opposer of popery; and from him the reformed
received the appellation of Waldoys, or Waldenses. Waldo
was a man eminent for learning and benevolence; his
doctrines were very generally admired, and he was followed by multitudes of all classes. The Bishop of Lyons
taking umbrage at the freedom with which he treated the
pope and the Romish clergy, sent to admonish him to
refrain in future from such discourses; but Waldo answered that he could not be silent in a cause of such
importance as the salvation of men's souls, wherein he
must obey God rather than man. When Pope Alexander III
was informed of these transactions, he excommunicated
Waldo and his adherents, and commanded the Bishop of
Lyons to exterminate them. Thus began the papal persecutions against the Waldenses.

Waldo remained three years undiscovered in Lyons,
though the utmost diligence was used to apprehend him,
but at length he found an opportunity of escaping from the
place of his concealment to the mountains of Dauphiny.
He soon after found means to propagate his doctrines in
Dauphiny and Picardy, which so exasperated Philip, King
of France, that he put the latter province, which contained
most of his followers, under military execution; destroying
above 300 gentlemen's seats, erasing some walled towns,
burning many of the reformed, and driving others into
Normandy and Germany.

Notwithstanding these persecutions, the reformed religion continued to flourish, and the Waldenses, in various
parts, became more numerous than ever. The pope, incensed at their increase, used all manner of arts for their
extirpation; by which they were rendered incapable of
holding places of trust, honour, or profit; their lands were
seized, their goods confiscated, and they were not permitted
to be buried in consecrated ground. Some of the Waldenses
having taken refuge in Spain, Aldephonsus, King of Arragon, at the instigation of the pope, published an edict,

strictly ordering all Roman Catholics to persecute them wherever they could be found; and decreeing that all who gave them the least assistance should be deemed traitors.

Peter Waldo continued to preach boldly against the Church of Rome. These proceedings of Waldo and his reformed companions occasioned the origin of the Inquisition; for Pope Innocent III elected certain monks inquisitors, to find and deliver over the reformed to the secular power. The monks, upon the least surmise or information, delivered over the reformed to the magistrate, and the magistrate delivered them to the executioner; for the process was short, as an accusation was deemed adequate to guilt, and a fair trial was never granted to the accused.

When the pope found that these cruel means had not the desired effect, he determined to try others of a more mild nature; he therefore sent several learned monks to preach among the Waldenses, and induce them to change their opinions. Among these was one Dominic, who was extremely zealous in the cause of popery. He instituted an order, which from him was called the order of Dominican friars; and the members of this order have ever since been principal agents in the various inquisitions of the world. The power of the inquisitors was unlimited; they proceeded against whom they pleased, without consideration of age, sex, or rank. If the accusers were ever so infamous, the accusation was deemed valid; and even anonymous informations sent by letter were thought sufficient evidence. To be rich was a crime equal to heresy; therefore many who had money were accused of it, or of being favourers of heretics. The dearest friends and kindred could not, without danger, serve any one who was imprisoned on account of religion: to convey to those who were confined a little straw, or give them a cup of water, was called favouring the heretics: no lawyer dared to plead even for his own brother, or to note or register anything in favour of the reformed. The malice of the papists, indeed, went beyond the grave, and the bones of many Waldenses who had been long dead were dug up and burnt. If a man on his death-bed were accused of being a follower of Waldo, his estates were confiscated, and the heir defrauded of his inheritance; and some were even obliged to make pilgrimages to the Holy Land, while the Dominicans took possession of their houses and properties, and when the owners returned would often pretend not to know them.

In the year 1380 a monk inquisitor, named Francis

Boralli, had a commission granted him by Pope Clement VII. to search for and punish the Waldenses in Aix, Ambrone, Geneva, Savoy, Orange, Arles, Vienna, Venice, and Avignon. He went to Ambrone, and summoned all the inhabitants to appear before him, when those who were found to be of the reformed religion were delivered over to the secular power and burnt, and those who did not appear were excommunicated for contumacy, and had their effects confiscated. In the distribution of these effects, the clergy had the lion's share—more than two-thirds of every man's property who was condemned—and the secular power less than one-third, and sometimes next to nothing. All the reformed inhabitants of the other places named in the commission of this ecclesiastic were equal sufferers.

In the year 1400 the Waldenses who resided in the valley of Pragela were, at the instigation of some priests, suddenly attacked by a body of troops, who plundered their houses, murdered the inhabitants, or drove them to the Alps, where great numbers were frozen to death, it being in the depth of winter. In 1460 a persecution was carried on in Dauphiny against the same people, by the Archbishop of Ambrone, who employed a monk, named John Vayleti; and this monk proceeded with such violence, that not only the Waldenses, but even many papists were sufferers: for if any of them expressed compassion or pity for the unoffending people, who were so cruelly treated, they were sure to be accused of partiality to heretics, and to share their fate. At length Vayleti's proceedings became so intolerable, that a great number of the papist themselves signed a petition against him to Louis XI, King of France, who granted the request of the petitioners, and sent an order to the governor of Dauphiny to stop the persecution. Vayleti, however, by order of the archbishop, still continued it; for taking advantage of the last clause of the edict, he pretended that he did nothing contrary to the king's precept, who had ordered punishment to such as affirmed anything against the holy catholic faith. This persecution at length concluded with the death of the archbishop, which happened in 1487.

Pope Innocent VIII in 1488, determined to persecute the Waldenses. To this end he sent Albert de Capitaneis, Archdeacon of Cremona, to France; who, on arriving in Dauphiny, craved the assistance of the king's lieutenant to exterminate them from the valley of Loyse. The lieutenant readily granted his assistance, and marched a body of troops to the place; but when they arrived in the valley, they found that it had been deserted by the inhabitants, who had retired to the mountains, and hid themselves in dens and caves of the earth. The archdeacon and lieutenant immediately followed them with their troops, and catching many, cast them headlong from precipices, by which they were dashed to pieces. Several, however, retired to the innermost parts of the caverns, and knowing the intricacies, were able to conceal themselves. The archdeacon and lieutenant not being capable of finding them, ordered the mouths of the caves to be filled with faggots, which being lighted, those within were suffocated.

When Louis XII came to the crown in 1598, the Waldenses petitioned him for a restitution of their properties. The king determined to have the affair impartially canvassed, and sent a commissioner of his own, together with a commissary from the pope, to make the proper inquiries. Witnesses against the Waldenses having been examined, the innocence of those poor people evidently appeared, and the king's commissioner therefore declared that he only desired to be as good a Christian as the worst of them. This favourable report being made to the king, he immediately gave orders that the Waldenses should have their property restored to them. The Archbishop of Ambrone, having the greatest quantity of their goods, protested that he would not restore any of the property, for it was incorporated and become part of his archbishopric. He, however, with an affection of candour, offered to relinquish several vineyards, of which he had dispossessed the sufferers, provided the lords of Dauphiny would restore all they had taken from them; but this the lords absolutely refused, being as fond of keeping their plunder as the archbishop himself.

The Waldenses finding that they were not likely to recover any of their property, again appealed to the king; and the monarch having attended to their complaints, wrote to the archbishop, who replied, "That at the commencement of the persecution the Waldenses had been excommunicated by the pope, in consequence of which their goods were distrained; therefore, till the sentence of excommunication was taken off, which had occasioned them to be seized, they could not be restored with propriety."

At length the Waldenses, having spread from Dauphiny into several other parts, became very numerous in Provence. At their first arrival Provence was almost a desert, but by their great industry it soon abounded with corn, wine, oil and fruit. The pope, by being often near them at his seat at Avignon, heard occasionally many things concerning their differences with the Church of Rome, which greatly exasperated him, and he determined to persecute them on this ground with severity. Proceeding to extremities, under the sanction of ecclesiastical authority only, without consulting the King of France, the latter became alarmed, and sent his master of requests and his confessor to examine the affair. On their return they reported that the Waldenses were not such dangerous people as they had been represented; that they lived with perfect honesty, caused their children to be baptised, had them taught the Lord's Prayer, Creed, and Ten Commandments, kept the Lord's day sacred, feared God, honoured the king, and wished well to the State.

"Then," said the king, "they are much better Christians than myself or my catholic subjects, and, therefore, they shall not be persecuted." The king was as good as his word, and sent orders to stop the persecution.

Some time after the inhabitants of Merindol received a summons, that the heads of the families of that town should appear before the ecclesiastical court. When they appeared and confessed themselves Waldenses, they were ordered to be burnt, their families outlawed, their habitations laid waste, and the woods that surrounded the town cut down two hundred paces square, so that the whole should be rendered desolate.

The president of Opede sent several companies of soldiers to burn some villages occupied by Protestants; this commission they too faithfully executed, exceeding it by a brutal treatment of the inhabitants, in which neither infancy, age, nor sex was spared. He next marched against Cabrieres, and began to cannonade it At this time there were not above sixty poor peasants with their families in the town; and they sent him word that he need not expend powder and shot upon the place, as they were willing to open the gates and surrender, provided they might be permitted to retire unmolested to Geneva or Germany. This was promised them; but the gates were no sooner opened, than the president ordered all the men to be cut to pieces, which cruel command was immediately executed. Several women and children were driven into a large barn, which was set on fire, and every one perished in the flames.

Other women and children having taken refuge in a church, the president ordered one of his officers to go and kill them all: the captain at first refused, saying, "Unnecessary cruelty is unbecoming a military man." The president, displeased at his reply, said, "I charge you, on pain of being accused of mutiny, immediately to obey my orders"; when the captain, afraid of the consequences, thought proper to comply. The president then sent a detachment of his troops to ravage the town of Costa, which was done with the greatest barbarity.

At length the judgment of God overtook this monster of cruelty; he was afflicted with a dreadful and most painful disease and expired in dreadful agony.

The Persecutions of the Albigenses.

The Albigenses were a people of the reformed religion, who inhabited the country of Albi. They were condemned on account of religion in the Council of Lateran, by order of Pope Alexander III, but they increased so rapidly, that many cities were inhabited exclusively by persons of their persuasion, and several eminent noblemen embraced their doctrines. Among the latter were two distinguished noblemen of the name of Raymond, Earls of Toulouse and Foix.

A friar, named Peter, having been murdered in the dominions of the Earl of Toulouse, the pope made the murder a pretence to persecute that nobleman and his subjects. He sent agents throughout Europe, to raise forces to act coercively against the Albigenses, and promised paradise to all who would enter this war, which he termed a holy war, and bear arms for forty days. The same indulgence was held out to all who entered for this purpose as to such as engaged in crusades to the Holy Land. He also sent orders to all archbishops and bishops to excommunicate the Earl of Toulouse every Sabbath and festival; at the same time absolving all his subjects from their oaths of allegiance, and commanding them to pursue his person, possess his land, destroy his property, and murder such of his subjects as continued faithful. The earl hearing of these mighty preparations against him, wrote to the pope in a very candid manner, desiring not to be condemned unheard, and assuring him that he had not the least hand in Peter's death. But the pope, being determined on his destruction, was resolved not to hear his defence: and a formidable army, with several noblemen and prelates at the

head of it, began their march against the Albigenses. The
earl had only the alternative to oppose force by force, or
submit: and he determined on the latter. The pope's legate
being at Valence, the earl repaired thither, and said he was
surprised that such a number of armed men should be sent
against him, before the least proof of his guilt had been
produced. He therefore came voluntarily to surrender
himself, armed with the testimony of a good conscience,
and hoped that the troops would be prevented from plundering his innocent subjects. The legate replied that he was
very glad that the earl had voluntarily surrendered; but,
with respect to the proposal, he could not pretend to
countermand the orders to the troops, unless he would
consent to deliver up seven of his best fortified castles as
securities for his future behaviour. At this demand the earl
perceived his error in submitting, but it was too late; he
knew himself to be a prisoner, and therefore sent authority
for the surrender of the castles. The pope's legate had no
sooner garrisoned these places, than he ordered the respective governors to appear before him. When they came, he
said that the Earl of Toulouse having delivered up his
castles to the pope, they must consider that they were now
the pope's subjects, and not the earl's; and that they must
therefore act conformably to their new allegiance. The
governors were astonished to see their lord thus in captivity, and themselves compelled into a new allegiance. But
what afflicted them still more were the affronts afterwards
put upon the earl; for he was stripped, led nine times round
the grave of Friar Peter, and severely scourged. They also
obliged him to swear that he would be obedient to the pope
during the remainder of his life, conform to the Church of
Rome, and make irreconcilable war against the Albigenses.
The legate even ordered him, by the oaths he had newly
taken, to join the troops, and inspect the siege of
Bezieres. The army proceeded to besiege Bezieres; and
the Earl of Bezieres, who was governor of that city,
thinking it impossible to defend the place, came out, and
presenting himself before the pope's legate, implored mercy
for the inhabitants; intimating that there were as many
Roman Catholics as Albigenses in the city. The legate
replied, that all excuses were useless; that the place must be
delivered up at discretion, or the most dreadful consequences would ensue.

The Earl of Bezieres returning to the city, told the
inhabitants he could obtain no mercy, unless the Albigenses

would abjure their religion and conform to the worship of the Church of Rome. The Roman Catholics pressed the Albigenses to comply with this request; but the Albigenses nobly answered, that they would not forsake their religion for the base price of a frail life: that God was able, if he pleased, to defend them; but if he would be glorified by the confession of their faith unto death, it would be a great honour to them to die for his sake. They added, that they had rather displease the pope, who could but kill their bodies, than God, who could cast both body and soul into hell. On this their enemies, finding importunity ineffectual, sent their bishop to the pope's legate, beseeching him not to include them in the chastisement of the Albigenses, and representing that the best means to win the latter over to the Roman Catholic persuasion was by gentleness, and not by rigour. Upon hearing this the legate flew into a violent passion with the bishop, and declared that if all the city did not acknowledge their fault, they should taste of one curse, without distinction of religion, sex, or age. The inhabitants refusing to yield upon such terms, a general assault was made, and the place taken by storm, when every cruelty that barbarous superstition could devise was practised. The city being fired in various parts, new scenes of confusion arose: in several places the streets were streaming with blood. Those who hid themselves in their dwellings had only the dreadful alternative to remain and perish in the flames, or rush out and fall by the swords of the soldiers. The bloody legate cried out to the troops, "Kill them! kill them all! kill man, woman, and child! kill Roman Catholics as well as Albigenses! for when they are dead, the Lord knows how to select his own." Thus the beautiful city of Bezieres was reduced to a heap of ruins; and 60,000 persons of different ages and both sexes were murdered.

The Earl of Bezieres and a few others made their escape, and went to Carcasson, which they endeavoured to put into the best posture of defence. The legate, not willing to lose an opportunity of shedding blood during the forty days which the troops were to serve, led them immediately against Carcasson. As soon as the place was invested, a furious assault was made, but the besiegers were repulsed. Two miles from Carcasson was a small town of the same name, which the Albigenses had likewise fortified. The legate being enraged at the repulse he had received from the city, determined to wreak his vengeance upon the town: the next morning he made a general assault; and, though the place was bravely defended, the legate took it by storm, and put all within it to the sword.

During these events the King of Arragon arrived at the camp, and after paying obedience to the legate, told him he understood the Earl of Bezieres, his kinsman, was in the city of Carcasson, and that if he would grant him permission, he would go thither, and endeavour to make him sensible of the duty he owed both to the Pope and Church: the legate acquiescing, the king repaired to the earl, and asked him from what motives he shut himself up in the city against so great an army. The earl answered it was to defend his life, goods, and subjects; that he knew the pope, under pretence of religion, resolved to destroy his uncle, the Earl of Toulouse, and himself; that he saw the cruelty which they had used at Bezieres, even against the priests; adding also what they had done to the town of Carcasson, and that they must look for no mercy from the legate or his army; he, therefore, rather chose to die, defending himself with his subjects, than fall into the hands of so inexorable an enemy as the legate.

The king reported to the legate what the earl had said: the legate, after considering for a time, replied, "For your sake, sir, I will receive the Earl of Bezieres to mercy, and with him twelve others shall be safe, and be permitted to retire with their property; but as for the rest, I am determined to have them at my discretion." This answer displeased the king; and when the earl heard it, he absolutely refused to comply with such terms. The legate determined to act by stratagem. He sent a gentleman who was well skilled in dissimulation and artifice to the Earl of Bezieres, with a seeming friendly message. The design was, by any means to induce the earl to leave the city, in order to have an interview with the legate. The infamous plot succeeded: the earl, believing the promises made him of personal security, by the agent, left the city and went with him. The legate no sooner saw him, than he told him he was a prisoner, and must remain so till Carcasson had surrendered, and the inhabitants were taught their duty to the pope.

The people, on hearing of the captivity of the earl, were thrown into the utmost consternation, when one of the citizens informed the rest that there was a subterraneous passage, leading from thence to the castle of Camaret, three leagues distant. The information was joyfully received and early in the evening the inhabitants began their flight. They reached the castle by the morning, and escaped to Arragon, Catalonia, and such other places as they thought would secure them from the power of the sanguinary legate. Next morning the troops were astonished, not hearing any noise, nor seeing any stir in the city; yet they approached the walls with much fear, lest it should be but a stratagem to endanger them; but finding no opposition, they mounted the walls, crying out that the Albigenses were fled; and thus was the city with all the spoils taken, and the Earl of Bezieres committed to prison in one of the strongest towers of Carcasson, where he soon after died.

The deceased Earl of Bezieres was succeeded in title and dignity by Earl Simon, a bigoted Roman Catholic, who threatened vengeance on the Albigenses, unless they conformed to the worship of the Church of Rome. But the King of Arragon, who was in his heart of the reformed persuasion, secretly encouraged the Albigenses, and gave them hopes that, if they acted with prudence, they might cast off the yoke of the tyrannical Earl Simon. They took his advice, and while Simon was gone to Montpellier, they surprised some of his fortresses and were successful in several expeditions against his officers.

These proceedings so enraged Earl Simon, that returning from Montpellier, he collected together some forces, marched against the Albigenses, and ordered every prisoner he took to be immediately burnt. But not succeeeding in some of his enterprises, he grew disheartened, and wrote to every Roman Catholic power in Europe to send him assistance, otherwise he should not be able to hold out against the Albigenses. He soon received assistance, with which he attacked the castle of Beron, and making himself master of it, ordered the garrison to be cruelly mutilated and deprived of sight, one person alone excepted, and he was but partially blinded, that he might conduct the rest to Cabaret. Simon then undertook the siege of Menerbe, which, on account of the want of water, was obliged to yield to his forces. The lord of Termes, the governor, was put in prison, where he died; his wife, sister, and daughter were burnt, and 180 persons were committed to the flames.

In the meantime the Earl of Toulouse, through letters of recommendation from the King of France, was reconciled to the pope. But the legate, by the connivance of the pope, did all he could to ruin the earl. Altercations having passed between them, the legate excommunicated the earl; and the Roman Catholic Bishop of Toulouse, upon such encouragement, thought proper to send this impudent message to the earl—That as he was an excommunicated person, he commanded him to depart the city; for an ecclesiastic could not say mass with propriety while a person of such a description was near him.

Greatly exasperated at the bishop's insolence, the earl sent him an order immediately to depart from the place on pain of death. This order was all the prelate wanted, as it would give him some reason to complain of his lord. The bishops, with the canons of the cathedral, marched out of the town in solemn procession, barefooted and bareheaded, taking with them the cross, banner, and host, and proceeded in that array to the legate's army, where they were received with great respect as persecuted martyrs, and the legate thought this a sufficient excuse to proceed against the Earl of Toulouse for having, as he termed it, relapsed from the truth. The legate attempted to get him into his power by stratagem, but the earl being apprised of the design, escaped. Enraged at his disappointment, the legate laid siege to the castle of Montferrand, which belonged to the earl, and was governed by Baldwin his brother. On the first summons, Baldwin not only surrendered, but abjured his religion and turned papist. This event, which severely afflicted the Earl of Toulouse, was followed by another that gave him still greater mortification; for his old friend the King of Arragon forsook his interest; and it was stipulated that the king's daughter should be married to Earl Simon's eldest son.

The Earl of Toulouse now did all he could to recover the friendship of the King of Arragon; and as the marriage ceremony between that monarch's daughter and Earl Simon's son had not been performed, he entreated him to break off the preposterous match, and proposed another more proper, that his eldest son and heir to the earldom of Toulouse should wed the Princess of Arragon. His majesty was easily persuaded, not only to agree to this proposal, but to form a league with the principal Albigenses, and to put himself as captain-general at the head of their united forces.

As soon as the army of the Albigenses was ready, the King of Arragon began his operations by laying siege to Marat, a town near Toulouse, belonging to the Roman Catholics. Earl Simon, by forced marches, came to the assistance of the place at a time when the King of Arragon, who kept very little discipline in his army, was feasting and revelling. Simon suddenly attacked the Albigenses while they were in confusion, when the united forces of the reformed were defeated, and the King of Arragon was killed. The loss of this battle was imputed to the negligence of the king, who would have as much entertainment in a camp as if he had been securely at peace in his capital. The victory made the popish commanders declare they would entirely extirpate the whole race of the Albigenses.

Soon after, Earl Simon marched towards the city of Toulouse, when the earl, who had retired to Montalban, sent word to the citizens of the former city to make the best terms they could with the Roman Catholics, as he was confident they could not hold out a siege. The citizens of Toulouse, on receiving this intimation, sent deputies to Earl Simon with offers of immediate surrender, provided the city itself, and the persons and properties of its inhabitants, should be protected from devastation. These conditions were agreed to immediately, and Earl Simon, to ingratiate himself at court, wrote a letter to Prince Louis, the son of Philip, King of France, informing him that the city of Toulouse had offered to surrender to him; but, being willing that the prince should have the honour of receiving the keys and homage of the people, he begged that he would repair to the camp for that purpose. The prince, pleased with the invitation, went directly to the army, and had the city of Toulouse surrendered to him. The pope's legate was greatly displeased at the mild conditions granted to the people of Toulouse, and insisted that though the prince might take upon him the sovereignty of the place, and receive the homage of the people, yet the plunder belonged to the holy pilgrims (so the popish soldiers employed in these expeditions were called); and that the place, as a receptacle of heretics, ought to be dismantled. The prince and Earl Simon in vain remonstrated against proceedings so contrary to the conditions granted at the surrender. The legate immediately set his holy pilgrims, as he termed them, to work, and they soon dismantled the city, and plundered the inhabitants of all their property.

The legate, finding that among the Albigenses many lucrative places would fall to the disposal of the prince, determined, by an artifice, to deprive him of any advantage which might accrue from this source; he, therefore, gave absolution to the Albigenses, which, though they had not in the least changed their religious opinions, were reconciled

to the Church. The legate informed the prince that he had
no power to dispose of those places. The prince demanded
an explanation of his meaning. "My meaning," replied the
legate, "is, that the people have received absolution, and,
being reconciled to the Church, are consequently under its
protection; therefore, all places among or connected with
them are in the disposal of the Church only."

The prince, offended and highly displeased, put the
troops under his command in motion, and marched to
attack some other fortresses. He found, however, that the
legate had played the same trick. Disgusted, he left the
army and returned to court. On this Earl Simon undertook
the siege of Foix, being chiefly incited to it by the death of
his brother, who was slain by the Earl of Foix, who was of
the reformed persuasion. He lay before the castle of Foix
for the space of ten days, during which time he frequently
assaulted it, but was always repulsed. Hearing that an army
of Arragonians were in full march towards him, to revenge
the death of their king, he raised the siege and went to
meet them. The Earl of Foix immediately sallied out and
harassed his rear, while the Arragonians in front gave him
a total defeat, which compelled him to shut himself up in
Carcasson.

Soon after, the pope's legate called a council at Montpellier, for renewing military operations against the Albigenses, and for doing proper honour to Earl Simon, who
was present; for the Arragonians, not taking advantage of
their victory, had neglected to block up Carcasson, by
which omission Earl Simon had an opportunity to repair to
Montpellier. On meeting the council, the legate, in the
pope's name, paid many compliments to Earl Simon, and
declared that he should be prince of all the countries that
might in future be taken from the Albigenses: at the same
time, by order of the pontiff, he styled him the active and
dextrous soldier of Jesus Christ, and the invincible defender of the Catholic faith. Just then a messenger brought
word that the people had heard Earl Simon was in the
council, and that they had taken up arms, and were coming
thither to destroy him as a common disturber. This intelligence threw the whole council into great confusion; and
Earl Simon, though a minute before styled an invincible
defender of the faith, was glad to jump out of the window
and steal away from the city. The pope soon after called a
council to be held at Lateran, in which great powers were
granted to Roman Catholic inquisitors, and many Albi-

genses were immediately put to death. This council likewise confirmed to Earl Simon all the honours intended him by the council of Montpellier, and empowered him to raise another army against the Albigenses. Earl Simon immediately repaired to court, received his investiture from the French king, and began to levy forces. Having now a considerable number of troops, he determined, if possible, to exterminate the Albigenses, when he received advice that his countess was besieged in Narbonne by the Earl of Toulouse. He proceeded to her relief, when the Albigenses met him, gave him battle, and defeated him; but he found means to escape from the field into the castle of Narbonne. After this Toulouse was recovered by the Albigenses; but the pope espousing Earl Simon's cause, raised forces on his account, and enabled him once more to undertake the siege of that city. The earl assaulted the place furiously, but being repulsed with great loss, he sunk into affliction.

To complete his misfortune, before the troops could recover from their confusion, the Earl of Foix made his appearance at the head of a formidable army, attacked the already dispirited forces of Earl Simon, and easily put them to the rout. The pope's legate offered to raise him another army, which promise, with some difficulty and three years' delay, he at length performed, and that bigoted nobleman was once more enabled to take the field. On this occasion he turned his whole force against Toulouse, which he besieged for the space of nine months, when, in one of the sallies made by the besieged he was killed and the seige was raised.

The legate, whose name was Bertrand, being very old, grew weary of following the army and begged to be recalled on account of his age and infirmities. The pope recalled Bertrand, and appointed Conrade, Bishop of Portua, to be legate in his room. The latter determined to follow the steps of his predecessor, and to persecute the Albigenses with the greatest severity. The legate prevailed upon the King of France to undertake the siege of Toulouse in person, and reduce to the obedience of the Church those obstinate heretics, as he called the brave Albigenses. The Earl of Toulouse hearing of the great preparations made by the King of France, sent the women, children, and cattle into secret and secure places among the mountains, ploughed up the land, that the king's forces should not obtain forage, and did all that a skilful general could perform to distress the enemy. By these expedients the

French army, soon after entering the earldom of Toulouse, suffered all the extremities of famine, which obliged the troops to feed on the carcasses of horses and dogs, which unwholesome food produced the plague.

This unexpected distress broke the king's heart; but his son, who succeeded him, determined to carry on the war, when he was soon defeated in three engagements by the Earl of Toulouse. The king, the queen-mother, and three archbishops raised another formidable army, and had the art to persuade the Earl of Toulouse to come to conference, when he was treacherously seized upon, made a prisoner, forced to appear bare-footed and bare-headed before his enemies, and compelled to subscribe to the following ignominious conditions;—1. That he should abjure the faith that he had hitherto defended. 2. That he should be subject to the Church of Rome. 3. That he should give his daughter Joan in marriage to one of the brothers of the King of France. 4. That he should maintain in Toulouse six popish professors of the liberal arts, and two grammarians. 5. That he should take upon him the cross, and serve five years against the Saracens in the Holy Land. 6. That he should level the walls of Toulouse with the ground. 7. That he should destroy the walls and fortifications of thirty of his other cities and castles, as the legate should direct. 8. That he should remain prisoner in the Louvre at Paris till his daughter was delivered to the king's commissioners. After these cruel conditions a severe persecution took place against the Albigenses, many of whom suffered for the faith; and express orders were issued that *the laity should not be permitted to read the sacred writings!*

The persecution against the Albigenses was again very great in 1620. At a town called Tell, while the minister was preaching to a congregation of the reformed, the papists attacked and murdered many of the people. A lady of considerable eminence being exhorted to change her religion, if not for her own sake, at least for that of the infant she held in her arms, said, with undaunted courage, "I did not quit Italy, my native country, nor forsake the estate I had there, for the sake of Jesus Christ, to renounce Him here. With regard to my infant, why should I not deliver him up to death, since God delivered up His Son to die for us?" Dominico Berto, a youth of sixteen, refusing to turn papist, was set upon an ass with his face to the tail, which he was obliged to hold in his hand. In this condition he was

led to the market-place, amidst the acclamations of the
populace; after which they burnt holes in several parts of
his body, till at last he died with the pain. An Albigense
young lady of a noble family was seized, and carried
through the streets with a paper mitre upon her head. After
mocking and beating her, they told her to call upon the
saints; when she said, "My trust and salvation is in Christ
only; for even the Virgin Mary, without the merits of her
Son, could not be saved." On this the multitude fell upon
and destroyed her.

Account of the
Persecutions in France
Previous to and During the Civil Wars
of That Nation.

Almericus, a learned man, and six of his disciples, were,
in the third century, ordered to be burnt at Paris for
holding that God was no more present in the sacramental
than in any other bread; that it was idolatry to build altars
or shrines to saints, or to offer incense to them, and absurd
to kiss relics. The martyrdom of Almericus and his pupils
did not prevent many from acknowledging the justice of
his notions, so that the faith of Christ continued to increase; and in time it spread not only over many parts of
France, but various other nations.

In the year 1524, at a town in France called Melden,
one John Clerk affixed a bill on the church door, in which
he called the pope Antichrist: for this offence he was
repeatedly whipped, and then branded in the forehead. His
mother, who saw the chastisement, cried with a loud voice,
"Blessed be Christ, and welcome these marks for His sake."
He went afterwards to Metz, in Lorraine, and demolished
some images, for which he had his right hand and nose cut
off, and his arms and breast torn by pincers: while suffering
these cruelties, he was sufficiently at ease to sing the 115th
Psalm, which expressly forbids superstition. On concluding
the psalm he was thrown into the fire and burnt to ashes.
About the same time several persons of the reformed
persuasion were beaten, racked, scourged, and burnt to
death, in several parts of France; but particularly at Paris,
Limosin, and Malda.

At Paris, Alexander Kanus, a reformed clergyman was
burnt in a slow fire; and four men were committed to the
flames for distributing papers that ridiculed the performance of mass. Peter Gaudet, a Genoese, was burnt by the

desire of his own uncle, a bigoted Roman Catholic; and
John Pointer, a surgeon, had his tongue cut out, and was
then burnt. At Arras, Fontanis, and Rutiers many were
martyred for being of the reformed religion. At the latter
place in particular one Stephen Brune was condemned to
be burnt for refusing to attend mass.

Aymond de Lavoy, a minister of Bourdeaux, had a
complaint lodged against him by the Romish clergy of that
city. His friends advised him to abscond, but he refused so
to do. He remained nine months in prison on the information only. Being brought to trial, he was ordered to be
racked; and when in the extremity of torture, he comforted
himself with this expression: "This body must once die, but
the soul shall live; for the kingdom of God endureth for
ever." At length he swooned; but on recovering, prayed for
his persecutors. The question was then put to him whether
he would embrace the Roman Catholic persuasion; which
positively refusing, he was condemned to be burnt. At the
place of execution he said, "O Lord, make haste to help
me; tarry not; despise not the work of thy hands." And
perceiving some who used to attend his sermons, he addressed them thus: "My friends, I exhort you to study and
learn the Gospel; for the word of God abideth for ever:
labour to know the will of God, and fear not them that kill
the body, but have no power over the soul." The executioner then strangled him, and his body was afterwards
burned.

Francis Bribard, secretary to Cardinal de Bellay, for
speaking in favour of the reformed, had his tongue cut out,
and was burnt A.D. 1554. James Cobard, a schoolmaster in
the city of St. Michael, was burnt A.D. 1545, for saying that
mass was useless and absurd. About the same time fourteen
men were burnt at Malda, their wives being compelled to
behold their martyrdom. Peter Chapot brought a number
of Bibles in the French tongue to France, and publicly sold
them there in the year 1546, for which he was condemned
to be burnt. Soon after a cripple of Meaux, a schoolmaster
of Fera, named Stephen Polliot, and a man named John
English, were burned for their religion. Michael Michelot
being told either to recant and be spared, or to persevere
and be burned, he chose the latter, making use of these
words: "God has given me grace not to deny the truth, and
will give me strength to endure the fire." At Langres five
men and two women suffered for being of the reformed
religion; on which occasion the youngest woman encour-

aged the other, saying "This day we shall be married to Jesus Christ, and be with him for ever."

Immediately after the coronation of Henry the Second, King of France, many singular circumstances happened. An artisan was apprehended for working on a saint's day; being asked why he gave such an offence to religion, his reply was, "I am a poor man, and have nothing but my labour to depend upon; necessity requires that I should be industrious, and my conscience tells me there is no day but the Sabbath which I ought to keep sacred from labour." Having expressed himself thus, he was committed to prison, and later burned to death.

A Genoese youth, called Thomas, having rebuked a Roman Catholic for profane swearing, was informed against as a heretic, and burnt at Paris; as were three men at Lyons: two of them with ropes about their necks, but the third, having been an officer in the king's service, was exempted from that disgrace. He, however, begged to be treated in the same manner as his companions, in honour of the Lord: his request was complied with; and having sung a psalm with great fervency, they were all three consumed.

A citizen of Geneva, Simon Laloe; Matthew Dimonet, a converted libertine; and Nicholas Naile, a bookseller of Paris, were burnt for professing the reformed religion. Peter Serre was originally a priest, but reflecting on the errors of popery, he at length embraced the reformed religion, and learned the trade of shoemaker. Having a brother at Toulouse, a bigoted Roman Catholic, Serre, out of fraternal love, made a journey to that city, in the hope of dissuading him from his superstitions: the brother's wife not approving of his design, lodged a complaint against him, on which he was apprehended, and made a full declaration of his faith. The judge asked him concerning his occupation, to which he replied, "I have of late practised the trade of a shoemaker." "Of late!" said the judge; "and what did you practise formerly?" "That I am almost ashamed to tell you," exclaimed Serre, "because it was the vilest and most wicked occupation imaginable." All who were present supposed, from these words, that he had been a murderer or a thief, and that what he spoke was through contrition. The judge, however, ordered him to explain precisely what he meant, when Serre, with tears in his eyes, exclaimed, "Oh, I was formerly a popish priest!" This reply so much exasperated the judge, that he condemned Serre first to be degraded, then to have his tongue cut, and afterwards to be publicly burnt.

The Rise, Progress, and Cruelties of the Inquisition.

In the time of Pope Innocent III the reformed religion had occasioned such a noise throughout Europe, that the Catholics began to fear their church was in danger. The pope was determined to impede as much as possible the progress of the Reformation and he accordingly instituted a number of inquisitors—*i.e.*, persons who were to make inquiry, and punish the reformed heretics. Dominic and the other inquisitors spread themselves over various Roman Catholic countries, and treated the Protestants with the utmost severity. At length the pope, not finding the inquisitors so useful as he had imagined, resolved upon the establishment of fixed courts of inquisition; the first office of which was established in the city of Toulouse, and Dominic became the first regular inquisitor.

Courts of inquisition were speedily erected in other countries; but the Spanish inquisition became the most powerful of any. Even the kings of Spain themselves, though arbitrary in all other respects, were taught to dread the power of the Inquisition; and the cruelties they exercised compelled multitudes, who differed but slightly in opinion from the Catholics, carefully to conceal their sentiments. The Dominicans and Franciscans were the most zealous of all the monks: these, therefore, the pope invested with an exclusive right of presiding over the different courts of inquisition. The friars of those two orders were selected from the very dregs of the people, and therefore were not much troubled with scruples of conscience.

The pope gave the inquisitors the most unlimited powers, as judges representing his person: they were permitted to excommunicate, or sentence to death, whom they thought proper, upon the slightest information of heresy; were allowed to publish crusades against all whom they deemed heretics, and enter into leagues with sovereign princes, to join those crusades with their forces. About the year 1244 their power was further increased by the Emperor Frederic the Second, who declared himself the protector of all inquisitors, and published two cruel edicts—viz., that all heretics who continue obstinate should be burnt; and that all who repented should be imprisoned for life.

The officers of the Inquisition are, three inquisitors or judges, a proctor fiscal, two secretaries, a magistrate, a messenger, a receiver, a gaoler, an agent of confiscated possessions and several assessors, counsellors, executioners, physicians, surgeons, doorkeepers, familiars, and visitors, who are all sworn to profound secrecy. Their chief accusation against those who are subject to this tribunal is heresy, which comprises all that is spoken or written against any of the articles of the creed, or the traditions of the Roman Catholic Church. The other articles of accusation are, renouncing the Roman Catholic persuasion, and believing that persons of any other religion may be saved, or even admitting that the tenets of any but papists are reasonable. There are two things which incur the most severe punishments—to disapprove of any action done by the Inquisition, or disbelieve anything said by an inquisitor.

All Roman Catholics were commanded, under pain of excommunication, to give immediate information, even of their nearest and dearest friends, if they judged them to be heretics, or any ways inclining to heresy. All who give the least assistance to Protestants are called fautors or abettors of heresy, and the accusations against these are for comforting such as the Inquisition have begun to prosecute; assisting, or not informing against them, if they should happen to escape; concealing, abetting, advising, or furnishing heretics with money; visiting, or writing to, or sending them subsistence; secreting or burning books and papers, which might serve to convict them. The Inquisition also takes cognisance of such as are accused of being magicians, witches, blasphemers, soothsayers, wizards, common swearers; and of such as read or even possess the Bible in the common language, the Talmud of the Jews, or the Koran of the Mohammedans. Upon all occasions the inquisitors carry on their process with the utmost severity. A Protestant is seldom shown any mercy; and a Jew, who turns Christian, is far from being secure; for if he be known to keep company with another converted Jew, suspicion arises that they privately practise together some Jewish ceremonies; if he keep company with a person who was lately a Protestant, but now professes popery, they are accused of plotting together; but if he associate with a Roman Catholic, an accusation is often laid against the

Catholic for only pretending to be a papist, and the consequence is, a confiscation of his effects and the loss of life if he complain of ill-usage. A defence is of little avail; for even suspicion is deemed cause of condemnation, and the greater his wealth the greater his danger.

When the inquisitors have taken umbrage against an innocent person, all expedients are used to facilitate condemnation; false oaths and testimonies are employed to find the accused guilty; and all laws and institutions are sacrificed to bigoted revenge. If a person accused be arrested and imprisoned, his treatment is deplorable. The gaolers may begin by searching him for books and papers which may tend to his conviction, or for instruments which might be employed in self-murder or escape, and on this pretext they often rob him of his wearing apparel. When the prisoner has been searched and robbed, he is committed to prison. The mildest sentence is imprisonment for life; yet the inquisitors proceed by degrees at once subtle, slow, and cruel. The gaoler first insinuates himself into the prisoner's favour, by pretending to wish him well, and advise him; and among other hints falsely kind, tells him to petition for an audit. When he is brought before the consistory, the first demand is, "What is your request?" To this the prisoner very naturally answers that he would have a hearing. Hereupon, one of the inquisitors replies, "Your hearing is this—confess the truth, conceal nothing, and rely on our mercy." If now the prisoner make a confession of any trifling affair, they immediately found an indictment upon it; if he is mute, they shut him up without light, or any food but a scanty allowance of bread and water, till he overcome his obstinacy, as they call it; and if he declare his innocence, they torment him till he either dies with the pain or confesses himself guilty.

On the re-examination of such as confess, they continually say, "You have not been sincere, you tell not all; you keep many things concealed, and therefore must be remanded to your dungeon." When those who have been mute are recalled for further examination, if they continue silent, such tortures are ordered as will either make them speak or kill them; and when those who proclaim their innocence are re-examined, a crucifix is held before them, and they are solemnly exhorted to take an oath of their confession of faith. This brings them to the test; they must either swear they are Roman Catholics or acknowledge they are not.

After a person impeached is condemned, he is either severely whipped, violently tortured, sent to the galleys, or sentenced to death; in either case the effects are confiscated. After judgment, a procession is formed to the place of execution, and the ceremony is called an *Auto da Fé*, or act of faith. The following is an exact account of one of these atrocious and grotesque solemnities, performed at Madrid in the year 1683:—

The officers of the Inquisition, preceded by trumpets, kettledrums, and their banner, marched on the 30th of May, in cavalcade, to the palace of the great square, where they declared by proclamation that on the 30th of June the sentence of the prisoners would be put in execution. There had not been a spectacle of this kind at Madrid for several years before, for which reason it was looked forward to by the inhabitants with as much impatience as a day of the greatest festivity and triumph. When the appointed day arrived, a prodigious number of people appeared dressed as splendidly as their respective circumstances would admit. In the great square was raised a high scaffold; and thither, from seven in the morning till the evening, were brought criminals of both sexes; all the inquisitions in the kingdom sending their prisoners to Madrid. Twenty men and women, with one renegade Mohamamedan, were ordered to be burned; fifty Jews and Jewesses, having never before been imprisoned, and repenting of their crimes, were sentenced to a long confinement, and to wear a yellow cap; and ten others, indicted for bigamy, witchcraft, and other crimes, were sentenced to be whipped, and then sent to the galleys. On this great occasion the whole Court of Spain was present. The grand inquisitor's chair was placed in a sort of tribunal more exalted than that of the king. The nobles acted the part of the sheriffs' officers in England, leading such criminals as were to be burned, and holding them when fast bound with thick cords: the rest of the prisoners were conducted by familiars of the Inquisition. There was among the sufferers a young Jewess of exquisite beauty, and but seventeen years of age. Being on the same side of the scaffold where the queen was seated, she addressed her, in hope of obtaining pardon, in the following pathetic speech:—"Great Queen! will not your royal presence be of some service to me in my miserable condition? Have regard to my youth; and, oh! consider that I am about to die for professing a religion imbibed from my earliest infancy!" Her majesty seemed greatly to pity her distress, but turned away her eyes, as she did not dare speak a word on behalf of a person who had been declared a heretic by the Inquisition. Mass now began, in the midst of which the priest came from the altar placed near the scaffold, and seated himself in a chair prepared for that purpose. Then the chief inquisitor descended from the amphitheatre, dressed in his cope, and having a mitre on his head. After bowing to the altar, he went up towards the king's balcony, attended by some of his officers, carrying a cross and the Gospels, with a book containing the oath by which the kings of Spain oblige themselvss to protect the Catholic faith, to extirpate heretics, and support with all their power the prosecutions and the decrees of the Inquisition. On the approach of the Inquisitor, and on his presenting this book to the king, his majesty rose up bare-headed, and swore to maintain the oath, which was read to him by one of his counsellors: after which the king continued standing till the inquisitor had returned to his place, when the secretary of the holy office mounted a sort of pulpit, and administered a like oath to the counsellors and the whole assembly. The mass began at about twelve at noon, and did not end till nine in the evening, being protracted by a proclamation of the sentences of the several criminals, which were all separately rehearsed aloud one after the other. Next followed the burning of the twenty-one men and women, whose intrepidity in suffering that horrid death was truly astonishing: some thrust their hands and feet into the flames with the most dauntless fortitude, and all yielded to their fate with such resolution, that many of the amazed spectators lamented that such heroic souls had not been more enlightened. The situation of the king was so near to the criminals, that their dying groans were audible to him. He could not, however, be absent, even if he wished it, from this heart-rending scene, as it is considered a religious ceremony, and the coronation-oath binds the monarch to give the sanction of his presence to all the acts of the tribunal.

Sometimes a prisoner passes months without knowing of what he is accused, or having the least idea when he is to be tried. The gaoler at length informs him that he must petition for a trial. This ceremony being gone through, he is taken bare-headed for examination. When they come to the door of the tribunal, the gaoler knocks three times, to give the judges notice of their approach. A bell is rung by one of the judges, when an attendant opens the door, admits the prisoner, and accommodates him with a stool. The prisoner is then ordered by the president to kneel down, and lay his right hand upon a book, which is presented to him close shut. This being complied with, the following question is put to him: "Will you promise to conceal the secrets of the holy office, and to speak the truth?" Should he answer in the negative, he is remanded to his cell and cruelly treated. If he answer in the affirmative, he is ordered to be again seated, and the examination proceeds; when the president asks a variety of questions, and the clerk minutes both them and the answers. When the examination is closed, the bell is again rung, the gaoler appears, and the prisoner is ordered to withdraw with this exhortation: "Tax your memory, recollect all the sins you have ever committed, and when you are again brought here, communicate them to the holy office." The gaolers and attendants, when apprised that the prisoner has made an ingenuous confession, and readily answered every question, make him a low bow, and treat him with simulated kindness as a reward for his candour. He is brought in a few days to a second examination, with the same formalities as before. The inquisitors often deceive prisoners by promising the greatest lenity, and even to restore them to freedom, if they will accuse themselves: the unhappy persons who in their power frequently fall into this snare, and are sacrificed to their own simplicity.

Though the inquisitors allow the torture to be used only three times, yet on each of these occasions it is so severely inflicted, that the prisoner either dies under it or continues a cripple for life. The following is a description of the severe torments occasioned by the torture, from the account of one who suffered it.

THE FIRST TIME OF TORTURING

A prisoner on refusing to comply with the iniquitous demand of the inquisitors, by confessing all the crimes with which they thought proper to charge him, was immediately conveyed to the torture-room. The prisoner was surrounded by six wretches, who, after preparing the tortures, stripped

him naked to his drawers. He was then laid upon his back
on a kind of stand, elevated a few feet from the floor. They
commenced by putting an iron collar round his neck, and a
ring to each foot, which fastened him to the stand. His
limbs being thus stretched out, they wound two ropes
round each arm and two round each thigh; which being
passed under the scaffold, through holes made for that
purpose, were all drawn tight at the same instant of time,
by four of the men, on a given signal. The pains which
immediately succeeded were intolerable; the ropes, which
were of a small size, cut through the prisoner's flesh to the
bone, making the blood gush out at all the different places
which were bound. If he persisted in not making any
confession of what the inquisitors required, the ropes were
drawn in this manner four times successively. A physician
and surgeon attended, and often felt his temples, so as to
judge of the danger he might be in. By these means his
agonies were for a short time suspended, but only that he
might have sufficient opportunity of recovering his vitality
to sustain further torture. The last time the ropes were
drawn tight, he grew so exceedingly weak, by the stoppage
of the circulation of his blood, and the pains he endured,
that he fainted away; upon which he was unloosed and
carried back to his dungeon.

THE SECOND TIME OF TORTURING

Six weeks later the prisoner was exposed to another
kind of torture, the manner of inflicting which was as follows: they forced his arm backwards, so that the palms of
his hands were turned outward behind him; when by means
of a rope that fastened them together at the wrists, and
which was turned by an engine, they drew them by degrees
nearer each other, in such a manner that the back of each
hand touched, and stood exactly parallel to each other. In
consequence of this violent contortion, both his shoulders
became dislocated, and a considerable quantity of blood
issued from his mouth. This torture was repeated thrice,
after which he was again taken to the dungeon, and
delivered to the physician and surgeon, who, in setting the
dislocated bones, put him to the most exquisite torment.

THE THIRD TIME OF TORTURING

About two months after the second torture, the prisoner, having recovered a little, was again ordered to the torture-room, and there, for the last time, made to undergo another kind of punishment, which was inflicted twice without any intermission. The executioners fastened a thick iron chain twice round his body, which, crossing upon his stomach, terminated at the wrists. They then placed him with his back against a thick board, at each extremity whereof was a pulley, through which there ran a rope that caught the ends of the chain at his wrists. Then the executioner, stretching the end of this rope by means of a roller placed at a distance behind him, pressed or bruised his stomach in proportion as the ends of the chain were drawn tighter. They tortured him in this manner to such a degree that his wrists, as well as his shoulders, were quite dislocated. They were, however, soon set by the surgeons; but the barbarians, not yet satisfied with this series of cruelty, made him immediately undergo the same torture a second time, which he sustained (although the pains were, if possible, keener) with equal constancy and resolution. He was then remanded to his dungeon, attended by the surgeon to dress his bruises and adjust the parts dislocated; and here he continued till the time of their gaol-delivery.

It may be judged from this relation under what dreadful agony the sufferer must have laboured by being so frequently put to the torture. Most of his limbs were disjointed; so much was he bruised and exhausted as to be unable, for weeks, to lift his hands to his mouth; and his body became greatly swelled from the inflammation caused by frequent dislocations. After his discharge he felt the effects of this cruelty for the remainder of his life, being frequently seized with excruciating pains. The unhappy females who fall into the hand of the inquisitors have not more favour shown them on account of the tenderness of their sex, but are tortured with as much severity as the male prisoners.

An Account of Proceedings Against Publications.

Having now mentioned the barbarities with which the prisoners are treated by the inquisitors, we shall proceed to recount the severity of their proceedings against publications. When a book is published, it is carefully read by some of the familiars belonging to the Inquisition. They scrutinize not for the merits, but for the defects of an author, and pursue the slips of his pen with unremitting diligence. Hence they read with prejudice, judge with partiality, pursue errors with avidity, and that which is innocent into an offensive meaning. Any trivial charge causes the censure of a book. There is a catalogue of condemned books annually published under three different heads of censures (viz., "wholly condemned," "partly condemned," and "incorrect"), and being printed on a large sheet of paper, is hung up in the most public and conspicuous places. After this, people are obliged to destroy all such books as come under the first censure, and to keep none condemned by the other two censures, unless the exceptionable passages have been expunged and the corrections made, as in either case disobedience would be of the most fatal consequence, for the possessing or reading the proscribed books are deemed very atrocious crimes. Every publisher of such books is usually ruined in his circumstances, and sometimes obliged to pass the remainder of his life in a prison of the Inquisition.

Barbarities Exercised by the Inquisitions of Spain and Portugal, from the Most Authenticated Records.

Francis Romanes, a native of Spain, was employed by the merchants of Antwerp to transact some business for them at Bremen. He had been educated in the Romish persuasion; but going one day into a Protestant church, he was struck with the truths which he heard, and, beginning to perceive the errors of popery, he determined to search farther into the matter. Perusing the sacred Scriptures and the writings of some Protestant divines, he perceived the error of the principles he had formerly embraced, and renounced the impositions of popery for the doctrines of the Reformed Church, in which religion appeared in all its genuine purity. Resolving to think only of his eternal salvation, he studied religious truth more than trade, and purchased books rather than merchandise, convinced that the riches of the body are trifling when compared with those of the soul. He resigned his agency to the merchants of Antwerp, giving them an account at the same time of his conversion; and then, resolving to convert his parents, he went without delay to Spain for that purpose. But the Antwerp merchants writing to the inquisitors, he was arrested, imprisoned for some time, and then condemned to the stake as a heretic. As he passed by a wooden cross on the way to his execution, one of the priests bade him kneel to it; but he absolutely refused to do so, saying, "It is not for Christians to worship wood." Having been placed on a pile of wood, the fire quickly reached him, when he lifted up his head suddenly and repeated part of the 7th Psalm.

A carver, named Rochus, who lived at St. Lucar, in Spain, and whose principal business was making images of saints and popish idols, becoming convinced of the errors of the Romish persuasion, embraced the Protestant faith, left off carving images, and, for subsistence, followed the business of a seal-engraver only. He had, however, retained one image of the Virgin Mary for a sign, when an inquisitor, passing by, asked if he would sell it. Rochus mentioned a price; the inquisitor objected to it, and offered half the money. Rochus replied, "I would rather break it to pieces than take such a trifle." "Break it to pieces!" said the inquisitor; "break it to pieces, if you dare!" Rochus being provoked at this expression, snatched up a chisel, and cut off the nose of the image. This was sufficient. The inquisitor went away in a rage, and soon after sent to have him arrested. In vain did he plead that what he defaced was his own property, and that if it was not proper to do as he would with his own, it was not proper for the inquisitor to bargain for the image in the way of trade. Nothing, however, availed him; his fate was decided—he was condemned to be burned and the sentence was executed immediately.

A Dr. Cacalla, his brother Francis, and sister Blanche, were burned at Valladolid for having spoken against the inquisitors. A gentlewoman with her two daughters and niece were apprehended at Seville, on account of their professing the Protestant religion. They were all put to the torture, and when that was over, one of the inquisitors sent for the youngest daugher, pretended to sympathise with her and pity her sufferings; then, binding himself with a solemn oath not to betray her, he said, "If you will disclose all to me, I promise you I will procure the discharge of your

mother, sister, cousin, and yourself." Made confident by
this oath, she revealed the whole of the tenets they professed, when the perjured wretch, instead of acting as he
had sworn, immediately ordered her to be put to the rack,
saying, "Now you have revealed so much, I will make you
reveal more." On her refusal, however, to say anything
further, all the prisoners were sentenced to be burned,
which sentence was executed at the next *Auto da Fé*.

The keeper of the castle of Triano, belonging to the
inquisitors of Seville, happened to be of a more humane
character than is usual with persons in his situation. He
gave all the indulgence he could to the prisoners, and
showed them every favour in his power with as much
secrecy as possible. At length the inquisitors became acquainted with his kindness, and determined to punish him
severely for it. They superseded him, threw him into a
dismal dungeon, and used him with such dreadful barbarity
that he lost his senses. His deplorable situation, however,
procured him no favour; for, frantic as he was, they
brought him from prison at an *Auto da Fé* to the usual
place of punishment. His sentence was then read—that he
should be placed upon an ass, led through the city, receive
two hundred stripes, and then be condemned six years to
the galleys.

A maid-servant to another gaoler belonging to the Inquisition was accused of humanity, and detected in bidding
the prisoners keep up their spirits. For this heinous crime,
as it was called, she was publicly whipped, banished her
native place for ten years, and had her forehead branded
with red hot irons with these words: "A favourer and aider
of heretics."

John Pontic, a Spanish gentleman and a Protestant, was,
principally on account of his great wealth, apprehended by
the inquisitors, and charged with heresy. On this charge all
his effects were confiscated to the use of the inquisitors,
and his body was burnt to ashes. John Gonsalvo, originally
a priest, but who now embraced the reformed religion, was
with his mother, brother, and two sisters, seized by the
inquisitors. Being condemned, they were led to execution
singing part of the 106th Psalm. On their arrival at the
place of execution they were ordered to say the Creed, with
which they complied, but coming to these words, "The
Holy Catholic Church," they were commanded to add the
monosyllables "of Rome," and, on their repeated refusals,

one of the inquisitors said, "Put an end to their lives directly!" The ferocious executioners immediately strangled them.

Four Protestant women were seized at Seville, tortured, and afterwards ordered for execution. On the way they began to sing psalms; but the officers, thinking that the words of the psalms reflected on themselves, put gags into their mouths to silence them. They were then burnt, and the houses where they resided were likewise demolished. A Protestant schoolmaster, of the name of Ferdinando, was apprehended, by order of the Inquisition, for instructing his pupils in the principles of Protestantism; and, after being severely tortured, was committed to the flames.

A Spanish Roman Catholic, named Juliano, travelling into Germany, became a convert to the Protestant religion, and undertook to convey to his own country a great number of Bibles, concealed in casks, and packed up like Rhenish wine. He succeeded so far as to distribute the books. A pretended Protestant, however, who had purchased one of the Bibles, betrayed him, and laid an account of the affair before the Inquisition. Juliano was seized, and, means being used to find out the purchasers of the Bibles, 800 persons were apprehended. They were indiscriminately tortured, and then most of them were sentenced to various punishments. Juliano was burnt, twenty were roasted upon spits, several imprisoned for life, some were publicly whipped, many sent to the galleys, and a very few were acquitted.

A young lady having been put into a convent, absolutely refused to take the veil, and on leaving the cloister she embraced the Protestant faith, on which she was apprehended and condemned to the flames. An eminent physician and philosopher, of the name of Christopher Losada, became obnoxious to the inquisitors on account of exposing the errors of popery and professing the tenets of Protestantism. He was apprehended, imprisoned, and racked; but these severities not making him confess the Roman Catholic Church to be the only true one, he was sentenced to the fire, which he bore with exemplary patience, and resigned his soul to his Creator.

A young lady named Maria de Coccicao, who resided with her brother at Lisbon, was arrested by the inquisitors, and ordered to be put to the rack. The torments she felt made her confess the charges against her. The cords were then slackened, and she was re-conducted to her cell, where she remained till she had recovered the use of her limbs; she was then brought again before the tribunal, and ordered to ratify her confession. This she absolutely refused to do, telling them that what she had said was forced from her by the excessive pain she had undergone. The inquisitors, incensed at this reply, ordered her to be racked again, when the weakness of nature once more prevailed, and she repeated her former confession. She was immediately remanded to her cell; and being a third time brought before the inquisitors, they ordered her to sign her first and second confessions. She answered as before, but added, "I have twice given way to the frailty of the flesh, and perhaps may, while on the rack, be weak enough to do so again: but depend upon it, if you torture me a hundred times, as soon as I am released from the rack I shall deny what was extorted from me by pain." The inquisitors then ordered her to be racked a third time; and, during this last trial, she bore the torments with the utmost fortitude, and could not be persuaded to answer any of the questions put to her. As her courage and constancy increased, the inquisitors, instead of putting her to death, condemned her to a severe whipping through the public streets, and banishment for ten years.

A lady of a noble family of Seville, named Jane Bohorquia, was apprehended on the information of her sister, who had been tortured and burnt for professing the Protestant religion. While on the rack, she confessed that she had frequently conversed with her sister concerning Protestantism, and upon this extorted confession Jane was arrested, and sentenced to the rack. Her tortures were so severe that she expired from their effects, only a few days afterwards.

Isaac Orobio, a learned physician, having beaten a Moorish servant for stealing, was accused by him of professing Judaism, and the inquisitor seized the master upon the charge. He was kept three years in prison before he had the least intimation of what he was to undergo, and then suffered the following various modes of torture:—a coarse linen coat was put upon him, and then drawn so tight that the circulation of the blood was nearly stopped, and the breath was almost pressed out of his body. After this the strings were suddenly loosened, when the air forcing its way hastily into his stomach, and the blood rushing into its channels, he suffered the most incredible pain. Not content with this, the executioners fastened ropes round his wrists, and then drew them about his body.

Placing him on his back with his feet against the wall, they pulled with the utmost violence, till the cord had penetrated to the bone. He suffered the last torture three times, and then lay seventy days before his wounds were healed.

An inhabitant of Toledo was fond of producing fine specimens of writings, and having them framed to adorn the different apartments of his house. Among other examples of penmanship was a large piece containing the Lord's Prayer, the Creed, and Ten Commandments in verse. This piece, which hung in a conspicuous part of the house, was one day seen by a person belonging to the Inquisition, who observed that the numeration of the commandments was not according to the Church of Rome, but according to that of the Protestant Church. The Inquisition soon had information of the circumstance, and this gentleman was seized, prosecuted, and burnt, only for embellishing his house with a specimen of his skill.

A Singular Discovery of Some Enormities of the Inquisition.

When the crown of Spain was contested for by two princes, who equally pretended to the sovereignty, France espoused the cause of one competitor, and England of the other. The Duke of Berwick, a natural son of James II who abdicated England, commanded the Spanish and French forces, and defeated the English at the celebrated battle of Almanza. The army was then divided into two parts: the one consisting of Spaniards and French, headed by the Duke of Berwick, advanced towards Catalonia; the other body, consisting of French troops only, commanded by the Duke of Orleans, proceeded to the conquest of Arragon. On the troops approaching the city of Arragon, the magistrates came to offer the keys to the Duke of Orleans; but he told them, haughtily, they were rebels, and that he would not accept the keys, for he had orders to enter the city through a breach. Accordingly, he made a breach in the walls of his cannon, and then entered the city through it, together with his whole army. When he had made regulations here, he departed to subdue other places, leaving a strong garrison under the command of his lieutenant-general, M. de Legal. This gentleman, though brought up a Roman Catholic, was totally free from superstition; he united great talents with great bravery, and was at once the accomplished gentleman and skilful officer. Before his departure, the duke had ordered that heavy contributions should be levied upon the city.

The money levied upon the magistrates and principal inhabitants, and upon every house, was paid as soon as demanded; but when the persons applied to the heads of the convents and monasteries, they found that the ecclesiastics were not so willing as other people to part with their cash.

Of the donatives to be raised by the clergy, the College of Jesuits was to pay 2,000 pistoles; Carmelites, 1,000 pistoles; Augustines, 1,000 pistoles; and Dominicans, 1,000 pistoles.

M. de Legal sent to the Jesuits a peremptory order to pay the money immediately. The superior of the Jesuits returned for answer that for the clergy to pay money to the army was against all ecclesiastical immunities, and that he knew of no argument that could authorise such a procedure. M. de Legal then sent four companies of dragoons, to quarter themselves in the college, with this sarcastic message: "To convince you of the necessity of paying the money, I have sent four substantial arguments to your college, drawn from the system of military logic, and therefore hope you will not need any further admonition to direct your conduct."

The Jesuits, greatly perplexed at these proceedings, dispatched an express to court to the king's confessor, who was of their order; but the dragoons were much more expeditious in plundering and doing mischief than the courier in his journey; so that the Jesuits, seeing everything going to ruin, paid the money before the return of the messenger. The Augustines and Carmelites, taking warning by what had happened to the Jesuits, prudently went and paid the money, and by that means escaped the study of military arguments, and of being taught logic by the dragoons.

On the other hand, the Dominicans, who are all familiars of or agents dependent on the Inquisition, imagined that that very circumstance would be their protection. The chief of the Dominicans sent word to the military commander that his order was poor, and had not any money whatever to pay the donative; "for," says he, "the whole wealth of the Dominicans consists only in the silver images of the apostles and saints which are placed in our church, and which to remove would be accounted sacrilege."

This insinuation was meant to terrify the French commander, whom the inquisitors imagined would not dare to be so profane as to wish for the possession of the precious idols. He, however, sent word that the silver images would make admirable substitutes for money, and would be more in character in his possession than in that of the Dominicans themselves; "for," says he, "while you possess them in the manner you do at present, they stand up in niches, useless and motionless, without being of the least benefit to mankind; but when they come into my possession, they shall be useful. I will put them in motion, for I intend to have them coined, when they may travel like the apostles."

The inquisitors were astonished at this treatment, which they never expected to receive even from crowned heads; they therefore determined to deliver their precious images in a solemn procession, that they might excite the people to an insurrection. The Dominican friars were accordingly ordered to march to De Legal's house, with the silver apostles and saints, in a mournful manner, having lighted tapers with them, and bitterly crying all the way, "Heresy! heresy!"

When M. de Legal heard of these proceedings, he ordered four companies of grenadiers to line the streets which led to his house; each grenadier was ordered to have his loaded fuzee in one hand, and a lighted taper in the other, so that the troops might either repel force with force, or do honour to the farcical ceremony. The silver images were therefore delivered up to M. de Legal, who sent them to the mint to be coined.

The inquisitors, however, determined to excommunicate M. de Legal, unless he would release their precious saints from imprisonment in the mint before they were melted down. The French commander absolutely refused to release the images, upon which the inquisitors drew up the form of excommunication, and ordered their secretary to go and read it to M. de Legal.

This commission the secretary punctually performed, and read the excommunication deliberately and distinctly. The French commander heard it with great patience, and politely told the secretary he would answer it next day. As soon as the secretary of Inquisition was gone, M. de Legal ordered his own secretary to prepare a form of excommunication exactly like that sent by the Inquisition, but instead of his name he put in those of the inquisitors.

The next morning he ordered four regiments under arms, and commanded them to accompany his secretary, and act according to his direction. The secretary went to the Inquisition, and insisted on admittance, which, after a great

deal of altercation, was granted. As soon as he entered, he
read, in an audible voice, the excommunicaton issued by
M. de Legal against the inquisitors. The inquisitors exclaimed against De Legal as an heretic, and declared that
his proceedings were an insult to the Church. But, to
surprise them still more, the French secretary told them
they must remove from their present lodgings, for the
French commander wanted to quarter the troops in the Inquisition, as it was the most commodious place in the
whole city. On this the inquisitors protested loudly, when
the secretary put them under a strong guard, and sent them
to a place appointed by M. de Legal to receive them. The
inquisitors immediately set out for Madrid, where they
made the most bitter complaints to the king; but the
monarch told them he could not grant them any redress, as
the injuries they had received were from the troops of his
grandfather, the King of France, by whose assistance alone
he could be firmly established in his kingdom.

In the meantime, M. de Legal opened all the doors of
the Inquisition, and released the prisoners, who amounted
altogether to four hundred, among whom were sixty beautiful young women, who appeared to form a seraglio for
the three principal inquisitors.

This discovery, which made the iniquity of the inquisitors so plain, greatly alarmed the archbishop, who desired
M. de Legal to send the women to his palace, and he would
take proper care of them; and at the same time he
published an ecclesiastical censure against all such as
should ridicule or blame the holy office of the Inquisition.

But the French commander sent word to the archbishop
that the prisoners had either run away or were securely
concealed by their friends, or even by his own officers; that
it was impossible for him to send them back again, and,
therefore, the Inquisition, having committed such atrocious
actions, must now put up with their exposure and shame.

Don Carlos, the amiable son of Philip II, King of Spain,
and grandson of the Emperor Charles V, intended to
abolish the Inquisition, but he lost his life before he
became king.

Don Carlos possessed all the good qualities of his
grandfather, without the bad ones of his father. He had
sense enough to see into the errors of popery, and abhorred
the very name of the Inquisition. He inveighed publicly
against the institution, ridiculed the affected piety of the
inquisitors, and declared that if he ever came to the crown,

he would abolish the holy office, and exterminate its agents.

This irritated the inquisitors against the prince; and they accordingly determined on his destruction. They therefore employed all their agents to spread the most artful insinuations against the prince, and at length excited such a spirit of discontent among the people, that the king was under the necessity of removing Don Carlos from court.

Shortly after, the prince, having shown great lenity and favour to the Protestants in the Netherlands, the Inquisition loudly exclaimed against him, declaring that, as the persons in question were heretics, the prince himself must be one, since he gave them countenance. Thus they gained so great an ascendancy over the mind of the king, who was absolutely a slave to superstition, that he sacrificed the feelings of nature to the force of bigotry, and afraid of incurring the anger of the Inquisiton, passed the sentence of death on his only son.

The prince had what they termed an indulgence; that is, he was permitted to choose the manner of his death. He chose bleeding and the hot bath; when the veins of his arms and legs being opened, he expired gradually, falling a martyr to the malice of the inquisitors, and the pitiless bigotry of his father.

Accounts of the Persecutions of Various Protestants Abroad.

Dr. Aegidio was educated at the University of Alcala, and applied himself to the study of the Scriptures. When the Professor of Theology died, he was elected into his place, and acted so much to the satisfaction of everyone, that his reputation speedily became known throughout Europe. The doctor's enemies, however, laid a complaint against him to the inquisitors, who sent him a citation, and on his appearance cast him into a dungeon.

As the greatest part of those who belonged to the cathedral church at Seville, and many persons belonging to the bishopric of Dortois, approved of the doctrines of Aegidio, which they thought consonant with true religion, they petitioned the emperor in his behalf. Though the monarch had been educated a Roman Catholic, he was not a bigot; and therefore sent an order for his liberation. Soon after he visited the church of Valladolid, did everything he could to promote religion, and returning home he fell sick, and died in an extreme old age.

The inquisitors having been disappointed of gratifying

their malice against him while living, ordered his remains to be dug up, and a legal process being carried on, they were condemned to be burnt, which was accordingly done.

ACCOUNT OF THE PERSECUTION OF DR. CONSTANTINE

Dr. Constantine was an intimate acquaintance of Dr. Aegidio, and was a man of uncommon abilities and profound learning. His eloquence rendered him a pleasing, and the soundness of his doctrines a profitable preacher.

When fully confirmed in Protestantism by Dr. Aegidio, he preached only such doctrines as were agreeable to Gospel purity, and uncontaminated by the errors which had from time to time crept into the Romish Church. For these reasons he had many enemies among the Roman Catholics, who were determined on his ruin. One Scobarta, having erected a school for divinity lectures, appointed Dr. Constantine to be reader therein. He immediately undertook the task, and read lectures on the Proverbs, Ecclesiastes, and Canticles; but while beginning to expound the Book of Job, the inquisitors seized him. When brought to examination, he answered with such precaution that they could not find any explicit charge against him, but remained doubtful in what manner to proceed, when the following circumstance occurred.

The doctor had deposited with a woman named Martin several books, which to him were very valuable, but which he knew were exceptionable in the eyes of the Inquisition. This woman was apprehended, and after a small process, her goods were confiscated.

The inquisitors, possessed now of Constantine's books and writings, soon found matter to form charges against him. When he was brought to re-examination, they presented one of his papers, and asked him if he knew the handwriting. Perceiving it was his own, he guessed the whole matter, confessed the writing, and justified the doctrine it contained, saying, "In that and all my other writings I have never departed from the truth of the Gospel, but have kept in view the pure precepts of Christ, as he delivered them to mankind." Having been detained upwards of two years in prison, he was at last seized with a dreadful disease, which put an end to his miseries. The process, however, was carried on against his body, which was publicly burnt at the ensuing *Auto da Fé*.

MR. NICHOLAS BURTON'S MARTYRDOM.

Mr. Burton was a merchant of London, who traded with Spain. Being at Cadiz, a familiar of the Inquisition called upon him one day at his lodgings, pretending that he wanted to send a quantity of merchandise to London. Having asked as many questions as he thought proper, he departed, and the next day one of the inquisitorial officers took Mr. Burton into custody. The president, on his examination, demanded if he had said or insinuated anything disrespectful to the Roman Catholic persuasion. Mr. Burton replied in the negative, saying that he was sensible, in whatever country we were, respect ought to be paid to its established religion. This defence, however, availed him nothing; they proceeded to torture him, in order to gain information. Failing in this, they condemned him for invincible obstinacy, and at the next *Auto da Fé* he was burnt. Several others of the English in Spain were, about the time of Mr. Burton's martyrdom, put to death by the inquisitors; particularly John Baker, William Burgate, and William Burgess, who were burnt, and William Hooker, who was stoned to death.

PARTICULARS OF WILLIAM GARDENER

William Gardener was born at Bristol, received a tolerable education, and was, at a proper age, placed under the care of one Paget, an eminent merchant. When twenty-six years of age, he was sent to Lisbon. Here he applied himself to the study of the Portuguese language, conversed privately with a few whom he knew to be zealous Protestants, and, at the same time, avoided giving offence to any who were Roman Catholics.

A marriage being concluded between the King of Portugal's son and the Infanta of Spain, upon the wedding-day the bridegroom, bride, and the whole court went to the cathedral church, attended by multitudes of all ranks of people, and, among the rest, William Gardener, who stayed during the whole ceremony, and was greatly shocked at the superstitions he beheld. He therefore formed the design of making a reform in Portugal. He settled his worldly affairs, paid his debts, closed his books, and consigned over his merchandise. On the ensuing Sunday he went to the cathedral church, and placed himself near the altar, with a New Testament in his hand. In a short time the king and

court appeared, and a cardinal began mass. At that part of
the ceremony in which the people adore the wafer, Gardener, springing toward the cardinal, snatched the host from
him, and trampled it under his feet. The whole congregation were thunderstruck, and one person, drawing a dagger, wounded Gardener in the shoulder. Thinking that he
hàd been stimulated by some other person to act as he had
done, the king demanded who was his abettor, to which he
replied, "My conscience alone. I would not hazard what I
have done for any man living, but I owe that and all other
service to my Creator." Hereupon he was sent to prison,
and a general order issued to apprehend all Englishmen in
Lisbon. This order was in a great measure put into execution, and many innocent persons were tortured, to make
them confess if they knew anything of the matter. Gardener himself was tormented in the most excruciating
manner. Being sentenced to death, a large fire was kindled
near a gibbet; Gardener was drawn up to the gibbet by
pulleys, and then let down near the fire, but not so close as
to touch it; for they burned, or rather roasted him by slow
degrees. Some of the sparks were blown from the fire
which consumed Gardener towards the haven, burnt one of
the king's ships of war, and did other considerable damage.
The Englishmen who were taken up on this occasion were
soon after Gardener's death, discharged.

ACCOUNT OF THE LIFE AND SUFFERINGS OF
MR. WILLIAM LITHGOW

William Lithgow was descended from a good family in
Scotland, and having a natural propensity to travelling,
rambled over France, Germany, and Switzerland, until he
arrived at Malaga, in Spain. While he resided here, he contracted with the master of a French ship for his passage to
Alexandria, but was prevented from going by the following
circumstances. In the evening of the 17th of October,
1620, the English fleet came to anchor before Malaga.

Many persons from the fleet came ashore the next day.
Among these were several known by Mr. Lithgow, who
invited him on board. When Mr. Lithgow returned to
shore, he proceeded towards his lodgings, when he was
surrounded by nine sergeants, who forcibly conducted him
to the governor's house. The governor began by inquiring
the quality of the English commander, and what were the
motives that prevented his accepting an invitation from

him to come on shore. He demanded the names of the English captains, and what knowledge Mr. Lithgow had of the departure of the ships from England. The junto seemed surprised at his denying any knowledge of the fitting out of the fleet. In short, they said he came from a council of war held that morning on board the admiral's ship, in order to put in execution the orders assigned him. They upbraided him with being accessory to the burning of the island of St. Thomas, in the West Indies; "wherefore," said they, "these Lutherans and sons of the devil ought to have no credit given to what they say or swear."

Mr. Lithgow in vain endeavoured to obviate every accusation. It was agreed that he should be confined in the governor's house, and the greatest secrecy observed. At midnight, two Turkish slaves released Mr. Lithgow from his confinement, but it was to introduce him to one more horrible. They conducted him to a remote chamber, where they loaded him with irons, and extended his legs by means of an iron bar above a yard long, the weight of which was so great that he could neither stand nor sit, but was obliged to lie continually on his back.

He received a visit from the governor the next day, who promised him his liberty if he would confess being a spy; but on his protesting that he was innocent, the governor left him in a rage, saying, he should see him no more till further torments constrained him to confess; commanding the keeper that his sustenance should not exceed three ounces of musty bread, and a pint of water every second day.

On the forty-eighth day of his imprisonment he was again examined and pressed to make a full discovery; that is, to accuse himself of crimes never committed. Mr. Lithgow persisting in his innocence, the governor ordered him to be tortured.

He was conducted where the rack was placed. The executioner struck off his irons, which put him to great pain, the bolts being so closely riveted that the sledge hammer tore away above half an inch of his heel in forcing off the bolt.

As soon as his irons were off, he fell on his knees, uttering a short prayer that God would enable him to undergo the trial he had to encounter. He was then stripped and fixed upon the rack.

It is impossible to describe all the tortures inflicted upon him. He lay on the rack for above five hours, during which time he received about sixty different tortures.

On being taken from the rack, he was loaded with irons and conducted to his dungeon, having received no other nourishment than a little warm wine.

Mr. Lithgow at length received information which gave him little hopes of ever being released. The substance of this was that an English priest had been employed by the governor to translate into Spanish his books and observations, and that it was said in the governor's house that he was an arch heretic. About two days after he had received the above information, the governor, an inquisitor, and a canonical priest, accompanied by two Jesuits, entered his dungeon, and the inquisitor asked Mr. Lithgow if he was a Roman Catholic and acknowledged the pope's supremacy? He answered that he neither was the one nor did the other. "As you have almost murdered me," said he, "for pretended treason, so now you intend to make a martyr of me for my religion."

The inquisitors returned in the morning, and asked the prisoner what difficulties he had on his conscience that retarded his conversion; to which he answered, he had not any doubts on his mind, being confident in the promises of Christ, and believing his revealed will signified in the Gospels, as professed in the Reformed Catholic Church. To these words the inquisitor replied, "Thou art no Christian, but an absurd heretic and a member of perdition." The prisoner then told him it was not consistent with religion and charity to convince by opprobrious speeches, racks, and torments, but by arguments deduced from the Scriptures, and that all other methods would be totally fruitless.

Lithgow received a sentence of eleven different tortures, and if he did not die in the execution of them, he was, after Easter holidays, to be carried to Grenada, and there burnt to ashes. The first part of the sentence was executed with great barbarity that night.

Mr. Lithgow now anxiously waited for the day which would end his torments; but his melancholy expectations were, by the interposition of Providence, rendered abortive, and his deliverance obtained from the following circumstances.

A Spanish gentleman came from Grenada to Malaga, whom the governor informed of what had befallen Mr. Lithgow from the time of his apprehension as a spy. He likewise told him that after it was known the prisoner was innocent, it gave him great concern; that on this account he would gladly have released him and made some atonement for the injuries he had received; but that, upon an inspection of his writings, several were found of a very blasphemous nature; that on his refusing to abjure these opinions, he was turned over to the Inquisition, who condemned him.

While the governor was relating this tale, the servant of the Spanish gentleman, who waited at table, was struck with amazement at the sufferings of the stranger. On his return to his master's lodging, he began to revolve in his mind what he had heard, which made such an impression on him that he could not rest in his bed; and when the morning came, without disclosing his intentions to any person whatever, he went into the town and inquired for an English factor. He was directed to the house of one Mr. Wild, to whom he related what he had heard pass between his master and the governor.

Mr. Wild, on the departure of the servant, immediately sent for the other English factors, to whom he related all the particulars relative to their countryman. After a short consultation it was agreed that an information should be sent by express to Sir Walter Aston, the English ambassador at Madrid. This was done, and the ambassador obtained an order for Mr. Lithgow's enlargement, and his delivery to the English factory. This order was received by the assembly of the Inquisition with the greatest surprise.

Mr. Lithgow was released on the eve of Easter Sunday, when he was carried from his dungeon to the house of one Mr. Busbich, where all comforts were given him. It fortunately happened that there was at this time a squadron of English ships in the road, commanded by Sir Richard Hawkins, who came ashore the next day with a guard, and received Mr. Lithgow from the merchants. The factory presented him with clothes and all necessary provisions, besides which they gave him 200 reals in silver, and Sir Richard Hawkins sent him two double pistoles. Sir Richard also demanded the delivery of his papers, money, and books, before his departure from the Spanish coast, but could not obtain any satisfactory answer on that head.

Having lain twelve days in the road, the ship weighed anchor, and in about two months arrived safe at Deptford. The next morning Mr. Lithgow was carried on a featherbed to Theobalds in Hertfordshire, where at that time were

the king and royal family. Mr. Lithgow was presented to
him, and related the particulars of his sufferings and his
happy delivery; at which the king was so affected that he
expressed the deepest concern, and gave orders that he
should be sent to Bath. By these means, under God, Mr.
Lithgow was restored from the most wretched spectacle to
a great share of health and strength; but he lost the use of
his left arm, and several of the smaller bones were so
crushed and broken as to be rendered unserviceable.

Notwithstanding every effort, Mr. Lithgow could never
obtain any part of his money or effects, though his majesty
and the ministers interested themselves in his behalf. Gon-
damore, the Spanish ambassador, promised that his effects
should be restored, with the addition of £1,000 English
money, as some atonement for the tortures he had undergone, which was to be paid to him by the governor of
Malaga. These engagements, however, were never kept;
and though the king was a kind of guarantee for the
performance of them, the cunning Spaniard found means
to elude the order.

A Brief Relation of the Horrible Massacre in France, A.D. 1572.

Our attention is now turned to the massacre of St.
Bartholomew. What wonder that retributive justice should
cause the Seine, the Loire, and the Rhone to run with the
blood of citizens in the great Revolution, when those
waters had been before reddened with the blood of the
martyrs of God! Charles IX and his mother Catharine,
finding open persecution only excited the Huguenots to
more obstinate resistance, determined to gain by subtlety
what they failed to obtain by force. They fixed on two
plans: first, the king commanded Coligny to take his army
into the Low Countries, that he might by that means find
out the number and names of his followers; secondly, a
marriage was proposed between the king's sister, the beautiful but dissolute Marguerite de Valois, and Henry of
Navarre, the head of the Huguenot princes and the heir to
the crown. All the leading Huguenot nobles were invited to
Paris, and received by the perfidious Catharine with every
mark of respect. The most illustrious of the guests was
Jeanne d'Albret, Queen of Navarre, the mother of Prince
Henry, and the firmest adherent to the Huguenot cause.
Her Protestant sympathies and her virtue both led her to
feel the deepest horror at the proposed alliance, and it was

with almost a breaking heart that she left her little kingdom of Navarre once more to visit the city of Paris. Before she had been there a week, she suddenly died, and it can scarcely be doubted that her death was hastened by poison, as her great talents and her strict integrity caused her to be a most dangerous opponent to the papists. Prince Henry was, however, persuaded that his mother's death arose from natural causes, and his marriage was accordingly solemnised in the following August, by the Cardinal of Bourbon upon a high stage erected outside the church walls.

In the evening they were conducted to a palace in the middle of the city to supper. The marriage having taken place on the 18th of August, the 24th was fixed for the massacre. At two a.m. the bell of St. Germain l'Auxerrois tolled, at which signal the Duke of Guise led his followers to Coligny's house: the duke remained below while his servants, headed by a young man named Besme, ascended to the admiral's room. After stabbing him several times they threw him out of the window; when his head and arms were cut off by the rabble, and the body hung up by the feet on a gibbet.

The martyrdom of this virtuous man had no sooner taken place than the armed soldiers ran about slaying all the Protestants they could find within the walls of the city. This continued for several days; but the greatest slaughter took place during the first three days, in which above 10,000 men and women, of all ages and conditions, are said to have perished.

These brutal deeds were not confined within the walls of Paris, but extended into other cities and quarters of the realm, especially to Lyons, Orleans, Toulouse, and Rouen, where the cruelties were unparalleled. Within the space of one month 60,000 Protestants are said to have been slain in France alone, as is credibly reported by those who testify of the matter. When intelligence of the massacre was received at Rome, the greatest rejoicings took place, and a medal was struck to commemorate this victory of the faith. The pope and his cardinals went in solemn procession to the church of St. Mark, to give thanks to God. A jubilee was also published, and the ordnance fired from the castle of St. Angelo. To the person who brought the news the Cardinal of Lorraine gave 1,000 crowns. Similar rejoicings were also celebrated all over France for this imagined overthrow of the faithful.

The following are among the particulars recorded of the above enormities:—

The admiral, on being wounded in both his arms, immediately said to Maure, preacher to the Queen of Navarre, "Oh, my brother! I now perceive that I am beloved of my God, seeing that for his most holy name's sake I do suffer these wounds." He was slain by Besme, who afterwards declared that he never saw any man suffer death more courageously.

2,000 were murdered in the city of Poictiers in one day, and the licence of massacre continued several days afterwards.

At Meldis 200 were cast into prison; and, being brought out as sheep to the slaughter, were pitilessly cut to pieces.

At Orleans 1,000 men, women, and children were slain.

The citizens of Augustobona, hearing of the massacre at Paris, shut the gates of their town that no Protestants might escape, and cast all they suspected into prison, who were afterwards killed.

At Lyons 800 perished most miserably; the children hanging on their fathers' necks, and the fathers embracing their children. 300 were slain in the archbishop's house, and the monks would not suffer their bodies to be buried.

At Toulouse 200 were murdered.

At Rouen 500 were put to death. The following is the testimony of Thuanus:—"This example passed unto other cities, and from cities to towns and villages, so that it is reported that in all the kingdom above 30,000 were destroyed in these tumults."

Bricamotius, a man of the age of seventy, and Cavagnius, were laid upon hurdles and drawn to execution; and, after being subjected to every species of personal indignity, were hanged. The first might have been pardoned if he would publicly confess that the admiral had conspired against the king, which he refused to do.

At Bourdeaux, by the instigation of a monk named Angerius, 264 persons were slaughtered, some of whom were senators.

At Agendicum, in Main, a cruel massacre of Protestants was committed by the instigation of Aemarus, inquisitor of criminal causes. A rumour being spread abroad that the Protestants had taken counsel to spoil the churches, above 100 of every estate and of both sexes were, by the enraged people, thrown into the river Igonna, which runs by the city.

On entering Blois, the Duke of Guise (to whom the city had opened its gates) gave it up to rapine and slaughter; houses were spoiled; and many Protestants who had remained were slain or drowned in the Loire. The duke proceeded from Blois to a town called Mere, about two leagues distant, where the Huguenots were accustomed to hold their meetings. He ordered Cassebonius, the pastor of the parish, to be cast into the river, and put many of the unfortunate inhabitants to death.

John Burgeolus, President of Turin, an old man, and suspected of being a Protestant, having bought his life and safety with a great sum of money, was, notwithstanding, taken and beaten cruelly with clubs, and, being stripped, was brought to the bank of the river Loire, and hanged with his head downward in the water, until he perished miserably.

The papists obtained possession of Matiscon by corrupting the keeper of the city keys, who, notwithstanding his perfidy, was put to death. They then treated the inhabitants with great cruelty, cutting off the legs and arms of many in mere sport.

At Albia of Cahors, upon the Lord's day, the 16th of December, the papists, at the ringing of a bell, broke open the doors where the Protestants were assembled, and killed, without distinction, all they could find, among whom was one Guacerius, a rich merchant, whom they drew into his house, and murdered with his wife and children.

Bordis, a captain under the Prince of Condé, at Mirabellum, was, contrary to promise, assassinated, and his body cast into the street to be devoured by the dogs.

The Prince of Condé, being taken prisoner, was shot in the neck by Montisquius, captain of the Duke of Anjou's guard.

At Orleans 100 men and women being committed to prison, were torn in pieces by the fanatic mob.

The inhabitants of Rochelle, a town in the province of Aunis, hearing of the cruelties committed on their brethren, resolved to defend themselves against the power of the king; and their example was followed by various other towns, with whom they entered into a confederacy, inspiriting one another in the common cause. To crush this, the king, having summoned the whole power of France and the greatest of his nobility, invested Rochelle by land and sea, and commenced a furious siege, which, but for the providential care of God, must have ended in its immediate destruction.

Seven principal assaults were made against the poor town of Rochelle, none of which succeeded. At one time a breach was made by the tremendous cannonade; but through the undaunted valour of the citizens, assisted even by their wives and daughters, who could not be restrained, the soldiers were driven back with great slaughter.

The siege lasted seven months, when the Duke of Anjou having been proclaimed King of Poland, he, in concert with the King of France, entered into a treaty with the people of Rochelle. The conditions, containing twenty-five articles, which were drawn up by the latter, and embraced many immunities both for themselves and the Protestant body in France, were confirmed by the king, and proclaimed with great rejoicings at Rochelle and other cities.

The year following, Charles IX died, the tyrant who had been so instrumental in the calamities above recorded.

The History of Robert Oguier and His Wife, and Baudicon and Martin Their Sons, who were Burned at Lisle.

On Saturday, March 6, 1556, about ten o'clock at night, the provost of the city, with his sergeants, sallied forth to search for any Protestants assembled together in houses for religious worship. Being, however, unsuccessful, they came to the house of Robert Oguier, where both rich and poor were familiarly instructed in the Scriptures.

Having entered into the house in pursuit of their prey, they found certain books, which they carried away. But he whom they principally sought was not there, namely, Baudicon, the son of the said Robert Oguier, who at that time had gone out to read the Word of God with some of the brethren. On his return home, he knocked at the door, when Martin, his younger brother, watching his coming, bade him be gone: but Baudicon, thinking his brother mistook him for some one else, said, "It is I; open the door." With that the sergeants opened the same and let him in, saying, "Ah! sir, you are well met!" to whom he answered, "I thank you, my friends; you are also welcome hither." Then said the provost, "I arrest you all in the emperor's name," and with that he commanded each of them to be bound, viz., the husband, his wife, and their two sons, and confined them in separate prisons. A few days after the prisoners were brought before the magistrates, and examined concerning their course of life. They

directed their speech first to Robert Oguier in these words:
—"It is told us that you never come to mass, yea, and also
dissuade others from coming thereto; we are further informed that you maintain conventicles in your house,
causing erroneous doctrines to be preached there, contrary
to the ordinance of our holy mother the Church, whereby
you have transgressed the laws of his imperial majesty."

Robert Oguier answered, "Whereas, first of all, you lay
to my charge that I go not to mass; I refuse so to do
indeed, because the death and precious blood of the Son of
God, and his sacrifice, are utterly abolished there, and
trodden under foot. 'For Christ by one offering hath
perfected for ever them that are sanctified'; that is by the
sacrifice of himself. For do we read in all the Scriptures
that either the prophets, Christ, or any of the apostles, ever
said mass? They knew not what it meant. Christ indeed
instituted the holy supper, in which all Christians communicate together, but they sacrifice not. If you please to
read the Bible over, you will never find the mass once
mentioned therein; therefore it is the mere invention of
men.

"As for the second accusation, I will not deny but there
have met together in my house honest people fearing God;
I assure you, not with intention to wrong any, but rather
for the advancement of God's glory and the good of many.
I knew, indeed, that the emperor had forbidden it, but
what then? I knew also that Christ, in his Gospel, had
commanded it. 'Where two or three (saith he) are gathered
together in my name, there am I in the midst of them.'
Thus, you see, I could not well obey the emperor but I
must disobey Christ. In this case, then, I chose rather to
obey my God than man."

One of the magistrates demanded what they did when
they met together. To which Baudicon, the eldest son,
answered, "If it please you to give me leave, I will open the
business at large unto you."

The sheriffs, seeing his promptness, looking upon one
another, said, "Well let us hear it." Baudicon, lifting up
his eyes to heaven, began thus:—"When we meet together
in the name of our Lord Jesus Christ, to hear the word of
God, we first of all prostrate upon our knees before God,
and in the humility of our spirits do make a confession of
our sins before His Divine Majesty. Then we pray that the
word of God may be rightly divided, and purely preached;
we also pray for our sovereign lord the emperor and for all

his counsellors, the the commonwealth may be peaceably governed to the glory of God."

While they were thus examined, each of them made an open confession of their faith, and, not long after, were put to the torture, to make them reveal who frequented their house. Four or five days after they were convened again before their judges, and after many words passed, they asked them whether they would submit themselves to the will of the magistrates. Robert Oguier and Baudicon his son, with some deliberation, said, "Yea, we will."

Then demanding the same of Martin, the younger brother, he answered that he would not submit himself thereto, but would accompany his mother; so he was sent back again to prison, whilst the father and the son were sentenced to be burnt to ashes. One of the judges, in pronouncing sentence, spake as if he were transported with fury in beholding the great patience of these two servants of Christ. Having received the sentence of death, they returned to the prison joyful that the Lord conferred on them the honour of enrolling them in the number of his martyrs. They no sooner entered the prison than a band of friars came; one amongst the rest told them the hour was come when they must die. Robert Oguier and his son answered, "We know it well; but blessed be the Lord our God, and now, delivering our bodies out of this vile prison, will receive our souls into His glorious and heavenly kingdom."

One of the friars endeavoured to turn them from their faith, saying, "Father Robert, thou art an old man; let me entreat thee in this thy last hour, to think of saving thine own soul; and if thou wilt give ear unto me, I warrant thee thou shalt do well."

The old man answered, "Poor man! how darest thou attribute that to thyself which belongs to the eternal God, and so rob him of his honour? For it seems by thy speech, that if I will hearken to thee, thou wilt become my saviour. No, no; I have only one Saviour, Jesus Christ, who by-and-by will deliver me from this miserable world. I have one teacher whom the heavenly Father hath commanded me to hear, and I purpose to hearken to none other."

Another exhorting him to take pity on his soul, "Thou willest me (said Robert) to pity mine own soul; dost thou not see what pity I have on it, when, for the name of Christ, I willingly abandon this body of mine to the fire, hoping to-day to be with him in paradise? I have put all my confidence in God, and my hope is wholly fixed upon the merits of Christ, his death and passion; he will direct me the right way to his kingdom. I believe what the holy prophets and apostles have written, and in that faith will I live and die." The friar, hearing this, said, "Out, dog! thou art not worthy the name of a Christian; thou, and thy son with thee, are both resolved to perish."

As they were about to separate Baudicon from his father, he said, "Let my father alone, and trouble him not thus: he is an old man, and hath an infirm body; hinder him not, I pray you, from receiving the crown of martyrdom."

When at the place of execution, the son pulled a cross of wood out of his father's hands, saying, "What cause hath the people to be offended at us for not receiving a Jesus Christ of wood? We bear upon our hearts the cross of Christ, the Son of the ever-living God, feeling his holy word written therein in letters of gold."

A band of soldiers attended them to execution, just as if it had been a prince who was being conducted into his kingdom. Baudicon was then dragged to the stake, where he began to sing the 16th Psalm. The friar cried out, "Do you not hear, my masters, what wicked errors these heretics sing to beguile the people with?" Baudicon, hearing him, replied, "How, simple idiot, callest thou the psalms of the prophet David errors?" Then, turning his eyes towards his father, who was about to be chained to the stake, he said, "Be of good courage, father; the worst will be past by-and-by." Then he often reiterated these short breathings: "O God, Father everlasting, accept the sacrifice of our bodies, for thy well-beloved Son Jesus Christ's sake." And thus, during these conflicts, Baudicon bent his eyes to heaven, and, speaking to his father, said, "Behold, I see the heavens open, and millions of bright angels ready to receive us, rejoicing to see us thus witnessing the truth in the view of the world. Father, let us be glad and rejoice, for the joys of heaven are opened unto us." Fire was forthwith put to the straw and wood. In the end, the fire growing hot, the last words they were heard to pronounce were, "Jesus Christ, thou Son of God, into thy hands we commend our spirits." And thus they fell asleep in the Lord.

Many of the popish rabble now went to Martin and his mother to turn them from their faith. In order that their devilish enterprise might succeed the better, they separated the one from the other, and after a time the poor woman began to waver and let go her first faith. At this their enemies rejoiced, whilst the little flock of Christ, hearing such sad news, were in perplexity; but the Lord left them not in their mournful condition.

One day one of the monks waited on her in the prison, counselling her to win over her son Martin, and to draw him from his errors, which she promised to do. But when he was come to his mother, and perceived that she was not only fallen, but also turned out of the right way, he began with tears to bewail her miserable state. "Oh, mother!" said he, "what have you done? Have you denied Him who hath redeemed you? Ah! good God! that I should live to see this, which pierces me to the very heart!" His mother, hearing these his pitiful complaints, and seeing the tears which her son shed for her, began again to renew her strength in the Lord, and with tears cried out, "O Father of mercies! be merciful unto me a miserable sinner, and cover my transgressions under the righteousness of thy blessed Son. Lord, enable me with strength from above to stand to my first confession, and make me to abide steadfast therein, even unto my last breath." It was not long after this change that the same instruments of Satan who had seduced her came in, supposing to find her in the same mind wherein they left her, whom she no sooner espied but with detestation said, "Away, Satan! get thee behind me; for henceforth thou hast neither part nor portion in me. I will, by the help of God, stand to my first confession, and if I may not sign it with ink, I will seal it with my blood." And so from that time this frail vessel, who for a while wavered, grew stronger and stronger. A certain temporiser said to Martin, "Thou silly youth; thou sayest thou knowest not what. Seest thou not all these people here about thee? They believe not as thou dost, and yet I doubt not but they shall be saved." The good woman hearing this, answered, "Sir, Christ Jesus our Lord saith that it is the wide gate and broad way which leads to destruction, and therefore many go in thereat: but the gate," saith she, "is narrow that leads to life, and few there be that find it. Do ye then doubt whether we are in the straight way or no, when ye behold our sufferings? Compare our doctrine with that of your priests and monks: we, for our parts, are determined to have but one Christ, and him crucified; we only embrace the Scriptures of the Old and New Testament.

Soon after Martin and his mother were bound and

brought to the place of their martyrdom. Being bound to the stake, she spake, in the hearing of the spectators, "We are Christians, and that which we now suffer is not for murder or theft, but because we will believe no more than that which the Word of God teacheth us:" both rejoicing that they were counted worthy to suffer for the same. The fire being kindled, the vehemency thereof did not abate the fervency of their zeal, but they continued constant in the faith, and, lifting up their hands to heaven, in holy accord, said, "Lord Jesus, into thy hands we commend our spirits." And thus mother and son slept in the Lord.

A Brief Relation of the Massacre at Vassy, in the Country of Champaigne, in France.

The Duke of Guise, on his arrival at Joinville, asked whether the Protestants of Vassy used to have sermons preached to them by their minister. On hearing that they had, he fell into a grievous passion; and upon Saturday, the last day of February, 1562, that he might the more secretly execute his wrath against the heretics at Vassy, he departed from Joinville, and lodged in the village of Dammartin, distant about two French miles and a half.

The next day, after he had heard high mass, attended by about 200 armed men, he left Dammartin, passing along to Vassy.

Now there were certain soldiers and archers accompanying the duke, who compassed about Vassy, most of them being lodged in the houses of papists. On the Saturday before the slaughter, they were observed preparing their weapons; but the faithful, not dreaming of such a conspiracy, thought the duke would treat them honourably, as the king's subjects.

The Duke of Guise marched with all his troops to the town of Vassy, determined to execute fearful vengeance on the unfortunate Protestants. He took his men direct to the Romish monastery, and sent out orders that all Romanists should retire into the monastery, and on no account go out into the streets, at the risk of their lives. This being done, he marched his soldiers on to a large barn, where the Huguenots were assembled for their usual service. On approaching the building, the soldiers fired into the windows. The terrified people within, who numbered about 1,200, one hearing the report, rushed to the doors, hoping to escape to the woods. A fearful scene followed: those who endeavoured to escape by the doors were cut down and murdered by the soldiers outside, who then rushed in with drawn swords, killing man, woman, and child, without mercy; others, with their guns, fired at the people in the gallery, who broke open the roof, and, jumping down over the city wall, which was very high, fled into the woods for safety, some of them being wounded by the shots, others stabbed or cut in their heads or arms by the swords. Mr. Morel, the preacher, who, even when the massacre commenced, remained in the pulpit exhorting the people and praying to God to have mercy on them, was seized and taken before the duke. "Come hither," exclaimed the latter. "Art thou the minister of this place? who made thee so bold to seduce this people thus?" "Sir," said the minister, "I am no seducer, for I have preached to them the Gospel of Jesus Christ." The duke perceiving that his answer condemned his cruel outrages, began to curse, saying, "Doth the Gospel preach sedition? Provost, go and let a gibbet be set up, and hang this fellow!" at which words the minister was delivered into the hands of two pages, who misused him vilely. The women of the city, being ignorant papists, caught up dirt to throw in his face, and, with outcries, said, "Kill him! kill this varlet, who hath been the cause of the death of so many!" In the meantime the duke went into the barn, to whom they presented a great Bible which they used for the service of God. The duke, taking it into his hands, calling his brother the cardinal, said, "Lo, hear the title of the Huguenot books!" The cardinal, viewing it, said, "There is nothing but good in this book, for it is the Holy Scriptures." The duke being offended at his brother's difference of feeling on the subject, became more enraged, saying, "How now? What! the Holy Scripture! It is 1,500 years ago since Jesus Christ suffered, and it is but a year since these books were printed; how, then, say you that this is the Gospel? You say you know not what."

The massacre continued a full hour, while the duke's trumpeters sounded the attack. When any of the victims desired to have mercy showed them for the love of Jesus Christ, the murderers would scornfully reply, "You use the name of Christ, but where is your Christ now?"

Fifty or threescore persons died in this massacre; besides which, there were about 250 who were wounded, whereof some died, one losing a leg, another an arm, another his fingers. The poor-box, which was fastened to the door of the church by two iron hooks, containing £12, was wrenched from its place and never restored.

The minister was closely confined and threatened to be sewed up in a sack and drowned. He was, however, on the 8th of May, 1563, liberated at the earnest suit of the Prince of Portien.

Brief Account of Sancerre During the Siege.

Sancerre, a town in the department of Cher, on the left bank of the river Loire, was the place to which the faithful fled for refuge in the year 1573. It was closely encompassed with enemies from the beginning of April. Owing to this, a dearth of provisions was soon felt by the inhabitants, on which they collected all the asses and mules they had in the city, which were eaten up in less than a month. They then killed the horses and dogs; after these were exhausted, they seized the cats, rats, moles, mice, and every other animal and vermin they could find. Having eaten these, they fed on ox and cow-hides, sheep-skins, parchment, old shoes, bullocks' and horse-hoofs, horns and lanterns, ropes, horse-harness, and leather girdles. Towards the end of June, a third part of the besieged had not bread to eat. Such as could get hemp-seed ground it in mortars, and made bread of it; which they also did with all sorts of herbs, mingling them with bran.

All children under twelve years of age perished from inability to endure the famine.

A boy of ten years old being at the point of death, seeing his father and mother weeping over him, said unto them, "Wherefore weep ye thus in seeing me famished to death, mother? I ask for no bread, I know you have none; but seeing it is God's will I must die this death, let us be thankful for it. Did not the holy man Lazarus die of famine? have I not read it in my Bible?" With these utterances he expired.

The reason that all the people did not die of famine was that some horses had been reserved for service, and six cows, which were left to give milk for the support of young infants. These beasts were killed, and their flesh sold for the relief of the survivors. A pound of wheat was sold for as much as half a crown.

Not more than eighty-four persons died by the hand of the enemy, but more than 500 perished from famine. Many soldiers, in order to avoid the lingering death of hunger, fled from the city, preferring to perish by the sword of the enemy; whereof some were slain, others imprisoned, and the rest put to death.

Every hope seemed cut off from the besieged, and death stared them in the face; for the King of France, so far from relenting at their state, being enraged at their courage, swore that they should eat up one another. But the election of the Duke of Anjou to the throne of Poland caused a general pacification, and the Protestants once more enjoyed liberty of conscience and freedom from persecution.

Particular Account of the Persecutions in Bohemia and Germany Under the Papacy.

The severity exercised by the Roman Catholics over the Bohemian churches induced the members to send two ministers and four laymen to Rome, in the year 977, to seek redress from the pope. After some delay their request was granted, and their grievances redressed. Two things in particular were conceded to them—vis., to have divine service in their own language, and to give the sacramental cup to the laity. The disputes, however, soon broke out again; the succeeding popes exerting all their power to enslave the minds of the Bohemians, and the latter with great spirit struggling to preserve their religious liberties.

Some friends, zealous of the Gospel, applied to Charles, King of Bohemia, A.D. 1375, to call a council for an inquiry into the abuses that had crept into the Church, and to effect a thorough reformation. Charles, at a loss how to proceed, sent to the pope for advice; the latter, incensed at the affair, only replied, "Punish those presumptuous heretics." The king accordingly banished every one who had been concerned in the application, and to show his zeal for the pope, imposed many additional restraints upon the religious liberties of the country.

The martyrdom of John Huss and Jerome of Prague increased the indignation of the reformed, and gave life to their cause. These two great and pious men were condemned by order of the Council of Constance, when fifty-eight of the principal Bohemian nobility interposed in their favour. Nevertheless, they were burnt; and the pope, in conjunction with the Council of Constance, ordered the Romish clergy everywhere to excommunicate all who adopted their opinions, or pitied their fate. In consequence of these orders great contentions arose between the papists and reformed Bohemians, which produced a violent persecution against the latter. At Prague it was extremely severe, till at length the reformed, driven to desperation, armed

themselves, attacked the senate-house, and cast twelve of
its members, with the speaker, out of the windows. The
pope, hearing of this, came to Florence, and publicly
excommunicated the reformed Bohemians, exciting the
Emperor of Germany, and all other kings, princes, and
dukes, to take up arms, to extirpate the whole race;
promising, by way of encouragement, full remission of sins
to the most wicked person who should kill one Bohemian
Protestant. The result of this was a bloody war; for several
popish princes undertook the extirpation of the proscribed
people: while the Bohemians prepared to repel them in the
most vigorous manner. The popish army prevailing against
the Protestant forces at the battle of Cuttenburgh, conveyed their prisoners to three deep mines near that town,
and threw several hundreds into each, where they perished
in a miserable manner.

The Emperor Ferdinand, whose hatred to the Protestants was unlimited, thinking he had not sufficiently oppressed them, instituted a high court of reformers, upon
the plan of the Inquisition, with this difference, that the
reformers were to remove from place to place, and always
to be attended by a body of troops. The greater part of this
court consisted of Jesuits, from whose decisions there was
no appeal. This bloody court, attended by its military
guard, made the tour of Bohemia, and seldom examined or
saw a prisoner; but suffered the soldiers to murder the
Protestants as they pleased, and then to report the matter
in their own fashion.

Not long afterwards a secret order was issued by the
emperor for apprehending all noblemen and gentlemen
who had been principally concerned in supporting the
Protestant cause, and in nominating Frederick, Elector
Palatine of the Rhine, to be King of Bohemia. Fifty of
these were suddenly seized in one night, and brought to the
castle of Prague; while the estates of those who were
absent were confiscated, themselves made outlaws, and
their names fixed upon a gallows as a mark of public
ignominy.

The high court of reformers afterwards proceeded to try
those who had been apprehended, and two apostate Protestants were appointed to examine them. Their examiners
asked many unnecessary and impertinent questions, which
so exasperated one of the noblemen, that he exclaimed,
opening his breast at the same time, "Cut here; search my
heart; you shall find nothing but the love of religion and

liberty: those were the motives for which I drew my sword, and for those I am willing to die."

As none of the prisoners would renounce their faith, or acknowledge themselves in error, they were all pronounced guilty; the sentence was, however, referred to the emperor. When that monarch had read their names, and the accusations against them, he passed judgment on all, but in a different manner; his sentences being of four kinds—viz., death, banishment, imprisonment for life, and imprisonment during pleasure. Twenty of them being ordered for execution, were informed they might send for Jesuits, monks, or friars, to prepare for their awful change, but that no communication with any Protestants would be permitted. This proposal they rejected, and strove all they could to comfort one another upon the solemn occasion. The morning of the execution having arrived, a cannon was fired as a signal to bring the prisoners from the castle to the principal market-place, in which scaffolds were erected, and a body of troops drawn up to attend. The prisoners left the castle, and passed with dignity and cheerfulness through soldiers, Jesuits, priests, executioners, and a prodigious concourse of people assembled to see the exit of these martyrs.

The following are among the principal who suffered on this occasion:—

Lord Schilik, a nobleman about the age of fifty. On being told that he was to be quartered, and his parts scattered in different places, he smiled, and said, "The loss of a sepulchre is but a trifling consideration." A gentleman who stood by, crying, "Courage, my lord," he replied, "I possess the favour of God, which is sufficient to inspire any one with courage: the fear of death does not trouble me. I have faced him in fields of battle to oppose Antichrist." After repeating a short prayer, he told the executioner he was ready, who cut off his right hand and head, and then quartered him.

Another victim was Viscount Winceslaus. This venerable nobleman had attained the age of seventy, and was noted equally for his piety, learning, and hospitality. He was so little affected by the loss of worldly riches, that on his house being broken open, his property seized, and his estates confiscated, he only said, with great composure, "The Lord hath given, and the Lord hath taken away. I am now full of years, and wish to lay down life, that I may not be a witness of the evils which await my country. You have long thirsted for my blood; take it, for God will be my avenger." He then approached the block, stroked his grey beard, and said, "Venerable hairs, the greater honour now attends you; a crown of martyrdom is your portion."

Lord Harant was a gentleman whose natural abilities were much refined and improved by travelling, having visited the principal places in Europe, Asia, and Africa. The accusations against him were, his being a Protestant, and having taken an oath of allegiance to Frederick, the Elector Palatine of the Rhine, as King of Bohemia. When he ascended the scaffold, he said, "I have travelled through many countries, and traversed many barbarous nations, yet have I never found so much cruelty as at home. I have escaped innumerable perils both by sea and land, and have surmounted all, to suffer innocently in my native place. My blood is likewise sought by those for whom I and my ancestors have hazarded our lives and fortunes; but, Almighty God! forgive them, for they know not what they do." Then approaching the block, he kneeled down, and exclaimed with great energy, "Into thy hands, O Lord! I commend my spirit; in thee have I always trusted; receive me, therefore, my blessed Redeemer."

Lord Henry Otto, on first coming upon the scaffold, seemed greatly agitated, and said, as if addressing himself to the emperor, "Oh, tyrant Ferdinand, your throne is established in blood; but if you kill my body, and disperse my members, they shall still rise up in judgment against you." He was then silent; and having walked about a while, recovered his fortitude, and growing calm, said to a gentleman, "For a few minutes I was discomposed, but now I feel my spirits revive; God be praised, death no longer appears as the king of terrors, but seems to invite me to participate in some unknown joys." Then kneeling before the block, he said, "Almighty God! to thee I commend my soul; receive it for the sake of Christ, and admit it to the glory of thy presence."

Sir Gasper Kaplitz. This nobleman was eighty-six years of age. On coming to the place of execution, he addressed the principal officer thus: "Behold a miserable ancient man, who hath often entreated God to take him out of this wicked world, but could not till now obtain his desire; for God reserved me till these years to be a spectacle to the world, and a sacrifice to himself; therefore God's will be done." An officer told him, that in consideration of his great age, if he would only ask pardon, he would immediately receive it. "Ask pardon!" exclaimed he; "I will ask pardon of God, whom I have frequently offended, but not of the emperor, whom I never offended. Should I sue for pardon, it might be justly suspected I had committed some crime for which I deserved this fate. No, no; as I die innocent, and with a clear conscience, I would not be separated from my noble companions in the faith:" so saying, he cheerfully resigned his neck to the block.

Christopher Chober. No sooner had this gentleman stepped upon the scaffold, than he said, "I come, in the name of God, to die for his glory; I have fought the good fight, and finished my course; so, executioner, do your office." On this he instantly received the crown of martyrdom.

Simeon Sussickey, not being of noble birth, was ordered to be hanged. He appeared impatient to be gone, saying, "Every moment delays me from entering into the kingdom of Christ."

Nathaniel Wodnianskey was hanged for having supported the Protestant cause. At the gallows the Jesuits used all their persuasions to make him renounce his faith, but without effect. His own son then approached the gallows, and said, "Sir, if life should be offered to you on condition of apostacy, I entreat you to remember Christ." To this his father replied, "It is very acceptable, my son, to be exhorted to constancy by you, but suspect me not; rather endeavor to confirm in their faith your brothers, sisters, and children, and teach them to imitate my constancy." He had no sooner concluded these words than he received his fate with great fortitude.

History of the Life, Sufferings, and Martyrdom of John Huss, Who Was Burnt at Constance, in Germany.

John Huss was a Bohemian by birth, and born in the village of Hussinetz, about the year 1380. His parents gave him the best education they could bestow, and, having acquired a tolerable knowledge of the classics at a private school, he was sent thence to the University of Prague, where he soon became conspicuous by his talents and industry.

In 1408 he commenced as bachelor of divinity, and was afterwards successively chosen pastor of the church of Bethlehem, in Prague, and rector of the university. These trusts he discharged with great fidelity, and became at length so celebrated for his preaching, and his bold utter-

ance of truth, that he soon attracted the notice and excited
the malignity of the pope and his creatures.

But the principal cause which aroused the indignation of
Huss was a bull published by Pope John XXIII, promising
remission of sins to all who would join his forces against
Ladislaus, King of Naples, who had now invaded the States
of the Church. When this bull was published in Prague,
Huss could not refrain from preaching against it as repugnant to the spirit of the Christian religion. The pope,
therefore, summoned him to Rome, and, upon his refusing
to comply, excommunicated him, and forbad divine service
being performed in all the churches of Prague except one,
so long as Huss remained in the city. To avoid disturb-
ances, Huss retired to Hussinetz.

The English reformer, Wycliffe, had so kindled the light
of the Reformation that it began to pierce the darkest
corners of popery. His doctrines were received in Bohemia
with eagerness and zeal by great numbers of people, and
especially by John Huss and his friend and fellow-martyr,
Jerome of Prague.

The influence of Huss in the university was very great,
not only on account of his learning, eloquence, and exemplary life, but also on account of some valuable privileges
he had obtained from the king on behalf of the Bohemians
in that seminary.

Sincerely attached to the doctrines of Wycliffe, Huss
strenuously opposed the decree of the archbishop, who
obtained a bull from the pope, authorising him to prevent
the publishing of Wycliffe's writings in his province. By
virtue of this bull the archbishop condemned the writings
of Wycliffe. Against these proceedings Dr. Huss, with some
other members of the university, protested, and entered an
appeal from the sentences of the archbishop. The pope no
sooner heard of this than he granted a commission to
Cardinal Colonna to cite John Huss to appear at the court
of Rome, to answer accusations laid against him of preaching both errors and heresies. From this appearance Dr.
Huss desired to be excused, and so greatly was he favoured
in Bohemia, that King Winceslaus, the queen, the nobility,
and the university desired the pope to dispense with such
an appearance; as also that he would not suffer the kingdom of Bohemia to lie under the accusation of heresy, but
permit them to preach the Gospel with freedom in their
places of worship.

Three proctors appeared for Dr. Huss before Cardinal

Colonna; they pleaded an excuse for his absence, and said
they were ready to answer in his behalf. But the cardinal
declared him contumacious, and, accordingly, excommunicated him. On this the proctors appealed to the pope, who
appointed four cardinals to examine the process; these
commissioners confirmed the sentence of the cardinal, and
extended the excommunication, not only to Huss, but to all
his friends and followers. Huss then appealed from this
unjust sentence to a future council, but without success;
and, notwithstanding so severe a decree, and an expulsion
from his church in Prague, he retired to Hussinetz, where
he continued to promulgate the truth, both from the pulpit
and with the pen.

In the month of November, in the year 1414, a general
council was assembled at Constance, in Germany, for the
purpose of determining a dispute then existing between
three persons who contended for the papal throne. These
were—John, proposed and set up by the Italians; Gregory,
by the French; and Benedict, by the Spaniards. The council
continued four years, in which the severest laws were
enacted to crush the Protestants. Pope John was deposed,
and obliged to fly.

John Huss was summoned to appear at this council; and
to dispel any apprehensions of danger, the emperor sent
him a safe-conduct, the wording being, "You shall let John
Huss pass, stop, stay, and return freely, without any
hindrance whatever." On receiving this information, he
told the persons who delivered it that he desired nothing
more than to purge himself publicly of the imputation of
heresy; and that he esteemed himself happy in having so
fair an opportunity of it as at the council to which he was
summoned to attend.

Notwithstanding the promise of the emperor to give him
a safe-conduct to and from Constance, no regard was paid
to the imperial pledge; but, according to the maxim of this
same council, that "faith is not to be kept with heretics,"
when it was known he was in the city, he was arrested, and
imprisoned in the palace. This breach of faith was noticed
by one of Huss's friends, who pleaded the imperial safe-
conduct; but the pope replied that he had not granted any
such thing, nor was he bound by the obligations of the
emperor.

While Huss was under confinement, the council acted
the part of inquisitors. They condemned the doctrines of
Wycliffe, and in their impotent malice ordered his remains

to be exhumed, and burnt to ashes; which orders were obeyed.

In the meantime the nobility of Bohemia and Poland used all their interest for Huss, and so far prevailed as to prevent his being condemned unheard, which had been resolved on by the commissioners appointed to try him.

At length he was brought before the council, when the articles exhibited against him were read: they were upwards of twenty-six in number, and chiefly extracted from his writings.

On his examination being finished, he was taken from the court, and a resolution was formed by the council to burn him as an heretic unless he retracted. He was then committed to a filthy prison, where, in the day-time, he was so laden with fetters that he could hardly move; and every night he was fastened by his hands to a ring against the walls of the prison.

He continued some days in this situation, during which time many noblemen of Bohemia interceded on his behalf. They drew up a petition for his release, which was presented to the council by several of the most illustrious nobles of Bohemia; notwithstanding which, so many enemies had Huss in that court, that no attention was paid to it, and the reformer was compelled to submit to the sentence of that merciless tribunal.

Shortly after the petition was presented, four bishops and two lords were sent by the emperor to the prison, in order to prevail on Huss to recant. But he called God to witness, with tears in his eyes, that he was not conscious of having preached or written anything against the truth of God, or the faith of his orthodox Church.

On the 4th of July he was, for the last time, brought before the council. After a long examination he was commanded to abjure, which, without hesitation, he refused to do. The council censured him for being obstinate and incorrigible, and ordained that he should be degraded from the priesthood, his books publicly burnt, and himself delivered to the secular power.

He received the sentence without the least emotion; and at the close of it kneeled down, and lifting his eyes towards heaven, exclaimed, with the magnanimity of a primitive martyr, "May thy infinite mercy, O my God! pardon this injustice of mine enemies. Thou knowest the injustice of my accusations: how deformed with crimes I have been represented; how I have been oppressed with worthless witnesses, and a false condemnation; yet, O my God! let that mercy of thine, which no tongue can express, prevail with thee not to avenge my wrongs."

A serenity appeared in his looks, which indicated that his soul was approaching the realms of everlasting happiness; and when the bishop urged him to recant, he turned to the people and addressed them thus:—

"These lords and bishops do counsel me that I should confess before you all that I have erred; which thing, if it might be done with the infamy and reproach of man only, they might, peradventure, easily persuade me to do; but now I am in the sight of the Lord my God, without whose great displeasure I could not do that which they require. For I well know that I never taught any of those things which they have falsely alleged against me, but I have always preached, taught, written, and thought contrary thereunto."

The bishops then delivered him to the emperor, who handed him over to the Duke of Bavaria. His books were burnt at the gates of the church; and on the 6th of July he was led to the suburbs of Constance to be burnt alive.

Having reached the place of execution, he fell on his knees, sung several portions of the Psalms, and looked steadfastly towards heaven, saying, "Into thy hands, O Lord! do I commit my spirit: thou hast redeemed me, O most good and faithful God."

As soon as the faggots were lighted, the martyr sung a hymn, with so cheerful a voice, that he was heard above the cracklings of the fire and the noise of the multitude. At length his voice was interrupted by the flames, which soon put an end to his existence.

Account of the Life, Sufferings, and Martyrdom of Jerome of Prague, Who Was Burnt at Constance, in Germany, for Maintaining the Doctrine of Wycliffe.

This hero in the cause of truth was born and educated at Prague, where he soon became distinguished for his learning and eloquence. Having completed his studies, he travelled over a great part of Europe, and visited many of the seats of learning, particularly the Universities of Paris, Heidelberg, Cologne, and Oxford. At the latter he became acquainted with the works of Wycliffe, and being a person of uncommon application, he translated many of them into his own language, having made himself master of English.

On his return to Prague, Jerome openly professed the

doctrines of Wycliffe, and finding that they had made considerable progress in Bohemia, from the industry and zeal of Huss, he became his assistant in the work of reformation.

On the 4th of April, A.D. 1415, Jerome went to Constance. This was about three months before the death of Huss. He entered the town privately, and consulting with some of the leaders of his party, was convinced that he could render his friend no service.

Finding that his arrival at Constance was known, and that the council intended to seize him, he prudently retired, and went to Iberling, an imperial town, a short distance from Constance. While here he wrote to the emperor, and stated his readiness to appear before the council, on the receipt of a safe-conduct; this, however, was refused. He then applied to the council, but also met with an unfavourable answer.

After this he caused papers to be put up in all the public places in Constance, particularly on the doors of the cardinal's house. In these he professed his willingness to appear at Constance in the defence of his character and doctrine, both of which, he said, had been greatly falsified. He farther declared that if any error should be proved against him, he would retract it; desiring only that the faith of the council might be given for his security.

Receiving no answer to these papers, he set out for Bohemia, taking the precaution to carry with him a certificate, signed by several of the Bohemian nobility then at Constance, testifying that he had used every means in his power to procure an audience.

He was, however, seized on his way, at Hirsaw, by an officer belonging to the Duke of Sultzbach, who hoped thereby to receive commendations from the council for so acceptable a service.

The Duke of Sultzbach immediately wrote to the council, informing them of what he had done, and asked directions as to how he should proceed with Jerome. The council, after expressing their obligations to the duke, desired him to send the prisoner to Constance. He was accordingly conveyed to a tower in Constance and fastened to a block, with his legs in stocks. He remained confined till the martyrdom of his friend Huss; after which he was brought forth and threatened with torments and death if he remained obstinate. Terrified at the preparations of torture, he, in a moment of weakness, abjured his doctrines, and

confessed that Huss merited his fate, and that both he and
Wycliffe were heretics. In consequence of this his chains
were taken off, and this harsh treatment suspended. His
enemies, however, suspecting his sincerity, proposed another form of recantation to him. He refused to answer
this, except in public, and was accordingly brought before
the council, when, to the astonishment of his auditors, and
to the glory of truth, he renounced his recantation, and
requested permission to plead his own cause, which being
refused, he thus vented his indignation:—

"What barbarity is this? For 340 days have I been
confined in a variety of prisons. There is not a misery,
there is not a want, which I have not experienced. To my
enemies you have allowed the fullest scope of accusation:
to me you deny the least opportunity of defence. You have
represented me as a heretic, without knowing my doctrine;
as an enemy of the faith, before you knew what faith I
professed. You are a general council; in you centre all
which this world can communicate of gravity, wisdom and
sanctity: but still you are men, and men are seducible by
appearances. The higher your character is for wisdom, the
greater ought your care to be not to deviate into folly. The
cause I now plead is not my own, it is the cause of men: it
is the cause of Christians: it is a cause which is to affect the
rights of posterity."

On the third day from this his trial commenced, and
witnesses were examined in support of the charge. The
prisoner was prepared for his defence, which appears
almost incredible, when we consider he had been nearly a
year shut up in loathsome prisons, deprived of daylight,
and almost starved for want of common necessaries.

The most bigoted of the assembly were unwilling he
should be heard, dreading the effects of eloquence in the
cause of truth, on the minds of the most prejudiced. At
length, however, it was carried by the majority that he
should have liberty to proceed in his defence; which he
began in such an exalted strain, and continued in such a
torrent of elocution, that the obdurate heart was seen to
melt. He began to deduce from history the number of great
and virtuous men who had, in their time, been condemned
and punished as evil persons, but whom after generations
had proved to have deserved honour and reward. He laid
before the assembly the whole tenor of his life and conduct. He observed that the greatest and most holy men had
been known to differ in points of speculation, with a view

to discover and not suppress the truth. He entered upon a high encomium on Huss, and declared he was ready to follow him to martyrdom. He then proceeded to defend the doctrines of the English luminary, Wycliffe; and concluded with observing that it was far from his intention to advance anything against the state of the Church of God; that it was only against the abuse of the clergy he complained; and that it was certainly impious that the patrimony of the Church, which was originally intended for the purposes of charity and benevolence, should be prostituted to the pride of the eye, in feasts, foppish vestments, and other reproaches to the profession of religion.

The trial being ended, Jerome received the same sentence as had been passed on Huss, and was delivered over the the secular power; but, being a layman, had not to undergo the ceremony of degradation. They had, however, prepared for him a cap of paper painted with red devils, which, being put on his head, he said, "Our Lord Jesus Christ, when he suffered death for me, a most miserable sinner, did wear a crown of thorns upon his head; and I, for his sake, will wear this cap."

On his way to the place of execution he sang several hymns; and on arriving at the spot where Huss had suffered, kneeled down and prayed fervently. He embraced the stake with great cheerfulness; and when the executioner went behind him to set fire to the faggots, he said, "Come here and kindle it before my eyes; for had I been afraid of it, I had not come here, having had so many opportunities of escape." When the flames enveloped him he sang a hymn; and the last words he was heard to say were "This soul in flames I offer, Christ, to thee!"

Account of the Persecutions in the Netherlands.

About the years 1543 and 1544 the storm of persecution raged with great violence in Flanders. Charles V, Emperor of Germany, and King of Spain, under whose dominion these provinces were, laboured vigorously to uproot heresy, and his efforts formed a bloody prelude to the more systematic onslaught of Alva and the Inquisition, under the reign of his son and successor, Philip II. Many of the reformed faith were sentenced to imprisonment or banishment for life; but the generality were martyred, by being hung, drowned, burned, racked, or buried alive. A zealous Protestant, by name John de Boscane, was arrested, in the city of Antwerp, on account of his faith. He was subjected

to the usual mockery of a trial, at which, on his boldly
avowing himself a Protestant, he was speedily condemned.
The authorities, however, were afraid to execute Boscane
in public, as from his great generosity and exemplary
piety, he was both popular and revered. They determined,
therefore, that he should be executed in private, and accordingly ordered him to be drowned in the prison.

In the year 1568 three persons—by name Scoblant,
Hues, and Coomans—were arrested at the above-men-
tioned city. In an epistle to some Protestant brethren,
written during their confinement, they expressed themselves as follows:—"Since it is the will of the Almighty that
we should suffer for his name, we patiently submit; though
the flesh may rebel against the spirit, yet the truths of the
Gospel shall support us, and Christ shall bruise the ser-
pent's head. We are comforted, for we have faith; we fear
not affliction, for we have hope; we forgive our enemies,
for we have charity. Be not alarmed for us; we are happy
through the promises of God, and exult in being thought
worthy to suffer for Christ's sake. We do not desire release,
but fortitude; we ask not for liberty, but for the power of
perseverance; we wish for no change but that which places
a crown of victory on our heads."

Scoblant was the first who was brought to trial, and,
persisting in his faith, was sentenced to death. On his
return to prison he requested the gaoler not to allow any
friar to visit him, saying, "They can do me no good, but
may greatly disturb me; I trust that my salvation is already
sealed in heaven, and that the blood of Christ, in which I
firmly trust, has washed away my sins. I now cast off this
mantle of clay, for robes of eternal glory. May I be the last
martyr to papal tyranny, that the Church of Christ may
have rest on earth, as she will hereafter." On the day of
execution he took a pathetic leave of his fellow-prisoners.
When bound to the stake, he sang the 40th Psalm, and
repeated, with great fervency, the Lord's Prayer—that
wondrous prayer, so sublime, yet simple, breathed by
millions since first the solitary Teacher uttered it on the
mountains of Galilee, and never possessing a sweeter
emphasis than when gasped with dying breath amidst the
crackling of the blazing pile. Having commended his soul
to God, the martyr soon perished in the flames.

A short time afterwards, Hues died in prison. After the
loss of Hues, Coomans thus writes to his friends:—"I am
now deprived of my companions: Scoblant is martyred,

and Hues is dead; yet I am not alone: the God of Israel is with me, who is my shield and my exceeding great reward." When brought to trial Coomans readily acknowledged himself to be of the reformed religion; and with manly firmness replied to every charge brought against him, proving his doctrine from the Gospel. "But," said the judge, "will you die for the faith you profess?" "I am not only willing to die for the truth," replied Coomans, "but also to suffer the utmost stretch of inventive cruelty for the Gospel's sake; after which my soul shall be received by God Himself in the midst of eternal glory." After his condemnation he went cheerfully to the place of execution, and perished with a holy resignation, the result of an enlightened faith.

Baltazar Gerard—a native of Franche Compté, a province of Burgundy—a bigoted papist, in hopes of advancing the cause of religion by one desperate act, determined to assassinate William of Nassau, the Prince of Orange. Having provided himself with firearms, he watched the prince as he passed through the hall of his palace to dinner, and demanded a passport. The Princess of Orange, observing something singular in his voice and manner, asked who he was, remarking she did not like his countenance. The prince answered it was some one who wanted a passport, with which he should be presently furnished. Nothing further transpired till after dinner, when, upon the return of the prince and princess through the same hall, the assassin, having secreted himself behind one of the pillars, fired at the prince, mortally wounding him. On receiving the wound the prince had only power to say, "Lord, have mercy on my soul, and on this poor people!" and immediately expired, in the fifty-first year of his age. The death of this prince spread universal grief throughout the united provinces; his funeral was the grandest ever witnessed in the Low Countries; and the lamentations over his loss were unfeigned, for he left behind him that character which should be always coveted by royalty, but, alas! is so seldom deserved, that of the "father of his people."

Account of the Persecutions in Lithuania.

The persecutions in Lithuania commenced in 1648, and were carried on with great severity by the Cossacks and Tartars. The cruelty of the former was such that even the Tartars revolted from it, and rescued some of the intended victims from their hands. The Russians, perceiving the devastation that had been made in the country, and its incapability of defence, entered it with a considerable army, and carried ruin wherever they went; everything was devoted to destruction, the country was wasted, the churches destroyed, villages burnt, the cities razed, the castles demolished, the people murdered, and the ministers of the Gospel singled out as objects of especial hatred.

Summary of the Persecutions Against the Christians in Abyssinia, or Ethiopia.

About the end of the fifteenth century, some Portuguese missionaries made a voyage to Abyssinia, and began to propagate their Roman Catholic doctrines among the Abyssinians, who professed Christianity before the arrival of the missionaries.

The priests gained such influence at court, that the emperor consented to abolish the established rites of the Ethiopian Church, and to admit those of Rome; and soon after consented to receive a patriarch from the pope, and to acknowledge his supremacy. This innovation, however, did not take place without great opposition. Several of the most powerful lords, and a majority of the people who professed the primitive Christianity, as at first established in Abyssinia, took up arms against the emperor. Thus, by the artifices of the court of Rome and its emissaries, the whole empire was thrown into commotion, and a war commenced which was carried on through the reign of many emperors, and which ceased not for above a century. All this time the Roman Catholics were strengthened by the power of the court, by means of which union the primitive Christians of Abyssinia were severely persecuted, and multitudes perished.

Some Account of the Persecutions in Japan.

Some Portuguese missionaries were the first to introduce Christianity into Japan. They landed on the island in the year 1552, and their efforts met with a degree of success beyond what they had ventured to anticipate. Their labours continued to be successful until the year 1616, when they were accused of being implicated in a conspiracy to overthrow the government and dethrone the emperor. For a few years they remained unmolested, though the greatest jealousy existed against them at the court, but in 1622 a dreadful persecution broke out against both the foreign and native Christians. It is asserted that during the first four years no less than 20,000 Christians were massacred. The churches were shut, and any profession of Christianity was punished with death. At length the Christians retired to the town of Siniabara, in the island of Ximio, where they determined to defend themselves to the last extremity. They were followed by the Japanese army, who besieged the place. The Christians, although much inferior in point of discipline, equipments, and resources, defended themselves with the greatest bravery, and resisted all attacks, for the space of three months; when, owing to scarcity of provisions and the weakening of their ranks, they were obliged to surrender. Every age and sex were then ruthlessly murdered by the conquerors, and Christianity, after its brief existence, was completely extirpated from the dominions of the Tycoon.

Summary of the Persecutions and Oppressions Against the Christians in Turkey.

That arch impostor Mohammed, in his early career, affected to respect the Christians. But no sooner was his power established, then he displayed himself in his true colours, as their determined and sanguinary enemy. This he proved by his persecutions of them in his lifetime, and by commanding those persecutions to be continued by his followers. From him the Turks received their religion, which they still maintain. Mohammed and his descendants, during the short period of thirty years, subdued Arabia, Palestine, Phoenicia, Syria, Egypt, and Persia. They soon, however, became divided among themselves. The princes of the Saracens, assuming the title of sultan, continued their rule over Syria, Egypt, and Africa, for the space of about 400 years, but when the Saracen King of Persia commenced war against the Saracen Sultan of Babylon, the latter brought to his aid the Turks. These Turks in time turned their arms against their masters, and by the valour of Ottomanus, from whom are descended the present family who fill the Turkish throne, they soon subdued the Saracens, and established the Ottoman Empire.

Constantinople, after having been for many ages an imperial Christian city, was invested in the year 1453 by the Turks under Mohammed II, whose army consisted of 300,000 men, and, after a bloody siege of six weeks, it fell into the hands of the Turks, who have retained it in their possession unto the present time. They no sooner found themselves masters of it than they began to exercise the most unrelenting barbarities on the inhabitants, destroying them by every method of cruelty. Some were roasted alive on spits, others were starved, some were flayed alive, many were sawn asunder, and others were torn to pieces by horses.

About the year 1521, Solyman I took Belgrade from the Christians. Two years after, with a fleet of 450 ships, and an army of 300,000 men, he attacked Rhodes, then defended by the knights of Jerusalem. These heroes resisted the infidels till all their buildings were levelled with the ground, their provisions exhausted, and their ammunition spent, when, receiving no succours from the Christian princes, they surrendered.

Mad with conquest, Solyman now proceeded westward to Vienna, glutting himself with slaughter on his march, and indulging in the vain hope that he would speedily prostrate Europe in the dust, and root out Christians from the earth.

Having pitched his tent before the walls of Vienna, he sent three Christian prisoners into the town to terrify the citizens with an account of the strength of his army. Happily for the Germans, three days only before the arrival of the Turks, the Earl Palatine Frederic, to whom was assigned the defence of Vienna, had entered the town with 14,000 chosen veterans. Solyman sent a summons for the city to surrender; and on receiving the defiance of the Germans, commenced the siege. It is well known that the religion of Mohammed promises to all soldiers who die in battle, whatever be their crimes, immediate admission to the joys of paradise. Hence arises that fury and temerity they usually display in fighting. They began with a most tremendous cannonade, and made many attempts to take the city by assault. But the steady valour of the Germans was superior to their enemies. Solyman, filled with indignation at this unusual check to his fortune, determined to exert every power to carry his project; to this end he planted his ordnance before the king's gate, and battered it with such violence, that a breach was soon made, whereupon the Turks, under cover of the smoke, poured in torrents into the city, and the soldiers began to give up all for lost. But the officers, with admirable presence of mind, causing a great shouting to be made in the city, as if fresh troops had just arrived, their own soldiers were inspired with fresh courage, while the Turks fled in a panic.

Grown more desperate by resistance, Solyman resolved

upon another attempt to storm the city by undermining the
Corinthian gate. They succeeded in reaching the foundations of the tower; but they were discovered by the wary
citizens, who with amazing activity, countermined them;
and having prepared a train of gunpowder, even to the
trenches of the enemy, set fire to it, blowing up about
8,000, and by that means rendered their attempts abortive.
Foiled in every attempt, the courage of the Turkish chief
degenerated into madness; he ordered his men to scale the
walls, in which attempt they were destroyed by thousands,
their very numbers tending to their own defeat, till, at
length, the valour of his troops fainted; and, dreading the
hardihood of their European adversaries, they began to
refuse obedience. Sickness also seized their camp, and
numbers perished from famine; for the Germans, by their
vigilance, had found means to cut off their supplies: and
Captain Rogendorffius, a brave and generous soldier, had
one time, in a sally, slain about 5,000 Turks whom he had
perceived from the walls estranged from the camp. Foiled
in every attempt, dispirited in his prospects, Solyman at
length, after having lost above 80,000 men, abandoned his
enterprise, and sending his baggage before him, proceeded
homewards, freeing Europe from the impending terror of
universal Mohammedanism.

Account of the Persecutions in Calabria.

About the fourteenth century, a great many Waldenses
of Pragela and Dauphiny emigrated to Calabria.

The nobles of Calabria were highly pleased with their
new tenants, finding them honest, quiet, and industrious;
but the priests, filled with jealousy, soon preferred several
negative complaints against them.

To these the Calabrian lords replied, that these people
were extremely harmless, giving no offence to the Roman
Catholics, but cheerfully paying the tithes to the priests,
whose revenues were considerably increased by their coming into the country, and who, consequently, ought to be
the very last person to make a complaint.

Things went on peacefully for a few years, during which
the Waldenses formed themselves into two corporate
towns, annexing several villages to their jurisdiction. At
length they sent to Geneva for two clergymen, one to
preach in each town. This being known, intelligence was
conveyed to Pope Pius IV, who determined to exterminate
them from Calabria without delay. To this end Cardinal

Alexandrino, a man of a violent temper, and a furious
bigot, was sent, together with two monks, to Calabria,
where they were to act as inquisitors. They came to St.
Xist, one of the towns built by the Waldenses, where,
having assembled the people, they told them that they
should receive no injury if they would accept the preachers
appointed by the pope; but if they refused, they should be
deprived both of their properties and lives; and that to
prove them, mass should be publicly said that afternoon, at
which they must attend.

But the people of St. Xist, instead of obeying this, fled
with their families into the woods, and thus disappointed
the cardinal and his coadjutors. Then they proceeded to La
Garde, the other town belonging to the Waldenses, where,
to avoid the like disappointment, they ordered the gates to
be locked, and all the approaches guarded. The same
proposals were made to the inhabitants, backed by this
artifice: the cardinal assured them that the inhabitants of
St. Xist had accepted his proposals, and agreed that the
pope should appoint their preachers. This falsehood succeeded; for the simple people of La Garde, thinking that
what the cardinal had told them was the truth, said they
would follow the example of their brethren at St. Xist.

The cardinal, having gained his point by a lie, sent for
two companies of soldiers to massacre the people of St.
Xist. The troops entered the woods, and many Waldenses
fell a prey to their ferocity. However, they determined to
sell their lives as dearly as possible, when several conflicts
took place, in which the half-armed Waldenses performed
prodigies of valour, and many were slain on both sides. At
length, the greater part of the troops being killed in the
different encounters, the remainder were compelled to
retreat, which so enraged the cardinal, that he wrote to the
Viceroy of Naples for reinforcements. Hereupon, the viceroy proclaimed throughout the Neapolitan territories, that
all outlaws, deserters, and other proscribed persons should
be freely pardoned for their crimes, on condition of making a campaign against the inhabitants of St. Xist, and of
continuing under arms till those people were destroyed. On
this several persons of desperate fortunes joined together,
and being formed into light companies, were sent to scour
the woods, and put to death all they could meet with of the
reformed religion. The viceroy also joined the cardinal, at
the head of a body of regular forces; and they mutually

strove to accomplish their bloody purpose. The inhuman chase was continued till all these poor people perished.

The inhabitants of St. Xist being exterminated, those of La Garde engaged the attention of the cardinal and viceroy. The fullest protection was offered to themselves, their families, and their children, if they would embrace the Roman Catholic persuasion; but, on the contrary, if they refused this mercy, the utmost extremities would be used and the most cruel deaths would be the consequences of refusal. In spite of the promises on one side, and menaces on the other, the Waldenses refused to renounce their religion, or to embrace the errors of popery. The cardinal and viceroy were so filled with rage at this, that they ordered thirty of them to be put to the rack, as a terror to the others. These barbarities, however, did not answer the end for which they were intended; for those who survived the torments of the rack, and those who had not felt it, remained equally constant to their fatih, and boldly declared that no torments whatever should ever induce them to renounce their God, or bow down to idols. The effect of this upon the obdurate cardinal was, that he ordered several of them to be stripped naked, and whipped to death with iron rods: some were hacked to pieces with large knives; others were thrown from the top of a high tower; and many, after the example of the pagan emperor, were cased over with pitch and burnt alive.

The four principal men of La Garde were hanged, and the clergyman was thrown from the top of his church steeple.

Many were put to death by various means; and so jealous and arbitrary were those fiends, that if any Roman Catholic, more compassionate than the rest, interceded for the reformed, he was immediately apprehended and sacrificed as a favourer of heretics.

The viceroy being obliged to return to Naples, and the cardinal having been recalled to Rome, the Marquis of Butiane was commissioned to complete what they had begun; which he at length effected, by acting with such barbarous rigour, that there was not a single person of the reformed religion left in all Calabria, A great number of inoffensive and harmless people were thus deprived of their possessions, robbed of their property, driven from their homes, and at length murdered by various means, only because they would not sacrifice their consciences to the superstitions of others, embrace doctrines which they abhorred, and listed to teachers whom they could not believe.

Account of the Persecutions in the Valleys of Piedmont.

The Waldenses, in consequence of the continued persecutions they met with in France, fled for refuge to various
parts of the world; among other places, many of them
sought an asylum in the valleys of Piedmont, where they
increased and flourished exceedingly for a considerable
time.

Notwithstanding their harmless behaviour, and their
payment of tithes to the Romish clergy, the latter could not
remain contented, but sought to disturb them, and accordingly complained to the Archbishop of Turin, that the
Waldenses of the valleys of Piedmont were heretics. They
alleged the following reasons: that they did not believe in
the doctrines of the Church of Rome; that they made no
offerings for the dead; that they did not go to mass; that
they neither confessed nor received absolution; that they
did not believe in purgatory, nor pay money to get the
souls of their friends released. Upon these charges the
archbishop ordered a persecution to be commenced.

At Revel, Catelin Girard being at the stake, desired the
executioner to give him a stone, which he refused, thinking
that he meant to throw it at somebody; but Girard assuring
him that he had no such intention, the executioner complied; when Girard, looking earnestly at the stone, said,
"When it is in the power of a man to eat and digest this
solid stone, the religion for which I am about to suffer shall
have an end, and not before." He then threw the stone on
the ground, and submitted cheerfully to the flames. A great
many more were maltreated or put to death, till, wearied
with their sufferings, the Waldenses flew to arms in their
own defence, and formed themselves into regular bodies.
Full of revenge at this, the Archbishop of Turin sent a
number of troops against them; but in most of the skir-
mishes the Waldenses were victorious.

Philip VII was at this time Duke of Savoy and Lord of
Piedmont. He determined at length to interpose his authority, and stop these bloody wars, which convulsed the
internal policy of his kingdom. Unwilling to offend the
pope or the Archbishop of Turin, he nevertheless sent them
both messages, to the effect that he could not any longer
tamely see his dominions overrun with troops, who were
commanded by prelates in the place of generals, nor would

he suffer his country to be depopulated, while he himself
had not been even consulted upon the occasion.

The priests, perceiving the determination of the duke,
endeavoured to prejudice his mind against the Waldenses.
The duke told them that though he was unacquainted with
the religious tenets of these people, yet he had always
found them quiet, faithful, and obedient, and was therefore
determined that they should be persecuted no longer. The
priests then assured the duke that he was mistaken in the
Waldenses, for they were a wicked set of people, and
addicted to intemperance, uncleanness, blasphemy, adul-
tery, and many abominable crimes. But the duke was not
to be imposed upon, though the priests affirmed these
things in the most solemn manner. In order to arrive at the
truth, he sent twelve learned gentlemen into the Piedmontese valleys, to examine into the real characters of the
people.

These gentlemen, after travelling through all their towns
and villages, and conversing with the Waldenses of every
rank, returned to the duke, and gave him the most favourable account of them; affirming, before the faces of the
priests, that they were harmless, loyal, friendly, industrious,
and pious: that they abhorred the crimes of which they
were accused; and that, should an individual, through his
depravity, fall into any of those crimes, he would, by their
laws, be punished in the most exemplary manner. "And to
convince your highness of what we have said," continued
one of the gentlemen, "we have brought twelve of the
principal inhabitants, who are come to ask pardon in the
name of the rest, for having taken up arms without your
leave, though in their own defence, and to preserve their
lives from their merciless enemies. We have likewise
brought several women, with children of various ages, that
your highness may have an opportunity of judging for
yourself." His highness then accepted the apology of the
twelve delegates, and afterwards graciously dismissed them.
He then commanded the priests to leave the court, and
gave strict orders that the persecution should cease
throughout his dominions.

During the reign of this virtuous prince, the Waldenses
enjoyed repose in their retreats; but, on his death, this
happy scene changed, for his successor was a bigoted
papist. About the same time some of the principal Waldenses proposed that their clergy should preach in public,
that every one should know the purity of their doctrines;

for hitherto they had preached only in private, and to such congregations as they well knew consisted of none but persons of the reformed religion.

When this reached the ears of the new duke, he was greatly exasperated, and sent a considerable body of troops into the valleys, swearing that if the people would not conform to the Roman faith, he would have them flayed alive. The commander of the troops soon found the impracticability of conquering them with the number of men under his command; he, therefore, sent word to the duke, that the idea of subjugating the Waldenses with so small a force was ridiculous; that they were better acquainted with the country than any that were with him; that they had secured all the passes, were well armed, and determined to defend themselves. Alarmed at this, the duke commanded the troops to return, determining to act by stratagem. He, therefore, offered rewards for the capture of any of the Waldenses who might be found straying from their places of security; and these, when taken, were either flayed alive or burnt.

Pope Paul III, a furious bigot, ascending the pontifical chair, immediately solicited the Parliament of Turin to prosecute the Waldenses, as the most pernicious of all heretics. To this the Parliament readily assented, when several were suddenly seized and burnt by their order. Among these was Bartholomew Hector, a bookseller and stationer of Turin. He was brought up a Roman Catholic, but some treatises written by the reformed clergy having fallen into his hands, he was fully convinced of their truth, and of the errors of the Church of Rome,

A consultation was again held by the Parliament of Turin, in which it was agreed that deputies should be sent to the valleys of Piedmont with the following propositions: —1. That if the Waldenses would return to the bosom of the Church of Rome, they should enjoy their houses, properties, and lands, and live with their families, without the least molestation. 2. That to prove their obedience, they should send twelve of their principal persons, with all their ministers and schoolmasters, to Turin, to be dealt with at discretion. 3. That the pope, the King of France, and the Duke of Savoy, approved of and authorised the proceedings of the Parliament of Turin upon this occasion. 4. That if the Waldenses of Piedmont rejected the propositions, persecution and death should be their reward.

In answer to these hostile articles, the Waldenses made

the following noble replies:—1. That no consideration whatever should make them renounce their religion. 2. That they would never consent to entrust their best and most respectable friends to the custody and discretion of their worst enemies. 3. That they valued the approbation of the King of kings, who reigns in heaven, more than any temporal authority. 4. That their souls were more precious than their bodies.

As may be conjectured, these spirited and pointed answers greatly exasperated the Parliament of Turin; in consequence of which they continued with more zeal than ever to kidnap such Waldenses as fell into their hands, who were sure to suffer the most cruel deaths. Among these it unfortunately happened that they caught Jeffrey Varnagle, minister of Angrogna, whom they accused of being a heretic, and committed to the flames.

They soon after solicited from the King of France a considerable body of troops, in order to exterminate the reformed from the valleys of Piedmont; but just as the troops were about to march, the Protestant princes of Germany interposed, and threatened to send troops to assist the Waldenses. On this the King of France, not caring to enter into a war, remanded the troops, and sent word to the Parliament of Turin that he could not spare them at present to act in Piedmont. At this those Sanguinary members of the Parliament were greatly disappointed, and for want of power the persecution gradually ceased.

After a few years' tranquillity, they were again disturbed by the following means: the pope's nuncio coming to Turin to the Duke of Savoy upon business, told that prince he was astonished he had not either rooted out the Waldenses from the valleys of Piedmont nor yet compelled them to return to the Church of Rome: that such conduct in him awakened suspicion, and that he really thought him a favourer of those heretics, and should accordingly report the affair to the pope. Roused by this reflection, and fearful of being misrepresented to the pope, the duke determined to banish those suspicions; and to prove his zeal, resolved to let loose the reins of cruelty on the unoffending Waldenses. He accordingly issued express orders for all to attend mass regularly, on pain of death. This they absolutely refused to do, on which he entered the Piedmontese valleys with a great body of troops, and began a most furious persecution, in which great numbers were hanged, drowned, tied to trees, pierced with prongs, thrown from precipices, burnt, stabbed, racked to death, worried by dogs, and crucified with their heads downwards. If any whom they took seemed wavering in their faith, they did not put them to death, but sent them to the galleys, to be converted by dint of hardships.

In this expedition the duke was accompanied by three men who were very cruel, viz.—1. Thomas Incomel, an apostate, brought up in the reformed religion, but who had renounced his faith, embraced the errors of popery, and turned monk. He was a great libertine, abandoned to every crime, and solicitous for the plunder of the Waldenses. 2. Corbis, a man of a very ferocious and cruel nature, whose business was to examine the prisoners. 3. The provost of justice, an avaricious miser, anxious for the execution of the Waldenses, as every execution added to his hoards.

These three monsters were unmerciful to the last degree; wherever they came, the blood of the innocent was sure to flow. But, besides the cruelties exercised by the duke with these three persons and the army in their different marches, many local barbarities took place.

The Roman Catholic inhabitants of the valley of St. Martin did all they could to torment the neighbouring Waldenses: they destroyed their churches, burnt their houses, seized their properties, stole their cattle, converted their lands to their own use, committed their ministers to the flames; and drove the people to the woods, where they had nothing to subsist on but wild fruits and the bark or roots of trees.

The monks of Pignerol having a great desire to get into their possession a minister of a town in the valleys, called St. Germain, hired a band of ruffians for the purpose of seizing him. These fellows were conducted by a treacherous person, formerly a servant to the clergyman. The guide knocked at the door, and being asked who was there, answered in his own name. The clergyman, expecting no injury from a person on whom he had heaped favour, immediately opened the door; but, perceiving the ruffians, he fled, when they rushed in, and seized him. They murdered his family; after which they proceeded with their captive towards Pignerol. He was confined a considerable time in prison, and then burnt.

The troops of ruffians belonging to the monks continuing their assaults about the town of St. Germain, murdering and plundering many of the inhabitants, the reformed of

Lucerne and Angrogna sent some armed men to the assistance of their brethren. These bodies of armed men frequently attacked and routed the ruffians, which so alarmed the monks, that they left their monastery of Pignerol for some time, till they could procure regular troops for their protection.

The Duke of Savoy, not thinking himself so successful as he at first imagined he should be, augmented his forces by the incorporation of every criminal, and commanded that a general release should take place in the prisons, provided the liberated would bear arms, and assist in the extermination of the Waldenses.

No sooner were the Waldenses informed of these proceedings than they secured as much of their properties as they could, and, quitting the valleys, retired to the rocks and caves among the Higher Alps.

The army no sooner reached their destined places than they began to plunder and burn the towns and villages wherever they came; but the troops could not force the passes of the Alps, gallantly defended by the Waldenses.

Determined, if possible, to expel their invaders, the Waldenses entered into a league with the Protestant Powers in Germany, and with the reformed of Dauphiny and Pragela. These were respectively to furnish bodies of troops; and the Waldenses resolved, when thus reinforced, to quit the mountains of the Alps, where they soon must have perished, as the winter was coming on, and to force the duke's army to evacuate their native valleys.

But the Duke of Savoy himself was tired of the war, it having cost him great fatigue and anxiety of mind, a vast number of men, and very considerable sums of money. For these reasons, and fearing that the Waldenses, by the treaties they had entered into, would become too powerful for him, he determined to return to Turin with his army, and to make peace with them.

This resolution he put in practice, greatly against the will of the ecclesiastics. Before the articles of peace could be ratified, the duke himself died soon after his return to Turin; but on his death-bed he strictly enjoined his son to perform what he had intended, and to be as favourable as possible to the Waldenses.

Charles Emmanuel, the duke's son, succeeded to the dominions of Savoy, and fully ratified the peace with the Waldenses.

A Farther Account of the Persecutions in the Valleys of Piedmont in the Seventeenth Century.

Pope Clement VIII sent missionaries into the valleys of Piedmont, with a view to induce the Protestants to renounce their religion. These missionaries erected monasteries in several parts of the valleys, and soon became very troublesome to the reformed, to whom the monasteries appeared not only as fortresses to curb, but as sanctuaries for all to fly to as had injured them in any degree.

The insolence and tyranny of these missionaries increasing, the Protestants petitioned the Duke of Savoy for protection. But instead of getting any redress, the duke published a decree, in which he declared that one witness should be sufficient in a court of law against a Protestant, and that any witness who convicted a Protestant of any crime whatever should be entitled to a hundred crowns reward.

In consequence of this, as may be imagined, many Protestants fell martyrs to perjury and avarice.

To encourage, as much as possible, the apostacy of the Protestants, the Duke of Savoy published a proclamation, wherein he said, "To encourage the heretics to turn Catholics, it is our will and pleasure, and we do hereby expressly command, that all such as shall embrace the holy Roman faith shall enjoy an exemption from all and every tax for the space of five years, commencing from the day of their conversion." He likewise established a court, called the council for extirpating the heretics. This court was to enter into inquiries concerning the ancient privileges of the Protestant churches, and the decrees which had been, from time to time, made in favour of them.

After this the duke published several successive edicts, prohibiting the Protestants from acting as schoolmasters or tutors; from teaching any art, science, or language; from holding any places of profit, trust, or honour; and, finally, commanding them to attend mass. This last was the sure signal for a persecution, which soon followed.

One of the first persons who attracted the notice of the papists, was Mr. Sebastian Basan, a zealous Protestant, who was seized by the missionaries, confined, tormented fifteen months, and then committed to the flames.

Before the persecution commenced, the missionaries employed kidnappers to steal away the children of the Protestants, that they might privately be brought up Roman Catholics; but now they took away the children by open force, and if the wretched parents resisted, they were immediately murdered.

The Duke of Savoy, in order to inspirit the persecution, called a general assembly of the Roman Catholic nobility and gentry, and issued a solemn edict against the reformed, setting forth several reasons for extirpating them, among which the following were the principal: "For the preservation of the papal authority; that the church livings may be all under one mode of government; to make a union among all parties; in honour of all the saints, and of the ceremonies of the Church of Rome."

This was followed by a most cruel order, published on January 25, A.D. 1655, under the sanction of the duke, by Andrew Gastaldo, doctor of civil laws. That order set forth, that every head of a family, with the individuals of that family, of the reformed religion, of what rank, degree, or condition soever, none excepted, inhabiting and possessing estates in Lucerne, St. Giovanni, Bibiana, Campiglione, St. Secondo, Lucernetta, La Torre, Fenile, and Bricherassio, should, within three days after the publication thereof, depart, and be withdrawn, out of the said places, and translated into the places and limits tolerated by his highness during his pleasure; particularly Bobbio, Angrogno, Villaro, Rorata, and the county of Bonetti. And all this to be done on pain of death, and confiscation of house and goods, unless within the limited time they turned Roman Catholics.

The suddenness of the order affected all, and to add to the distress, the winter was remarkably severe. Notwithstanding this, the papists drove them from their habitations at the time appointed, without even sufficient clothes to cover them; and many perished in the mountains through the severity of the weather, or from want of food. Those who remained behind after the publication of the decree were murdered by the popish inhabitants, or shot by the troops. A particular description of these cruelties is given in a letter, written by a Protestant, who was upon the spot, and who happily escaped the carnage. "The army," says he, "having got footing, became very numerous by the addition of a multitude of the neighbouring popish inhabitants, who, finding we were the destined prey of the plunderers, fell upon us with impetuous fury. Exclusive of the Duke of Savoy's troops, and the Roman Catholic inhabitants, there were several regiments of French auxiliaries, some companies belonging to the Irish brigades, and several bands formed of outlaws, smugglers, and prisoners, who had been promised pardon and liberty in this world, and absolution in the next, for assisting to exterminate the Protestants from Piedmont.

"This armed multitude being encouraged by the Roman Catholic bishops and monks, fell upon the Protestants in a most furious manner. All now was horror and despair: blood stained the floors of the houses, dead bodies bestrewed the streets, and groans and cries shocked the ears of humanity from every quarter. Some armed themselves and skirmished with the troops; and many, with their families, fled to the mountains.

There were several men, women, and children, flung from the rocks, and dashed to pieces. Among others was Magdalen Bertino, a Protestant woman of La Torre, who was stripped, and thrown down one of the precipices. Mary Raymondet, of the same town, had her flesh sliced from her bones till she expired; Magdalen Pilot, of Villaro, was cut to pieces in the cave of Castelus; Ann Charboniere had one end of a stake thrust through her body, and the other end being fixed in the ground, she was left in that manner to perish; and Jacob Prins the elder, of the church of Villaro, with David, his brother, were flayed alive.

Giovanni Andrea Michialin, an inhabitant of La Torre, with four of his children, was apprehended; three of them were hacked to pieces before him, the soldiers asking him at the death of every child if he would recant, which he constantly refused. One of the soldiers then took up the last and youngest by the legs, and putting the same question to the father, he replied as before, when the inhuman brute dashed out the child's brains. The father, however, at the same moment started from them and fled; the soldiers fired after him, but missed him; he escaped to the Alps, and there remained concealed.

Giovanni Pelanchion, on refusing to abjure his oath, was tied by one leg to the tail of a mule, and dragged through the streets of Lucerne, amidst the acclamations of an inhuman mob, who kept stoning him, and crying out, "He is possessed of the devil." They then took him to the river side, chopped off his head, and left that and his body unburied upon the bank of the river.

Peter Fontaine had a beautiful child ten years of age, named Magdalene, who was murdered by the soldiers. They roasted alive another girl, of about the same age, at Villa Nova; and a poor woman, hearing the soldiers were coming towards her house, snatched up the cradle in which her infant son was asleep, and fled towards the woods. The soldiers, however, saw and pursued her, when she lightened herself by putting down the cradle and child, which the soldiers no sooner came to than they murdered the infant, and continuing the pursuit found the mother in a cave, and cut her to atoms.

Jacobo Michelino, elder of the church of Bobbio, and several other Protestants, were hung up by the means of hooks, and left to expire. Giovanni Rostagnal, a venerable Protestant, upwards of fourscore years of age, had his nose and ears cut off, and slices cut from the fleshy parts of his body, till he bled to death.

Jacob Birone, a schoolmaster of Rorata, for refusing to change his religion, was stripped naked; and after having been so exposed, had the nails of his toes and fingers torn off with red-hot pincers, and holes bored through his hands with the point of a dagger. He next had a cord tied round his middle, and was led through the streets with a soldier on each side of him. At every turning the soldier on his right-hand side cut a gash in his flesh, and the soldier on his left-hand side struck him with a bludgeon, both saying, at the same instant, "Will you go to mass? Will you go to mass?" He still replied in the negative to these interrogatories, and being at length taken to the bridge, they cut off his head on the balustrades, and threw both that and his body into the river.

Paul Garnier, a Protestant, beloved for his piety, had his eyes put out, was then flayed alive, and being divided into four parts, his quarters were placed on four of the principal houses of Lucerne. He bore all his sufferings with the most exemplary patience, praised God as long as he could speak, and plainly evinced the courage arising from a confidence in God.

A man named Paul Giles, on attempting to run away from the soldiers, was shot in the neck; they then slit his nose, sliced his chin, stabbed him, and gave his carcase to the dogs.

Some of the Irish troops having taken eleven men of Garcigliana prisoners, they heated a furnace red hot, and forced them to push each other in till they came to the last man, whom they themselves pushed in.

Michael Gonet, a man about ninety years old, was burnt to death; Baptista Oudri, another old man, was stabbed; and Bartholomew Frasche had his heels pierced, through which ropes being put, he was dragged by them to the gaol, where, in consequence of his wounds mortifying, he soon died.

Cipryana Bastia being asked if he would renounce his religion, and turn Roman Catholic, he replied, "I would rather renounce life, or turn dog." To which a priest answered, "For that expression you shall both renounce life and be given to the dogs." They, accordingly, dragged him to prison, where they confined him till he perished of hunger, after which they threw his corpse into the street before the prison, and it was devoured by dogs.

Lucy, the wife of Peter Besson, who lived in one of the villages of the Piedmontese valleys, being in an advanced state of pregnancy, determined, if possible, to escape from such dreadful scenes as everywhere surrounded her: she accordingly took two young children, one in each hand, and set off towards the Alps. But on the third day of the journey she was delivered of an infant, who perished through the inclemency of the weather, as did the other two children; for all three were found dead by her side, and herself just expiring, by the person to whom she related the above circumstances.

The Sieur Thomas Margher fled to a cave, where, being discovered, the soldiers shut up the mouth, and he perished with famine.

Jacob Roseno was commanded to pray to the saints, and upon his refusal, the soldiers beat him violently with bludgeons to make him comply, but he continued faithful, whereupon they fired, and lodged many balls in his body. While in the agonies of death, they cried to him, "Will you pray to the saints?" to which he answered, "No!" when one of the soldiers, with a broad sword, clove his head asunder, and put an end to his sufferings.

Giovanni Pallias, being apprehended as a Protestant by the soldiers, was ordered by the Marquis of Pianessa to be executed in a place near the convent. When brought to the gallows, several monks attended, to persuade him to renounce his religion. But he told them he never would embrace idolatry, and that he was happy in being thought worthy to suffer for the name of Christ. They then represented to him what his wife and children, who depended on his labour, would suffer after his decease: to which he replied, "I would have my wife and children, as well as myself, consider their souls more than their bodies, and the next world before this; and with respect to the distress I may leave them in, God is merciful, and will provide for them while they are worthy of his protection." Finding the inflexibility of this poor man, the monks commanded the executioner to perform his office.

Paul Clement, an elder of the church of Rossano, being apprehended by the monks of a neighbouring monastery, was carried to the market-place of that town, where some Protestants had just been executed. On beholding the dead bodies, he said calmly, "You may kill the body, but you cannot prejudice the soul of a true believer. With respect to the dreadful spectacles which you have here shown me, you may rest assured that God's vengeance will overtake the murderers of those poor people, and punish them for the innocent blood they have spilt." The monks were so exasperated at this reply, that they ordered him to be hung up directly; and while he was hanging the soldiers amused themselves by shooting at the body.

Daniel Rambaut, of Villaro, the father of a numerous family, was seized, and, with several others, committed to the gaol of Paysana. Here he was visited by several priests, who, with continual importunities, strove to persuade him to turn papist: to do this he peremptorily refused, when the priests, finding his resolution, pretended to pity his numerous family, and told him that he might yet have his life, if he would subscribe his belief to the following articles:

1. The real presence in the host. 2. Transubstantiation. 3. Purgatory. 4. The pope's infallibility. 5. That masses said for the dead will release souls from purgatory. 6. That praying to saints will procure the remission of sins.

To these proposals Rambaut replied that neither his religion, his understanding, nor his conscience would suffer him to subscribe to any of these articles; "for," said he, "1. To believe the real presence in the host is blasphemy and idolatry. 2. To fancy the words of consecration perform what the papists call transubstantiation, by converting the water and wine into the identical body and blood of Christ, which was crucified, and which afterwards ascended into heaven, is too gross an absurdity for even a child to believe; and nothing but the most blind superstition could make the Roman Catholics put confidence in anything so ridiculous. 3. The doctrine of purgatory is more inconsistent and absurd than a fairy tale. 4. The infallibility of the popes is an impossibility, and the pope arrogantly lays claim to what can belong to God only, as a perfect being. 5. Saying masses for the dead is ridiculous, and only meant to keep up a belief in the fable of purgatory, as the fate of all is finally decided in the departure of the soul from the body. And, 6. Praying to saints for the remission of sins is misplacing adoration, as the saints themselves have occasion for an intercessor in Christ; therefore, as God only can pardon our errors, we ought to sue to him alone for pardon."

Filled with rage at these answers, the priests determined to shake his resolution by the most cruel method imaginable; they ordered one joint of his fingers to be cut off every day, till all his fingers were gone; they then proceeded in the same manner with his toes; afterwards they alternately cut off, daily, a hand and a foot; and finding that he bore his sufferings with the most unconquerable fortitude, and maintained his faith with steadfast resolution, they stabbed him to the heart, and then gave his body to be devoured by dogs.

Peter Gabriola, a Protestant gentleman, of considerable eminence, being seized by a troop of soldiers, and refusing to renounce his religion, they hung several bags of gunpowder about his body, and then setting fire to them, blew him up.

Also, Mary Nigrino, and her daughter, a poor idiot, were cut to pieces in the woods, and their bodies left to be devoured by wild beasts.

A Protestant lady, named Constantia Bellione, was apprehended on account of her faith, and asked by a priest if she would renounce the devil and go to mass; to which she replied, "I was brought up in a religion by which I was always taught to renounce the devil: but should I comply with your desire, and go to mass, I should be sure to meet him there in a variety of shapes." The priest was highly incensed at this, and told her to recant, or she should suffer cruelly. She, however, boldly answered that she feared not any sufferings he could inflict, and in spite of all the torments he could invent, she would keep her faith inviolate. The priest then ordered slices of her flesh to be cut off from several parts of her body. This she bore with the most singular patience, only saying to the priest, "What horrid and lasting torments will you suffer in hell, for the trifling and temporary pains which I now endure!" Exasperated at this expression, and willing to stop her tongue, the priest ordered a file of musketeers to draw up and fire upon her, by which she was soon dispatched.

Paul Genre and David Paglia, attempting to escape to

the Alps, with their sons, were pursued and overtaken by the soldiers in a large plain. Here they hunted them for their diversion, goading them with their swords, and making them run about till they dropped down with fatigue. When they found that their spirits were quite exhausted, and that they could not afford them any more barbarous sport by running, the soldiers hacked them to pieces.

Michael Greve, a young man of Bobbio, was apprehended in the town of La Torre, and being led to the bridge, was thrown over into the river. Being, however, an expert swimmer, he swam down the stream, thinking to escape, but the soldiers and mob followed on both sides of the river, and kept stoning him, until he received a blow on one of his temples, when he sank and was drowned.

Isaiah Mandon, a pious Protestant, in the wane of life, fled from the merciless persecutors to a cleft in a rock, where he suffered the most dreadful hardships; for, in the midst of the winter, he was forced to lay on the bare stone, without any covering: his food was the roots he could scratch up near his miserable habitation; and the only way by which he could procure drink was to put snow in his mouth till it melted. Here, however, some of the soldiers found him, and after beating him unmercifully, they drove him towards Lucerne, goading him all the way with the points of their swords. Being exceedingly weakened by his manner of living, and exhausted by the blows he had received, he fell down in the road. They again beat him to make him proceed; till on his knees he implored them to put him out of his misery. This they at last agreed to do; and one of them shot him through the head, saying, "There, heretic, take thy request."

Mary Revel, a Protestant, received a shot in her back while walking along the street, which brought her to the ground, but recovering sufficient strength, she raised herself upon her knees, and lifting her hands towards heaven, prayed in a most fervent manner to the Almighty; when a number of soldiers, near at hand, fired a whole volley of shot at her, and in an instant put an end to her miseries.

To screen themselves from danger, a number of men, women, and children fled to a large cave, where they continued for some weeks in safety, two of the men going, when it was absolutely necessary, to procure provisions. These were, however, one day watched, by which the cave was discovered, and soon after a troop of Roman Catholics appeared before it. Many of these were neighbours and

intimate acquaintances, and some even relations of those in
the cave. The Protestants, therefore, came out, and implored them, by the ties of hospitality, and by the ties of
blood and neighbourhood, not to murder them. But the
papists, blinded by bigotry, told them they could not show
any mercy to heretics, and therefore bade them all prepare
to die. Hearing this, and knowing the obduracy of their
enemies, the Protestants fell prostrate, lifted their hearts to
heaven, and patiently awaited their fate, which the papists
soon decided by cutting them to pieces.

The blood of the faithful being almost exhausted in all
the towns and villages of Piedmont, there was but one
place that had escaped from the general slaughter. This
was the little commonalty of Rora. Rora is the smallest
among the communes of the Waldenses, lying further south
than the rest, and isolated amid its mountains. The tops of
the Sea Bianca rise above it, and Monte Viso is just
eclipsed by the summits in whose ravines the village lies
embedded. It is separated from the valley of the Po by
Mount Friouland, upon whose steeps its hamlets are suspended over the torrent of Lucerna, and peep forth amid
the chestnuts. Of this place did Count Christopher, one of
the Duke of Savoy's officers, determine, if possible, to
make himself the master, and detached 500 men to take it
by surprise.

The inhabitants, however, had intelligence of the approach of these troops, and Captain Joshua Gianavel, a
brave Protestant officer, put himself at the head of a small
body of the peasants, and waited in ambuscade to attack
the enemy in a narrow pass.

As soon as the troops appeared, and had entered the
passage, the Protestants commenced a smart and well-directed fight against them, and still kept themselves concealed behind the bushes from the sight of the enemy. A
great number of soldiers were killed, and the rest, not
being able to discover their assailants, beat a precipitate
retreat.

The members of this little community immediately sent
a memorial to the Marquis of Pianessa, a general of the
Duke of Savoy, stating that they were sorry to be under the
necessity of taking up arms; but the secret approach of a
body of troops, without any previous notice sent of the
purpose of their coming, had greatly alarmed them; that as
it was their custom never to suffer any of the military to
enter their little community, they had repelled force by

force, and should do so again; but in all other respects, they professed themselves dutiful, obedient, and loyal subjects to their sovereign, the Duke of Savoy.

The Marquis, in order to delude and surprise the Protestants of Rora, sent them word that he was perfectly satisfied with their behaviour, for they had done right, and even rendered a service to their country, as the men who had attempted to pass the defile were not his troops, but a band of desperate robbers, who had, for some time, infested those parts.

The very day after, however (Easter Sunday, April 25, 1655), the marquis sent 500 men to storm the town, while the people, as he thought, were lulled into security by his artifice.

Captain Gianavel, however, was not thus to be deceived; he, therefore, laid a second ambuscade for these troops, and compelled them to retire with a proportionate loss.

Foiled in these two attempts, the sanguinary marquis determined on a third, which should be still more formidable.

He soon after sent 700 chosen men upon the expedition, who, in spite of the fire from the Protestants, forced the defile, entered Rora, and began to murder every person they met with, without distinction of sex or age. Captain Gianavel, at the head of his friends, though he had lost the defile, determined to dispute the passage through a fortified pass, that led to the richest and best part of the town. Here he succeeded, by keeping up a continual fire, which did great execution, his men being all excellent marksmen. The Roman Catholic commander was astonished at this opposition, as he imagined that he had surmounted all difficulties. He, however, strove to force the pass, but being able to bring up only twelve men in front at a time, and the Protestants being secured by a breastwork, he saw all his hopes frustrated.

Enraged at the loss of so many of his troops, and fearful of disgrace if he persisted in attempting what appeared so impracticable, he thought it wiser to retreat. Unwilling, however, to withdraw his men by the defile at which he had entered, on account of the danger, he determined to retreat towards Villaro, by another pass called Pianpra, which, though hard of access, was easy of descent. Here, however, he was again opposed by Gianavel, who, having posted his little band in the wood, greatly annoyed the troops, and even pursued their rear till they entered the open countty.

The Marquis Pianessa, finding all these attempts baffled, and that every artifice he used was useless, resolved to act openly; and therefore proclaimed that ample rewards should be given to any who would bear arms against the heretics of Rora, and that any officer who would exterminate them should be honoured accordingly.

Captain Mario, a bigoted Roman Catholic, and a desperate ruffian, stimulated by this, resolved to undertake the enterprise. He therefore obtained leave to raise a regiment in the towns of Lucerne, Barges, Bubiano, Cavour, and Bagnol. In these places he levied 1,000 men. With these he resolved to attempt gaining the summit of a rock, from whence he could pour his men into the town without much opposition or difficulty. But the Protestants, aware of his design, suffered his troops to gain almost the summit of the rock, without appearing in their sight: when they made a most furious attack upon them; one party keeping up a well-directed and constant fire, and another party rolling down stones of a great weight. Thus were they suddenly stopped in their career. Many were killed by the musketry, and more by the stones, which beat them down the precipices. Captain Mario himself, having fallen from a craggy place into a river at the foot of the rock, was taken up senseless, and remained ill of the bruises a long time; and, at length, fell into a decline at Lucerne, where he died.

The Marquis of Pianessa, enraged at being thus foiled by such a handful of men, determined on their expulsion or destruction.

To this end he ordered all the Roman Catholic militia of Piedmont to be called out and disciplined. To these he joined 8,000 regular troops, and dividing the whole into three distinct bodies, he planned three formidable attacks to be made at once, unless the people of Rora, to whom he sent an account of his great preparations, would comply with the following conditions:—

To ask pardon for taking up arms; to pay the expenses of all the expeditions sent against them; to acknowledge the infallibility of the pope; to go to mass; to pray to the saints; to deliver up their ministers and schoolmasters; to go to confession; to pay loans for the delivery of souls from purgatory; and to give up Captain Gianavel and the elders of their Church at discretion.

The brave inhabitants, indignant at these proposals, answered, that sooner than comply with them they would suffer their estates to be seized, their houses to be burnt, and themselves to be murdered.

Swelling with rage at this, the marquis sent them the following laconic letter:—

"TO THE OBSTINATE HERETICS INHABITING RORA.

"You shall have your request, for the troops sent against you have strict injunctions to plunder, burn, and kill.

"PIANESSA."

The three armies were accordingly put in motion, and the attacks ordered as follows:—The first by the rocks of Villaro; the second by the pass of Bagnol; and the third by the defile of Lucerne.

As might be expected, from the superiority of numbers, the troops gained the rocks and defile, entered the town, and commenced the most horrid depredations. They hanged, burnt, racked to death, or cut to pieces men, women and children. On the first day of their gaining the town, 126 suffered in this manner.

Agreeably to the orders of the marquis, they likewise plundered the estates, and burnt the houses of the people. Several Protestants, however, made their escape, under the conduct of the brave Gianavel, whose wife and children were unfortunately made prisoners, and sent to Turin under a strong guard.

The marquis, thinking to conquer at least the mind of Gianavel, wrote him a letter, and released a Protestant prisoner, that he might carry it to him. The contents were, that if the captain would embrace the Roman Catholic religion, he should be indemnified for all his losses since the commencement of the war, his wife and children should be immediately released, and himself honourably promoted in the Duke of Savoy's army; but if he refused to accede to the proposals made to him, his wife and children should be put to death; and so large a reward should be given for his capture, dead or alive, that even some of his confidential friends should, from the greatness of the sum, be tempted to betray him.

To this Gianavel returned the following answer:—

"MY LORD MARQUIS,—

"There is no torment so great, or death so cruel, that I would not prefer to the abjuration of my religion: so that promises lose their effects, and menaces only strengthen me in my faith.

"With respect to my wife and children, my lord, nothing can be more afflicting to me than the thoughts of their confinement, or be more dreadful to my imagination than their suffering a violent death. I keenly feel all the tender sensations of a husband and a parent; I would suffer any torment to rescue them; I would die to preserve them.

"But having said thus much, my lord, I assure you that the purchase of their lives must not be the price of my salvation. You have them in your power, it is true; but my consolation is, that your power is only a temporary authority over their bodies: you may destroy the mortal part, but their immortal souls are out of your reach, and will live hereafter, to bear testimony against you for your cruelties. I therefore recommend them and myself to God, and pray for a reformation in your heart.

"JOSHUA GIANAVEL."

Gianavel now, with his followers, retired to the Alps, where, being afterwards joined by several Protestant officers, with a considerable number of fugitive Protestants, they conjointly defended themselves, and made several successful attacks upon the Roman Catholic towns and forces; carrying terror by the valour of their exploits, and the boldness of their enterprises.

It was on this occasion also that Oliver Cromwell endeavoured to interest most of the courts of Europe in his remonstrance to the Duke of Savoy, and the English nation proved their practical sympathy with the persecuted by collecting no less than £38,248 10s 6d. to alleviate their sufferings. The cruelties related above would be difficult to credit were it not that they are well authenticated, both by the history of Leger, an eye-witness of many things, and endorsed by Sir Samuel Morland, Cromwell's special envoy to the Duke of Savoy.

Some Particulars of the English Reformation, and the Circumstances Which Preceded it, From the Time of Wycliffe to the Reign of Mary.

The Protestant Church in England is the lineal descendant of the Church of Britain. Who was the original founder of Christianity in these islands is wrapped in mists of tradition, and cannot now, perhaps, be absolute determined; "but," writes Bishop Jewel, "it is certain the Church of Britain, now called England, received not first the faith from Rome." Various accounts are given of the conversion of Britain; some authors, amongst whom are Usher, Stillingfleet, and Godwin, believe that the British Church was founded by Paul, in the interval between his first and second imprisonment at Rome. Others incline to the opinion that Christianity was introduced about A.D. 58, by Bran, the father of Caractacus, who was detained seven years at Rome as a hostage for the loyalty of his son. In answer to the Romanists' assertion, that Pope Eleutherius was the apostle of the Britons, the learned apologist replies that "King Lucius was baptised nearly 150 years before Constantine, and that Constantine, the first christened emperor, was born in this island, and the faith had been planted here long before, either by Joseph of Arimathea, or Simon Zelotes, or by the Greeks," which seems credible, as the king, being already converted, requested Eleutherius to send hither some authorised persons for the purposes of clerical reformation, and the general regulation of ecclesiastical affairs. It would appear that the Church of Britain, by observing the Asiatic mode of celebrating Easter, by their difference from many of the rites of Rome, especially in baptism, their journeys to Palestine, and from other details, received their faith from the East, rather than the West.

"Augustine," writes a well-known author, "was the founder of the English Church, as distinguished from the British, but the existence of a British Church, before the arrival of Augustine in the year 597, is a fact clearly established."

Pope Gregory the Great was struck with the beauty of some British children whom he saw in the streets of Rome, and his sympathies being enlisted, he was anxious for the conversion of that nation, and accordingly sent Augustine to England, who laid the foundations of the claims of papal supremacy over the island.

King Edgar was so devoted an adherent of the Romish superstition, that he built as many monasteries and nunneries as there are Sundays in the year. The Saxon chronicles relate a story illustrating his pride and arrogance. When at Chester he received the homage of eight tributary kings, after which he embarked on the River Dee in a boat, and seating himself at the helm, commanded the eight kings to row him to his palace, in token of his sovereignty and their submission.

From this time the Church of Rome commenced a series of cautious and gradual encroachments in her efforts to subjugate Britain as a spiritual appanage of the see of Rome.

The first definite attempt towards the reformation of religion was made in the reign of Edward III, about the year 1350. Darkness covered the nation, and gross darkness the people. About this time John Wycliffe, the morning star of the Reformation, arose to shed abroad the light of obscured truth. He was public lecturer on divinity in the University of Oxford, and accounted well versed both in theology and philosophy. Being a person of shrewd sense and conscientious piety, Wycliffe published his belief with regard to several articles of faith on which his views differed from those generally received as orthodox by the Romish Church. Pope Gregory XI, hearing this, condemned some of the tenets, and commanded the Archbishop of Canterbury to oblige Wycliffe to retract his opinions; and, in case of non-compliance, to summon him to Rome.

This commission, however, could not be so easily executed, for Wycliffe had powerful friends, the chief of whom was John of Gaunt, Duke of Lancaster. Wycliffe accordingly appeared at the archbishop's synod, accompanied by the duke, when a dispute arose as to whether Wycliffe should answer sitting or standing, which led to a broil between the archbishop and the duke. The people generally sided with the archbishop, so that the duke returned, taking Wycliffe with him. An insurrection ensuing shortly after this, the people plundered the duke's palace, who, in revenge, ousted the Lord Mayor and aldermen from their municipal offices. After this the bishops met again, when Wycliffe explained his views about the sacrament, on which the bishops, not daring to have recourse to stronger measures, enjoined him to be silent.

Wycliffe, regardless of the episcopal censures, and bent rather on approving himself to God, continued to propagate his doctrines, and to unveil truth, which received a mighty emphasis from current events.

He wrote several books which gave great offence to the clergy, but possessing, in God's providence, a protector in the Duke of Lancaster, he was secure from their malice.

He translated the Bible into English, the effect of which on the gross ignorance of the times was akin to the bright light of the sun bursting forth after a total eclipse. He prefixed a preface to this translation, written in a bold and uncompromising spirit, in which he censured the clergy for their ignorance and immorality, condemned the worship of saints and images, and exhorted all persons to imitate the Bereans in searching for themselves the oracles of God.

Notwithstanding an insurrection which about this time disturbed the peace of the kingdom, and the efforts of the archbishop to root out heresy, Wycliffe's adherents increased, secretly but steadily. The progress of the new opinions became at length so marked that the Vice-Chancellor of Oxford, with the consent of the leading doctors of the University, put forth, under their common seal, certain edicts, threatening Wycliffe and his followers with excommunication and imprisonment unless he and they repented after three days' canonical admonition. On this it was Wycliffe's intention to have appealed to the king, but the Duke of Lancaster prevented him; when he was forced to make another confession of his doctrines, in which, to moderate the rigour of his enemies, he qualified certain statements. Wycliffe may be considered as the founder of the Reformation in England, and, indeed, in Europe, for Huss and Jerome, the apostles of Prague, derived their light from him. He was educated at Merton College, Oxford, after which he became rector of Christ Church. On his rejection, owing to the intrigues of the monks, he was presented to the living of Lutterworth, in Leicester, where he published his "Dialogues," "Trialogues," and some other pieces, calculated to enforce the truths he had maintained.

He died at his rectory, December 31st, 1348, and was buried there. As the number of his followers continued to increase after his death, Thomas Arundel, the successor of William Courtenay in the see of Canterbury, condemned again the chief articles in his doctrines in two councils, one held at London in 1396, and the other at Oxford in 1408. In a general council held at Rome in 1413, under John XXIII, his treatises were ordered to be burnt, and nine months were allowed to his followers to appear before the apostolic tribunal to vindicate his memory and prevent his being branded as an heretic. But Wycliffe's books, doctrines, and memory, were principally condemned in the eighth session of the Council of Constance, held on Saturday, May 4th, 1414.

Three hundred propositions and upwards advanced by him in different books, and at different times, were read in full council by the Archbishop of Genoa, and condemned with one consent. The principal and most offensive articles were: "The substance of material bread, and the substance of material wine, remain in the sacrament of the altar; the accidents of the bread do not remain without a subject in the sacrament of the altar; Christ is not himself identically and really, in his proper corporeal presence, in the sacrament; a bishop or priest in mortal sin cannot ordain, nor consecrate, nor baptise; it cannot be proved from the Gospel that Christ instituted the mass; it is contrary to the Holy Scriptures for ecclesiastics to have any temporal possessions; the Church of Rome is the synagogue of Satan; it is lawful for a priest or deacon to preach the Word of God without the authority of the Apostolic See, or of any bishop; the election of the pope by the cardinals is an invention of the devil."

The above articles, and many others, were all condemned, some of them as notoriously heretical, others as rash, seditious, and offensive to pious ears. John Wycliffe was declared to be a most obstinate and impenitant heretic; his works were forbidden, his memory anathematised, and his bones ordered to be dug up, burnt, and cast to the winds. His body was accordingly exhumed, burnt, and the ashes thrown into the river Swift, the stream that flows at the foot of the hill on which the town of Lutterworth is built.

At the beginning of the reign of Henry V, about the year 1413, the anger of the clergy was especially excited against the Lollards, and they fabricated a report of a pretended conspiracy among them, headed by Sir John Oldcastle, or, as he was also called, Lord Cobham. Lord Cobham has the honour of being the first author and the first martyr among the nobility of England. He was a man of considerable natural abilities, proficient in literature, of a ready wit, and skilled in affairs in the cabinet or in the field. In his love of philosophy, he had perused the writings of Wycliffe, and in so doing unconsciously absorbed the leaven of evangelical and spiritual religion. When persuaded of the truth of those doctrines, he enrolled himself as a zealous disciple, and did all in his power for their spread, both by his gifts and personal efforts. He transcribed the works of Wycliffe; he supported various preachers, and became the acknowledged leader of the rising reformation. The hostility of the Church was, of course, an inevitable result. Henry, though himself averse to persecution, was, through the malicious instigation of the clergy, induced to organise a persecution against the Lollards, on the ground of conspiracy. It was reported that they intended to murder the king and the royal family, with most of the lords spiritual and temporal, in hopes that the confusion which would ensue therefrom might prove favourable to their sect. Upon this rumour was spread that Lord Cobham had secretly collected 20,000 men in St. Giles-in-the-Fields—a place at that time covered with bushes and underwood. The king went there at midnight, but found only some fourscore persons assembled for religious worship, many of whom, however, were inhumanely slaughtered by the royal troops. Some were taken prisoners, and when examined and put to the rack, admitted the design, and accused Lord Cobham of being its ringleader. The king, believing in his guilt, set a thousand marks upon his head, and promised remission of taxes to any town who should deliver him up to the authorities. Sir John was accordingly apprehended and imprisoned in the Tower of London; but having effected his escape, was not re-captured until four years afterwards. He was condemned to be executed in the most barbarous manner—viz., to be roasted to death by a slow fire. He was suspended to a gallows by chains, and a fire being kindled under him, he died in the most exquisite and protracted agonies, amidst the imprecations of the priests and monks, who used their utmost endeavours to prevent the people encouraging him with their prayers.

Such was the tragical end of Sir John Oldcastle, Baron of Cobham, who left the world with a resolution and constancy worthy of the brave spirit with which he had maintained the cause of truth and of his God.

Not satisfied with his death, the clergy got the Parliament to make fresh statutes against the Lollards. It was enacted, among other things, that whoever read the Scriptures in English should forfeit land, chattels, goods, and life; and be condemned as heretics to God, enemies to the Crown, and traitors to the kingdom; that they should not have the benefit of any sanctuary; and that, if they continued obstinate, or relapsed after being pardoned, they should first be hanged for treason against the king, and then burned for heresy against God. This act was no

sooner passed, than a violent persecution was raised against
the Lollards. Several were burnt alive, some escaped from
the kingdom, and others abjured rather than suffer the
horrible torments perpared for them by popish intolerance
and cruelty.

During the reign of King Henry VIII, Britain began as a
body to cast from herself the errors of Rome.

The progress of Martin Luther's doctrines during this
reign are well known, and they spread rapidly in England,
engrafted as they were on the similar tenets of his predecessor, Wycliffe. The state of the Church was deplorable.
The bishops, steeped in ignorance, rarely visited their
dioceses, except to riot at high festivals; the abbots and
monks were notorious for their unbridled profligacy; and
the inferior clergy were despised and hated for their vices
and crimes. Everything seemed tending to a crisis, and to
portend an inevitable reformation. The invention of printing and the revival of classic learning had disenthralled the
minds of many of the laity, so that when books were
introduced from Germany into England, and translated,
they were devoured by a large class of earnest inquirers
after a purer faith.

Upon this a violent persecution arose, and six men and
women were burnt in Coventry in Passion Week, only for
teaching their children the Creed, the Lord's Prayer, and
the Ten Commandments in the English tongue.

King Henry VIII came forward on this occasion as the
champion of the Church, and entered the lists of polemic
theology with the dauntless Luther.

The divorce of the king was the occasion for that
arbitrary monarch to swerve from his allegiance to the see
of Rome, and for asserting the independence of the English
Church and the royal supremacy, which events tended to
accelerate the onward path of reformation in faith and
practice. This result was further advanced by the fall of
Cardinal Wolsey, and by the rise of Thomas Cranmer,
whose energies and influence were devoted to the cause of
the English Reformation.

About this time Tyndale's translation of the New Testament appeared, which excited the indignation of the clergy,
whose desire was not to be expounders of the Word of
God, but to keep it altogether out of the hands of the
people.

Tyndale and others resided at Antwerp, and every year
they wrote or translated fresh books against popish errors,

which books they had secretly conveyed to England. Tonstall, the Bishop of London, becoming aware of this, entered into a negotiation with an English merchant to obtain for him as many of Tyndale's Testaments as money could procure. Tyndale gladly received the order, and sold off the remainder of an old edition. Tonstall purchased the whole of them, and burnt them publicly in Cheapside. But the next year a large number of the revised and later edition came over to England, and when Constantine, one of Tyndale's partners, was arrested and promised his liberty if he would disclose the persons who patronize this heretical version, he replied that Tonstall, Bishop of London, was the best friend Tyndale had, for it was through him that the old edition had been cleared off, and a newer and a better one had appeared.

Among the martyrdoms which took place during the reign of Henry VIII, when religious opinions were in a transition state, not being as yet clearly wrought out by conflict and study, we may instance the following examples.

Story and Martyrdom of Thomas Bilney.

Thomas Bilney was brought up at Cambridge. On leaving the university, he went into several places and preached; and in his sermons spoke with great boldness against the pride and insolence of the clergy. This was during the ministry of Cardinal Wolsey, who hearing of his attacks, caused him to be imprisoned. Overcome with fear, Bilney abjured, was pardoned, and returned to Cambridge in the year 1530. Here he fell into great horror of mind in consequence of his denial of the truth. He became overwhelmed with shame, and bitterly repenting of his sin, resolved to make some atonement by a public confession of his sentiments. To prepare himself for his task, he studied the Scriptures with deep attention for two years, at the expiration of which he quitted the university, went into Norfolk, and preached up and down that county against idolatry and superstition; exhorting the people to live well, to give much alms, to believe in Christ, and to offer up their souls and wills to him in the sacrament. He openly confessed his own sin of denying the faith; and, using no precaution as he went about, was soon taken by the bishop's officers, condemned as a relapse, and degraded. Parker, afterwards archbishop, was an eye-witness of his sufferings, which he bore with great fortitude and resignation, and continued very cheerful after his sentence. He ate up the poor provisions that were brought him, saying he must keep up a ruinous cottage till it fell. He had these words of Isaiah often in his mouth, "When thou walkest through the fire, thou shalt not be burned;" and by burning his finger in the candle, he prepared himself for the fire, and said it would only consume the stubble of his body, and would purify his soul.

On the 10th of November he was brought to the stake, where he repeated the Creed, as a proof that he was a true Christian. He then prayed earnestly, and with the deepest feeling repeated these words, "Enter not into judgment with thy servant." Dr. Warner, who attended, embraced him, shedding many tears, and wishing he might die in as good a frame of mind as Bilney then was. The friars requested him to inform the people that they were not instrumental to his death, which he did, so that the last act of his life was full of charity.

The officers then put the reeds and faggots about his body, and set fire to the first, which made a great flame and disfigured his face; he held up his hands, and struck his breast, crying sometimes "Jesus!" sometimes "Credo!" but the flame was blown away from him several times, the wind being very high, till at length the wood taking fire, the flame was stronger, and so he yielded up the ghost.

His body being shrunk up, leaned down on the chain, till one of the officers with his halbert struck out the staple of the chain behind him, on which his body fell down into the bottom of the fire, when they heaped up wood upon it and consumed it.

The sufferings, the confession, and the heroic faith of this martyr inspired and animated others with like courage.

Byfield, who had formerly abjured, was taken dispersing Tyndale's books; and he, with one Tewkesbury, were condemned by Stokesly, and burnt. Two men and a woman suffered also the same fate at York. Upon this the Parliament complained to the king; but this did not check the sanguinary proceedings of the clergy. One Bainham, a counsellor of the Temple, was taken on suspicion of heresy, and whipped in the presence of Sir T. More, and afterwards racked in the Tower, yet he could not be wrought on to accuse any, but through fear he abjured. After this, however, being discharged, he was in great trouble of mind, and could find no quiet till he went publicly to church, where he openly confessed his sins, and declared the torments he felt in his conscience for what he had done. Upon this he was again seized on, and condemned for having said that in the sacrament Christ's body was received by faith, and not chewed with the teeth. Sentence was passed upon him by Stokesly, and he was burnt. Soon after this More delivered up the great seal, in consequence of which the preachers had some ease.

The rage of persecution stopped not with the living, but vented itself even on the dead. Lord Tracy made a will by which he left his soul to God, in hopes of mercy through Christ, without the help of any other saint, and therefore he declared that he would leave nothing for soul-masses. This will being brought to the Bishop of London's Court to be proved, Tracy provoked them so much, that he was condemned as an heretic, and an order was sent to the Chancellor of Worcester to exhume his body; but he proceeded farther, and burnt it, which could not be justified, since he was not a relapse. Tracy's heir sued him for it, and he was turned out of his place, and fined £400. The clergy proclaimed an indulgence of forty days' pardon to any that carried a faggot to the burning of an heretic, that so cruelty might seem the more meritorious.

The reformed now enjoyed a respite of two years, when the crafty Gardiner represented to the king that it would give him great advantages with the pope if he would take some occasion to show his hatred of heresy. Accordingly a young man named Frith was chosen as a sacrifice for this affected zeal for religion.

Story and Martyrdom of Frith.

Frith was a young man much famed for learning, and was the first in England who wrote against the corporeal presence in the sacrament. He followed Zwingli's doctrine on these grounds: Christ received in the sacrament gave eternal life, but this was given only to those who believed, from which he inferred that he was received only by faith. These reasons he put in writing, which falling into the hands of Sir Thomas More, were answered by him; but Frith never saw his publication till he was put in prison; and then, though he was loaded with irons, and had no books allowed him, he replied.

For these offenses he was seized in May, 1533, and brought before Stokesly, Gardiner, and Longland. They charged him with not believing in purgatory and transubstantiation. He gave his reasons that determined him to

look on neither of these as articles of faith; but thought
that neither the affirming nor denying them ought to be
determined positively. The bishops seemed unwilling to
proceed to sentence; but he continuing resolute, Stokesly
pronounced it, and delivered him to the secular power, at
the same time desiring that his punishment might be
moderated, so that the rigour might not be too extreme,
nor yet the gentleness of it too much mitigated—a piece of
hypocrisy which deceived no one.

Frith, with a fellow-martyr, one Hewitt, were brought to
the stake at Smithfield on the 4th of July, 1533. On
arriving there, Frith expressed great joy, and hugged the
faggots with transport. The fire was then kindled, and
consumed the martyrs to ashes.

This was the last martyrdom which occurred for some
time, as an act was passed soon afterwards, which diminished the power of the priests.

Phillips was accused of heresy, and arrested, but was
released on appealing to the king, though it was not
known whether he had been heard by him. After this the
reformed preachers had some respite. The king had united
himself with the German princes for political purposes,
and they made it an article in their treaty that no one
should be persecuted for their religious opinions. They also
enjoyed the favour of the queen: she appointed Latimer
and Shaxton to be her chaplains, and bestowed on them the
bishoprics of Worcester and Salisbury. Cranmer, meanwhile, was actively engaged in collecting the opinions of
the old fathers on all points of religion. His work, when
completed, comprised six folio volumes, He was admirably
fitted for the work before him, as he was a man of great
candour, industry, and patience. Cromwell was always his
earnest friend and assistant in promoting the Reformation.

The visitation of the monasteries commenced in October. Strict instructions were given to those employed in
the work, as to what questions and inquiries they were to
make—whether the houses had their full number; whether
the services were performed in the appointed hours; how
the heads were chosen; what statutes they had; how their
vows were observed; whether the severities of their orders
were kept up; what hospitality was shown; how the officers
performed their duties; how the revenues and lands were
managed; how the novices were cared for; what benefices
they possessed, and how they were disposed of. They were
also ordered to give them injunctions in the king's name,

declaring them absolved from their oaths of obedience to
the pope, and commanding that all statues so binding them
should be erased from their books. The abbots were
forbidden to have choice dishes, and the Scriptures were to
be read aloud during the meals. The monks were to be
instructed in true religion, and taught that it consisted in
worshipping God in spirit, and not in outward observances.
Rules were also given about the management of the revenues, and no one under twenty was to be permitted to
enter the house.

The visitors had power to punish any offenders, and to
bring them before the Visitor-General. Some monasteries
were privileged as sanctuaries for any who fled to them.

The belief in purgatory, and that their masses could
lessen the sufferings and at last deliver the souls of the
dead, was the great source of their wealth. For this reason
the abbeys were largely endowed with lands, on condition
of so many masses being said for the donor, in proportion
to the gift. The monks were greatly corrupted by their vast
wealth, and their lives were a scandal to the people: they
were in general grossly ignorant and very dissolute. The
begging friars succeeded easily in carrying off the public
esteem from them, by following an exactly opposite course
of conduct; they, under the show of poverty and self-de-
nial, rose high in the public estimation, and became almost
the only confessors in the world. They were useful to the
pope in a much greater degree than the monks had been.
The school learning was also in their hands, which served
to increase their general popularity. But they were unable
to conceal their vices so well as the monks could, in
consequence of being so much before the world, and they
all in their turn fell into contempt. Cranmer and the king
being anxious to found new bishoprics, and needing funds
to carry out their plans, thought the best way would be to
publish the vices of the monks, so as to bring the wealth
into their own hands.

The visitation was accordingly carried on all over England: dreadful crimes were discovered in some houses; in
others, factions and fearful cruelties; and in some, tools for
coining. Many accounts were returned in the report not fit
to be mentioned; three houses were compelled to sign a
resignation in the king's favour, and in the following year
four more surrendered.

A convocation sat soon after, when Cranmer endeavoured to show the imposition put upon the world by the

priests declaring their absolution more efficacious than
contrition, and the encouragement given to outward ceremonies, in consequence of the gain derived from them by
the priests. He urged the king to carry out the work of
reformation vigorously, and to determine nothing without
having Scripture proofs. Many things were declared contrary to the Word of God, which a short time before many
had suffered death for not believing: such as the existence
of purgatory, the invocation of saints, and the sanctity of
images. The king was exhorted to hear these points well
discussed before passing a judgment.

The next step was to examine all the lesser monasteries,
and to take their seals away. All who would return to a
secular life were sent to the Archbishop of Canterbury or
the Lord Chancellor for licences, and those who preferred
a monastic life were removed to the large establishments.
Pensions were given to the abbots for their lives. By these
means 10,000 monks were driven to seek their own livings,
with one gown and forty shillings a-piece. Their goods
were estimated at £100,000, and the rents of their houses
at £32,000; but this was scarcely a tenth part of their real
value. Many churches and cloisters were pulled down, and
the sale of the materials produced almost incredible sums.
The monks were now pitied almost as much as they were
formerly hated. Strangers who, when travelling, found the
abbeys places of reception, had much cause to lament the
change. Cromwell advised the king to sell the lands on easy
terms to the nobility, and oblige them to keep up the
former hospitality.

The translation of the Bible into English was completed
in this year. It was sent first to Paris to be printed, the English workmen not being sufficiently skilled for the
work. On the remonstrance of the French clergy, the
printing was stopped, and most of the copies confiscated. It
was then brought to England, and finished by Grafton.
Cromwell procured a warrant from Henry allowing his
subjects to read it, for which Cranmer thanked Cromwell,
saying that he rejoiced to see the star of the Reformation
arise in England, for the light of God's Word might now
shine without a cloud.

Soon after this Cromwell ordered the clergy to set Bibles
in their churches, and to exhort the people to read them.
The clergy were required to teach the Creed, the Lord's
Prayer, and the Ten Commandments in English; and to

direct the people to alms deeds, and not to trust in pilgrimages and other superstitious observances.

Thus a severe blow was given to the cardinal points of superstition, and the free circulation of the Scriptures did more than aught else to dispel popular superstition.

This year Prince Edward was born, an event adverse to the popish party, whose hopes were built on the accession of Lady Mary to the crown. Lee, Gardiner, and Stokesley now emulated the bishops of the reforming party, as to who should most zealously execute the king's injunctions. Gardiner had been ambassador in France, but Cromwell had caused Bonner to be appointed, who appeared a steadfast adherent to the Reformation. Notwithstanding schemes to ruin him, Gardiner, through his intrigues and flatteries, remained in favour during the king's life. He urged one point which had much weight with the king, that his zeal against heresy advantaged him greatly in the eyes of Europe, and therefore he besought him to begin with the sacramentarians, or those who denied the corporeal presence in the sacrament. This advice falling in with the king's own convictions, had much weight with him, and an opportunity speedily manifested itself for the display of his zeal in the memorable indictment of John Lambert.

Martyrdom of John Lambert.

John Lambert was born in the county of Norfolk, and educated at the university of Cambridge. Having been converted by Bilney, he became disgusted at the corruption of the Church; and apprehensive of persecution, he crossed the sea and joined Tyndale and Frith, with whom he remained more than a year; and, from his piety and ability, was appointed chaplain to the English at Antwerp. But there the persecuting spirit of Sir T. More reached him, and on the accusation of a person named Barlow, he was carried from Antwerp to London, where he was brought up for examination first at Lambeth, then at Oxford, before Warham, the Archbishop of Canterbury, having five-and-forty articles preferred against him, to which he returned answers written with a perspicuity and strength excelled by none of his age.

These answers were directed to Dr. Warham about the year 1532, at which time Lambert was in custody in the archbishop's house at Oxford. The following year Warham died and whereby Lambert was delivered.

It happened that in the year 1538 he was present at a

sermon preached by Dr. Taylor, afterwards Bishop of Lincoln, and one of the noble army of martyrs in the time of Queen Mary.

Dr. Taylor having said something upon the corporeal presence, Lambert believing him to be in error, felt obliged to argue the subject with him. At the conclusion of the sermon he went to the doctor, but Taylor, excusing himself for other business, wished him to state his views in writing, and to come again at his leisure.

The sum of Lambert's arguments were ten, proving the truth by the Scriptures, by reason, and by the doctors. These were written with great force and authority. The first reason was the following, founded upon Christ's words, "This cup is the new testament."

"And if," said he, "these words do not change either the cup or the wine corporeally into the new testament, by the same reason it is not agreeable that the words spoken of the bread should turn the bread corporeally into the body of Christ."

Another was this: "That it is not agreeable to a natural body to be in two places or more at one time: wherefore it must follow of necessity that either Christ had not a natural body or else truly, according to the common nature of a body, it cannot be present in two places at once, that is to say, in heaven and in earth; on the right hand of his Father, and in the sacrament."

This being the origin of Lambert's quarrel, it soon became a matter of public talk. He was summoned by Archbishop Cranmer into court, and compelled to defend his cause; for Cranmer, though afterwards an earnest believer in the reformed doctrines on the sacrament, favoured as yet the Romish view. Gardiner, ever alive to his own interests, and anxious to avail himself of every opportunity for thwarting the Reformation, which he hated, learning the particulars of the affair, went privately to the king. Having with much craft and subtlety insinuated that the world began to suspect him as a favourer of heretics, he suggested that vigorous proceedings against Lambert would effectually crush all unfavourable suspicions. Henry listened to this advice with more zeal than prudence, and issued a commission commanding all the bishops and peers of the realm to come to London to be the king's assessors, when his majesty sat in judgment on heretics.

When these preparations were completed, a day was

appointed for the trial of Lambert, a great assembly was gathered together from all parts of the country, and all the places round the judgment seat were crowded with eager auditors of this singular case. A guard of soldiers conducted Lambert from the prison, and placed him opposite the king's throne. At last the king himself arrived with a numerous escort, clothed all in white. The king having seated himself on his throne, beheld Lambert with a stern countenance, and then turning himself to his councillors, commanded the Bishop of Chichester to explain to the public the cause of the present assembly.

The king then commanded him to state his opinions with reference to the sacrament of the altar.

Then Lambert, beginning to speak, thanked God that the king did not disdain to hear the controversies of religion, for that it often happened, through the cruelties of the bishops, that many innocent men were murdered without the knowledge of their sovereign; but now, as God had endued the king with such judgment and knowledge, he doubted not but that the king would judge rightly, and that the result would tend to the furtherance of Divine truth.

At this point Henry interrupted him, and with an angry voice said, "I came not hither to hear my own praises thus painted in my presence; go to the matter in hand, without any more circumstance."

Lambert was somewhat abashed at the king's angry words, and contrary to all expectation, paused, considering what he might best do in this emergency.

Upon which the king, overcome by his vehement passion, said, "Why standest thou still? answer as touching the sacrament of the altar. Dost thou say that it is the body of Christ, or dost thou deny it?"

Lambert.—I answer with Augustine, "That this is the body of Christ after a certain manner."

The King.—Answer me neither out of Augustine nor any other authority; but tell me plainly, dost thou believe it is the body of Christ or not?

Lambert.—Then I deny that it is the body of Christ.

The King.—Mark well, for now thou shalt be condemned by Christ's own words: *"Hoc est corpus meum."*

He then commanded Cranmer to refute his assertion, who, first making a short preface unto the hearers, began his disputation with Lambert, modestly saying, "Brother Lambert, let this matter be handled between us indifferently, that if I do prove this your argument to be false by the

Scriptures, you will willingly retract the same; but if you shall prove it true by the Scripture, I do promise to embrace the same."

Cranmer and Lambert argued for hours. When they were disputing about St. Paul's conversion, Lambert maintained his own ground, the king seemed greatly moved, and the archbishop appeared to be somewhat entangled. Gardiner, fearing lest the accused should get the better of the argument, in violation of all order, and without the king's permission shamelessly interrupted the discussion.

When the argument was concluded, the bishops were greatly elated, assured of victory by this philosophical transmutation of elements. Lambert, in the meantime, being encompassed with so many difficulties, dispirited on the one side with insults and taunts, restrained on the other by the authority and threats of the audience, partly oppressed with the majesty of the king's presence, and wearied with standing from twelve o'clock till five, despairing that any further argument would profit him, now held his peace. Upon this the bishops argued their own case, without interruption; for Lambert, overcome by weariness and grief, defended himself rather by his silence than by his arguments. At last, when evening was closing in, and the torches were lighted, the king, desirous of breaking up this pretended disputation, said to Lambert, "What sayest thou now after all these great labours which thou hast taken upon thee, and all the reasons of these learned men? Art thou not yet satisfied? Wilt thou live or die? What sayest thou? Thou hast yet free choice."

Lambert answered, "I yield and submit myself wholly unto the will of your majesty."

"Then," said the king, "commit thyself into the hand of God, and not into mine."

Lambert replied, "I commend my soul into the hands of God, but my body I submit unto your clemency."

Then said the king, "If you commit yourself unto my judgment, you must die, for I will not be a patron unto heretics;" and turning himself unto Cromwell, commanded him to read the sentence of condemnation.

Cromwell, taking the schedule of condemnation in hand, read the same; wherein was contained the burning of heretics, who either spake or wrote anything repugnant to the Papistical Church and tradition touching the sacrament of the altar.

Thus was John Lambert condemned to death by the

king. Upon the day appointed he was brought out of the prison at eight o'clock, to the house of Lord Cromwell, where, it is reported, Cromwell desired forgiveness for what he had done. From hence he was carried straight to the place of execution at Smithfield.

The manner of his death was dreadful; for after his legs were burned up to the stumps, and his wretched tormentors had withdrawn the fire from him, so that but a small portion was left under him, then two who stood on each side of him hoisted him upon their halberts as far as the chain would reach; while he, lifting up such hands as he had, cried unto the people in these words: "None but Christ, none but Christ;" and so, being let down again from their pikes, fell into the fire, and there expired.

Sufferings and Martyrdom of Dr. Robert Barnes.

Dr. Barnes was educated at the University of Louvain, in Brabant. On his return to England he went to Cambridge, where he was made prior of the House of the Augustines. That scene of learning was wrapped in the grossest ignorance and barbarity, there being but a very small number of intelligent and disciplined minds. Barnes, anxious to promote enlightenment, began to instruct the students in the ancient classics; and, before long, a higher tone was given to the university. He then began to read openly the Epistles of St. Paul, and inveighed with great warmth against the hypocrisies of the times, and the luxuries of the dignitaries of the Church, singling out Cardinal Wolsey by name. But he was as yet ignorant of the true cause of these evils—the idolatry of the Church—until, having made the acquaintance of Bilney, he was, through his instrumentality, converted to Christ. Not long after this, he preached a sermon in Trinity Hall, the subject being the epistle for the Sunday. On account of his statements he was accused of heresy by two fellows of King's College, and much disputation ensued throughout the university. His adversaries then accused him to the Vice-Chancellor, and Barnes was commanded to recant. This Barnes refused to do, and wrote to King Henry, refuting the judgment of Cardinal Wolsey and the rest of the popish bishops. He continued some time in Cambridge, until, suddenly, a sergeant-at-arms was sent down from London, who arrested him in the Convocation House. He was conveyed to London on the Wednesday, and remained at Mr. Parnel's house. Next day he was taken to Cardinal

Wolsey, at Westminster, but was kept waiting all day without an audience; but Gardiner, who was secretary to Wolsey, presented him the same night to the cardinal in his chamber of state.

"Is this," asked the cardinal, "Dr. Barnes, who is accused of heresy?"

"Yes, please your grace," they replied; "and we trust you will find him reformable, for he is learned and wise."

"What!" said Wolsey, "had you not a sufficient scope in the Scriptures to teach the people, but that my golden shoes, my pole-axes, my pillars, my golden cushions, my crosses, did so sore offend you, that you must make us *ridiculum caput* amongst the people, who that day laughed us to scorn?"

Dr. Barnes answered, "I spake nothing but the truth out of the Scriptures, according to my conscience, and according to the old doctors." And then he delivered him six sheets of paper written, to confirm and corroborate his sentiments.

The cardinal received them smiling, saying, "We perceive, then, that you intend to stand to your articles, and to show your learning."

"Yea," said Barnes, "that I do, by God's grace, with your lordship's favour."

He answered, "Such as you bear us little favour, and the Catholic Church. I will ask you a question: whether you do think it more necessary that I should have all this royalty, because I represent the king's majesty in all the high courts of this realm, to the terror and keeping down of all corrupt members of this commonwealth; or to be as simple as you would have us, to sell all these things, and to give them to the poor, who shortly will cast them in the dirt, and to pull away this princely dignity, which is a terror to the wicked, and to follow your counsel."

"I think it necessary," said Barnes, "to be sold and given to the poor. For this is not becoming your calling; nor is the king's majesty maintained by your pomp and pole-axes, but by God, who saith, 'By me kings reign.' "

Then answered the cardinal, "Lo, master doctors, he is the learned wise man that you told me of."

Then they kneeled down and said, "We desire your grace to be good unto him, for he will be reformable."

"Then," said Wolsey, "stand you up; for your sakes and the university we will be good unto him. How say you, master doctor? do you not know that I am *legatus de latere,* and that I am able to dispense in all matters concerning religion within this realm, as much as the pope may?"

He said, "I know it to be so."

"Will you then be ruled by us? and we will do all things for your honesty, and for the honesty of the university."

Barnes answered, "I thank your grace for your good will; I will stick to the Holy Scripture and to God's book, according to the simple talent that God hath lent me."

He would then have been sent to the Tower, but Gardiner and Fox standing sureties for him, he returned to Mr. Parnel's again, and devoted the whole night to writing. Next morning he was brought into the Chapter House at Westminster, before the bishops.

At the same time there were five Still Yard men to be examined about Luther's book and Lollardism; who, after they were examined, were all committed to the Fleet. Then they called Dr. Barnes again, and asked him whether he would subscribe to his articles: he subscribed willingly, when they committed him and young Parnel to the Fleet also with the others.

Soon after he was again brought before the bishops in the Chapter House, and he was asked whether he would abjure or be burned. Overcome by the persuasions of Gardiner and Fox, he consented to abjure, and, kneeling down, subscribed with his own hand the written declaration, and promised on oath to do all that was commanded him. The warden of the Fleet then conveyed him and his fellows back to prison, and was ordered to provide five faggots for Dr. Barnes and the four Still Yard men, and to conduct them with all formality to St. Paul's on the following morning. At the appointed hour St. Paul's church was crowded to excess: the cardinal had a high platform made for himself, on which he sat, clothed in purple, surrounded by six-and-thirty abbots and mitred bishops, and spiritual doctors, in gowns of damask and satin. There was also a new pulpit erected for the Bishop of Rochester to preach against Luther and Barnes; great basketfuls of books stood near the altar rails, which were to be burned in a great fire made before the rood of Northen; and after the sermon the heretics were to go thrice round the fire, and cast in their faggots. During the sermon, Barnes and his companions were commanded to kneel down and ask forgiveness of God, the Church, and the cardinal. This farce ended, the cardinal departed under a canopy. The accused were brought down from the stage, when the bishops, seating themselves, commanded the warden of the Fleet to carry them round the fire before they gave them absolution, and received them into the Church again. They were then sent to the Fleet, to await the cardinal's pleasure. Barnes remained there for half a year, but learning from a friend that a writ was issued to burn him, he escaped to Antwerp, where he met Luther, and wrote several works. After this he went to and fro from England, in the character of an ambassador from the King of Denmark to Henry, and from Henry to the Duke of Cleves, until he was apprehended, taken before the king at Hampton Court, and conducted to the Tower, where he remained until he was brought out to martyrdom. On the 30th of June following, Barnes, together with Thomas Garret, curate, of London, and William Jerome, Vicar of Stepney, were brought from the Tower to Smithfield, where, before they were committed to the flames, they addressed the people.

"I am come hither," said Dr. Barnes, "to be burned as an heretic, and now hearken to my faith.

"I believe in the blessed Trinity, three Persons and one God, that created the world, and that this blessed Trinity sent down the second person, Jesus Christ, into the womb of the Virgin Mary. I believe that he was conceived by the Holy Ghost, and took flesh of her, and that he suffered hunger, thirst, cold, and other passions of our body, sin excepted, according to the saying of St. Peter, 'He was made in all things like to his brethren, yet without sin.' And I believe that this his death and passion was the sufficient ransom for sin. And I believe that through his death he overcame sin, death, and hell, and that there is none other satisfaction unto the Father, but this his death and passion only; and that no work of man did deserve anything of God, but his passion only as touching our justification, for I know the best work that ever I performed is impure and imperfect." And with this he cast abroad his hands, and desired God to forgive him his trespasses:—"Wherefore I beseech thee, O Lord, not to enter into judgment with me, according to the saying of the prophet David. Wherefore, I trust in no good work that ever I did, but only in the death of Christ. I do not doubt but through him to inherit the kingdom of heaven. But imagine not that I speak against good works, for they are to be done, and verily they that do them not shall never come into the kingdom of God. We must do them, because they are commanded us of God, to show and set forth our profession, not to deserve or merit, for that is only by the death of Christ."

He then desired all men to forgive him and to pray for him.

Jerome then addressed the people as follows: "I say unto you, good brethren, that God hath bought us all with no small price, neither with gold nor silver, or other such things of small value, but with his most precious blood. Be not unthankful, therefore, to him again, but fulfil his commandments—that is, love your brethren. Love hateth no man, love fulfilleth all things. If God hath sent thee plenty, help thy neighbour that hath need. Give him good counsel. And again, bear your cross with Christ. Consider what reproof and reproach he suffered for his enemies, and how patiently he suffered all things. Consider that all that Christ did was for his mere goodness, and not of our deserving. For if we could merit our own salvation, Christ would not have died for us. But for Adam's breaking of God's precepts, we had been all lost, if Christ had not redeemed us again. And like as Adam broke the precepts, and was driven out of Paradise, so we, if we break God's commandments, shall have damnation, if we do not repent and ask mercy. Now, therefore, let all Christians put no trust nor confidence in their works, but in the blood of Christ, to whom I commit my soul, beseeching you all to pray to God for me and for my brethren here present with me, that our souls, leaving these wretched bodies, may depart in the true faith of Christ."

After he had concluded, Garret thus spoke: "I also detest all errors, and if I have taught any, I am sorry for it, and ask God's mercy. Or if I have been rash in preaching, whereby any person hath taken any offence, I desire forgiveness. Notwithstanding, to my remembrance, I have never preached anything against God's holy Word; but have ever endeavoured, with my little learning and wit, to set forth the honour of God and the right obedience to his laws, and also the king's accordingly. And I pray God send for the king's grace good and godly counsel, to his glory, to the king's honour, and the increase of virtue in his realm. And thus do I now yield my soul up unto Almighty God, believing that he, of his infinite mercy, according to his promise made in the blood of his Son Jesus Christ, will take it and pardon all my sins, of which I ask him mercy, and desire you all to pray with and for me, that I may patiently suffer this pain, and die in true faith, hope, and charity."

The three martyrs then took each other by the hand, and after embracing, submitted themselves to the executioners, who, having fastened them to the stake, lighted the faggots, which speedily terminated their mortal sufferings.

Condemnation of Testwood and His Companions.

When King Henry was about to appear in public again, after his marriage with Catherine Parr, Gardiner had so skilfully played his cards, that no man had more influence than he had, and much apprehension was consequently felt, as he was known to be antagonistic to the reformed opinions. In the meantime three or four persons were arrested, and sent to the town gaol at Windsor—namely, Anthony Pearson, Henry Filmer, and Testwood. A session was then specially appointed, and held on the following Thursday, in which many well-known judges presided. They were severally indicted for having spoken reproachfully of the sacrament of the altar; and as the jury was formed of papists, they were speedily pronounced to be guilty.

As the prisoners passed to execution, they desired the people to pray for them, and to stand fast in the truth of the Gospel, and not to be moved at their afflictions, for it was the happiest thing that ever happened to them. When they came to the place, Anthony Pearson, with a cheerful countenance, said, "Now welcome mine own sweet wife; for this day shalt thou and I be married together in the love and peace of God."

All three were bound to the post. Testwood, lifting up his hands and eyes to heaven, desired the Lord above to receive his spirit. And so yielded they up their souls to their Father in heaven, in the faith of his dear Son, Jesus Christ, with such humility and steadfastness, that many who saw their patient suffering confessed that they could have found in their hearts to have died with them.

Martyrdom of Adam Damlip.

Another earnest and learned man was soon called to follow in the steps of the former martyrs. George Bucher, more commonly called Adam Damlip, had been chaplain for some time to Fisher, Bishop of Rochester, and was known as an earnest papist. He went to travel on the

Continent after the bishop's death, and journeyed as far as Rome, expecting that there, in the city of the pope, he would find true religion and piety. So great was his horror at discovering the real state of the place and people, that, notwithstanding the most flattering offers which were made to him by Cardinal Pole, if he would take an office as lecturer in his house, he determined to leave Italy and return to England.

At Calais he met some men who were also tired and disgusted with Romanism, and at their request he promised to stay there and preach, if the authorities gave him license.

Lord Lisle, who was the king's deputy at that time, immediately granted the desired permission, giving his license, and that of Sir John Butler, the commissary. So greatly was his lordship pleased with Damlip's preaching, that he offered to provide for him in his own house, and also gave him money to buy books with, if he would only stay and preach in the town.

Damlip gratefully refused all these generous offers, and requested to be provided with quiet lodgings, where he could live comfortably and have time for study, promising to preach twice a day. Lodgings were accordingly provided for him in the house of William Stevens, one of the men who had been instrumental in detaining him in Calais. For nearly a month he continued to labour earnestly, preaching strongly against the errors of popery, especially against transubstantiation and the sacrifice of the mass. His listeners increased so much that the chapter-house of the White Friars was no longer able to contain them; and he therefore began to preach in the public meeting-place, in front of the Town Hall. The anger of the priests was soon awakened, and a prior of the White Friars, in concert with Lord Lisle's chaplain, began to write against him to the clergy in England; in consequence of which, Damlip received an order to appear before the Archbishop of Canterbury, and answer the charges made against him. He immediately obeyed the summons, and replied to the accusations made against him with such skill and boldness that the bishops who heard him were both astonished at his wisdom and enraged at their own inability to cope with his arguments.

He was dismissed, and commanded to appear again the next day; but Cranmer, the archbishop, told him privately that, if he appeared, he would surely be condemned to death; therefore he escaped and fled into another part of the country, where he remained concealed for two years, when he was again apprehended, and sent to Calais to be tried there. An Act of Parliament having been passed forbidding the punishment of death for religious belief, the charge against him of heresy was unavailing; his enemies therefore accused him of treason, for having accepted a French crown from Cardinal Pole, to pay for his travelling expenses; and on this trifling charge he was condemned to be hung, drawn, and quartered.

The Condemnation of Mr. George Wishart, Gentleman, Who Suffered Martyrdom for the Faith of Christ, at St. Andrew's, in Scotland, March 1, 1546, with the Articles Brought Against Him, and His Answers to the Same.

Before we enter upon the examination of this bright character of the Church of Christ, we will give to the reader a testimonial of his manners, written by one of his scholars, to Mr. Foxe:—

"About the year of our Lord 1543, there was in the university of Cambridge one Mr. George Wishart, commonly called Mr. George, of Bennet's College, who was a man of tall stature, bald-headed, long-bearded and comely of personage. He was well spoken after his country of Scotland, courteous, lowly, lovely, glad to teach, desirous to learn, and was well travelled. He wore a mantle or frieze gown to the shoes, a black millian fustian doublet, and plain black hose, coarse new canvas for his shirts, and white falling bands and cuffs at his hands. All the which apparel he gave to the poor, some weekly, some monthly, some quarterly, as he liked.

"He was a man modest, temperate, fearing God, hating covetousness; for his charity had never end, night, noon, nor day; he forbare one meal in three, one day in four, for the most part, except something to comfort nature. He lay hard upon a puff of straw, and coarse new canvas sheets, which, when he changed, he gave away. He taught me with great modesty and gravity, so that some of his people thought him severe, and would have slain him, but the Lord was his defence. And he, after due correction for their malice, by good exhortation amended them and went his way. His learning was no less sufficient than his desire; always pressed and ready to do good in that he was able, both in the house privately and in the school publicly, professing and reading divers authors.

"All this I testify with my whole heart, and truth, of this godly man.—EMERY TYLNEY."

George Wishart was by birth a Scotchman, but received his education at Cambridge. The year before his death he returned to his own country, and on his way preached in many places against idolatry. He made some stay at Dundee; but he was expelled thence, and at his departure denounced heavy judgment on them for rejecting the Gospel. He then went and preached in many other places, and entrance to the churches being denied him, he preached in the fields. He would not suffer the people to open the church doors by violence, for that, he said, became not the Gospel of peace which he preached. He heard that the plague had broken out in Dundee within four days after he was banished; so he returned thither, and took care of the sick, and did all the offices of a faithful pastor among them. He foretold several extraordinary things, particularly his own sufferings, and the spreading of the Reformation over the land. He preached last in Lothian, and there the Earl of Bothwell took him, but promised upon his honour that no harm should be done him; yet he delivered him to the cardinal, who brought him to St. Andrew's, and called a meeting of bishops there, to destroy him with more solemnity.

While imprisoned in the castle, the Dean of St. Andrew's was sent by the cardinal to summon him to appear before the judge, to render an account of his heretical doctrine.

Wishart answered, "What need my lord cardinal to summons me, when I am thus in his power, and bound in irons? Can he not compel me to answer? or does he believe that I am unprovided with the means of defending my doctrine?"

Upon the next morning the lord cardinal caused his servants to apparel themselves in their warlike array, with jack, knapskal, splent, spear, and axe—an equipment more suitable for the battle than for the preaching of the true word of God.

And when these armed champions, marching in warlike order, had conveyed the bishops into the abbey, they sent for George, who was conveyed into church by the captain of the castle, accompanied with a hundred men dressed in like manner. The sub-prior of the abbey, Dean Winryme, preached to the congregation assembled, taking his matter out of the thirteenth chapter of Matthew.

And when he ended the sermon, they caused Wishart to

ascend the pulpit, to hear his accusation. And right against them stood by one John Lauder, laden full of cursings written in paper, of which he took out a roll full of cursings, and words of devilish malice, addressing to the innocent George many cruel words. Notwithstanding, Wishart stood still with great patience, hearing their sayings, not once moving or changing his countenance.

When Lauder had read through his menacings, he spit at Wishart's face, saying, "What answerest thou to these sayings, thou runagate, traitor, thief, which we have duly proved by sufficient witness against thee?" Wishart hearing this, kneeled down in the pulpit, making his prayer to God. When he had ended his prayer, he sweetly answered as follows:

"Many horrible sayings ye have spoken this day, which not only to teach, but even to think, I hold in abomination. Wherefore I pray your discretions quietly to hear me, that ye may know what were my sayings, and the manner of my doctrine.

"First, since the time I came into this realm, I taught nothing but the ten commandments of God, the twelve articles of the faith, and the prayer of the Lord in the mother tongue. Moreover, in Dundee, I taught the Epistle of St. Paul to the Romans. And I shall show you faithfully what manner I used when I taught, without any human dread; so that your discretions give your ears benevolence and attention."

Suddenly, then, with a high voice cried the accuser, "Thou heretic, runagate, traitor, and thief, it was not lawful for thee to preach. Thou hast taken the power at thine own hand, without any authority of the Church. We forethink that thou hast been a preacher so long."

Then all the whole congregation of the prelates, with their accomplices, said these words: "If we give license to preach, he is so crafty, and in the Holy Scripture so exercised, that he will persuade the people to his opinion, and raise them against us."

He, seeing their malicious intent, appealed from the lord cardinal to the lord governor, as to an impartial judge. To whom John Lauder answered, "Is not my lord cardinal the second person within this realm, Chancellor of Scotland, Archbishop of St. Andrew's, Bishop of Meropois, *Legatus natus, Legatus a Latere?*" "Is not he," quoth Lauder, "a judge for thee? What other desirest thou to be thy judge?"

"I refuse not my lord cardinal," said Wishart, "but I

desire the Word of God to be my judge, and the temporal estate, with some of your lordships mine auditors, because I am here my lord governor's prisoner."

To be brief, these were the articles of condemnation, with his answers, as far as they would give him leave to speak. For when he intended to show the manner of his doctrine, they stopped his mouth with another article.

"Thou false heretic, runagate, traitor, and thief, deceiver of the people, thou despisest the holy Church, and contemnest my lord governor's authority. And this we know, that when thou preachedst in Dundee, and was charged by my lord's authority to desist, nevertheless thou wouldest not obey, but perseveredst in the same; and therefore the Bishop of Brothen cursed thee, and delivered thee into the devil's hands, and gave thee in commandment that thou shouldest preach no more, which, notwithstanding, thou didst continue obstinately."

"My lords, I have read in the Acts of the Apostles that it is not lawful to desist from the preaching of the Gospel for the threats and menaces of men. Therefore it is written, 'We ought to obey God rather than men.' "

"Thou preachedst against the sacrament, saying that there were not seven sacraments."

"My lords, if it be your pleasures, I never taught the number of the sacraments, whether they were seven or eleven. So many as are instituted by Christ are showed to us by the Evangel."

"Thou hast openly taught that auricular confession is not a blessed sacrament, and sayest that we should only confess to God, and to no priest."

"My lords, I say that auricular confession, seeing that it hath no promise of the Evangel, cannot be a sacrament. Of the confession to be made to God, there are many testimonies in Scripture. When I exhorted the people, I reproved no manner of confession."

When he had said these words the bishops and their accomplices cried, and grinned with their teeth, saying, "See ye not what colours he hath in his speaking, that he may beguile us to his opinion?"

"Heretic, thou didst say openly that it was necessary to every man to understand his baptism, contrary to general councils and the holy Church."

"My lords, I believe there be none so unwise here that will make merchandise with a Frenchman; so likewise I would that we understood what thing we promise in the name of the infant unto God in baptism. For this cause I believe ye have confirmation."

Then said Bleiter, the chaplain, that he had the devil within him, and the spirit of error. On which a little child who was present, and heard the chaplain, said, "The devil cannot speak such words as yonder man doth speak."

"Heretic, traitor, thief, thou saidst that the sacrament of the altar was but a piece of bread baked upon the ashes, and no other thing, and all which is there done is against the commandment of God."

"As concerning the sacrament of the altar, my lords, I never taught anything against the Scripture, the which I shall, by God's grace, make manifest this day, I being ready therefore to suffer death."

"False heretic, thou saidst that a man hath no free will, but that all cometh by God, whatsoever kind it be of."

"My lords, I said not so, truly; I say, that as many as believe in Christ firmly, unto them is given liberty, conformable to the saying of St. John, 'If the Son make you free, ye shall be free indeed.' Of the contrary, as many as believe not in Christ Jesus, they are bond-servants of sin: 'He that sinneth is servant to sin.'"

"Thou saidst it is as lawful to eat flesh upon the Friday as on Sunday."

"I have read in the epistles of St. Paul, that who is clean unto him all things are clean. But the creature maketh no man acceptable unto God. To the faithful man all things are sanctified by the Word of God and prayer."

At this all the bishops, with their accomplices, said, "What need we any witness against him? hath he not openly here spoken blasphemy?"

"Heretic, thou dost say that we should not pray to saints, but to God only. Say whether thou hast said this or not."

"My lords, there are two things worthy of note; the one is certain, the other uncertain. It is found plainly in Scripture that we should worship one God, according to the first commandment, 'Thou shalt worship the Lord thy God with all thy heart.' But as for praying to saints, there is a great doubt whether they hear or not invocation made unto them. Therefore I exhorted all men in my doctrine, that they should leave the unsure way, and follow that way which was taught us by our Master, Christ. He is the only Mediator, and maketh intercession for us to God his Father; he is the door by which we must enter in: he that entereth not by this door, but climbeth another way, is a thief and a murderer. Christ is the truth and life."

"Thou hast preached saying there is no purgatory, and that it is a feigned thing for any man after this life to be punished in purgatory."

"As I have said heretofore, without express witness of the Scripture I dare affirm nothing. I have oft read over the Bible, and yet such a term found I never, nor yet any place of Scripture applicable thereunto. Therefore I was ashamed ever to teach that thing which I could not find in the Scripture."

"False heretic, thou sayest thou wilt not obey our general nor provincial councils."

"My lords, what your general councils are I know not; I was never exercised in them; but to the pure Word of God I gave my labours. Read here your general councils, or else give me a book wherein they are contained, that I may read them. If they agree with the Word of God, I will not disagree."

"Thou hast preached openly, saying that the soul of man shall sleep till the latter day of judgment, and shall not obtain life immortal until that day."

"God, full of mercy and goodness, forgive them that say such things of me. I know surely, by the Word of God, that he which hath begun to have the faith of Jesus Christ, and believeth firmly in him, I know surely that the soul of that man shall never sleep, but ever shall live an immortal life; which life, from day to day is renewed in grace, and augmented; nor yet shall ever perish, but immortal shall live with Christ; to which life all that believe in him shall come, and rest in eternal glory. Amen."

When the bishops, with their accomplices, had thus accused this innocent man, they next condemned him to be burnt as a heretic.

When the fire and the gallows were being prepared, the cardinal, fearing lest he should have been taken away by his friends, commanded to direct all the ordnance of the castle against that part, and his gunners to be ready beside their guns, until such time as he were burned. All this being done, they bound the martyr's hands behind his back, and led him forth with soldiers from the castle to the place of execution.

When he came to the fire he knelt down upon his knees and rose again, and thrice repeated these words:—"Oh, thou Saviour of the world, have mercy on me! Father of heaven, I commend my spirit into thy holy hands." Then he turned him to the people and said—

"I beseech you, Christian brethren and sisters, that ye be not offended in the Word of God for the torments which ye see prepared for me; but I exhort you that you love the Word of God, and suffer with a comfortable heart for the Word's sake, which is your undoubted salvation and ever-lasting comfort.

"For this cause I was sent, that I should suffer this fire for Christ's sake. This grim fire I fear not. If that any persecution come to you for the Word's sake, do not fear them that slay the body, and afterward have no power to slay the soul. Some have said of me that I have taught that the soul of man should sleep until the last day; but I know surely, and my faith is such, that my soul shall sup with my Saviour Christ this night, ere it be six hours, for whom I suffer this. I beseech thee, Father of heaven, to forgive them that have of any ignorance or else have of any evil mind forged any lies upon me: I forgive them with all my heart. I beseech Christ to forgive them that have con-demned me to death this day ignorantly; and, last of all, I beseech you, brethren and sisters, to exhort your prelates to the learning of the Word of God, that they at the last may be ashamed to do evil, and learn to do good."

The hangman fell upon his knees and said, "I pray you forgive me, for I am not guilty of your death;" to whom he answered, "Come hither to me." When he was come to him, he kissed his cheek, and said, "Lo, here is a token that I forgive thee. My heart, do thine office;" and by-and-by he was put upon the gibbet and hanged, and burnt to powder.

Story and Martyrdom of Anne Askew.

Anne Askew was descended from a good family, and had received an accomplished education: but the reader will best form his judgment of her by what follows, and which was written by herself.

"To satisfy your expectation, good people," said she, "this was my first examination, in the year of our Lord 1545, in the month of March.

"First, Christopher Dare examined me at Sadler's Hall, being one of the quest, and asked if I did not believe that the sacrament hanging over the altar was the very body of Christ really. Then I demanded this question of him: 'Wherefore was St. Stephen stoned to death?' and he said he could not tell. Then answered I that no more would I answer his vain question.

"Then he said he had sent for a priest to examine me, who was at hand.

"The priest asked me what I said to the sacrament of the altar, and required much to know my meaning therein. But I desired him again to hold me excused concerning that matter; no other answer would I make him, because I perceived him to be a papist.

"He asked me if I did not think that private masses helped the departed souls. I said it was great idolatry to believe more in them than in the death which Christ died for us.

"Then they brought me unto my lord mayor, and he examined me as they had before.

"Then the lord mayor commanded me to prison. I asked him if sureties would not serve me; he made me short answer, that he would take none. Then was I forced to the Compter, where I remained eleven days, no friend admitted to speak with me. But in the meantime, there was a priest sent unto me, who said that he was commanded by the bishop to examine me, and to give me good counsel, which he did not. But first he asked me for what cause I was put in the Compter, and I told him I could not tell.

"He said it was told him that I denied the sacrament of the altar. I answered again, 'What I have said I have said.'

"A short time later, the Bishop of London sent for me, and as I came before him, he said he was sorry for my trouble, and desired to know my opinions in such matters as were laid against me.

"In the meanwhile he commanded his archdeacon to commune with me, who said, 'Mistress, wherefore are you accused and thus troubled here before the bishops?'

"I answered, 'Sir, ask my accusers, for I know not as yet.'

"Then he took my hand, and said, 'Such a book as this has brought you to the trouble you are in. Beware!' said he, 'beware! for he that made this book, and was the author thereof, was a heretic and burned in Smithfield.'

"I asked him if he was certain and sure that it was true what he had spoken. He said he knew well the book was of John Frith's making. Then I asked him if he was not ashamed to judge of the book before he saw it within, or yet knew the truth thereof. Then I opened the book and showed it him. He said he thought it had been another, for he could find no fault therein.

"Then inquired the bishop of me, 'What if the Scripture doth say that it is the body of Christ?'

" 'I believe,' said I, 'as the Scripture doth teach.'

"Then he asked again, 'What if the Scripture doth say that it is not the body of Christ?'

"My answer was still, 'I believe as the Scripture informeth me.'

"Then he asked me, why I had so few words; and I answered, 'God hath given me the gift of knowledge, but not of utterance.'

"Then my lord went away, and said he would entitle some of my meaning in writing; but what it was I have not in my memory, for he would not suffer me to have the copy thereof, only I remember this small portion of it:—

" 'Be it known of all men, that I, Anne Askew, do confess this to be my faith and belief, notwithstanding many reports made afore to the contrary.'

"Then he read it to me, and asked me if I did agree to it.

"And I said again, 'I believe so much thereof as the Holy Scripture doth agree unto; wherefore I desire you that you will add that thereunto.'

"Then he answered that I should not teach him what he should write.

"Then my lord sat down, and gave me the writing to set thereto my hand, and I wrote after this manner: 'I, Anne Askew, do believe all manner of things contained in the faith of the catholic Church.'

"Then because I did add unto it the 'catholic Church,' he went into his chamber in great fury.

"After this we thought that I should be put to bail immediately, according to the order of the law. At the last, after much ado and reasoning to and fro, they took a bond of them of recognisance for my forthcoming: and thus I was at the last delivered.

"Written by me, ANNE ASKEW."

Thus ends her first persecution, from which, for a time, she escaped; but not conforming to the erroneous doctrine of the sacrament, she was, in 1546, again apprehended, of which, before her martyrdom, she wrote as follows:—

"SUM OF MY EXAMINATION BEFORE THE KING'S COUNCIL
AT GREENWICH.

"I being before the council, was asked of Mr. Kyme. I answered that my lord chancellor knew already my mind in that matter. Then my lord chancellor asked of me my opinion in the sacrament. My answer was this, 'I believe that so oft as I, in a Christian congregation, do receive the bread in remembrance of Christ's death, and with thanksgiving according to his holy institution, I receive therewith the fruits also of his most glorious passion. The Bishop of Winchester bade me make a direct answer. I said I would not sing a new song of the Lord in a strange land.

"They then drew out a confession respecting the sacrament, urging me to set my hand thereunto; but this I refused. On the following Sunday I was so extremely ill, that I thought death was upon me. In the height of my illness I was conveyed to Newgate, where the Lord was pleased to renew my strength.

"MY FAITH BRIEFLY WRITTEN TO THE KING'S GRACE, AND SENT BY THE HANDS OF THE CHANCELLOR.

"I, Anne Askew, of good memory, although God hath given me the bread of adversity and the water of trouble, yet not so much as my sins have deserved, desire this to be known unto your grace, that forasmuch as I am by the law condemned for an evil doer, here I take heaven and earth to record, that I shall die in my innocency; and according to that I have said first, and will say last, I utterly abhor and detest all heresies. And as concerning the supper of the Lord, I believe so much as Christ hath said therein, which he confirmed with his most blessed blood; I believe so much as he willed me to follow, and believe so much as the catholic Church of him doth teach. For I will not forsake the commandment of his holy lips. But look what God hath charged me with his mouth, that I have shut up in my heart. And thus briefly I end for lack of learning.

"ANNE ASKEW."

"MY EXAMINATION AND TREATMENT AFTER MY DEPARTURE FROM NEWGATE.

"On Tuesday I was sent from Newgate to the sign of the 'Crown,' where Mr. Rich and the Bishop of London, with all their power and flattering words, went about to persuade me from God; but I did not esteem their glossing pretences.

"Then Mr. Rich sent me to the Tower, where I remained till three o'clock, when Rich came and one of the council, charging me upon my obedience to show unto them if I knew any man or woman of my sect. My answer was that I knew none. Then they asked me of Lady Suffolk, Lady Sussex, Lady Hertford, Lady Denny, and Lady Fitzwilliam. To whom I answered, if I should pronounce anything against them, that I was not able to prove it.

Then they commanded me to show how I was maintained in the Compter, and who willed me to stick to my opinion.

"I said, that there was no creature that therein did strengthen me. And as for the help that I had in the Compter, it was by the means of my maid. For as she went abroad in the streets, she told my case to the apprentices, and they by her did send me money, but who they were I never knew.

"Then they did put me on the rack, because I confessed no ladies or gentlewomen to be of my opinion, and thereon they kept me a long time.

"The lieutenant then caused me to be loosed from the rack. After that I sat two hours reasoning with my lord chancellor upon the bare floor, when he, with many flattering words, tried to persuade me to leave my opinion; but my Lord God, I thank his everlasting goodness, gave me grace to persevere.

"Then was I brought to a house and laid in a bed. Then my lord chancellor sent me word, if I would leave my opinion I should want for nothing; if I would not, I should forthwith to Newgate, and so be burned. I sent him again word that I would rather die than break my faith."

THE CONFESSION OF HER FAITH WHICH SHE MADE IN NEWGATE.

"I, Anne Askew, of good memory, although my merciful Father hath given me the bread of adversity, do confess myself here a sinner before the throne of his heavenly majesty, desiring his forgiveness and mercy. And for so much as I am by the law unrighteously condemned for an evil-doer, concerning opinions, I take the same most merciful God of mine, which hath made both heaven and earth, to record that I hold no opinions contrary to his most holy

Word; and I trust in my merciful Lord, which is the giver of all grace, that he will graciously assist me against all evil opinions which are contrary to his blessed verity.

"But this is the heresy which they report me to hold, that after the priest had spoken the words of consecration, there remaineth bread still. They both say and also teach it for a necessary article of faith, that after these words be once spoken, there remaineth no bread, but even the selfsame body that hung upon the cross of Good Friday, both flesh, blood, and bone. To this belief of theirs say I, Nay. For then were our common creed false, which saith, that He sitteth on the right hand of God the Father Almighty, and from thence shall come to judge the quick and the dead. But as touching the holy and blessed supper of the Lord, I believe it to be a most necessary remembrance of his glorious sufferings and death.

"Finally, I believe all those Scriptures to be true which he hath confirmed with his most precious blood; yea, and as St. Paul saith, those Scriptures are sufficient for our learning and salvation, that Christ hath left here with us; so that I believe we need no unwritten verities to rule his Church with.

"There be some that say I deny the eucharist, or sacrament of thanksgiving; but those people untruly report of me, for I both say and believe it, that if it were ordered as Christ instituted and left it, a most singular comfort it were unto us all. But as concerning your mass as it is now used in our days, I say and believe it to be the most abominable idol that is in the world. For my God will not be eaten with teeth, neither yet dieth he again; and upon these words that I have now spoken will I suffer death.

"O Lord, I have more enemies now than there be hairs on my head. Yet, sweet Lord, let me not set by them which are against me, for in thee is my whole delight; and, Lord, I heartily desire of thee that thou wilt, of thy most merciful goodness, forgive them that violence which they do and have done unto me. Open also thou their blind hearts, that they may hereafter do that thing in thy sight which is only acceptable before thee, and set forth thy verity aright, without all vain phantasy of sinful men. So be it, O Lord, so be it.

"ANNE ASKEW."

Hitherto we have given the words of this good lady; now it remains for us to speak of her martyrdom. Being born of such a kindred as would have enabled her to live in wealth and prosperity, if she had chosen rather to have followed the world than Christ, yet she had been so tortured that she could not live long. The day of her execution being appointed, she was brought to Smithfield in a chair, because she could not go on her feet from the cruel effects of the torments. Three others were also brought to suffer with her, and for the same offence these were Nicholas Belenian, a priest, of Shropshire; John Adams, a tailor; and John Lacels, a gentleman of the court and household of King Henry. The martyrs being all chained to the stake, and all things ready for the fire, Dr. Shaxton, then appointed to preach, gave his sermon.

The sermon being finished, the martyrs, standing there, tied at three several stakes ready for their martyrdom, began their prayers. There was a great concourse of people; the place where they stood being railed about to keep out the press. Upon the bench, under St. Bartholomew's Church, sat Wrisley, the Chancellor of England, the old Duke of Norfolk, the old Earl of Bedford, the Lord Mayor, with divers others.

Then the Lord Chancellor sent letters to Anne Askew, offering to her the king's pardon if she would recant, but she refused to look at them, answering again that she came not thither to deny her Lord and Master. Then were the letters likewise offered unto the others, who, in like manner, following the constancy of the woman, refused not only to receive them, but even to look at them; whereon they continued mutually to exhort each other by the glory they were about to enter; after which the Lord Mayor commanded fire to be put to them.

And thus Anne Askew, with these blessed martyrs, were compassed about with flames of fire, as sacrifices unto God.

Life and Martyrdom of William Tyndale.

We shall now rehearse the story and martyrdom of William Tyndale, who, although he did not suffer in England, ought to be ranked with the martyrs of our country, of which, from his great zeal, perseverance, and dispersing of truth, he may properly be esteemed the apostle.

William Tyndale was born about the borders of Wales, and brought up in the University of Oxford, where he grew up and increased in the knowledge of the liberal arts, and in his acquaintance with the Scriptures.

After this he removed to Cambridge, and then to Gloucestershire, and engaged himself to a knight, named Welch, as tutor to his children. To this gentleman's table several abbots, deans, and other beneficed men used to resort, with whom Tyndale conversed of learned men, particularly of Luther and Erasmus, and of questions relative to the Scriptures.

In course of time it happened that the bishop's chancellor held a court, at which the priests were summoned to appear, among whom was Tyndale. The latter had his doubts as to the formation of a conspiracy against him; and on his way thither he earnestly prayed to God to enable him to bear witness to the truth of his word. The chancellor reviled him grievously; but no definite accusation could be proved against him.

There dwelt not far off a certain doctor, named Munmouth, who had been an old acquaintance of Tyndale's. Tyndale went to him to disclose his heart. After some discourse, the doctor said—

"Do you not know that the pope is very Antichrist, whom the Scripture speaketh of? But beware what you say: for if you be perceived of that opinion, it will cost you your life. I have been an officer of his; but I have given it up, and defy him and all his works."

Not long after, Tyndale happened to be in company of a certain divine, and in disputing with him he pressed him so hard that the doctor burst out into these blasphemous words: "We were better to be without God's laws than the pope's."

Tyndale full of godly zeal, replied: "I defy the pope and all his laws;" and added, that if God spared him life, ere many years, he would cause a boy that driveth the plough to know more of the Scripture than he did.

After this the priests became more bitter against Tyndale, saying that he was a heretic. Being so molested by the priests, he was obliged to remove from that part. On coming to London he was recommended to Tonstall, Bishop of London, by Sir Henry Guildford. He remained in London almost a year, greatly distressed with the pomp, pride, and ignorance of the clergy, insomuch that he perceived not only no room in the bishop's house for him to translate the New Testament, but also that there was no place for him in all England. He departed to Germany, and

studied by what possible means he could bring his countrymen to the understanding of God's Word, and to the
possession of the same privileges which he himself enjoyed.
He perceived that the cause of the people's blindness, and
of the errors and superstitions of the Church, was ignorance of the Scriptures. The truth was entombed in the
sepulchre of a dead language; the efforts of the priests were
directed to keep men from inquiring of the oracles of God;
and when reference was ever made to the sacred text, these
doctors of the law did what they could to perplex the
inquirers, wresting the Scriptures to suit their own purposes. From these considerations Tyndale felt moved, by
the Spirit of God, to translate the Scriptures into his
mother tongue, for the benefit of the simple people of
England. He first began with the New Testament, which
was translated about the year 1527, prefixing a short
preface to every book, after which, in like manner, he
translated the five books of Moses, and wrote sundry other
godly works. His books were published and sent over to
England, and became like holy fire from the altar, to give
light in the night season.

On Tyndale's departure from England he went to Germany, after which he moved to the Netherlands, and
resided principally at Antwerp. Having finished his translation of the five books of Moses, he sailed to Hamburg,
intending to print them in that city. On his voyage he was
shipwrecked, and lost all his manuscripts, and almost all he
possessed. However, with true moral heroism, he proceeded to Hamburg, and began the work again, in company with Mr. Coverdale, in the house of Miss Emmerson,
anno 1529. When the translation of the New Testament
was first issued, Tyndale appealed to the learned for help,
for the correction of accidental errors; but the dignitaries
of the Church, indignant that the people should possess the
Word of God, clamorously inveighed against it, as being so
full of heresy, sedition, and inaccuracies, that its suppression was the duty of the faithful. They scanned it with a
microscopic jealousy, and magnified the inadvertent omission of a letter into a flagrant and wilful perversion of the
original. The English prelates were filled with wrath, and
did not rest until they had persuaded the king to take
hostile proceedings in the matter. A proclamation was then
issued, under authority, which condemned and prohibited
Tyndale's translation of the New Testament. But not con-

tent with this, they studied how they might entangle and destroy its author.

Accordingly, after some stratagem and the employment of treachery, Tyndale was betrayed at Antwerp by one Philips, and conveyed to the castle of Filford, eighteen miles from Antwerp, where he remained until his death.

At last, after the lapse of a year and a half, and much fruitless disputation, he was condemned by virtue of the emperor's decree made in the assembly at Augsburg. When he was brought out for execution, and was being tied to the stake, he cried with a loud and earnest voice, "Lord, open the King of England's eyes!" He was then strangled, and his remains burnt to ashes. Such was the power and excellence of this truly good man, that during his imprisonment he converted his keeper, with his daughter, and others of his attendants. Several of those who came in contact with him during his imprisonment reported of him, that if he were not a good Christian, they did not know whom to trust; and the procurator-general left this testimony about him, that he was "a learned, a good, and a godly man."

Progress of the Reformation in the Reign of Edward VI.

The events that marked the progress of the Reformation in the reign of Henry VIII were the rejection of the papal supremacy, the suppression of the monasteries, and the circulation of the Scriptures in the vulgar tongue. The invention of printing was one of those providential discoveries whose innate importance was augmented tenfold by the peculiar circumstances under which it became current; for the revival of literature, the desire for knowledge, and freedom of inquiry, would all tend to unshackle the minds of men, and to prove favourable to the new opinions which made enlightened truth their basis. King Henry VIII died in 1547, in the fifty-sixth year of his age, and the thirty-eighth year of his reign.

The severities he used against many of his subjects, in matters of religion, made both parties write unfavourably of him; his temper was imperious and cruel: he was violent in his revenge, and stuck at nothing by which he could gratify his lust or his passion. This was much provoked by the sentence the pope thundered against him, by the virulent books Cardinal Pole and others published, by the rebellions that were raised in England, and the apprehensions he was in of the Emperor Charles' greatness, together with what he had read in history of the fate of those princes whom the popes had excommunicated: all these considerations made him think it necessary to keep his people under the terror of a severe government, and, by some public examples, to secure the peace of the nation, and thereby prevent a greater effusion of blood.

Edward was the only son of King Henry, by his beloved wife, Jane Seymour, who died the day after his birth. He was born October 12, 1537, and came to the throne in 1547, being only ten years of age. The funeral of the deceased king was performed with the ordinary ceremonies at Windsor. He left £600 a year to the church at that place for masses for his soul, for the annual commemoration of his death, and for the maintenance of thirteen poor knights.

The Parliament was opened on the 4th of November, and proceeded to repeal various statutes passed in the late reign, with reference to treason and the persecution of dissentients. Another Act was passed, permitting the laity to receive the sacrament in both kinds; that bishops should be nominated by the Crown; and for the dissolution of the chantries. Many ceremonies connected with external worship were abolished, and a new communion office was promulgated, which was followed, before long, by the issue of a new liturgy. In February, 1549, an Act was passed permitting the clergy to marry. King Edward was much pleased with the advice tendered to him by Bucer, and formed a scheme for amending many things which were amiss in his government. This he embodied in the form of a treatise, which he wrote out with his own hand. He also wrote a discourse in French, being a collection of Scriptural passages against idolatry, to which he prefixed a preface, and dedicated it to the Protector, the Duke of Somerset. Notwithstanding the changes in religion, which were enforced by law, the Princess Mary refused to conform to them, and maintained the service of mass. She refused to comply with the orders of the Council, who did not venture to proceed to extremities with her, as she was under the guardianship of the emperor, who threatened England with war if she were molested. Some time afterwards the Council remonstrated with her again, on her public observance of mass; and being then more indifferent to the emperor's displeasure, pressed her more closely on the point.

She was, however, resolved not to conform to the new

services, and would leave her house rather than comply. Bishop Ridley went to visit her at Hunsden. After the bishop had saluted her grace, he said that he had come to do his duty to her. Then she thanked him for his pains, and for a quarter of an hour talked with him very pleasantly, and said that she knew him in the court when he was chaplain to her father, and could well remember a sermon that he made before King Henry, her father, and so dismissed him to dine with her officers.

After dinner was done, the bishop being called for by the said Lady Mary, resorted again to her grace, between whom this communication was—first, the bishop beginneth in manner as followeth:

Bishop. Madam, I came not only to do my duty to see your grace, but also to offer myself to preach before you on Sunday next, if it will please you to hear me.

At this her countenance changed.

And after many bitter words against the form of religion then established, and against the government of the realm, and the laws made in the young years of her brother, which she said she was not bound to obey till her brother came to perfect age, and then she affirmed she would obey them, she asked the bishop whether he were one of the Council: he answered, "No." "You might well enough," said she, "as the Council goeth now-a-days."

And so she concluded with these words: "My lord, for your gentleness to come and see me, I thank you; but for your offering to preach before me, I thank you never a whit."

Then the said bishop was brought by Sir Thomas Wharton to the place where they dined, and was desired to drink. And after he had drunk, he paused awhile, looking very sadly, and suddenly broke out into these words: "Surely I have done amiss." "Why so?" quoth Sir Thomas Wharton. "For I have drunk," said he, "in that place where God's word offered hath been refused: whereas, if I had remembered my duty, I ought to have departed immediately, and to have shaken off the dust of my shoes for a testimony against this house." This done, the said bishop departed, and so returned to his house.

Fall and Death of the Duke of Somerset.

At this time a great creation of peers took place. Warwick was made Duke of Northumberland, the Percies being then under an attainder: Paulet was made Marquis of

Winchester; Herbert, Earl of Pembroke; and a little before
this, Russell had been created Earl of Bedford, and Darcy
was raised to the peerage. There was none so likely to take
the king out of Northumberland's hands as the Duke of
Somerset, who was beginning to form a new party. Therefore, upon some informations, both the Duke of Somerset
and his duchess, Sir Ralph Vane, Sir Thomas Palmer, Sir
Thomas Arundel, and several others, of whom some were
gentlemen of quality, and others the duke's servants, were
all committed to the Tower. The committing of Palmer
was a mere delusion, for he had betrayed the duke, and
was seized as an accomplice, after which he pretended to
discover a plot: he said the duke intended to have raised
the people, and that Northumberland, Northampton, and
Pembroke, having been invited to dine at the Lord Paget's,
he intended to have set on them by the way, or have killed
them at dinner: that Vane was to have 2,000 men ready;
Arundel was to have seized on the Tower, and all the
gendarmery were to have been killed. All these things were
told the young king with such specious circumstances, that
he was deluded by them, and unhappily became alienated
from his uncle, judging him guilty of so foul a conspiracy.
It was added by others, that the duke intended to have
raised the city of London; one Crane confirmed Palmer's
testimony, and both the Earl of Arundel and Paget were
also committed as accomplices. On the 1st of December,
the duke was brought to his trial. The particulars charged
on him were, a design to seize on the king's person, to
imprison Northumberland, and to raise the city of London.
He was not deeply skilled in law, and neither objected to
the indictment nor desired counsel to plead for him, but
only answered to matters of fact: he denied all designs of
raising the people, or of killing Northumberland. He desired the witnesses might be brought face to face, and
raised many objections to them, chiefly to Palmer; but this
common act of justice was denied him, and only their
depositions were read. All the sharpness which the King's
counsel expressed, in pleading against him, did not provoke
him to any indecent passion. But when sentence was given,
his courage sank a little, and he asked the three lords, who
were his enemies, pardon for his ill designs against them,
and made suit for his life, and for his wife and children. It
was generally thought that nothing being found against him
but an intention to imprison a privy councillor, one so
nearly related to the king would not have been put to death

on that account. It was, therefore, necessary to raise in the king a great aversion to him. Accordingly, a story was brought to him, as if in the Tower he had confessed a design to employ some persons to assassinate those lords; and those named for that wicked service were persuaded to affirm it. This being believed by the king, he took no care to preserve him, assassinaton being a crime of so bad a nature, that it filled him with horror, even of his uncle, when he thought him guilty of it; and thus the duke was given up to death. Stanhope, Partridge, Arundel, and Vane were next tried: the two first were not much pitied, for they had made an ill use of their interest in the duke during his greatness: the last two were much lamented. Partridge and Vane were condemned to be hanged, the other two were condemned to be beheaded.

On the 22nd of January, 1552, King Edward's uncle, the Duke of Somerset, was brought out of the Tower of London, and delivered up to the sheriffs of the city, who were accompanied by a great number of armed men and guards. When brought upon the scaffold, he maintained the utmost serenity; and kneeling down, he lifted up his hands, and commended his soul to God.

After having offered up a few short prayers, he arose and turned round, apparently quite undismayed at the sight of the executioner and his axe; but with the most perfect cheerfulness and composure addressed the people, in almost the following words:

"Dearly beloved friends, I am brought here to suffer death, although I have never offended, by word or deed, against the king. Nevertheless, as the law has sentenced me to death, I acknowledge that I, as well as any other man, have no appeal from it. Therefore, to show my obedience to the laws, I have come here to die, heartily thanking God for having allowed me this time for repentance, instead of cutting me off by sudden death.

"There is yet something, beloved friends, regarding the Christian religion, which I must put you in mind of; and which, when I was in authority, I always set forth to the utmost of my power. Not only do I not repent of my actions, but I rejoice in them, since now the forms of our Christian religion have come nearer to the order of the primitive Church; which I look upon as a great benefit unto you and me, and exhort you all with thankfulness to accept and embrace what is so purely set forth before you, and to show the same in your lives."

Just as he concluded these words, the assembly was suddenly alarmed by a loud and extraordinary noise. Though all heard the noise, no one could see any cause for it. The terrified people ran in all directions. Those who remained in their places scarcely knew where they were, so great was the general panic. During this commotion the people espied Sir Anthony Brown riding under the scaffold, which raised a fresh tumult, for all hoped that the king had sent his uncle pardon by this messenger; and throwing their caps up in the air, with great rejoicings, they cried, "Pardon, pardon is come; God save the king!" Thus the duke saw before his death what a popular favourite he was, and few dukes ever had more tears shed for them, for all men saw in his fall the ruin of England.

Somerset meanwhile remained standing quietly in his place, without displaying any excitement or emotion. At length, making a sign to the crowd with his hand to maintain silence, he thus addressed them:—

"Dearly beloved friends, there is no such matter here in hand as you vainly hope or believe. It seemeth thus good unto Almighty God, whose ordinance it is meet and necessary that we all be obedient unto. Wherefore I pray you all to be quiet, and to be contented with my death, which I am most willing to suffer. And let us now join in prayer unto the Lord for the preservation of the king's majesty, unto whom, hitherto, I have always showed myself a most faithful and true subject. I have always been most diligent about his majesty, in his affairs both at home and abroad, and no less diligent in seeking the common good of the whole realm."

"Moreover, I do wish unto all his councillors the grace and favour of God, whereby they may rule in all things uprightly with justice; unto whom I exhort you all in the Lord to show yourselves obedient, as it is your bounden duty, under the pain of condemnation, and also most profitable for the preservation and safeguard of the king's majesty.

"Moreover, as heretofore I have had oftentimes affairs with divers men, and hard it is to please every man, therefore, if there be any who hath been offended and injured by me, I most humbly require and ask him forgiveness; but especially Almighty God, whom throughout all my life I have most grievously offended. And all other, whatsoever they be, that have offended me, I do with my whole heart forgive them. Now I once again require you, dearly beloved in the Lord, that you will keep yourselves quiet and still, lest through your tumult you might trouble me. For albeit the spirit be willing and ready, the flesh is frail and wavering, and through your quietness I shall be much more composed."

After this, he again knelt down, when Dr. Cox, who had accompanied him in order to let him have the benefit of his counsel and advice, if needed, presented him with a scroll of paper, on which was written a brief confession to God. The duke, after hearing it, again stood up, without any appearance of emotion, and bade farewell to the sheriffs, the Lieutenant of the Tower, and all others who were on the scaffold; then, giving some money to the executioner, he took off his gown, and, kneeling down, untied his shirt strings. The executioner removed his collar and other things, which would have proved a hindrance; and the duke, lying down, called out, "Lord Jesus, save me!" As the name of Jesus was on his lips, the fatal blow was struck, and in a moment he was freed for ever from all the cares and anxieties of this troubled world.

The Death of King Edward

Before long the king became ill; he bore his sickness with great submission, and expressed much anxiety about the state of the Church after his death. His illness originated in a severe cold, followed by an obstinate cough, which baffled the skill of his attendants. A rumour spread abroad that he had been poisoned, but no certain proofs could be obtained to justify the suspicion. Bishop Ridley, who visited him during his illness, pressed on him the duty of men who held high stations to endeavour to alleviate the sufferings of the poor. The king was so impressed with his remarks, that he asked the bishop's opinion as to the best way of performing some public national benefit. After consulting with the lord mayor and aldermen of the City, it was decided to found an asylum for idiots, another for orphans, and a hospital for the sick poor of London. Nothing pressed so much on the king's mind as the troubles that would probably fall on the Church after his death. Great efforts were made by Northumberland to obtain the succession for his daughter-in-law, the Lady Jane Grey, the daughter of the Duke of Suffolk; and the king, who was much attached to her, was ready to yield his consent, and ordered the judges and his council to make some alterations in the law of succession. But when the council

met, Montague, who was chief justice, spoke in the name
of the rest, and declared that they could not alter the law
in this reign. On this Northumberland became greatly
enraged, and denounced the judges as traitors, for refusing
to obey the king's orders. At length, after much importunity from the king, they agreed to sign the patent; but
Cranmer resisted for a long time, positively refusing to aid
in any efforts to disinherit his late master's daughters. But
he at last was overcome by the solicitations of the young
dying monarch, and signed his name with the others.
Northumberland, meanwhile, had full power over the king,
and putting away his physicians, introduced into the court
a woman who professed herself able to cure him; and from
that time his malady increased, which led to the general
belief that he was being poisoned by the duke's agency.

Northumberland's next step was to persuade the king to
write and ask his sisters to come and visit him in his illness;
and they, not having heard of the bill of exclusion, immediately commenced their journey.

On the 6th of July the king felt his end must be rapidly
approaching, and often engaged in earnest prayer that God
would preserve England from the miseries of popery, and
allow the true religion to prosper in the land. The last
words he uttered were, "Lord, I am faint; have mercy on
me, and receive my spirit!" Efforts were made to conceal
his death, in order that his sisters might be brought into the
duke's power; but it could not be concealed.

Edward was only in his sixteenth year when he died, and
was considered a perfect wonder, being learned in languages, sciences, and the state of his kingdom. He studied
fortifications, and knew the Mint well; he knew all the
harbours in the kingdom, the depth of water in them, and
the way of coming into them. The ambassadors from the
various courts published extraordinary accounts of his
wisdom and sagacity. He was distrustful of his memory,
and made notes of what he heard in the Greek characters,
that those around him should not know what it was that he
was writing; and afterwards he copied them out in the
journal that he kept.

The king's virtues were extraordinary, and he only
abandoned his uncle when he was persuaded that he
conspired against the lives of the other councillors.

He was very merciful in his disposition, which was
proved by his unwillingness to sign the warrant for burning
the Maid of Kent. He took great care to have his debts

regularly paid, reckoning that a prince who breaks faith and loses credit throws up that which he can never recover, and makes himself liable to perpetual distrust and extreme contempt. He took special care of the petitions that were given him by poor and oppressed people. But his great zeal for religion was the crowning glory of his character. It was not merely a temporary zeal that actuated him, but a true tenderness of conscience, founded on the love of God and his neighbour.

These extraordinary qualities, set off with great sweetness and affability, made him universally beloved by all his people. All people concluded that the sins of England must have been very great, since they provoked God to deprive the nation of so signal a blessing as the rest of his reign would, to all appearance, have proved. Bishop Ridley, and the other good men of that time, made great lamentations of the vices which had become then so common that men had passed all sense of shame. Luxury, oppression, and a hatred of religion had over-run the higher rank of people, who had countenanced the Reformation merely to rob the Church, but by that and their other practices were become a great scandal to so good a work. The inferior sort were so much in the power of the priests, who were still, notwithstanding their outward compliance, papists in heart, and were so much offended at the spoil they saw made of all good endowments, without substituting other and more useful ones in their room, that they who understood little of religion laboured under great prejudice against everything that was advanced by such instruments.

The Reign of Queen Mary.

On the death of King Edward, the crown legally devolved on Mary, his eldest sister, who was then within half a day's journey of London, having been persuaded by Northumberland to come there, under pretence of seeing her sick brother, but in reality that her person might be in his power when he declared the succession of Lady Jane. Immediately that the princess heard of her brother's death, and of the patent for Lady Jane's succession, she retreated to Framlingham, a sea-port in Suffolk, in order that she might be able at any time, if necessary, to escape to Flanders, and also because Northumberland was held in especial abhorrence in that neighbourhood. She wrote at once to the council, telling them that, having heard of her brother's death, she wondered that she had received no

intimation of her succession; that their treasonable con-
spiracies were known to her, but that she was ready to
forgive all who returned to their loyalty, and declared her
title to her crown.

On receiving this letter, the council found it impossible
any longer to conceal the news of the king's death; they
accordingly proceeded to Lady Jane Grey's, and declared
her their queen. She was greatly troubled at hearing of the
king's death, as she was much attached to him; and the
knowledge that she was chosen as queen served greatly to
increase her distress. She was a most remarkable person,
being mistress of both the Greek and Latin languages, and
devoted to study; she took no pleasure in the usual pursuits
of the young people of her time, and was not tainted in
any way with the levities and vices of those in her rank and
position. She rejected the crown when it was first offered,
declaring that it belonged to the king's sisters, and that she
had no right to it; and she was only overcome by the
importunities of her husband, who inherited much of his
father's ambition, and at length gave her consent to its
acceptance.

On this the privy councillors wrote to Mary, saying that
the marriage between her father and mother was null, and
thus her succession to the crown was forfeited; they therefore required her to yield up her pretensions, and submit to
the present arrangements, promising her much favour if
she gave a ready obedience to their wishes. Jane was
accordingly proclaimed queen. The councillors declaring
that the late king had excluded his sisters, they being
illegitimate, by sentences passed both in Parliament and in
the ecclesiastical courts.

Mary meanwhile was actively engaged in making preparations to assert her rights. The men of Suffolk were
generally in favour of the Reformation, but a large body
who came to speak to her on the subject, being assured
that she would make no changes, but be satisfied with the
private exercise of her religion, joined her party, and swore
to maintain her rights to the death. The Earl of Sussex
raised a large force on her behalf, and several others
followed his example.

The rapidly increasing strength of Mary's forces, the
emperor's indignation, and the protestations of the foreign
ambassadors, raised the alarm of the councillors, who
determined to declare for Mary. They announced this to
the mayor and aldermen. The Earl of Arundel was sent to

apprehend Northumberland. Immediately he received the intelligence, he hastened to the market-place and proclaimed Mary, and falling down at Arundel's feet, he implored his favour.

Every one now flocked to Queen Mary to seek her forgiveness, and among the number was Ridley, who was at once committed to the Tower.

On the 3rd of August the queen reached London, when her sister Elizabeth met her with 1,000 horsemen, whom she was bringing to the queen's assistance. Thus Mary became seated on the throne. She was superstitious, bigoted, and cruel, and determined to use every effort to uproot the Reformation. Power being now in her hands, she soon used it against Lady Jane, who was kept a prisoner. Northumberland was beheaded within a month. He died unpitied, as the people could not forget the part he had taken against Somerset. Other executions rapidly followed, and every act testified how little the queen regarded the promise she had made to the men of Suffolk.

Rebellion of Wyatt.—Lady Jane Grey's Letters, Sentiments, and Conduct: Her Execution.

The first month of 1554 commenced with persecution. Dr. Crome was committed to the Fleet for preaching without licence on Christmas Day; and Thomas Wotton, Esq., on account of religion.

The publication of Mary's intended marriage with Phillip of Spain was very ill received by the people and several of the nobility; and it was not long before a rebellion broke out, of which Sir Thomas Wyatt was one of the chief ringleaders. He said that the queen and council would, by this marriage, bring upon the realm that slavery and despotism, religious and civil, which is one of the natural results of developed popery.

Wyatt advanced towards London, early in February, when the queen repaired to Guildhall, and made a vehement oration against him.

At the conclusion of her speech Gardiner, who stood by her, exclaimed aloud, with great admiration, "Oh, how happy are we, to whom God hath given so wise and learned a queen!"

On the 3rd of February Lord Cobham was committed to the Tower. Wyatt, whose forces now amounted to 4,000, came to Southwark, but could not force the bridge of

London. He was informed the City would all rise if he
should come to their aid; but he could not find boats to
take him over into Essex, so he was forced to go to the
bridge of Kingston. On the 4th of February he came
thither, but found it broken; his men, however, mended it,
and he reached Hyde Park next morning. His troops were
weary and disheartened, and did not now amount to more
than 500; so that though the queen's forces could have
easily dispersed them, yet they let them advance that they
might cast themselves into their hands. Wyatt accordingly
marched through the Strand and Ludgate Hill. Returning
from thence, he was opposed at Temple Bar, and there
surrendered himself to Sir Clement Parson, who brought
him to court; and with him, the remains of his army were
also taken, and about 100 killed. A great number of the
captives were hanged, and Wyatt was executed on Tower
Hill.

It was soon after resolved to proceed against Lady Jane
Grey and her husband: she had lived six months in the
daily meditations of death, so she was not much surprised
at the reality. Fecknam, who was sent to prepare her for
death, acknowledged that he was astonished at her calm
behaviour, her great knowledge, and the extraordinary
sense she had of religion.

The following are among the letters written by this
accomplished but unfortunate young lady during her imprisonment; and which, for their originality, force, and
eloquence, would do honour to a father of the Church.

"TO MR. HARDING.

"So oft as I call to mind the dreadful and fearful saying
of God, that he which layeth hold upon the plough, and
looketh back, is not meet for the kingdom of heaven; and,
on the other side, the comfortable words of our Saviour
Christ to all those that, forsaking themselves, do follow
him, I cannot but marvel at thee, and lament thy case,
which seemed sometime to be the lively member of Christ,
but now the deformed imp of the devil; sometime my
faithful brother, but now a stranger and apostate; sometime
a stout Christian soldier, but now a cowardly runaway.
Yea, when I consider these things, I cannot but speak to
thee, and cry out up on thee, thou seed of Satan and not of
Judah, whom the devil hath deceived, the world hath
beguiled, and the desire of life subverted, and made thee,

of a Christian, an infidel. Wherefore hast thou taken the testament of the Lord in thy mouth? Wherefore hast thou preached the law and the will of God to others? Wherefore hast thou instructed others to be strong in Christ, when thou thyself dost so shamefully shrink, and so horribly abuse the testament and law of the Lord? When thou thyself preachest not to steal, yet most abominably stealest, not from men, but from God, and committing most heinous sacrilege, robbest Christ thy Lord of his right members, thy body and soul, and choosest rather to live miserably, with shame in the world, than to die, and gloriously, with honour, reign with Christ, in whom even death is life— why dost thou now show thyself most weak, when indeed thou oughtest to be most strong? And wilt thou resist thy Maker, that fashioned and framed thee? Wilt thou now forsake him that called thee from the custom-gathering among the Romish anti-Christians, to be an ambassador and messenger of his eternal word? He that first framed thee, and since thy first creation and birth preserved thee, nourished and kept thee—yea, and inspired thee with the spirit of knowledge (I cannot say grace), shall he not now possess thee? Darest thou deliver up thyself to another, being not thine own, but his? Wilt thou torment again, rend and tear the most precious body of our Saviour Christ, with thy bodily and fleshly teeth? Wilt thou take upon thee to offer any sacrifice unto God for our sins, considering that Christ offered up himself (as St. Paul saith) upon the cross, a lively sacrifice once for all? Can neither the punishment of the Israelites (which, for their idolatry, they so oft received), nor the terrible threatenings of the prophets, nor the cures of God's own mouth, make thee afraid to honour any other God than him? Dost thou so regard him that spared not his dear and only Son for thee? so diminishing, yea, utterly extinguishing his glory, that thou wilt attribute the praise and honour due unto him to the idols which have mouths and speak not, eyes and see not, ears and hear not, which shall perish with them that made them?

"God saith he is a jealous God, which will have all honour, glory, and worship given to him only. And Christ saith in the fourth of Matthew, to Satan which tempted him, even to the same Beelzebub, the same devil which hath prevailed against thee: 'It is written,' said he, 'Thou shalt worship the Lord thy God, and him only shalt thou serve.'

"These and such like do prohibit thee and all Christians to worship any other God than he who was before all worlds, and laid the foundations of heaven and earth; and wilt thou honour a detestable idol, invented by Romish popes. Christ offered himself up once for all, and wilt thou offer him up again daily at thy pleasure? But thou wilt say thou doest it for a good intent. Oh, sink of sin! Dost thou dream therein of a good intent, where thy conscience beareth thee witness of God's threatened wrath against thee? How did Saul, who, for that he disobeyed the word of the Lord for a good intent, was thrown from his worldly and temporal kingdom? Shalt thou then, that dost deface God's honour, and rob him of his right, inherit the eternal and heavenly kingdom? Wilt thou for a good intent dishonour God, offend thy brother, and endanger thy soul, for which Christ shed his most precious blood? Wilt thou for a good intent pluck Christ out of heaven, and make his death void, and deface the triumph of his cross by offering him up daily? Wilt thou, either for fear of death or hope of life, deny and refuse thy God, who enriched thy poverty, healed thy infirmity, and yields to thee his victory, if thou couldest have kept it? Dost thou not consider that the thread of thy life hangeth upon Him that made thee. Remember the saying of Christ in his Gospel: 'Whosoever seeketh to save his life shall lose it; but whosoever will lose his life for my sake shall find it.'

"Last of all, let the lively remembrance of the last day be always before your eyes, remembering the terror that such shall be in at that time, with the runagates and fugitives from Christ, which, setting more by the world than by heaven, more by their life than by him that gave them that life, did shrink, yea, did clean fall away from him that forsook not them: and contrariwise, the inestimable joys prepared for them that, fearing no peril, nor dreading death, have manfully fought, and victoriously triumphed over all the powers of darkness, over hell, death, and damnation, through their most redoubted captain Christ, to whom, with the Father and the Holy Ghost, be all honour, praise, and glory everlasting. Amen."

The following letter was written the night before her execution, at the end of a Greek New Testament, which she sent as her last present to her sister, the Lady Katherine.

"TO THE LADY KATHERINE.

"GOOD SISTER KATHERINE,—I have here sent you a book which although it be not outwardly trimmed with gold, yet inwardly is more worth than precious stones. It is the book, dear sister, of the law of the Lord. It is his testament and last will, which he bequeathed unto us wretches, which shall lead you to the path of eternal joy, and if you with a good mind read it, and with an earnest mind do purpose to follow it, it shall bring you to an immortal and everlasting life. It shall teach you to live, and learn you to die. It shall win you more than you should have gained by the possession of your woeful father's lands. For as, if God had prospered him, you should have inherited his lands so, if you apply diligently this book, seeking to direct your life after it, you shall be an inheritor of such riches as neither the covetous shall withdraw from you, neither thief shall steal, neither yet the moths corrupt. Desire with David, good sister, to understand the law of the Lord God. Live still to die, that you by death may purchase eternal life. And trust not that the tenderness of your age shall lengthen your life; for as soon (if God call) goeth the young as the old; and labour always to learn to die. Defy the world, deny the devil, despise the flesh, and delight yourself only in the Lord. Be penitent for your sins, and yet despair not; be strong in faith, and yet presume not; and desire with St. Paul to be dissolved and to be with Christ with whom even in death there is life. Rejoice in Christ, as I do. Follow the steps of your master Christ, and take up your cross; lay your sins on his back, and always embrace him. And as touching my death, rejoice as I do, good sister, that I shall be delivered of this corruption and put on incorruption. For I am assured that I shall, for losing of a mortal life, win an immortal life, the which I pray God grant you, and send you of his grace to live in his fear, and to die in the true Christian faith, from the which, in God's name, I exhort you that you never swerve, neither for hope of life nor for fear of death. For if you will deny his truth, to lengthen your life, God will deny you, and shorten your days. And if you cleave unto him, he will prolong your days to your comfort and his glory: to which glory God bring me now, and you hereafter, when it pleaseth him to call you. Fare you well, good sister, and put your only trust in God."

She was at first much affected when she saw her husband, Lord Guildford Dudley, led out to execution, but recovered herself when she considered how soon she was to follow him; and when he desired they might take leave of one another, she declined it, for she thought it would increase their grief. She now continued so perfectly calm, that when she saw the lifeless body of her husband conveyed to the chapel in the Tower, she expressed no emotion thereat.

On mounting the scaffold, she addressed the spectators thus: "Good people, I am come hither to die, and by a law I am condemned to the same. The fact against the queen's highness was unlawful, and the consenting thereunto by me; but touching the procurement and desire thereof by me or on my behalf, I do wash my hands in innocency before God and the face of you, good Christian people, this day. I pray you all to bear me witness that I die a true Christian woman, and that I do look to be saved by no other means but only by the mercy of God in the blood of his only Son, Jesus Christ: and I confess that when I did know the Word of God, I neglected the same, loved myself and the world, and therefore this plague and punishment is happily and worthily happened unto me for my sins: and yet I thank God that of his goodness he hath thus given me a time and respite to repent: and now, good people, while I am alive, I pray you assist me with your prayers." Then kneeling down, she turned to Fecknam, saying, "Shall I say this psalm?" and he said, "Yea." Then she repeated the psalm of *Miserere mei Deus,* in English, in a most devout manner, to the end. She then stood up, and gave her maid her gloves and handkerchief, and her book to Mr. Bruges. After this she untied her gown, when the executioner pressed forward to help her, but she, desiring him to let her alone, turned towards her two gentlewomen, who helped her off with it, and also with her frowes, paaft, and neckerchief, giving to her a fair handkerchief to bind round her eyes.

Then the excutioner kneeled down and asked her forgiveness, which she willingly granted. He then desired her to stand upon the straw, when she saw the block, whereon she said, "I pray you dispatch me quickly." She then kneeled, saying, "Will you take if off before I lay me down?" The executioner said, "No, madam." She then tied the handkerchief about her eyes, and feeling for the block, she said, "What shall I do? where is it? where is it?" One of the bystanders guiding her thereunto, she laid her head down upon it, and then stretching forth her body, said, "Lord, into thy hands I commend my spirit!" Thus this noble, learned, and saintly lady finished her life, in the year of our Lord 1554, the 12th of February, about the seventeenth year of her age.

Her death was as much lamented as her life had been admired. It affected Judge Morgan, who had pronounced the sentence, so much, that he went mad, and thought she still followed him. The queen herself was troubled at it; for it was rather reasons of state than private resentment that induced her to enact the tragedy.

Her father, the Duke of Suffolk, was soon after tried by his peers, and condemned and executed. He was the less pitied, because by his means his daughter was brought to her untimely end.

Injunctions were now given to the bishops to execute such ecclesiastical laws as had been in force in King Henry's time; that in their courts they should proceed in their own names; that the oath of supremacy should be no more exacted; none suspected of heresy were to be put in orders; they were required to suppress heresy and heretics, to turn out all married clergymen, and to separate them from their wives. If they left their wives, they might put them in some other cure, or reserve a pension for them out of their livings; no one who had vowed chastity was to be suffered to live with his wife: those who were ordained by the book, set out in King Edward's time, were to be confirmed by all the other rites then left out, and the first was declared to be no valid ordination.

The queen gave also a special commission to Bonner, Gardiner, Tonstall, Day, and Kitchin, to proceed against the Archbishop of York, and the Bishops of St. David's, Chester, and Bristol, and to deprive them of their bishoprics, for having contracted marriage, and thereby having broken their vows and defiled their function. She also authorized them to call before them the Bishops of Lincoln, Gloucester, and Hereford, who held their bishoprics only during their good behaviour; and since they had done things contrary to the laws of God and the practice of the universal Church, to declare their bishoprics void. And thus were seven of the reformed bishops discharged, as it were, by a single stroke.

History and Martyrdom of the Rev. John Rogers, Who Was Burned at Smithfield, February 4, 1555.

Mr. John Rogers was born at Deritend, near Birmingham, A. D. 1500. He was M.A. of both universities, having taken his degree of B.A. at Pembroke college, Cambridge, in 1525, after which he was chosen to the Cardinals' College (now Christ Church) on account of his learning, and soon afterwards entered into holy orders. He was first a priest in the Romish Church. He resigned that living in 1534, on account of the incipient change in his religious sentiments, and soon after accepted the office of Chaplain to the "Merchants of the Company of St. Thomas à Becket," at Antwerp, where he became acquainted with Tyndal. The latter, together with Coverdale and other eminent Protestants, had been driven from England on account of the retrograde and intolerant Act of the "Six Articles," passed in the latter part of the reign of Henry VIII. From intercourse with these pious servants of God, the religious views of Mr. Rogers were soon matured; and casting off the popish yoke of bondage, his soul rejoiced in the glorious light of Christ's Gospel. Whilst at Antwerp he translated the first authorized English Bible, known as "Matthew's Bible," which was published in 1537, by Grafton and Whitchurch.

Mr. Rogers returned to England in 1547, and was presented to the rectory of St. Margaret Moyses, and the vicarage of St. Sepulchre, simultaneously, on the 10th of May, 1550. On the 24th of August, 1551, he was chosen to a prebendal stall in St. Paul's Cathedral; in 1553 was elected a divinity lecturer by the chapter. Familiar with the Scriptures, Mr. Rogers had found that, according to those sacred oracles, matrimony was an estate honourable to all, and had, in 1537, married Adryana de Weyden, of an Antwerp family, called also Adriana Pratt, by whom he had eleven children—namely, eight born in Germany, and three in England. He obtained an Act of Parliament for the naturalization of his children born abroad. He continued at his post until the accession of Mary, who again introduced the idolatry of the Church of Rome.

When Mary was in the Tower of London, imbibing Gardiner's pernicious counsels, Mr. Rogers preached at Paul's Cross, confirming those doctrines which he and others had taught there in King Edward's days, and exhorted the people, with peculiar energy, to continue steadfast in the same, and to beware of the false tenets that were about to be introduced. For this sermon the preacher was summoned before the Council, then filled with popish bishops, before whom he pleaded his own cause with such piety, boldness, and prudence, as to obviate their displeasure for that time, and was accordingly dismissed. But after Mary's proclamation, prohibiting the doctrines of the reformed religion, Mr. Rogers, for contempt of the same, was again summoned before a council of bishops, who, after having debated upon the nature of his offence, ordered him to keep close prisoner in his own house, where he remained a considerable time, till, at the instigation of the sanguinary Bonner, Bishop of London, he was removed to Newgate, and placed among the common felons. He was brought before Bishop Gardiner, and others of the council of bishops, on January 22, 1555, and we leave him to give the account in his own words:—

"First, the lord chancellor said unto me thus: 'Sir, you have heard the state of the realm in which it standeth now.'

"*Rogers.*—No, my lord, I have been kept in close prison, and except there have been some general things said at the table, when I was at dinner or supper, I have heard nothing.

" 'General things!' said the lord chancellor; 'you have heard of my lord cardinal's coming, and that the Parliament hath received his blessing, not one resisting it, except one man who spoke against it. Such a unity and such a miracle hath not been seen. And all they, of which there are eightscore in one house, have with one assent received pardon of their offences, for the schism that we have had in England, in refusing the holy father of Rome to be head of the Catholic Church. How say you? Are you content to unite yourself to the faith of the Catholic Church with us, in the state in which it is now in England?'

"*Rogers.*—The catholic Church I never did nor will dissent from.

"*Lord Chancellor.*—Nay, but I speak of the state of the Catholic Church, in that wise in which we stand now in England, having received the pope to be supreme head.

"*Rogers.*—I know no other head but Christ of his catholic Church, neither will I acknowledge the Bishop of Rome to have any more authority than any other bishop hath by the Word of God.

"*Lord Chancellor.*—Why didst thou then acknowledge King Henry VIII to be supreme head of the Church, if Christ be the only head?

"*Rogers.*—I never granted him to have any supremacy in spiritual things, as are the forgiveness of sins, giving of the Holy Ghost, authority to be a judge above the Word of God.

"*Lord Chancellor.*—Yea, if thou hadst said so in his days thou hadst not been alive now. What sayest thou? Make us a direct answer, whether thou wilt be one of this Catholic Church or not, with us in that state in which we are *now?*

"*Rogers.*—My lord, without fail I cannot believe that ye yourselves think in your hearts that he is supreme head in forgiving of sins, seeing you and all the bishops of the realm have now twenty years long preached, and some of you also written to the contrary, and the Parliament hath so long ago condescended unto it.

"*Lord Chancellor.*—Tush! that Parliament was with great cruelty constrained to abolish and put away the supremacy from the Bishop of Rome. Here are two things, mercy and justice; if thou refuse the queen's mercy now, then shalt thou have justice ministered unto thee.

"*Rogers.*—I never offended, nor was disobedient unto her grace, and yet I will not refuse her mercy.

"*Lord Chancellor.*—If thou wilt not receive the Bishop of Rome to be supreme head of the Catholic Church, then thou shalt never have her mercy, thou mayest be sure.

"*Rogers.*—I will find it first in the Scripture, and see it tried thereby, before I receive him to be supreme head.

"*Worcester.*—Why, do you not know what is in your creed—'I believe in the holy catholic Church?'

"*Rogers.*—I find not the Bishop of Rome there. For the word *catholic* signifieth not the Romish Church: it signifieth the consent of all true teaching churches of all times and all ages. But how should the Bishop of Rome's church be one of them, which teacheth so many doctrines that are plainly and directly against the Word of God?

"*Lord Chancellor.*—Show me one of them, one; let me hear one.

"*Rogers.*—The Bishop of Rome and his church say, read, and sing all that they do in their congregations in Latin, which is directly and plainly against 1 Cor. xiv.

"*Lord Chancellor.*—I deny that; I deny that it is against the Word of God. Let me see you prove that.

"*Rogers.*—Thus I began to say the text from the beginning of the chapter, 'He that speaketh in an unknown tongue. To speak with tongues is to speak with a strange tongue, as Latin, or Greek, and so to speak is not to speak unto men, but to God. But ye speak in Latin, which is a strange tongue; wherefore ye speak not unto men, but unto God. This he granted, that they spake not unto men, but unto God.

" 'This is a point of sophistry,' quoth Secretary Bourne.

"Then the lord chancellor began to tell the Lord Haward, that when he was in High-Dutchland, they at Hale, which had before prayed and used the service all in Dutch, began then to turn part into Latin and part into Dutch.

"Worcester.—Yes, and at Wittenberg too.

"Here I would have declared how they ought to proceed in these days, and so have come again to my purpose, but it was impossible; for one asked one thing, another said another; so that I was fain to hold my peace, and let them talk. And even when I would have taken hold on my proof, the lord chancellor ordered me to prison again.

"Then Sir Richard Southwell, who stood by a window, said to me, 'Thou wilt not burn in this cause when it cometh to the purpose, I know well.'

"Rogers.—Sir, I cannot tell, but I trust in my Lord God, yes; lifting up mine eyes unto heaven.

"Then my lord of Ely told me much of the queen's pleasure and meaning, and set out with large words, saying that she took them that would not receive the pope's supremacy to be unworthy to have her mercy.

"Rogers.—I said I would not refuse her mercy; and yet I never offended her in all my life.

"Divers spake at once. 'No!' quoth many of them; 'a married priest, and have not offended the law?'

"Rogers.—I said I had not broken the queen's law, nor yet any point of the law of the realm therein; for I married where it was lawful.

" 'Where was that?' said they, thinking that to be unlawful in all places.

"Rogers.—In Dutchland. And if you had not here in England made an open law that priests might have had wives, I would never have come home again: for I brought a wife and eight children with me.

"And one said that there was never a Catholic man or country who ever yet granted that a priest might have a wife.

"I said the catholic Church never denied marriage to priests, nor yet to any other man.

"Then the Bishop of Worcester turned his face towards me, and said that I knew not where that Church was or is.

"I said, yes, that I could tell where it was, but therewith the sergeant went with me out of the door."

THE SECOND EXAMINATION, 28TH OF JANUARY, 1555.

"Being asked again by the lord chancellor what I thought concerning the blessed sacrament—whether I believed in the sacrament to be the very body and blood of our Saviour Christ, really and substantially—I answered, I had often told him that it was a matter in which I was no meddler, and therefore suspected of my brethren to be of a contrary opinion. 'Notwithstanding, even as the most part of your doctrine, in other points, is false, and the defence thereof only by force and cruelty, so in this matter I think it to be as false as the rest. For I cannot understand the words *really* and *substantially* to signify otherwise than corporally: but corporally Christ is only in heaven. And here I somewhat set out his charity after this sort: 'My lord,' said I, 'you have dealt with me most cruelly, for you have put me in prison without law, and kept me there now almost a year and a half; for I was almost half a year in my house. And now have I been a full year in Newgate, at great costs and charges, having a wife and ten children to provide for, and have not received a penny from my livings, which was against the law.'

"I asked him wherefore he put me in prison. He said because I preached against the queen.

"I answered that it was not true; and I would be bound to prove it, and to stand to the trial of the law, that no man should be able to disprove it, and thereupon would set my life. I preached, I confessed, a sermon at the Cross, after the queen came to the Tower; but there was nothing said against the queen.

"'But you read lectures after,' said he, 'against the commandment of the Council.'

"'That I did not,' said I; 'let that be proved, and let me die for it.'

"I might and would have added, if I had been suffered to speak, that it had been time enough to take away men's livings, and then to have imprisoned them, after that they had offended the laws; for they are good citizens that break not laws, and worthy of praise, and not of punishment. But their purpose is to keep men in prison, until they may catch them in their laws, and so kill them. I would have added that I most humbly desired to be set at liberty, sending my wife to him with a supplication to Richmond, while I was yet in my house.

"I wrote likewise two petitions to him out of Newgate, and sent my wife many times to him. Mr. Gosnold also, a worthy man in the Lord, laboured for me, and so did divers others also take pains in the matter. These things declare my lord chancellor's anti-Christian charity, which is, that he hath and doth seek my blood, and the destruction of my wife and my ten children.

"This is a short sum of the words which were spoken on the 28th of January, in the afternoon, after that Mr. Hooper had been the first and Mr. Cardmaker the second in examination before me.

"Then the clock being, as I guessed, about four, the lord chancellor said that he and the Church must yet use charity with me, and gave me respite till to-morrow, to see whether I would return to the Catholic Church again, and repent, and they would receive me to mercy.

"And thus was I brought up by the sheriffs to the Compter in Southwark."

THE THIRD EXAMINATION AND CONDEMNATION, JANUARY 29, 1555.

"The next day, January 29, we were sent for in the morning, about nine o'clock, and by the sheriffs brought from the Compter in Southwark, to St. Mary Overy's: and when Mr. Hooper was condemned, as I understood afterwards, then sent they for me. My lord chancellor said—

"'Rogers, we gave thee liberty to remember thyself last night, whether thou would come to the holy Catholic Church of Christ again or not. Tell us now what thou hast determined, whether thou wilt be repentant and sorry.'

"'My lord,' said I, 'when I yesterday desired that I might be suffered by the Scripture and authority of the first, best, and purest Church, to defend my doctrine by writing (meaning not only of the primacy, but also of all the doctrine that ever I had preached), you answered that it might not and ought not to be granted me, for I was a private person; and that the Parliament was above the authority of all private persons. Yet, my lord, I am able to show examples that one man hath come into a general council, and after the whole had determined and agreed upon an act or article, some one man coming in afterwards hath by the Word of God proved so clearly that the council had erred in decreeing the said article, that he caused the whole council to change and alter their act or article before determined.

" 'I could also show the authority of a learned lawyer, Panormitanus, who saith that unto a simple layman that bringeth the Word of God with him, there ought more credit to be given than to a whole council gathered together. By these things will I prove that I ought not to be denied to speak my mind, and to be heard against a whole parliament bringing the Word of God for me, and the authority of the old Church 400 years after Christ, albeit that every man in the Parliament had willingly and without respect of fear and favour agreed thereunto, which thing I doubt not a little of; especially seeing the like had been permitted in the old Church, even in general councils, yea, and that in one of the chiefest councils that ever was, unto which neither any acts of this Parliament nor yet any of the late general councils of the bishops of Rome ought to be compared.'

"Here my lord chancellor would suffer me to speak no more, but bade me sit down, mockingly saying that I was sent for to be instructed of them.

" 'My lord,' said I, 'I stand, and sit not: shall I not be suffered to speak for my life?'

" 'Shall we suffer thee to tell a tale, and prate?' said he. And with that he stood up, and began to face me, after his old arrogant proud fashion, for he perceived that I was in a way to have touched him somewhat, which he thought to hinder by dashing me out of my tale, and so he did; but he had much like communication with me as he had the day before, taunt upon taunt, and check upon check. For in that case, being God's cause, I told him he should not make me afraid to speak.

"Lord Chancellor.—See what a spirit this fellow hath, finding fault at mine accustomed earnestness and hearty manner of speaking.

"Rogers.—I have a true spirit, agreeing to and obeying the Word of God. I would further have said that I was never the worse, but the better, to be earnest in a just and true cause, and in my master Christ's matters: but I could not be heard. And at length he proceeded towards his excommunication and condemnation.

"To be short, he read my condemnation before me. He caused me to be degraded and condemned, and put into the hands of the laity, and then he gave me over into the sheriff's hands.

"After this sentence was read, Bishop Gardiner sent Mr. Hooper and me to the Clink, there to remain till night. When it was dark they carried us, Mr. Hooper going before with one sheriff, and I coming after with the other, with bills and weapons, out of the Clink, and over the bridge in procession to Newgate, through the city. When the bishop had read the condemnation, I petitioned to see and speak to my wife, who was a stranger, and had ten children; but he said she was not my wife. I declared she was, for we had been married eighteen years. He still denied it, said I maintained open sin, and that I should not see her."

Mr. Rogers was confined for a long time, lodged in Newgate amongst thieves, and often harshly examined by Gardiner and others. He was at length condemned by the Bishop of Winchester.

When he was led to Bishop Bonner to be degraded, which being done, he craved one petition of the bishop—that he might speak a few words to his wife before he was burned. Even this was denied to him. "Then," said he, "you declared what your charity is."

The sheriffs now led him away to Smithfield. Here he was asked if he would recant his opinion. He answered that what he had preached he would seal with his blood. "Then," said the sheriff, "thou art a heretic." To which the unshaken hero of God replied, "That shall be known at the day of judgment." "Well," said the sheriff, "I will never pray for thee." "But I will pray for you," said Mr. Rogers.

All the way to the stake he was singing psalms, all the people rejoicing at his constancy. On the way he was met by his wife and his eleven children, one an infant in her arms. This sad sight did not move him, but he cheerfully and patiently went on his way to Smithfield, where he was burnt to ashes in the presence of a great number of people.

Life and Martyrdom of Rowland Taylor, Vicar of Hadley, in Suffolk, Who Was Burned at Aldham Common, Feb. 9, 1555.

The little town of Hadley first heard the pure Gospel of Christ from the lips of the Rev. Thomas Bilney, who preached there with great earnestness, and whose work was greatly blessed, numbers of both men and women becoming convinced of the errors and idolatries of Popery, and gladly embracing the faith as it is in Christ Jesus.

After the martyrdom of Bilney, Dr. Rowland Taylor was appointed vicar of the parish. He possessed the friendship of Cranmer, who favoured him on account of his attachment to the Reformed principles, and it was through the archbishop that he obtained the living of Hadley. Throughout Edward's reign, Taylor was unmolested, and was truly a "living epistle," which could be "seen and read of all men," his daily life carrying out all he preached, and bearing witness of his love towards his Master and his work.

When Mary succeeded to the crown, dark clouds gathered round Taylor and all others who were like-minded, and an opportunity was soon seized of bringing him into trouble. Two men in Hadley, Clark and Foster, the one a tradesman and the other a lawyer, determined to have mass publicly performed in the parish church, according to the rites of the Romish priests. They accordingly persuaded the minister from a neighbouring parish to come over and perform the service during Passion week. Dr. Taylor, hearing the bells ringing at an unusual hour, hastened to the church to inquire the cause. Finding the large doors fastened, he entered through the chancel, and was astonished to see a priest in Romish vestments preparing to celebrate mass, and guarded by a body of armed men. Dr. Taylor, as vicar, demanded of him what right he had to be there without his consent, to which the lawyer, Foster, insolently replied, "Thou traitor! how darest thou to intercept the execution of the queen's orders?" but the doctor undauntedly denied the charge of traitor, and asserted his mission as a minister of Christ, and delegation to that part of his flock, commanding the priest to depart. A very violent altercation then ensued between Foster, the lawyer, and Dr. Taylor, the former asserting the queen's prerogative, and the other the authority of the canon law, which commanded that no mass be said but at a consecrated altar.

The priest, intimidated by the intrepid behaviour of the Protestant minister, would have departed without saying mass, but Clark said to him, "Fear not, you have a *super altare;* proceed and do your duty."

They then forced the doctor out of the church, celebrated mass, and informed the Bishop of Winchester of his behaviour, who summoned him to answer the complaints laid against him.

Dr. Taylor, upon receipt of the summons, cheerfully

prepared to comply: and on some of his friends advising him to fly beyond the sea, in order to avoid the cruelty of his inveterate enemies, he told them that he was determined to go to the bishop, and he accordingly repaired to London.

When Gardiner saw him, he reviled him, which Dr. Taylor having patiently heard, at last replied—

"My lord, I am neither traitor nor heretic, but a true subject and a faithful Christian, and am come according to your commandment, to know the cause of your lordship's sending for me."

"Art thou come, thou villain?" said Gardiner; "How darest thou look me in the face for shame? Knowest thou not who I am?"

"Yes," said Dr. Taylor, "I know who you are, Dr. Stephen Gardiner, Bishop of Winchester, and Lord Chancellor, and yet but a mortal man. But if I should be afraid of your lordly looks, why fear you not God, the Lord of us all? How dare you for shame look any Christian in the face, seeing you have forsaken the truth, denied our Saviour Christ and his Word, and done contrary to your own oath and writing? With what countenance will you appear before the judgment-seat of Christ, and answer to your oath made first unto King Henry, and afterwards unto Edward, his son?"

The bishop answered, "That was Herod's oath, unlawful; and therefore worthy to be broken: I have done well in breaking it; and I thank God I am come home again to our mother, the Catholic Church of Rome; and so I would thou shouldst do."

"Should I forsake the Church of Christ?" said Dr. Taylor: "God forbid."

"Thou hast resisted the queen's proceedings." said Gardiner, "And would not suffer the minister of Aldham, Mr. John Averth, a very virtuous and devout priest, to say mass in Hadley."

Dr. Taylor answered, "My lord, I am vicar of Hadley, and it is against all right, conscience, and laws, that any man should come into my charge, and presume to infect the flock committed unto me with the venom of the popish idolatrous mass."

With that the bishop waxed very angry, and taking off his cap, said, "Thou art a blasphemous heretic indeed, that blasphemest the blessed sacrament, and speakest against the holy mass."

"Christ," said the undaunted veteran of truth, "gave himself to die for our redemption upon the cross, whose body there offered was the propitiatory sacrifice, full, perfect, and sufficient unto salvation for all them that believe in him."

Then the bishop called his men and said, "Take this fellow hence, and carry him to the King's Bench." So he was sent to prison, where he was kept almost two years.

THE LAST EXAMINATION OF DR. TAYLOR, WHO, WITH MR. BRADFORD AND MR. SAUNDERS, WERE BROUGHT BEFORE THE BISHOP OF WINCHESTER AND OTHER PRELATES.

In January, 1555, Dr. Taylor was summoned to appear before the Bishops of London, Durham, Norwich, Salisbury, and Winchester, and required to give a determinate answer to the charge of heresy made against him, either to abjure his errors or receive the sentence of condemnation. He boldly answered that he would not depart from the truth he had preached nor submit to the authority of the pope, and that he thanked God for his graciousness in counting him worthy to suffer for his name. On this the bishops at once proceeded to read the sentence of death on him, and committed him to the Compter.

About a week later the sheriff came before dawn to take him to the "Woolpack," an inn outside the town. Mrs. Taylor, who suspected that he would be removed that night, had remained in St. Botolph's porch, in company with her daughter Mary, and Elizabeth, an orphan whom they had adopted.

As the sheriff and his party passed the church, little Elizabeth perceived them, and cried out, "Oh, my dear father! Mother, mother, here is my father led away!"

"Rowland, Rowland." exclaimed Mrs. Taylor. "where art thou?" for the morning was so dark she could not distinguish him.

"Dear wife, I am here," said the doctor, stopping.

The men in charge would have forced him on, but the sheriff said, "Stay a little, I pray you, and let him speak to his wife."

She then came to him, when he took his daughter Mary in his arms, and he, his wife, and Elizabeth kneeled down and said the Lord's Prayer. When the prayer was finished, the doctor, embracing his wife, said, "Farewell, my dear wife; be of good comfort, for I am quiet in my conscience:

God shall stir up a father for my children." He then kissed the children, warning them to continue in the faith, and to shrink from idolatry.

As he was led on, his wife followed him, saying, "God be with thee, dear Rowland. I will, with God's grace, meet thee at Hadley."

On coming out of the "Woolpack," the doctor seeing his servant, John Hull, standing at the rails with his son, called them, saying, "Come hither, my son Thomas." John Hull lifted the child up, and set him on the horse before his father. Dr. Taylor then took off his hat, and said to the people, "Good people, this is mine own son, begotten in lawful matrimony; and God be blessed for lawful matrimony." Then he lifted his eyes towards heaven and prayed for his child, laid his hat upon his head and blessed him, and then delivered him to his faithful servant. After this they rode forth; the sheriff of Essex, four yeomen of the guard, and the sheriff's men leading them.

At Chelmsford Dr. Taylor was delivered to the sheriff of Suffolk, and conducted by him to Hadley. When they arrived there, and were riding over the bridge, there was a poor man waiting with five children: and when he saw Dr. Taylor, he and his children fell down upon their knees, and holding up their hands, cried with a loud voice, "Oh, dear father and good shepherd, God help and succour thee, as thou hast many a time succoured me and my poor children!" Such witness had this servant of God of his virtuous and charitable life. The streets of Hadley were crowded with men and women of the town and country, who waited to see him; and on beholding him led to death, with weeping eyes and lamentable voice they cried one to another, "Ah, good Lord! there goeth our good shepherd from us, who so faithfully hath taught us, so fatherly hath cared for us, and so religously hath governed us!"

On arriving at Aldham Common, the place where he should suffer, seeing a great multitude, he asked, "What place is this, and what meaneth it that so much people are gathered hither?" It was answered, "It is Aldham Common, the place where you must suffer: and the people are come to behold you." Then, said he, "Thanked be God, I am even at home."

On alighting, he desired leave of the sheriff to speak; but the latter refused it, bidding him remember his promise to the Council.

Dr. Taylor, perceiving that he would not be suffered to

speak, sat down, and seeing one named Soyce, he called him, and said, "Soyce, I pray thee come and pull off my boots, and take them for thy labour: thou hast long looked for them, now take them." Then he rose up and pulled off his clothes unto his shirt, and gave them away; which done, he said with a loud voice, "Good people, I have taught you nothing but God's holy Word, and those lessons that I have taken out of God's blessed book, the Holy Bible: and I am come hither this day to seal it with my blood." With that Holmes, yeoman of the guard, who had used Dr. Taylor very cruelly all the way, gave him a great stroke upon the head, and said, "Is that keeping thy promise, thou heretic?" Then he, seeing they would not permit him to speak, kneeled down and prayed and a poor woman who was among the people stepped in and prayed with him; but they thrust her away, and threatened to tread her down with their horses: notwithstanding this, she would not move, but remained and prayed with him. When he had prayed he went to the stake and kissed it, and placed himself in a pitch-barrel, which they had set for him to stand in, and so stood with his back upright against the stake, with his hands folded together, and his eyes towards heaven, and kept praying continually.

At last they kindled the fire; when the martyr, holding up his hands, called upon God, and said, "Merciful Father of heaven, for Jesus Christ my Saviour's sake, receive my soul into thy hands." He then folded his hands together, and bore his sufferings without a murmur.

Story and Martyrdom of Dr. Robert Farrar, Bishop of St. David's Who Was Burned at Carmarthen, March 30, 1555.

This excellent and learned prelate had been promoted to his bishopric by the Lord Protector, in the reign of Edward; but after the fall of his patron, he also had fallen into disgrace, through the malice and false accusations of several enemies, among whom was George Constantine, his own servant. Articles, to the number of fifty-six, were preferred against him, in which he was charged with many negligences and contumacies of the Church government. These he answered and denied. But so many and so bitter were his enemies, that they prevailed, and he was in consequence thrown into prison. He was now prosecuted on different charges—namely, such as related to doctrine; and he had been called up in company with the glorious martyrs, Hooper, Rogers, Bradford, and Saunders, on the

4th of February, and with them would have been condemned; but from the want of leisure, or some such cause,
among his judges, he was remanded to prison, where he
remained till the 14th of the same month. As much of the
examination and answers as could be collected we here
present to our readers.

At his first appearance before the lord chancellor, Ste-
phen Gardiner, Bishop of Winchester, and the Bishops of
Durham and Worcester, the lord chancellor said unto him,
"Now, sir, have you heard how the world goeth here?"

Farrar.—If it please your honour, I know not.

Win.—What say you? Do you not know things abroad,
notwithstanding you are a prisoner?

Far.—No, my lord, I know not.

Win.—Lo! what froward fellow is this!

Far.—If it please your lordship, how should I know
anything abroad, being a prisoner?

Win.—Have you not heard of the coming in of the lord
cardinal?

Far.—I know not my lord cardinal; but I heard that a
cardinal was come in, but I did not believe it, and I believe
it not yet.

Wor.—I pray your lordship tell him yourself, that he
may know what is done.

Win.—The queen's majesty and the Parliament hath
restored religion to the same state it was in at the beginning
of the reign of our King Henry VIII. Ye are in the queen's
debt, and her majesty will be good unto you, if you will
return to the Catholic Church.

Far.—In what state I am concerning my debts to the
queen's majesty, in the Court of Exchequer, my lord
treasurer knoweth: and the last time that I was before your
honour, and the first time also, I showed you that I had
made an oath never to consent nor agree that the Bishop of
Rome should have any power or jurisdiction within this
realm: and further I need not rehearse to your lordship;
you know it well enough.

Bourne.—You were once abjured for heresy at Oxford.

Far.—That was I not.

Bourne.—You were.

Far.—I never was; it is not true.

Bourne.—You supplanted your master.

Far.—That did I never in my life.

Bourne.—By my faith you did.

Far.—Forsooth, I did not, never in my life; but did

shield and save my master from danger, and that I obtained of King Henry VIII, for my true service, I thank God therefore.

Bourne.—(To my lord chancellor.) My lord, he hath an ill name in Wales, as ever had any.

Far.—That is not so. Whosoever saith so, they shall never be able to prove it.

Bourne.—He hath deceived the queen in divers sums of money.

Far.—That is utterly untrue; I never deceived the king nor queen of one penny in my life, and you shall never be able to prove that you say.

Win.—Thou art a false knave.

Then Farrar stood up unbidden, for all that while he kneeled, and said, "No, my lord: I am a true man, I thank God for it. I was born under King Henry VII, I served King Henry VIII and King Edward VI truly, and have served the queen's majesty that now is, truly with my poor heart and word: more I could not do, and I was never false, nor shall be, by the grace of God."

Win.—How sayest thou? wilt thou be reformable?

Far.—My lord, I have made an oath to God, and to King Henry VIII, and also to King Edward, and in that to the queen's majesty, the which I can never break while I live, to die for it.

Dur.—You have made another oath before.

Far.—No, my lord, I never made another oath before.

Dur.—You made a vow.

Far.—That did I not.

Win.—You made a profession to live without a wife.

Far.—No, my lord, that did I never: I made a profession to live chastely; but not without a wife.

Wor.—You were sworn to him that was master of your house.

Far.—That was I never.

Win.—Well, you are a froward knave: we will have no more to do with you, seeing that you will not come; we will be short with you, and that you shall know within this seven-night.

Far.—I am as it pleaseth your honour to call me; but I cannot break my oath, which your lordship yourself made before me, and gave in example, the which confirmed my conscience. Then I can never break that oath whilst I live, to die for it.

Dur.—Well, saith he, he standeth upon his oath; call another.

My lord chancellor then rang a little bell; and Mr. Farrar said, "I pray God save the king and queen's majesties long to continue in honour to God's glory and their comfort, and the comfort of the whole realm; and I pray God save all your honours," and so departed.

After these examinations, Bishop Farrar remained in prison uncondemned, till the 14th day (as is aforesaid) of February, and then was sent down into Wales, to receive sentence of condemnation.

On the appointed day this true servant of God appeared before Henry, the pretended bishop of St. David's, and was asked whether he would renounce his heresies, schisms, and errors which hitherto he had maintained, and if he would subscribe to the Catholic articles.

Upon this Bishop Farrar did exhibit a certain schedule written in English; appealing withal by express word of mouth from the bishop, as from an incompetent judge, to Cardinal Pole.

Notwithstanding this, Morgan, proceeding in his rage, pronounced the definitive sentence against him, contained in writing: by which sentence he denounced him as a heretic excommunicate, and to be given up forthwith to the secular power—namely, to the sheriff of the town of Carmarthen, Mr. Leyson; after which his degradation followed as a matter of course.

Thus this godly bishop, being condemned and degraded, was committed to the secular power, and not long after was brought to the place of execution in the town of Carmarthen, where he, in the market-place on the south side of the cross, on the 30th of March, most patiently sustained the torments of fire.

The Life and Martyrdom of John Bradford, Who Was Burned in Smithfield.

John Bradford was born in Manchester, and received such a good education from his parents, that he was able at an early age to take a respectable situation and maintain himself. He entered the service of Sir John Harrington, to whom he proved such an efficient assistant, that he soon obtained his master's entire confidence, and might have risen high in office, had not the Spirit of God opened his eyes to see the truth of the Gospel, and the errors of the religion in which he had been trained. Renouncing all his

bright worldly prospects, he determined to devote his life
to the Scriptures, and the ministry of the Word.

In order to carry out his plan, he went to Cambridge
University, where he applied himself with such diligence,
that in a few years the degree of Master of Arts was
conferred on him. He was then made a Fellow of Pembroke College, and was befriended by Martin Bucer, who
strongly urged him to use his talents in preaching. Bradford
replied that he could not preach, as he did not consider
himself qualified for such an office; to which his friend
would answer, "If thou hast not fine wheat bread, yet give
the poor people barley bread, or whatsoever else the Lord
hath committed unto thee."

Bradford was appointed by Dr. Ridley as a prebendary
of St. Paul's, where he laboured diligently for three years.

It was in the first year of Queen Mary's reign that the
Bishop of Bath, Dr. Bourne, preached at Paul's Cross on
the merits of popery, which raised the indignation of the
people to such a pitch, that they would have pulled him out
from the pulpit by force, had not the bishop, seeing his
danger, called to Mr. Bradford, who was standing near, to
come forward and take his place. Bradford obeyed this
request, and so greatly was he respected and beloved, that
he soon quelled the rising tumult, and dismissed the people
quietly to their homes. Within three days he was summoned before the queen's council, and accused of having
saved Bourne's life, and of having put himself forward to
preach in the bishop's stead; being found guilty, he was
committed to the Tower.

For two years he remained closely confined there; and
then he was brought before the lord chancellor, and other
councillors, to be examined on the accusation of seditious
behaviour at Paul's Cross.

On entering the council room, the chancellor told him he
had been justly imprisoned for his arrogancy in preaching
without authority; "but now," he said, "the time for mercy
has come, and the queen's highness hath by us sent for
you, to declare and give the same, if you will with us
return; and if you will do as we have done, you shall find
as we have found."

To this Bradford answered, "My lords, I know that I
have been long imprisoned, and—with humble reverence
be it spoken—unjustly, for that I did nothing seditiously,
falsely, or arrogantly, in words or fact, by preaching or
otherwise, but rather sought truth, peace, and all godly

quietness, as an obedient and faithful subject, both in going about to serve the present Bishop of Bath, then Mr. Bourne, and in preaching for quietness accordingly."

The chancellor angrily made answer, "I know thou hast a glorious tongue, and goodly shows thou makest; but all is lies thou speakest. And again, I have not forgot how stubborn thou wast when thou wast before us in the Tower, whereupon thou wast committed to prison concerning religion."

The councillors and bishops then began to question him on religious opinions, that they might find some reason to sentence him to death; and after much argument, the lord chancellor again offered him mercy, to which Bradford nobly and simply answered that mercy with God's mercy would be welcome, but otherwise he would have none. On this the chancellor rang a bell, and when the under-marshal entered, said to him, "You shall take this man with you, and keep him close, without conference with any man but by your knowledge, and suffer him not to write any letters, for he is of another manner of charge to you now than he was before." And so the first examination ended, Bradford testifying by his looks, as well as his words, that he was ready and willing, yea, even desirous, to lay down his life in confirmation of his faith and doctrine.

In about a week he was again brought before the council.

The chancellor began by making a long speech and stating that Bradford's act at Paul's Cross was arrogant and presumptuous. He then accused him of having written seditious letters when in the Tower, and of having endeavoured to pervert the people, and finally questioned him closely as to his belief in the presence of Christ in the sacrament.

To this Bradford replied, "My lord, I have now been a year and almost three quarters in prison, and in all this time you have never questioned me hereabouts, when I might have spoke my conscience frankly without peril; but now you have a law to hang up and put to death, if a man answer freely and not to your liking, and so now you come to demand this question."

Here the lord chancellor, affecting astonishment and horror, replied that neither did he use such means, that he had ofttimes been charged with showing too much gentleness and forbearance.

Mr. Bradford answered, "Then, my lord, I pray you

stretch out your gentleness that I may feel it, for hitherto I have not."

The lord chancellor being now informed that his dinner was ready, arose, and Bradford was again led to his prison.

At seven the next morning, Mr. Thomas Hussey came into the room where he was confined, and, saying that he came to see and speak to him through love, said, "So wonderfully did you behave yourself before the chancellor and other bishops yesterday, that even the greatest enemies you have say they have no matter against you; therefore I advise you to desire a time, and men to confer with, so by that means you may escape danger, which is otherwise nearer to you than you suppose."

Bradford refused to make any such request, which would give occasion to people to think that he doubted the doctrine he confessed. While they were still talking, Dr. Seton entered the room, and began to speak of Ridley and Latimer, who, he said, were unable to answer anything, and had desired to confer with others, hinting that Bradford had better follow their example. Bradford, however, refused his suggestion as he had Mr. Hussey's, whereupon they both became enraged. Soon after they had quitted his cell, the prisoner was again brought before his judges, when, after a long discussion, during which he displayed as much gentleness as they did ferocity, the sentence of excommunication was read, when he knelt down and thanked God that he was thought worthy to suffer for His sake. It was proposed that he should be sent to Manchester, his native town, to be burnt; and while they were settling whether or not it should be so, he was once again committed to prison.

He remained there nearly five months; when one afternoon the keeper's wife came to him, and in much trouble, said, "Oh, Mr. Bradford, I come to bring you heavy news."

"What is that?" asked he.

"To-morrow," she replied, "you must be burned; and your chain is now a-buying, and you must soon go to Newgate."

Bradford, taking off his cap, and lifting up his eyes to heaven, exclaimed, "I thank God for it."

Then, after thanking the woman for the kindness she had always shown him, he went to his room, and remained in private prayer for some time. At midnight he was removed to Newgate, and the next morning conducted by a large body of armed men to Smithfield, where he suffered death by being burnt alive, in company with a young man only twenty years of age, being joyful to the last moment of his life that he was thought worthy to die for his Saviour.

Martyrdom of Robert Glover.

A few miles from Coventry is the village of Mancetter.

The family of the Glovers had possessed large estates in Mancetter for more than two hundred years, and also held smaller lands in the neighbourhood. The three brothers—John, Robert, and William—lived together at the manor house at Mancetter, and were known to be zealous in the Reformed doctrines; but John being the eldest, was the one singled out by the Church of Rome as her victim.

Soon after Mary's accession, the Bishop of Coventry sent orders for his apprehension, but the mayor of the town, hearing of it, contrived to let him know his danger in time for him to effect his escape, in company with his brother William. When the officers reached the house, they instituted a rigid search for him, but failing to find him, they seized upon Robert, who had been for a long time confined to his bed by sickness. The sheriff, touched by his sufferings, would have allowed him to remain unmolested, but the other officers insisted on his apprehension, and he was taken before the bishop. He has left an account of what followed, in a letter written to his wife.

LETTER FROM MR. ROBERT GLOVER TO HIS WIFE, CONTAINING HIS TROUBLES.

"The peace of conscience which passeth all understanding, the sweet consolation, comfort, strength, and boldness of the Holy Ghost, be continually increased in your heart, through a fervent, earnest, and steadfast faith in our only Saviour Jesus Christ. Amen.

"After I came into prison, and had reposed myself there awhile, I wept for joy and gladness, musing much of the great mercies of God, and saying to myself, 'O Lord, who am I, on whom thou shouldst bestow this great mercy, to be numbered among the saints that suffer for the Gospel's sake?'

"Not long after, Mr. W. Brasbridge, Mr. C. Phineas, and Mr. N. Hopkins came unto me, persuading me to be dismissed upon bonds. But I answered that as the masters had nothing to burden me withal, if I should enter into bonds, I should in so doing accuse myself; and seeing they had no matter to lay to my charge, they might as well let me pass without bonds as with them.

"The second day after the bishop's coming to Coventry, Mr. Warren came to the Guildhall, and ordered the chief gaoler to carry me to the bishop. I laid to Mr. Warren's charge the cruel seeking of my death; and when he would have excused himself, I told him he could not wipe his hands so, for he was as guilty of my blood before God as though he had murdered me with his own hands.

"And so he departed from me, saying I needed not to fear if I would be of his belief.

"When I came before the bishop, in Mr. Denton's house, he began with this protestation, That he was my bishop for lack of better, and willed me to submit myself.

"Mr. Chancellor standing by, said I was a Master of Arts.

"Then my lord laid to my charge my not coming to the church.

"Here I might have dallied with him, and put him to his proofs, forasmuch as I had not been in his diocese for a long season, neither were any of the citizens able to prove any such matter against me. Notwithstanding, I answered him, through God's merciful help, that I neither had nor would come to their church, as long as their mass was used there, to save (if I had them) five hundred lives. I desired him to show me one jot or tittle in the Scriptures for the proof and defence of the mass.

"He answered he came to teach, and not to be taught.

"I was content, I told him, to learn of him, so far as he was able to teach me by the Word of God.

"*Bishop.*—Who shall judge the Word?

"*Glover.*—Christ was willing that the people should judge his doctrine by searching the Scriptures, and so was Paul; methinks you should claim no further privilege nor pre-eminence than they had. If you will be believed because you are a bishop, why find you fault with the people that believed Bishop Latimer, Bishop Ridley, Bishop Hooper, and others?

"*Bishop.*—Because they were heretics.

"*Glover.*—And may not you err as well as they? I expected my lord to use some learned arguments to persuade me, but instead of that, he oppressed me only with his authority. He said I dissented from the church, and asked me where my church was before King Edward's time.

"I desired him to show me where their church was in Elias's time, and what outward show it had in Christ's time.

"*Bishop.*—Elias's complaint was only of the ten tribes that fell from David's house, whom he called heretics.

"*Glover.*—You are notable to show any prophets that the other ten tribes had at the same time.

"My lord making no answer to that, Mr. Rogers, one of the masters of the city, cometh in the mean season, taking upon him as though he would answer to the text. But my lord forthwith commanded me to be committed to some tower, if they had any besides the common goal, saying he would, at the end of the visitation of his diocese, weed out such wolves. Mr. Rogers willed him to content himself for that night, till they had taken further order for me. 'Even where it pleaseth you,' said I to my lord, 'I am content;' and so I was returned at that time to the common gaol again from whence I came.

"Certain sergeants and constables at Coventry being appointed to convey us to Lichfield, to be delivered there to one Jephcot, the chancellor's man, sent from Coventry with us for the same purpose, we were commanded to be on horseback about eleven o'clock on Friday, it being a market day, in order that we might be the more gazed at: and to set the people's hearts more against us, they published a letter concerning a proclamation made for calling in and disannulling all such books as truly expounded the Scriptures.

"I was put into a prison that same night, where I continued till I was condemned, in a place next the dungeon, where was small room, strong building, and very cold, with little light; and there I was allowed a bundle of straw instead of my bed, without chairs, form, or anything else to rest myself upon.

"Then they consented that I should have a bed of my own procuring. But I was allowed no help, neither night nor day, nor company of any man, notwithstanding my great sickness; nor yet paper, pen, ink, or books, except my New Testament in Latin, and a Prayer-book, which I brought privily in.

"Within two days after, Mr. Chancellor and Mr. Temsey, a prebendary there, came into my prison. The first exhorted me to conform myself to my lord and to the Church.

"I answered that I refused not to be ruled by that church which was content to be governed by the Word of God.

"He said he came not to reason with me, and so departed. And I remained for the space of eight days without further conference with any man, until the bishop's coming: in which time I gave myself continually to prayer, and meditation of the merciful promises of God unto all, without exception of person, that call upon the name of his Son, Jesus Christ. I found in myself daily amendment of health of body, increase of peace of conscience, and many consolations from God, by the help of his Holy Spirit, and sometimes as it were a taste and glimmering of the life to come.

"At the bishop's first coming to Lichfield after my imprisonment, I was called into a bye chamber next to my prison, to my lord; before whom, when I came, and saw none but his officers, chaplains, and servants, except it were an old priest, I was partly amazed, and lifted up my heart to God for his merciful help and assistance.

"He asked me how I liked my imprisonment; I gave him no answer touching that question. He then proceeded to persuade me to be a member of his church, which had continued so many years. 'As for your church,' said he to me, 'it was not known but lately in Edward's time.'

" 'I profess myself to be a member of that Church,' said I, 'that is built upon the foundation of the apostles and prophets, Jesus Christ being the head corner-stone; and so alleged the place of St. Paul to the Ephesians. And this Church hath been from the beginning,' said I, 'though it bear no glorious show before the world, being ever, for the most part, under the cross and affliction, condemned, despised, and persecuted.' My lord contended, on the other side, that they were the Church.

"I desired him to lay something to my charge in particular, and then to convince me with some Scriptures and good learning.

"He began to move certain questions. I refused to answer him in corners, requiring that I might make my answer openly. He said I should answer him there. I stood with him upon that point till he said I should go to prison again, and there have neither meat nor drink till I had answered him.

"Then I lifted up my heart to God, that I might stand and agree with the doctrine of his most holy Word.

"The first question was this: How many sacraments Christ instituted to be used in the Church.

" 'The sacrament of baptism,' said I, 'and the sacrament that he instituted at his last supper.'

"He asked me, further, whether I allowed their confession.

"I answered, 'No.'

"Then the bishop would know what I thought of the presence of Christ's body in the sacrament.

"I answered that their mass was neither sacrifice nor sacrament, 'because,' said I, 'you have taken away the true institution, which, when you restore again, I will tell you my judgment.' "

This was the testimony which the worthy martyr of God left behind him, in his own handwriting, concerning his usage in prison and his disputations with the bishop and his chancellor. He was probably, examined more frequently by the bishop in the public consistory, whence he was brought forth for condemnation; and these records he would doubtless have left us, had length of life or leisure permitted him to finish his intentions; but by reason of the writ for his burning being sent from London, want of time prevented his being able to do so, and there are no records extant of his last examination; this incident is however, recorded by his friend Augustine Bernher. Mr. Glover, after his condemnation by the bishop, and when on the eve of his deliverance out of this world, felt himself destitute of all spiritual consolation, and a heavy unwillingness rather than a loving willingness to bear the bitter cross of martyrdom; he feared that the Lord had withdrawn his favour from him, and he complained of his spiritual barrenness to Augustine, stating how earnestly he had prayed, day and night, to God, yet without the sense of relief. Augustine desired him to wait the Lord's pleasure, seeing that the cause of his suffering was just and holy; he exhorted him to cleave, with full purpose of heart, to Christ, who, in his own good time, would visit him with his salvation. He spent his last night upon earth praying for that joy of the Lord which is the believer's strength, but without its experimental realization. The time for his martyrdom had at length arrived; and when he had come within sight of the stake, he was suddenly so filled with a sense of God's love and presence, that he clapped his hands together, crying out to his friend, "Austin! He is come, He is come!"

Account of a Public Disputation, Appointed by the Queen's Special Command, in a Convocation Held at St. Mary's Church, in Oxford, with the Circumstances Pertaining to the Said Disputation, in the Year 1554.

About the 10th of April, Cranmer, Archbishop of Canterbury, Ridley, Bishop of London, and Hugh Latimer, sometime Bishop of Worcester, were conveyed as prisoners from the Tower to Windsor, and from thence to the University of Oxford, there to dispute with the divines and learned men, both of Oxford and Cambridge, about the presence, substance, and sacrifice of the sacrament. The questions in dispute were— 1. Whether the natural body of Christ be really in the sacrament after the words of consecration or not. 2. Whether any other substance do remain therein, saving that of the body and blood of Christ. 3. Whether the mass be a propitiatory sacrifice for the sins of the quick and the dead.

On April 13 the three prisoners were separated, Dr. Ridley being taken to the house of Mr. Irish, Mr. Latimer to another, while Dr. Cranmer was kept in Bocardo, a prison in Oxford.

On April 14, at eight o'clock, the vice-chancellor of Cambridge, with the other doctors of that university went to St. Mary's Church, where, shortly after, all the commissioners (in number thirty-three) arrived, and sat on seats before the altar. Dr. Cranmer was then sent for, and shortly afterwards introduced by a number of trusty bill-men.

The reverend archbishop paid his respects to them with much humility, standing with his staff in his hand, and notwithstanding the offer of a stool, refused to sit.

The articles were now read before him, and a copy of them delivered to him, after which he was given in charge of the mayor, and remanded to prison.

Dr. Ridley was next brought in, who, hearing the articles read to him, immediately replied they were all false.

He was then asked whether he would dispute or not. He answered that as long as God gave him life, he should not only have his heart, but also his mouth and pen, to defend his truth; but he required time and books. Then they gave him the articles, and desired him to write his opinion upon them that night; after which they commanded the mayor to take him from whence he came.

Last of all Mr. Latimer was brought in, with a handkerchief and two or three caps on his head, his spectacles hanging by a string at his breast, and a staff in his hand, and was set in a chair. After his denial of the articles, when he had appointed Wednesday for disputation, he alleged age, sickness, disuse and lack of books, saying that he was almost as meet to dispute as to be a captain of Calais: but he would, he said, declare his mind either by writing or word, and would stand to all they could lay upon his back; complaining, moreover, that he was permitted to have neither pen nor ink, nor yet any book but only the New Testament there, in his hand, which he said he had read over seven times deliberately, and yet could not find the mass in it. At this the commissioners were not a little offended. There was so great a throng of people, that one of the beadles swooned in consequence of the heat. They then adjourned.

THE ARGUMENTS, REASONS, AND ALLEGATIONS USED IN THIS DISPUTATION.

On Monday, Dr. Weston, and the residue of the visitors, censors, and opponents, repairing to the Divinity School, installed themselves in their places. Dr. Cranmer was brought thither, and set in the answerer's place, with the mayor and aldermen by him.

Chedsey, the first opponent, began: "Rev. Mr. Doctor, these three conclusions are put forth unto us at present to dispute upon:—

"1. In the sacrament of the altar, is the natural body of Christ, conceived of the Virgin Mary, and also his blood, present really under the forms of bread and wine, by virtue of God's Word pronounced by the priest?

"2. There remaineth no substance of bread and wine after the consecration, nor any other substance, but the substance of God and man.

"3. The lively sacrifice of the Church is in the mass propitiatory, as well for the quick as the dead.

"These are the arguments on which our present controversy rests. Now to the end we might not doubt how you take the same, you have already given up unto us your opinion thereof. I term it your opinion, in that it disagreeth from the catholic. Wherefore I argue, Christ, when he instituted his last supper, spake to his disciples. 'Take, eat, this is my body, given for you.' But this true body was given for us. *Ergo,* his true body is in the sacrament."

Cran.—His true body is truly present to them that truly

receive him; namely, spiritually. And so it is taken in a spiritual sense. For when he said, "This is my body," it is as if he had said, "This is the breaking of my body, this is the shedding of my blood. As often as you shall do this, it shall put you in remembrance of the breaking of my body, and the shedding of my blood; that as truly as you receive this sacrament, so truly shall you receive the benefit promised by receiving the same worthily."

Ched.—Your opinion differeth from the Church, which saith that the true body is in the sacrament. *Ergo,* your opinion therein is false.

Cran.—I say and agree with the Church, that the body of Christ is in the sacrament effectually, because the passion of Christ is effectual.

Ched.—Christ, when he spake these words, "This is my body," spake of the substance, and not of the effect.

Cran.—I grant he spake of the substance, and not of the effect after a sort: and yet it is most true that the body of Christ is effectually in the sacrament. But I deny that he is there materially present in bread, or that under the bread is his original body.

Dr. Cranmer then observed that, to prevent loss of time, he would request the prolocutor to read to the court the following opinions he had written upon the three propositions.

DR. CRANMER'S EXPLICATION.

"In the assertions of the Church and of religion, trifling and new-fangled novelties of words are to be eschewed, whereof ariseth nothing but contention; and we must follow, as much as we can, the manner of speaking of the Scripture.

"In this first conclusion, if ye understand by this word 'really' *re ipsa,* that is, in very deed and effectually, so Christ, by the grace and efficacy of his passion, is indeed and truly present to all true and holy members.

"But if ye understand by this word 'really' *corporaliter,* that is, corporally, so that by the body of Christ is understood a natural and organical substance, the first proposition doth vary, not only from the usual phrase of Scripture, but also is contrary to the holy Word of God, and Christian profession: since both the Scripture doth testify by these words, and also the catholic Church hath professed from the beginning, that Christ has left the world, and sits at the right hand of the Father till he come to judgment.

"I answer likewise to the second question, that it swerveth from the accustomed manner and speech of Scripture.

"The third conclusion, as it is intricate, and wrapped in all doubtful and ambiguous words, and differing also much from the true speech of Scripture, so as the words thereof seem to import no open sense, is most contumelious against our only Lord and Saviour Christ Jesus, and a violating of his precious blood, which, upon the altar of the cross, is the only sacrifice and oblation for the sins of all mankind."

Chedsey then said, "By this interpretation which you have made upon the first conclusion, I understand that the body of Christ is to be in the sacrament only by the way of participation: insomuch as we, communicating thereof, do participate the grace of Christ; by which you mean only the effect thereof. But our conclusion standeth upon the substance, and not the efficacy only, which shall appear by the testimony both of Scripture and of all the fathers a thousand years after Christ.

Ched.—The Scriptures in many places affirm that Christ gave his natural body—Matt. xxvi., Mark xiv., Luke xxii. *Ergo,* I do conclude that the natural body is in the sacrament.

Cran.—To your argument I answer, if you understand by the body natural, *organicum,* that is, having such proportion and members as he had living here, then I answer negatively. Furthermore, concerning the Evangelists, this I say and grant, that Christ took bread, and called it his body.

Ched.—The text of the Scripture maketh against you, for the circumstance thereto annexed doth teach us not only there to be the body, but also teacheth us what manner of body it is, and saith, "The same body which shall be given"—that thing is here contained that is given for us. But the substance of bread is not given for us. *Ergo,* the substance of bread is not here contained.

Cran.—I understand not yet what you mean by this word 'contained:' if you mean 'really,' then I deny your major.

Ched.—The major is the text of Scripture. He that denieth the major denieth the Scripture. For the Scripture saith, "This is my body which is given for you."

Cran.—I grant he said it was his body which should be given, but he said it was not his body which is here contained, but the body that shall be given for you. As though he should say, "This bread is the breaking of my body, and this cup is the shedding of my blood." What will ye say then? Is the bread the breaking of his body, and the cup the shedding of his blood really? If you say so, I deny it.

Ched.—If you ask what is the thing therein contained, because his apostles should not doubt what body it was that should be given, he saith, "This is my body which shall be given for you, and my blood which shall be shed for many." *Ergo,* here is the same substance of the body which the day after was given, and the same blood which was shed. And here I urge the Scripture, which teacheth that it was no fantastical, no feigned, no spiritual body, nor body in faith, but the substance of the body.

Cran.—You must prove that it is contained, but Christ said not which is contained. He gave bread and called that his body. I stick not in the words of the Scripture, but in your word, which is feigned and imagined by yourself.

Ched.—When Christ took bread and brake it, what gave he?

Cran.—He gave bread, the bread sacramentally, and his body spiritually; and the bread there he called his body.

Ched.—This answer contradicts the Scripture, which saith that he gave his body.

Cran.—It did signify that which he did eat.

Ched.—They did not eat the body as the Capernaites did understand it, but the selfsame body which was given for the sins of the world. *Ergo,* it was his body which should be given, and his blood which should be shed. The same body is in the sacrament which was given for us on the cross. But bread was not given for us on the cross. *Ergo,* bread is not given in the sacrament.

Cran.—I deny the major, which is, that the same natural body is given in the sacrament which was given on the cross, except you understand it spiritually.

Weston now called upon Dr. Cranmer to answer one part, bidding him repeat his words; which, when he essayed to do, such was the uproar in the Divinity School, that his mild voice could not be heard. For here the prolocutor rudely interrupted him, and, substituting noise and insolence for argument, called him unlearned and impudent, at the same time pointing at him scornfully, urged the people to silence him with hissing, clapping of hands, and other species of tumult, which this reverend man most patiently

and meekly did abide, as one inured to the suffering of
such reproaches. And when the prolocutor, with rude and
unseemly demeanour, did call upon him to answer the
argument, he desired the notary to repeat his words again.

Ched.—Will you affirm that it is absurd which Chrysostom saith, that the body of Christ is touched? I touch the
body of Christ in the sacrament, as Thomas touched Christ.
Thomas touched Christ, saying, "My Lord and my God;"
therefore that which he touched was the Lord, the God.

Cran.—I deny your argument. He touched not God, but
him who was God. Neither is it sound doctrine to affirm
that God is touched.

Ched.—This is because of the union; so that God is said
to be touched, when Christ, who is both God and man, is
touched. Tertullian, speaking of the resurrection of the
body, saith, "Let us consider as concerning the proper
form of the Christian man, what great prerogative this vain
and foul substance of ours hath with God. Although it
were sufficient to it, that no soul could ever get salvation,
unless it believe while it is in the flesh; so much the flesh
availeth to salvation: by the which flesh it cometh, that
whereas the soul is so linked unto God, it is the said flesh
that causeth the soul to be linked: yet the flesh moreover
is washed, that the soul may be cleansed; the flesh is
anointed, that the soul may be consecrated; the flesh is
signed, that the soul may be defended; the flesh is shad-
owed by the imposition of hands, that the soul may be
illuminated with the Spirit; the flesh doth eat the body and
blood of Christ, that the soul may be fed of God."
Whereupon I gather this argument—the flesh eateth the
body of Christ; therefore the body of Christ is eaten with
the mouth. Phoceus also (1 Cor. xi.), upon these words, "Is
guilty of the body and blood," declareth, "That like as
Judas betrayed him, and the Jews were fierce and spiteful
against him, so do they dishonour him who receive his holy
body with their impure hands, and as the Jews did hold
him then, do now receive him with impure mouths." And
whereas he maketh mention of the body and blood of the
Lord, he declareth that it is not simply man that is
sacrificed, but the Lord himself; therefore the body of
Christ is touched with the hands.

Cran.—You vouch two authors against me upon sundry
things. I must first answer Tertullian, and then the other.
Unto Tertullian I answer, that he calleth that the flesh
which is the sacrament. For although God works all things

in us invisibly beyond men's reach, yet they are so manifest, that they may be seen and perceived of every sense.
Therefore he setteth forth baptism, unction, and, last of all,
the supper of the Lord unto us, which he gave to signify
his operation in us. The flesh liveth by the bread, but the
soul is inwardly fed by Christ. Inwardly we eat Christ's
body, and outwardly we eat the sacrament. So one thing is
done outwardly, another inwardly. Like as in baptism, the
external element, whereby the body is washed, is one; the
internal thing, whereby the soul is cleansed, is another.

Young.—This disputation is taken in hand that the truth
might appear. I perceive that I must go another way to
work than I had thought. It is a common saying, 'Against
those who deny principles we must not dispute;' therefore,
that we may agree on the principles, I demand whether
there be any other body of Christ than his instrumental
body?

Cran.—There is no natural body of Christ, but his
organical body.

Young.—Again, I demand whether sense and reason
ought to give place to faith?

Cran.—They ought.

Young.—Thirdly, whether Christ be true in all his
words?

Cran.—Yes, he is truth itself.

Young.—Fourthly, whether Christ, at his supper,
minded to do that which he spake, or not?

Cran.—In saying he spake, but in saying he made not,
but made the sacrament to his disciples.

Young.—Answer according to the truth, whether did
Christ that as God and man which he spake, when he said,
"This is my body?"

Cran.—This is sophistical cavilling. There is some deceit
in these questions.

Young.—I demand whether Christ by these words
wrought anything or no?

Cran.—He did institute the sacrament.

Young.—But answer whether he did work any thing.

Cran.—He did work in instituting the sacrament.

Young.—Now I have you; for before you said it was a
figurative speech. But a figure worketh nothing; therefore it
is not a figurative speech. A liar ought to have a good
memory.

Cran.—I understood your sophistry before. You by

working understanding converting into the body of Christ: but Christ wrought the sacrament, not in converting, but in instituting.

Young.—Woe be to them who make Christ a deceiver! Did he work any other thing than he spake, or the selfsame thing?

Cran.—He wrought the sacrament, and by these words he signified the effect.

Young.—A figurative speech is no working thing. But the speech of Christ is working; therefore it is not figurative.

Cran.—It worketh by instituting, not by converting.

Young.—The thing signified in the sacrament, is it not the sacrament?

Cran.—It is. For the thing is ministered in a sign. He followeth the letter that taketh the thing for a sign. Augustine separateth the sacrament from the thing. "The sacrament," saith he, "is one, and the thing of the sacrament another."

West.—Stick to this argument. It is a figurative speech; therefore it worketh nothing.

Young.—But the speech of Christ is a working thing; therefore it is not figurative.

Cran.—Oh, how many crafts are in this argument! they are mere fallacies. I said not that the words of Christ do work, but Christ himself, and he worketh by a figurative speech.

West.—If a figure work, it maketh of bread the body of Christ.

Cran.—A figurative speech worketh not.

West.—A figurative speech, by your own confession, worketh nothing. But the speech of Christ in the supper, as you grant, wrought somewhat; therefore the speech of Christ in the supper was not figurative.

Cran.—I answer these are mere sophisms. The speech doth not work, but Christ by the speech doth work the sacrament. I look for Scriptures at your hands, for they are the foundation of disputations.

At two o'clock this disorderly discussion, carried on sometimes in English, and sometimes in Latin, ended, with a universal cry of *Vincit veritas;* and the arguments were set down in writing, and delivered to the notary. Cranmer was again remanded, in the charge of the mayor of Oxford.

Life and Martyrdom of John Hooper, Bishop of Worcester and Gloucester.

John Hooper, when a student and graduate in the Oxford University, was filled with an earnest love and knowledge of the Scriptures. He advanced steadily in spiritual enlightenment, and gave proof of his opinions, which incurred the displeasure of several of the doctors of the college, who, at length, by the procurement of Dr. Smith, compelled him to leave the university. He then became steward to Sir Thomas Arundel, who favoured him very much, until he became aware of his religious views, from which he strongly dissented. Unwilling to part with so faithful a servant, Sir Thomas sent him to the Bishop of Winchester, hoping that a religious discussion might create a change in his feelings. The bishop, after conferring with Hooper for four or five days, seeing that he was unable to move him, sent him back to his master, secretly bearing a strong enmity towards him, though he praised his learning and talents. Not long after, Hooper had warning that dangers were gathering around him, so he left Sir Thomas Arundel's house, and borrowing a horse from a friend whose life he had on one occasion saved, set out for France. He succeeded in reaching Paris, but could not make up his mind to remain there, so returned to England. His enemies discovering him again, he was obliged to fly to Ireland, from whence he escaped through France to Germany. Here he formed friendships with many learned men, by whom he was hospitably entertained, particularly by a Mr. Bullinger. He travelled as far as Zurich, where he married, and applied himself with much earnestness to the study of the Hebrew language. When King Edward succeeded to the throne, many who had left their native country for conscience' sake returned, and among the number was Hooper, whose heart burned to preach the Gospel to his countrymen. Before leaving he went to thank all his friends for their kindness to him. Mr. Bullinger, on parting with him, said, "Mr. Hooper, although we are sorry to part with your company for your own cause, yet much greater cause have we to rejoice, both for your sake and especially for the cause of Christ's true religion, that you shall now return out of long banishment to your native country, where you may not only enjoy your own private liberty, but also the cause and state of Christ's Church by you may fare the better, as we doubt not but it will."

Then Hooper thanked them all, assuring them that

nothing could ever make him forget the kindness he had received during his stay among them, promising to write from time to time to tell them of his welfare. "But," said he, taking Mr. Bullinger's hand, "the last news of all I shall not be able to write; for there where I shall take most pains, there shall you hear of me to be burned to ashes; and that shall be the last news which I shall not be able to write unto you, but you shall hear of me."

Having said farewell to all his friends in Zurich, he returned to London, and preached regularly once a day, generally twice, and always inveighed strongly against the abuses which had crept into the Church. After some time he was sent for to preach before the king, who shortly afterwards appointed him Bishop of Gloucester. He remained at Gloucester for two years, and conducted himself with such truly Christian consistency, that his very enemies could find no fault with him.

At this time the dress of bishops resembled closely that worn by popish priests, consisting of a white rochet, over that a chymere, and a mathematical cap with four angles, representing the division of the world into four parts. Hooper was steadfast in his determination not to wear these superstitious robes; he wrote therefore to the king, requesting him either to discharge him from his bishopric or else to grant him leave to dispense with such ceremonials. The king immediately granted his request, and wrote in his favour to the archbishop. The Earl of Warwick also wrote to the archbishop, begging him to excuse Mr. Hooper from taking the usual oaths administered to bishops at their consecration.

Notwithstanding both these letters, the bishops stood out firmly in defence of the customary ceremonies, declaring that it was but a small matter, and that the fault lay in the abuse, and not in the use of the garments. They added that Bishop Hooper ought not to be so stubborn in so light a matter, and this his obstinacy could not be suffered. The contention ended by Mr. Hooper's agreeing to wear the usual episcopal robes when he preached. Being appointed to preach before the king, he accordingly appeared in the objectionable habiliments. He acted thus in respect of the public profit of the Church, which was his only desire, and he patiently bore the private injury and reproach. These trifling differences all vanished when the storm of persecution really broke out, and many affectionate letters passed between Hooper and his brother bishops while they were in prison.

After much vexation on these points, Hooper at length entered his diocese, and he employed his time there with such diligence, that he may well be taken for an example by all other bishops. He neglected no means that could benefit his flock, and laboured continually for their good. The time which he had to spare from preaching was occupied either in hearing public causes or else in private study, prayer, and in visiting schools. At home he omitted nothing that could conduce to his children's advantage, bringing them up carefully, both in regard to their manners and morals, and also their studies, so that it would be difficult to say whether he deserved most praise for his conduct at home or in his diocese. When you entered his palace, you might have supposed yourselves in a church or temple: there was the beauty of virtue, good example, honest conversation, and study of the Scriptures.

Bishop Hooper did not save anything out of the revenues of his bishoprics, but spent all in hospitality. Every day his manner was to have at dinner a certain number of the poor of the said city by course, who were served, by four at a mess, with wholesome meats; and when they were served (before being examined by him or his deputies in the Lord's Prayer, the Articles, and Ten Commandments), then he himself sat down to dinner, and not before. In this manner he laboured for more than two years, until the death of King Edward.

When Mary ascended the throne, he was one of the first who were summoned to London. His friends, warning him of his danger, entreated him to leave the country, but he refused, saying, "Once did I flee, and take me to my feet, but now, because I am called to this place and vocation, I am thoroughly persuaded to remain, and to live and die with my sheep." He was ordered to appear before Dr. Heath, who had been deprived of his bishopric in King Edward's time, on account of being a papist, and before Dr. Bonner, Bishop of London, because he had, in the previous reign, been one of his accusers. On arriving at London, before he saw Bonner and Heath, he was intercepted, and commanded to appear before the queen and her council. On coming before them, Gardiner received him very opprobriously, railing at him, and accusing him of his religion. He answered boldly and freely, but was, notwithstanding, committed to ward, being told that it was

not for his religion, but for certain sums of money which
he owed the queen, that he was imprisoned. In March
following, he was again called before Gardiner, and deprived of both his bishoprics, not being permitted to plead
his own cause.

AN ACCOUNT OF THE SEVERE TREATMENT OF BISHOP HOOPER, DURING NEAR EIGHTEEN MONTHS' CONFINEMENT IN THE FLEET, WRITTEN BY HIMSELF.

"The 1st of September, 1553, I was committed unto the
Fleet, from Richmond, to have the liberty of the prison;
and within six days after, I paid five pounds sterling to the
warden for fees, for my liberty; who, immediately upon
payment thereof, complained unto the Bishop of Winchester, upon which I was committed to close prison one
quarter of a year in the tower-chamber of the Fleet, and
used extremely ill.

"After one quarter of a year, Babington, the warden,
and his wife fell out with me, respecting the wicked mass;
and thereupon the warden resorted to the Bishop of
Winchester, and obtained to put me into the wards, where I
have continued a long time, having nothing appointed to
me for my bed but a little pad of straw, until, by God's
means, good people sent me bedding to lie on. On one side
of the prison is the sink and filth of the house, and on the
other the town ditch, so that the stench of the house hath
infected me with sundry diseases.

"During which time I have been sick, and the doors,
bars, hasps, and chains being all closed upon me, I have
mourned, called, and cried for help; but the warden, when
he hath known me many times ready to die, and when the
poor men of the wards have called to help me, hath
commanded the doors to be kept fast, and charged that
none of his men should come at me, saying, 'Let him
alone; it were a good riddance of him.'

"I have suffered imprisonment almost eighteen months;
my goods, livings, friends, and comfort taken from me; the
queen owing me, by just account, fourscore pounds or
more. She hath put me in prison, and giveth nothing to
keep me, neither is there suffered any one to come at me,
whereby I might have relief. I am with a wicked man and
woman, so that I see no remedy, saving God's help, but I
shall be cast away in prison before I come to judgment.
But I commit my just cause to God, whose will be done,
whether it be by life or death."

On the 28th of January the Bishop of Winchester and
the other commissioners sat in judgment at St. Mary
Overy's, when Mr. Hooper again appeared before them,
and after much reasoning and disputation, was commanded
to wait until Mr. Rogers had been examined. When these
examinations were over, the two sheriffs of London were
ordered to take them to the Compter in Southwark, and
keep them there until nine the following day, to see
whether they would return to the Catholic Church. Bishop
Hooper was led out first, Mr. Rogers following with the
other sheriff. On going out of the church door, Hooper
looked back, and seeing Mr. Rogers coming, he waited for
him, and said, "Come, brother Rogers, must we two take
this matter first in hand, and begin to fry these faggots?"
"Yes, sir," replied Rogers, "by God's grace." "Doubt not,"
answered Hooper, "but God will give us strength." They
then passed out into the street, which was crowded to
excess with people, who rejoiced at the constancy of these
two noble men.

They were given in charge to the keeper of the Compter,
who received orders to put them in separate chambers, and
not to allow them to converse with each other or with their
friends.

On the following day they were again brought before the
Bishop of Winchester, who examined them for a long time,
but found them resolute in maintaining their opinions.
Hooper was then degraded, and his condemnation was read
to him. The sheriff afterwards led him away to the Clink, a
prison near Gardiner's house, where he was kept until
night. At dark he was taken with a strong guard to
Newgate. Many people, who suspected what was happening, came out with lights to their doors, and saluted him,
praising God for his constancy, and exhorting him to
continue steadfast to the end.

Hooper asked them all to pray for him earnestly, and
was hastened on by the sheriff to Newgate, where he was
kept a close prisoner for six days. Bonner, Bishop of
London, came several times to see him, to persuade him to
recant, but his efforts were unavailing. He sent Fecknam,
Chedsey, Harpsfield, and some others for the same purpose, but they also found him immovable. When they
failed to convince him with their arguments, they affected
great gentleness towards him, promising him their friendship and great worldly wealth if he would join their church.
They then changed their promises into threats, but he

continued steadfast. Finding all their efforts useless, they endeavoured to bring him and the doctrines he professed into discredit with the people, by publishing a report that he had recanted. The frequent visits of the Bishop of London led many people to believe the report, which at length reached Hooper's ears, and it grieved him greatly to think that the people should give credit to such a statement. He wrote the following letter on this occasion:—

"The grace of our Lord Jesus Christ be with all them who unfeignedly look for the coming of our Saviour Christ. Amen.

"Dear brethren and sisters in the Lord, and my fellow-prisoners for the cause of God's Gospel, I do much rejoice and give thanks unto God for your constancy and perseverance in affliction, unto whom I wish continuance unto the end. I am credibly informed, that there is a report abroad that I John Hooper, recant and abjure that which heretofore I have preached. And that talk ariseth from this —that the Bishop of London and his chaplains resort unto me. Doubtless, if our brethren were as godly as I could wish them, they would think that in case I did refuse to talk with them, they might have just occasion to say that I was unlearned, and durst not speak with learned men, or else proud, and disdained to speak with them. Therefore, to avoid just suspicion of both, I have, and do daily speak with them when they come, not doubting but they report that I am neither proud nor unlearned. I fear not their arguments, neither is death terrible unto me. I am more confirmed in the truth which I have heretofore preached by their coming.

"I have hitherto left all things of the world, and suffered great pains and imprisonment, and I thank God I am as ready to suffer death as a mortal man can be.

"I have taught the truth with my tongue, and with my pen heretofore, and hereafter shortly shall confirm the same, by God's grace, with my blood. From Newgate, February 2, 1555.—Your brother in Christ,

"JOHN HOOPER."

On the following Monday Bonner degraded Hooper, with all the usual pomp and pride of the Romish Church. The same night, February 4th, the keeper gave the bishop a hint that he would probably be sent to Gloucester to be burned. This greatly rejoiced Hooper, who, raising his

hands to heaven, praised God for sending him to suffer
death among the people over whom he was pastor. Immediately he sent word to his servant, to bring him his boots,
spurs, and cloak, that he might be in readiness to ride
whenever the order came. At four o'clock the following
morning, the keeper, accompanied by some others, came
and searched him, to see whether he had concealed any
papers. He was then led by the sheriff to a place previously
appointed, where he was met by six of the queen's guard,
who had orders to take him to Gloucester. They reached
Gloucester about five o'clock the same evening. About a
mile from the town great numbers of people had congregated to meet their bishop, and they loudly bewailed his
sad fate, insomuch that one of the guard rode on with
speed to the town, to ask aid from the mayor and sheriffs,
lest the prisoner should be released by force. Hooper was
lodged at the house of a Mr. Ingram, in the city. During
the first part of the night he slept soundly, and afterwards
remained engaged in prayer until the morning.

Sir Anthony Kingston, a former friend of the bishop's,
had been appointed to attend at his execution. As soon as
he saw the bishop he burst into tears. Hooper did not at
first recognise him, when Sir Anthony said—

"Why, my lord, do not you know me—an old friend of
yours—Anthony Kingston? But I am sorry, my lord, to
see you in this case, for, as I understand, you are come
hither to die. But, alas! consider that life is sweet, and
death is bitter; therefore, seeing life may be had, desire to
live, for life hereafter may do good."

"Indeed, it is true, Sir Anthony; I am come hither to end
this life, and to suffer death here, because I will not gainsay
the truth that I have heretofore taught amongst you in this
diocese and elsewhere."

Sir Anthony then took leave of him, not without shedding bitter tears, and tears also ran down the face of the
good bishop. At eight the next morning, the commissioners
who were appointed to witness the execution arrived,
accompanied by a large band of men. Having been strictly
forbidden to speak, he went in silence to the appointed
place, smiling cheerfully on any whom he knew; he walked
with difficulty, as he was suffering from sciatica, which he
had caught in prison. Upwards of 7,000 persons were
congregated to see the last scene. Three iron hoops had
been prepared to fasten him to the stake, and he had three
bags of gunpowder tied to him. There was a strong wind,

and the greater part of the faggots being green, it was a
long time before they caught fire. Three times were they
lighted before they really began to burn up, and even when
the gunpowder exploded it did him no good. He was heard
to pray aloud, "Lord Jesus, have mercy upon me! Lord
Jesus, receive my spirit!" These were the last words he was
heard to utter; but when he was black in the mouth, and
his tongue so swollen that he could not speak, yet his lips
were seen to move. In three quarters of an hour his body
fell forwards, and he was released from his sufferings.

An Historical Account of Several Protestants, Who Were Persecuted, Tormented, and Most of Them Burned, Under the Tyranny of Bonner, Bishop of London.

Stephen Gardiner, having condemned and burned several great and learned men, presumed that these examples
would deter any in future from speaking against and
opposing the popish religion. But in this he found himself
deceived; for with eight or nine days after sentence had
been passed upon Bishop Hooper and others, on the 8th of
February, six other persons were brought up for examination for the same cause. Gardiner, seeing this, became
discouraged, and from that day meddled no more in such
kind of condemnations, but referred the whole of this cruel
business to the more sanguinary Bonner, Bishop of London, who summoned before him, in his consistory at St.
Paul's, the six persons, upon the 8th day of February, and
on the next day read the sentence of condemnation upon
them.

On the 18th of February, Queen Mary, after considerable delay, returned an answer to the King of Denmark,
who had written two letters to the queen on behalf of Mr.
Coverdale, who at that time was bailed by sureties, and was
in great danger, had he not been rescued by the suit and
letters of the Danish monarch.

On the 19th of February a certain intimation was
printed and set forth, in the name of Bishop Bonner, which
contained strict admonition to every person within his
diocese to prepare themselves against the approaching
Lent, to receive the tidings of peace and reconciliation
from Pope Julius III, conveyed by Cardinal Pole, the papal
legate.

About this time, Judge Hales, of Kent, was brought
before the lord chancellor, and examined respecting his
having resisted the ceremony of the mass, or rather for

having acted according to his duty as a justice, as the law then stood, when several Romish priests had been indicted and brought before him. Not giving satisfactory answers to the chancellor, he was committed to prison. While there he was waited upon by Mr. Day and Judge Portman, who by some means so worked upon his mind, that he was filled with despair, and after in vain attempting to destroy himself by a penknife, found a means of drowning himself in a shallow river. This unhappy gentleman had, at the death of King Edward, stood firmly in defence of Mary's title to the crown. But this service was found insufficient to protect him from the persecuting rage of the Roman Catholic bishops and priests.

I.

THE HISTORY OF THOMAS TOMKINS.

This plain honest Christian was by trade a weaver, and lived in the parish of Shoreditch, till he was summoned before the inhuman Bishop Bonner, and, with many others who had renounced the errors of popery, was confined in a prison in that tyrant's house at Fulham.

During his confinement, the treatment which he received at the bishop's hands was not only disgraceful to the character of the latter as a prelate, but even as a man; for Bonner's violence was such, because Tomkins would not assent to the erroneous doctrine of transubstantiation, that his lordship struck him in the face, and plucked out the greatest part of his beard.

On another occasion, because our martyr remained inflexible, and would not deviate in the least point from the uncorrupted truths of the Gospel, Bonner, in the presence of several of his visitors at his seat at Fulham, took the poor weaver by the fingers, and held his hand over the flame of a wax candle, having three or four wicks, supposing that, being terrified by the smart of the fire, he would abjure the doctrine which he then maintained.

Tomkins, expecting nothing but immediate death, commended himself unto the Lord, saying, "O Lord, into thy hands I commend my spirit." When relating the incident to one James Hinse, Tomkins declared that his spirit was so entranced in God, that he did not feel the pain.

When he had been half a year in prison, about the 8th of

February he was brought with several others before Bishop Bonner, in his consistory, to be examined; to whom first was brought forth a certain bill or schedule, subscribed (as appeareth) with his own hand, the fifth day of the same month, containing these words following:—

"Thomas Tomkins, of Shoreditch, and of the diocese of London, hath believed and doth believe, that in the sacrament of the altar, under the forms of bread and wine there is not the very body and blood of our Saviour Jesus Christ in substance, but only a token and remembrance thereof, the very body and blood of Christ being only in heaven and nowhere else.

"By me, THOMAS TOMKINS."

Whereupon he was asked whether he acknowledged the same subscription to be his own. He admitted it to be so. The bishop then endeavoured to persuade him with fair words, rather than with reasons, to relinquish his opinions, and to return to the unity of the Catholic Church, promising, if he would do so, to absolve him from the past. But he constantly refused.

When the bishop saw he could not convince him, he read to him another writing, containing articles and interrogatories, whereunto he should reply the next day; in the meantime he should deliberate with himself as to his course, and then either recant and reclaim himself, or else in the afternoon of the same day have justice (as the bishop called it) administered unto him. The copy of which articles here followeth:—

ARTICLES OBJECTED AND ADMINISTERED AGAINST
THOMAS TOMKINS, WITH HIS OWN HAND
SUBSCRIBING TO THE SAME.

"Thou dost believe that in the sacrament of the altar, under the forms of bread and wine, there is not by the omnipotent power of Almighty God, and his holy Word, really, truly, and in very deed, the very true and natural body of our Saviour Jesus Christ, as touching the substance thereof, which was conceived in the womb of the Virgin Mary, and hanged upon the cross, suffering death there for the life of the world."

"I do so believe."

"Thou dost believe that after the consecration of the

bread and wine prepared for the use of the sacrament of
the altar, there doth remain the substance of material bread
and material wine, not changed nor altered in substance by
the power of Almighty God, but remaining as it did
before."

"I do so believe."

"Thou dost believe that it is an untrue doctrine, and a
false belief, to think or say that in the sacrament of the
altar there is, after consecration of the bread and wine,
the substance of Christ's natural body and blood, by the
omnipotent power of Almighty God and his holy Word."

"I do so believe."

"By me, THOMAS TOMKINS."

THE SECOND EXAMINATION.

The next day Tomkins was again brought before the
bishop and his other assistants, where the aforesaid articles
were propounded unto him, whereunto he answered as
followeth:—

To the first he said that he did so believe, as in the same
is contained.

To the second he said that it was only bread and a
participation of Christ's death and passion, and so do the
Scriptures teach.

To the third he declared that it was a false doctrine to
believe and think as is contained in this article.

After this answer he also subscribed his name to the said
articles; whereupon the bishop, drawing out of his bosom
another confession subscribed with Tomkins' own hand,
and also that article that was the first day objected against
him, caused the same to be openly read, and then willed
him to revoke his opinions, which he refused to do; and
therefore he was commanded to appear before the bishop
again, in the same place, at two in the afternoon.

Agreeably to this mandate, being brought before the
bloody tribunal of bishops, and pressed to recant his errors
and return to the mother church, he maintained his fidelity,
nor would swerve in the least from the articles which he
had signed with his own hand.

Having, therefore, declared him to be an obstinate
heretic, they delivered him up to the secular power, and he
was burned in Smithfield, March 6th, 1555.

II.

THE HISTORY AND MARTYRDOM OF WILLIAM HUNTER, AN APPRENTICE IN LONDON, AGED NINETEEN YEARS, WHO WAS PURSUED TO DEATH BY JUSTICE BROWN, AND BURNED MARCH 27, 1555.

William Hunter had been trained to the doctrines of the Reformation from his earliest youth, being descended from pious parents, who carefully instructed him in the principles of true religion.

When Queen Mary succeeded to the crown, orders were issued to the priests of every parish, to summon all their parishioners to receive the communion at mass, the Easter after her accession; and Hunter, who was then nineteen years of age, refusing to obey the summons, was threatened with citation before the bishop.

His master, fearful of incurring ecclesiastical censure, desired him to leave him for a time; upon which he quitted his service, went down to Brentwood, and resided with his father for about six weeks.

One day, finding the chapel open, he entered, and began to read in the English Bible, which lay upon the desk, but was severely reprimanded by an officer of the bishop's court, who said to him, "William, why meddlest thou with the Bible? Understandest thou what thou readest? Canst thou expound Scripture?" He replied, "I presume not to expound Scripture; but finding the Bible here, I read for my comfort and edification."

The officer then informed a neighbouring priest of the liberty the young man had taken in reading the Bible; the priest, therefore, severely chid him, saying, "Sirrah, who gave thee leave to read the Bible and expound it?"

He answered as he had done to the officer: and on the priest's telling him that it became him not to meddle with the Scriptures, he frankly declared his resolution to read them as long as he lived, as well as reproved the vicar for discouraging persons from that practice, which the Scriptures so strongly enjoined.

The priest then upbraided him as a heretic. He denied the charge, and being asked his opinion concerning the corporal presence in the sacrament of the altar, he replied that he esteemed the bread and wine but as figures, and looked upon the sacrament as an institution in remembrance of the death and sufferings of our blessed Lord and Saviour Jesus Christ.

A neighbouring justice, named Brown, having heard that he maintained heretical principles, sent for his father, and inquired of him concerning his son. The old man assured him that he had left him, that he knew not whither he was gone; and on the justice's threatening to imprison him, unless he caused him to be apprehended and brought before him, he said, with tears in his eyes, "Would you have me seek out my son to be burned?"

The old man, however, was obliged to go, in pretence, at least, in quest of him, and by accident meeting him, was asked by him if he was seeking for him; he replied with tears he was, and told him that it was by command of the justice, who threatened to imprison him.

The son, to prevent his father from incurring any danger, said that he was ready to accompany him home, on which they returned together.

The following day he was taken by the constable, kept in the stocks for twenty-four hours, and then brought before the justice, who called for a Bible, and turning to John vi, desired him to give his opinion of the meaning of it, as it related to the sacrament of the altar.

Having given the same explanation as he had done to the priest, and persisting in his denial of the corporal presence in the eucharist, the justice upbraided him with damnable heresy, and wrote to the Bishop of London, acquainting him with the same, to whom this valiant young martyr was conducted by a constable.

After Bonner had read the letter, and the constable had returned home, the bishop caused William to be brought into a chamber, where he began to reason with him in this manner: "I understand William Hunter, by Mr. Brown's letter, that you have had certain communications with the vicar of Welde, about the blessed sacrament of the altar, and that you could not agree, whereupon Mr. Brown sent for thee to bring thee to the catholic faith, from which he saith that thou art gone. Howbeit, if thou wilt be ruled by me, thou shalt have no harm for anything that thou hast hitherto said or done in this matter."

William answered, "I am not fallen from the catholic faith of Christ, I am sure, but do believe it, and confess it with all my heart."

"Why," said the bishop, "how sayest thou to the blessed sacrament of the altar? Wilt thou recant thy saying, which thou confessedst before Mr. Brown, that Christ's body is not in the sacrament of the altar, the same that was born of the Virgin Mary?"

"My lord," answered he, "I understand that Mr. Brown hath certified you of the talk which he and I had together, and thereby you know what I said to him, which I will not recant, by God's help."

"Then," said the bishop, "I think thou art ashamed to bear a fagot, and recant openly; but if thou wilt recant thy sayings, I will promise thee that thou shalt not be put to open shame."

William then said, "My lord, if you let me alone, and leave me to my conscience, I will go to my father and dwell with him, or else with my master again, and so, if nobody will disquiet nor trouble my conscience, I will keep my conscience to myself."

Then said the bishop, "I am content, so that thou wilt go to the church and go to a confession, and so continue a good catholic Christian."

"No," returned the young Christian; "never while I live, God willing."

Upon this the bishop commanded his men to put him in the stocks in his gate-house, where he sat two days and nights only with a crust of brown bread and a cup of water.

After two days the bishop sent for him, and demanded whether he would recant or not. But William made answer that he would never recant that which he had confessed before men as concerning his faith in Christ. Then the bishop said that he was no Christian, but denied the faith in which he was baptised. But William answered, "I was baptised in the faith of the Holy Trinity, which I will not go from, God assisting me with his grace." The bishop then sent him to the convict prison, and commanded the keeper to lay as many irons upon him as he could bear; and, moreover, asked him how old he was. William said that he was nineteen years of age. "Well," said the bishop, "you will be burned before you be twenty, if you will not yield yourself better than you have done yet."

He now continued in prison three quarters of a year, during which time he was taken before the bishop five times, besides the time when he was condemned in the consistory of St. Paul's, on the 9th day of February.

The bishop again calling William, asked him if he would recant, and so read to him again his examination and confession, as above related, and then rehearsed that William had confessed he believed that he received Christ's body spiritually when he received the communion. "Dost thou mean," said the bishop, "that the bread is Christ's body spiritually?"

"I mean not so," replied William, "but rather, when I receive the holy communion rightly and worthily, I do feed upon Christ spiritually through faith in my soul, and am made partaker of all the benefits which Christ has brought unto all faithful believers through his precious death, passion, and resurrection, and not that the bread is his body, either spiritually or corporally."

"I have always found thee at this point, and I see no hope to reclaim thee unto the catholic faith, but thou wilt continue a corrupt member." He then pronounced sentence upon him, that he should go from that place to Newgate for a time, and so from thence to Burntwood, "where," said he, "thou shalt be burned."

The bishop then called for another, and when he had condemned them all, he called William Hunter, and reasoned with him, saying, "If thou wilt yet recant, I will make thee a free man in the city, and give thee forty pounds in good money to set thee up in thine occupation; or I will make thee steward of my house, and set thee in office."

"I thank you for your great offers," answered William; "but, notwithstanding, my lord, if you cannot persuade my conscience with Scriptures, I cannot find in my heart to turn from God for the love of the world; for I count all worldly things but loss and dung in respect of the love of Christ."

"If thou diest in this mind, thou art condemned for ever."

"God judgeth righteously, and justifieth them whom man condemneth unjustly," said William.

They then parted, William and the rest being committed to Newgate, where they remained about a month, after which they were sent down, William to Burntwood, and the others unto divers places of the country.

William's father and mother came to him at Burntwood, and desired heartily of God that he might continue to the end as he had begun, and his mother said to him that she was happy to have such a child, who could find in his heart to lose his life for Christ's sake.

William said to his mother, "For the little pain I shall

suffer, which will soon be at an end, Christ hath promised me, mother, a crown of joy; should you not be glad of that?"

Whereupon his mother kneeled down on her knees, saying, "I pray God strengthen thee, my son, to the end; yea, I think thee as well bestowed as any child I ever bore."

Next morning, Mr. Brocket, the sheriff, called to bid him prepare for his fate. At the same time the son of Mr. Brocket came to him and embraced him, saying, "William, be not afraid of these men with bows, bills, and weapons ready prepared to bring you to the place where you shall be burned." "I thank God I am not afraid," replied the undaunted youth, "for I have reckoned what it will cost me already." Then the sheriff's son could speak no more to him for weeping.

Hunter then took up his gown and went forward cheerfully, the sheriff's servant taking him by one arm, and his brother by another, and, going along, he met with his father who said to him, weeping, "God be with thee, son William." "God be with you, good father," said he, "and be of good comfort; for I hope we shall meet again, when we shall be joyful." "I hope so, William," said his father, and departed. He then went to the place where the stake stood, and taking a wet broom fagot, he kneeled thereon, and read the 51st Psalm till he came to these words: "The sacrifices of God are a broken spirit: a broken and a contrite heart, O God, thou wilt not despise."

"Thou liest, heretic! thou readest false!" exclaimed a person named Tyrill, "for the words are 'an humble spirit.' "

But William said, "The translation saith 'a contrite heart.' "

"Yes," quoth Tyrill, "the translation is false; you translate books as you please yourselves, like heretics."

"Well," said William, "there is no great difference."

Then said the sheriff, "Here is a letter from the queen; if thou wilt recant, thou shalt live; if not, thou shalt be burned."

"No," said William; "I will not recant, God willing." He then rose up and went to the stake, and stood upright against it. Richard Ponde, a bailiff, then came and made the chain fast about him.

Mr. Brown complained that there was not wood enough to burn a leg of him. "Good people," said William, "pray for me, and make speed and dispatch me quickly, and pray for me while you see me live, good people, and I will pray for you likewise."

"No," said Brown; "pray for thee! I will pray no more for thee than for a dog."

"Mr. Brown," returned the youthful martyr, "now you have that which you sought, and I pray God it be not laid to your charge in the last day; howbeit I forgive you."

"I ask no forgiveness of thee," retorted the savage.

"Well," said William, "if God forgive you, I shall not require my blood at your hands."

He then prayed, "Son of God, shine upon me!" and immediately the sun in the heavens shone out of a dark cloud so full in his face, that he was constrained to look another way; whereat the people wondered, because it was so dark a little time before. He then took up a fagot of broom and embraced it in his arms.

A gentleman was present who said, "I pray God have mercy upon his soul." To which the people said, "Amen, amen." Immediately after the fire was kindled.

William then cast his psalter into his brother's hand, who said, "William, think on the holy passion of Christ, and be not afraid of death."

"I am not afraid," answered William. Then, lifting up his hands to heaven, he said, "Lord, Lord, Lord, receive my spirit!" and casting down his head again into the smothering smoke, he yielded up his life for the truth.

Martyrdom of William Pygot, Stephen Knight, and John Lawrence.

We have already alluded to several persons who were brought before Bonner, the martyrdom of two of whom, Hooper and Hunter, we have just recorded. Two others, by name Pygot and Knight, suffered upon the 28th of March, and John Lawrence on the day after. They were first interrogated as to their opinions on the sacrament, to which they answered, affirming that there was not therein the actual body and blood of Christ, for that Christ's body was in heaven, and nowhere else. After this a series of articles was read to them, such as was read to Tomkins, to which they replied in like manner. Then the bishop addressed himself to the two laymen, and with an affected concern for their spiritual and temporal interests, warmly exhorted them to reject their heresies, and not expose themselves to death here, and damnation hereafter, by obstinately persisting in disobedience to the holy see. But

these steady Christians were too well grounded in the
doctrines of Christ's pure Gospel to be moved from their
faith. They therefore told the bishop that the could not
recant consistently with the dictates of their consciences,
nor would they abjure the opinions to which they had
subscribed.

Bonner afterwards entered into an argument with the
Rev. Mr. Lawrence alone, and having demanded of what
order he was, he answered that he had been admitted to
priests' orders eighteen years before, that he was some time
a black friar, and that he was betrothed to a maid, whom
he intended to marry.

The bishop then asked him his opinion of the corporal
presence in the sacrament, to which he replied that it was
an institution of our blessed Lord, in commemoration of
his death and sufferings; and that they were greatly deceived who believed that his body was verily present in the
same, for that he had long before ascended into heaven,
and was placed at the right hand of the glorious majesty of
the Father.

Mr. Lawrence was then for the present dismissed; but a
few days after he, with Pygot and Knight, was again
summoned before the bishop, who, with his usual hypocrisy, exhorted them to recant, embrace the Roman Catholic faith, and not to be the wilful causes of their own
destruction. But no arguments could induce them to recede
in a single point, all of them declaring that they would
abide by their opinions, because they were founded on the
Word of God, whereas the other was merely of human
invention.

Upon this frank confession, Bishop Bonner proceeded to
pass sentence on them as irreclaimable heretics, and then
degraded Mr. Lawrence with the usual ceremonies; after
which they were all three delivered to the sheriff, who
condemned them to Newgate, where they remained with
joy together, until they were carried into Essex, and there,
on the 28th of March, William Pygot was burned at
Braintree, and Stephen Knight at Malden, the latter of
whom, at the stake, kneeling upon the ground, said the
following prayer, which is not only exquisitely touching,
but morally sublime:—

"O Lord Jesus Christ, for whose love I leave willingly
this life, and desire rather the bitter death of thy cross, with
the loss of all earthly things, than to abide the blasphemy
of thy most holy name, or to obey men in breaking thy

holy commandment: thou seest, O Lord, that where I might live in worldly wealth to worship a false god, and honour thine enemy, I choose rather the torment of the body, and the loss of this life. Such love, O Lord, hast thou laid up in my breast, that I hunger for thee, as the wounded deer desireth the pasture. Send thy holy Comforter, O Lord, to aid, comfort, and strengthen this weak piece of earth, which is empty of all strength of itself. Thou rememberest, O Lord, that I am but dust, and able to do nothing that is good; therefore, O Lord, as of thine accustomed goodness and love thou hast invited me to this banquet, and accounted me worthy to drink of thine own cup amongst thine elect; even so give me strength, O Lord, against this raging element, which as to my sight it is most irksome and terrible, so to my mind it may at thy commandment be sweet and pleasant, that, through the strength of thy Holy Spirit, I may pass through the rage of this fire into thy bosom according to thy promise. Oh, heavenly Father, forgive me my sins, as I forgive all the world. Oh, sweet Son of God, my Saviour, spread thy wings over me. Oh, blessed and Holy Ghost, through whose merciful inspiration I am come hither, conduct me into everlasting life. Lord, into thy hands I commend my spirit."

The next day Mr. Lawrence was brought to Colchester, and there, being not able to move (for his legs were much worn with heavy irons in prison, and also his body weakened with low diet), was taken to the fire in a chair, and thus was consumed.

Life and Martyrdom of Thomas Cranmer, Archbishop of Canterbury, Burned at Oxford, March 21, 1556.

Thomas Cranmer was born at Aslacton, in Nottinghamshire, on the 2nd of July, 1489. On his father's death, in 1503, his mother placed him at Jesus College, in Cambridge, where he applied himself with great diligence to his studies, particularly to those of Greek, Hebrew, and theology. In 1510 he was chosen a fellow of his college, but in consequence of his marriage taking place shortly afterwards, he lost his fellowship. On this he became a reader in Buckingham College. In order that he might the more zealously apply himself to the duties of his readership, he boarded his wife with one of her relatives, who kept the Dolphin Inn,

His frequent visits were noticed by some Roman Catholics, and from these circumstances arose the various slanders which afterwards assailed him when promoted to the archbishopric of Canterbury. Mr. Cranmer continued at Buckingham College until the death of his wife, when the master and fellows of Jesus, in consideration of his eminent learning, re-elected him to a fellowship. His energy was now devoted more to theological studies, so that he became the divinity lecturer, and was generally selected by the university as one of the examiners of the candidates for degrees. Cranmer, desirous of promoting the knowledge of the Scriptures, would not permit any one to proceed with the divinity course unless they were well grounded in the knowledge of the Holy Scriptures, which proceeding brought upon him the enmity of certain friars and others, who had been brought up in the barren subtleties of the schoolmen, to the neglect of the practical truths of the Word of God.

Whilst Cranmer was at Cambridge, the vexed question of King Henry's divorce with the Lady Catherine of Arragon arose, which was debated for several years by the jurists, both ecclesiastical and civil. The cardinals Campeggio and Wolsey had been appointed as papal commissioners to decide the knotty point, but finding themselves beset with difficulties, from Henry's urgency on the one hand, and from the fact that Catherine was aunt to the Emperor Charles V on the other, procrastinated matters, in the usual hope that time and the chapter of accidents would befriend them, and bring the desired solution. The king, however, became enraged, when he saw that he was the dupe of the cardinals, and that no definite move was made towards the accomplishment of his wishes. He accordingly dismissed Cardinal Campeggio, and made an excursion into the neighbourhood of Waltham Abbey, in Essex, where Cranmer was staying. At Waltham Dr. Gardiner, afterwards Bishop of Winchester, and Fox, subsequently Bishop of Hereford, who were in attendance on the king, met Cranmer, and the conversation turned upon the pending controversy of the time.

In the course of conversation Cranmer suggested the expediency of "trying the question by the Word of God;" and that the matter might be as well settled in England by the universities as in Rome, or in any foreign court. When Fox, who was Royal almoner, repeated the substance of the conversation to the king, the king swore "that that man had the right sow by the ear." Cranmer was accordingly summoned to court, received into favour, and, on the disgrace of Wolsey, promoted to the see of Canterbury.

It is not for us to enter into a minute analysis of the difficulties of the archbishop's position, or of the motives which influenced his conduct at certain critical junctures. Allowance must be made for the dilemmas of a giant mind struggling to free itself from the shackles of association, education, and prejudice, and for its gradual advance towards the goal of truth. Cranmer's opinions passed through various transition states; and his mind was extricated from erroneous doctrines on the sacramental presence only by slow degrees. His conduct, with reference to his oath of consecration, the divorce of Anne Boleyn, the condemnation of John Frith and Joan of Kent, is open to the apologies of the casuist or the censure of the rigid moralist. He was a man of a vigorous understanding, and of many virtues; his influence was cast into the scale of enlightenment and truth; to him, as much as to any other, is England indebted for the legacy of an open Bible, and his master mind advanced the reformation of the Church of England to almost her present position.

We now pass over those events of his public career which have been related, and come to the close of his eventful life.

In September, 1555, Dr. Brooks, Bishop of Gloucester, came with authority from Cardinal Pole to judge him; and with him came two delegates to assist him in the name of their majesties. Dr. Cranmer, on being brought before them, paid the respect that was due to those who represented royalty; but would show none to the Bishop of Gloucester, since he was there by an authority derived from the pope, which, he said, he never would acknowledge. He would not serve two masters; and, since he had sworn allegiance to the Crown, he could never submit to the pope's authority. He also showed that the pope's power had been as unjustly used as it was ill-grounded; that they had changed the laws settled by Christ, which he instanced in denying the cup to the laity, in their worship in an unknown tongue, and in their assuming a power to depose princes. He reminded Brooks that he had sworn to maintain the king's supremacy; and when the latter studied to cast that back on him, as an invention of his, Cranmer told him that it was acknowledged in his predecessor Warham's time, and that Brooks had then set his hand to it. Brooks, and the two delegates, Martin and Scory, laid many complaints against him—as that he had flattered King Henry for the sake of preferment, and that he had condemned Lambert for denying the presence in the sacrament, and had been afterwards guilty of the same heresy himself. But Cranmer vindicated himself from all aspirings to the see of Canterbury, which appeared visibly by the slowness of his movement when he was called over out of Germany to be consecrated, for he was seven weeks on his journey. He confessed he had changed his opinion in the matter of the sacrament, and acknowledged that he had been twice married, which he thought was a liberty free to all men, and was certainly much better than to take other men's wives. After much discourse had passed on both sides, Brooks required him to appear before the pope within eighty days, and answer the things that should be brought against him. He said he would do it most willingly, but he could not possibly go if he were kept a prisoner.

In February, 1556, Bonner and Thirleby were sent to degrade him for his contumacy in not going to Rome, although he was all the while kept in prison.

Now many devices were set on foot to make him recant: both English and Spanish divines had many conferences with him, and great hopes were given him, not only of life, but of preferment, if he would do it; and these, at last, had a fatal effect upon him, for he signed a recantation of all his former opinions, and concluded it with a protestation that he had done it freely, for the discharge of his conscience. The queen, however, was resolved to sacrifice him to her resentments; and, she said, it was good for his own soul that he repented; but since he had been the chief spreader of heresy over the nation, it was necessary to make him a public example. Accordingly the writ was sent down to burn him, and, after some stop had been made in the execution of it, new orders came for doing it suddenly. This was kept from Cranmer's knowledge, for they intended to carry him to the stake without giving him any notice, and so hoped to make him die in despair; yet he, suspecting somewhat, wrote a long paper, containing a confession of his faith, such as his conscience, and not his fears, had dictated.

He was, on the 21st of March, carried to St. Mary's, where Dr. Cole preached, and vindicated the queen's justice in condemning Cranmer; but magnified his conversion much, and ascribed it to God's Spirit. He gave him great hopes of heaven, and promised him all the relief that masses could give.

All this time, with great grief, Cranmer stood hearing his sermon: one while lifting up his hands and eyes unto heaven, and then again, for shame, letting them down to the earth, while the tears gushed from his eyes.

After Cole had ended his sermon, he called back the people to prayers that were ready to depart. "Brethren," said he, "lest any man should doubt of this man's earnest conversion and repentance, you shall hear him speak before you, and, therefore, I pray you, Mr. Cranmer, to perform that now which you promised not long ago—namely, that you would openly express the true and undoubted profession of your faith, that you may take away all suspicion from men, and that all men may understand that you are a catholic indeed." "I will do it," said the archbishop, "and that with a good will;" and rising up, and putting off his cap, he began to speak thus unto the people:—

"Good people—my dearly beloved brethren in Christ, I beseech you most heartily to pray for me to Almighty God, that he will forgive me all my sins and offences, which are without number, and great above measure. But yet one thing grieveth my conscience more than all the rest, whereof, God willing, I intend to speak more hereafter." And here, kneeling down, he said the following prayer:—

"O Father of heaven, O Son of God, Redeemer of the world, O Holy Ghost, three persons and one God, have mercy upon me, most wretched caitiff and miserable sinner. To thee, therefore, O Lord, do I run; to thee do I humble myself, saying, O Lord my God, my sins be great, but yet have mercy upon me for thy great mercy. The great mystery that God became man was not wrought for little or few offences. Thou didst not give thy Son, O heavenly Father, unto death for small sins only, but for all the greatest sins of the world, so that the sinner return to thee with his whole heart, as I do at this present. Wherefore have mercy on me, O God, whose property is always to have mercy. I crave nothing for mine own merits, but for thy name's sake, that it may be hallowed thereby, and for thy dear Son Jesus Christ's sake." After repeating the Lord's Prayer, he continued:—

"Every man, good people, desireth at the time of his death to give some good exhortation, that others may remember the same before their death, and be the better thereby; so I beseech God grant me grace that I may speak something at this my departing, whereby God may be glorified, and you edified.

"My first exhortation is:—That you set not your minds over much upon this deceitful world, but upon God, and upon the world to come, and to learn to know what this lesson meaneth which St. John teacheth, that the love of this world is hatred against God.

"The second exhortation is, That next unto God you obey your king and queen willingly and gladly, without murmuring or grudging; not for fear of them only, but much more for the fear of God, knowing that they be God's ministers, appointed by God to rule and govern you; and, therefore, whosoever resisteth them, resisteth the ordinance of God.

"The third exhortation is, That you love altogether like brethren and sisters. For, alas! pity it is to see what contention and hatred one Christian man beareth to another, not taking each other as brother and sister, but rather as strangers and mortal enemies. For this you may be sure of, that whosoever hateth any person, and goeth about maliciously to hinder or hurt him, surely, and without all doubt, God is not with that man, although he think himself ever so much in God's favour.

"The fourth exhortation shall be to them that have great substance and riches of this world, That they will well consider and weigh three sayings of the Scripture: one is of our Saviour himself, who saith (Luke xviii.), 'It is hard for a rich man to enter into the kingdom of heaven.' A sore saying, and yet spoken by him who knoweth the truth. The second of St. John (1 John iii.), whose saying is this: 'He that hath the substance of this world, and seeth his brother in necessity, and shutteth up his mercy from him, how can he say that he loveth God?' The third is of St. James, who speaketh to the covetous rich man, after this manner: 'Weep you and howl for the misery that shall come upon you; your riches do rot, your clothes be moth-eaten, your gold and silver doth canker and rust, and their rust shall bear witness against you, and consume you like fire; you gather a hoard or treasure of God's indignation against the last day.' Let them that be rich ponder well these three sentences.

"And now, forasmuch as I am come to the last end of my life, whereupon hangeth all my life past and all my life to come, either to live with my master Christ for ever in joy, or else to be in pain for ever with wicked devils in hell, I shall therefore declare unto you my very faith how I believe, without any colour of dissimulation.

"First, I believe in God the Father Almighty, maker of heaven and earth. And I believe every article of the catholic faith, every word and sentence taught by our Saviour Jesus Christ, His apostles and prophets, in the New and Old Testament.

"And now I come to the great thing which so much troubleth my conscience, more than anything that ever I did or said in my whole life, and that is the setting abroad of a writing contrary to the truth; which now I here renounce and refuse, as things written with my hand contrary to the truth which I thought in my heart, and written for fear of death.

"And as for the pope, I refuse him, as Christ's enemy and Antichrist, with all his false doctrine.

"And as for the sacrament, I believe as I have taught in my book against the Bishop of Winchester, which my book teacheth so true a doctrine of the sacrament, that it shall stand at the last day before the judgment of God, where the papistical doctrine contrary thereto shall be ashamed to show her face."

As soon as the doctors heard these things, they began to rage and fret, and so much the more, because they could not revenge themselves, for they could no longer threaten nor hurt him; for the most miserable man in the world can die but once, and of necessity he must needs die that day.

And then Cranmer being pulled down from the stage, was led to the fire, accompanied with those friars, vexing, troubling, and threatening him most cruelly. "What madness," said they, "hath brought thee again into this error, by which thou wilt draw innumerable souls with thee into hell?" To whom he answered nothing, but directed all his talk to the people, saving that to one who troubled him as he went he spoke, and exhorted him to get home to his study, and apply to his book; saying, that if he did diligently call upon God, by reading more he should get knowledge.

When he had come to the place where the holy bishops and matryrs of God, Latimer and Ridley, were burnt before him for the confession of the truth, kneeling down, he prayed to God, and tarrying not long in his prayers, he put off his garment to his shirt, and prepared himself for death.

Then an iron chain was tied about Cranmer, and they commanded the fire to be set to the faggots.

And when the wood was kindled, and the fire began to burn near him, he stretched forth into the flames his right hand, which had signed his recantation, and there held it so steadfastly, that the people might see it burned to a coal before his body was touched. In short, he was so patient and constant in the midst of these extreme tortures, that he seemed to move no more than the stake to which he was bound; his eyes were lifted up to heaven, and often he repeated the words, "This unworthy right hand!" so long as his voice would suffer him; and often used the words of the blessed martyr St. Stephen, "Lord Jesus, receive my spirit!" till, the fury of the flames putting him to silence, he gave up the ghost.

Thus did Thomas Cranmer end his days, in the sixty-seventh year of his age. His last fall was the greatest blemish of his life, yet for that there was a full forgiveness, through Him who said to the thief on the cross, "To-day shalt thou be with me in paradise." And it seemed necessary that the reformation of the Church, being the restoring of the primitive and apostolical doctrine, should have been chiefly carried on by a man thus eminent for primitive and apostolical virtues.

History and Martyrdom of Bishop Ridley and Bishop Latimer.

On the 16th of October, 1555, those two pillars of Christ's Church, Dr. Nicholas Ridley, Bishop of London, and Mr. Hugh Latimer, some time Bishop of Worcester, were burnt in one fire at Oxford.

Dr. Ridley was born in the county of Northumberland, and was descended from a most respectable family. He was taught the rudiments of his education at Newcastle, and, when a child, discovered great promptness in learning. From Newcastle he was removed to the university of Cambridge, where he in a short time became so famous, that, for his singular aptness, he was called to higher functions and offices of the university, and was at length placed at the head of Pembroke Hall, and there made doctor of divinity. After this, departing from thence, he travelled to Paris, and at his return was made chaplain to King Henry VIII, and promoted afterwards to the bishopric of Rochester, and from thence, in King Edward's days, translated to that of London.

In his important offices he so diligently applied himself

by preaching and teaching the true and wholesome doctrine of Christ, that no good child was more singularly
loved by his dear parents than he by his flock and diocese.
Every holiday and Sunday he preached in one place or
other, except he were otherwise hindered by weighty affairs
and business; and to his sermons the people resorted,
swarming about him like bees; and so faithfully did his life
portray his doctrines.

He was also wise of counsel, deep of wit, and very
politic in all his doings. He was anxious to gain the
obstinate papists from their erroneous opinions, and sought
by gentleness to win them to the truth, as his kind and
courteous treatment of Dr. Heath, who was prisoner with
him in King Edward's time, in his house, for a year,
sufficiently proved.

He took all things in good part, bearing no malice nor
rancour in his heart, but straightway forgetting all injuries
and offences done against him. He was very kind and
natural to his relations, and yet his conduct to them was
regulated only by the laws of right, for he gave even his
own brother and sister to understand that if they did evil
they were to look for nothing at his hands, but would be as
strangers and aliens to him, and that to be acknowledged
by him as his brother and sister, they must live virtuous
lives.

When at his manor at Fulham, he used to read daily a
lecture to his family at the common prayer, beginning at
the Acts of the Apostles, and so went through all the
epistles of St. Paul, giving to every man that could read a
New Testament, hiring them, besides, with money, to learn
by heart certain principal chapters, but especially the 13th
chapter of the Acts of the Apostles; reading also unto his
household oftentimes the 101st Psalm, being marvellously
careful over his family, that they might be patterns of
virtue and honesty to others. In short, as he was godly and
virtuous himself, so nothing but virtue and godliness
reigned in his house, to the honour of our Saviour Jesus
Christ.

Dr. Ridley was first brought to a knowledge of Christ
and his Gospel by reading Bertram's book on the sacrament; and his conference with Archbishop Cranmer, and
with Peter Martyr, did much to confirm him in that belief.
Being now, by the grace of God, thoroughly converted to
the true way, he was as constant and faithful in the right
knowledge which the Lord had revealed unto him, as he

was before blind and zealous in his old ignorance, and so long as the power and authority of the State defended the Gospel, and supported the happiness of the Church, his influence was mighty for spiritual good. After the death of King Edward, the whole state of the Church in England was left desolate and open to the enemy's hand: so that Bishop Ridley, after the accession of Queen Mary, was one of the first upon whom they laid their hands, and sent to prison, as has been sufficiently declared: first in the Tower, and from thence conveyed, with the Archbishop of Canterbury and Mr. Latimer, to Oxford, and with them confined in the common prison of Bocardo; but being separated from them, he was committed to custody in the house of one Irish, where he was kept till the day of his martyrdom, a period reaching from the year of our Lord 1554 till October 16, 1555.

LETTER FROM BISHOP RIDLEY AND HIS FELLOW-PRISONERS
TO MR. BRADFORD AND HIS FELLOW-PRISONERS,
IN THE KING'S BENCH, IN SOUTHWARK, ANNO 1554.

"Well beloved in Christ our Saviour, we all with one heart wish to you, with all those that love God in deed and truth, grace and health, and especially to our dearly-beloved companions which are in Christ's cause, and the cause both of their brethren and of their own salvation, to put their neck willingly under the yoke of Christ's cross. How joyful it was to us to hear the report of Dr. Taylor, and of his godly confession, I assure you it is hard for me to express.

"Blessed be God, which was and is the giver of that, and of all godly strength and support in the time of adversity. As for the rumours that have or do go abroad, either of our relenting or massing, we trust that they which know God and their duty towards their brethren in Christ, will not be too light of belief. For it is not the slanderer's evil tongue, but a man's evil deed, that can with God defile a man; and, therefore, with God's grace, you shall never have cause to do otherwise than you say you do, that is, not to doubt but that we will, by God's grace, continue.

"It would much comfort us if we might have knowledge of the state of the rest of our most dearly beloved, which in this troublesome time do stand in Christ's cause, and in the defence of the truth thereof. We have heard somewhat of Mr. Hooper's matter, but nothing of the rest. We long to hear of Father Crome, Dr. Sands, Mr. Saunders, Veron, Beacon, and Rogers. We are in good health, thanks be to God, and yet the manner of using us doth change as sour ale in summer.

"My lord of Worcester passed through Oxford, but he did not visit us. The same day our restraint began to be more close, and the book of the communion was taken from us by the bailiffs, at the mayor's command. Sir, blessed be God, with all our evil reports, grudges, and restraints, we are merry in God; all our care is and shall be, by God's grace, to please and serve Him, of whom we look and hope, after these temporal and momentary miseries, to have eternal joy and perpetual felicity with Abraham, Isaac, and Jacob, Peter and Paul, and all the heavenly company of the angels in heaven, through Jesus Christ our Lord. As yet there has no learned man, nor any scholar, been to visit us since we came into Bocardo. Thus fare you well. We shall, by God's grace, one day meet together, and be merry. The day assuredly approacheth apace; the Lord grant that it may shortly come. For before that day come, I fear the world will wax worse and worse.

"We all pray you, as we can, to cause all our commendations to be made unto all such as you know did visit us and you when we were in the Tower, with their friendly remembrances and benefits. Mrs. Wilkson and Mrs. Warcup have not forgotten us, but ever since we came to Bocardo, with their charitable and friendly benevolence, have comforted us: not that else we did lack (for God be blessed, he hath always sufficiently provided for us), but that is a great comfort, and an occasion for us to bless God, when we see that he maketh them so friendly to tender us, whom some of us were never familiarly acquainted withal.—Yours in Christ,

"NICHOLAS RIDLEY."

LETTER TO THE BRETHREN IN CAPTIVITY, AND DISPERSED IN VARIOUS PRISONS, BUT UNITED TOGETHER IN SPIRIT AND HOLY RELIGION IN THE LORD JESUS.

"Grace, peace, and mercy be multiplied among you. What worthy thanks can we render unto the Lord for you, my brethren? namely, for the great consolation which, through you, we have received in the Lord, who, notwithstanding the rage of Satan, that goeth about by all manner of subtle means to beguile the world, and also busily laboureth to restore and set up his kingdom again, that of late began to decay and fall to ruin, remain yet still immovable, as men surely grounded upon a strong rock. And now, albeit that Satan, by his soldiers and wicked ministers, daily (as we hear) draweth numbers unto him, so that it is said of him that he plucketh the very stars out of heaven, while he driveth into some men the fear of death and loss of all their goods, and showeth to others the pleasant baits of the world—namely, riches, wealth, and all kinds of delights and pleasures, fair houses, great revenues, fat benefices, and what not. Blessed be God, the Father of our Lord Jesus Christ, which hath given unto you a manly courage, and hath so strengthened you in the inward man, by the power of his Spirit, that you can contemn as well all the allurements of the world, who also hath wrought, planted, and surely established in your hearts so steadfast a faith and love of the Lord Jesus Christ, joined with such constancy, that by no engines of Antichrist, be they ever so terrible or plausible, will you suffer any other Jesus, or any other Christ, to be forced upon you besides him the prophets have spoken of before, the apostles have preached, the holy martyrs of God have confessed and testified with the effusion of their blood.

> "Your brother in the Lord, whose name this bearer shall signify unto you, ready always by the grace of God to live and die with you."

LIFE OF BISHOP LATIMER.

Hugh Latimer was born about 1472, and was the only son of a yeoman who lived at Thurcaston, in Leicestershire. As he gave early evidences of possessing unusual abilities, his parents determined to give him all the educational advantages which lay in their power—a proof of discernment and enlightenment uncommon in that age. Hugh was sent in the first instance to the common schools of his own county, where his progress was so rapid and marked, that at the age of fourteen he was sent to the University of Cambridge. After passing through the usual course of secular studies, his inclinations turned to the study of divinity. although trammelled with the subtleties of the schoolmen, the servile worshippers of the cramping genius of Aristotle. In the early ages of Christianity its writers were strongly tinctured with the influence of Platonism, and in the Middle Ages a deference to the master-spirit of Aristotle tended to restrict anything like progression in the free kingdom of mind and morals. Latimer was both zealous and misguided, showing nevertheless a nobility of nature capable of achieving great results when under the empire of truth. He was of the straitest sect of his religion, and full of its Pharisaic scrupulousness as to the outside of the cup and the platter. Misguided by this blind zeal, he was a great enemy to the professors of Christ's Gospel. His wrath was strongly excited against Mr. Stafford, reader of the divinity lectures in Cambridge, at whom he railed most spitefully, and persuaded the students neither to believe his teachings and his doctrine, nor to follow his practices. Mr. Thomas Bilney, perceiving that Latimer had a great zeal, felt a brotherly pity towards him, and began to consider by what means he might expound to this ignorant brother the way of God more perfectly. After a short time he came to Mr. Latimer's study, and asked him to hear his own confession; the result of which interview was, that Latimer's understanding was so enlightened by God's good Spirit, that immediately he forsook the study of the school doctors, and other such philosophers and became an earnest student of the Bible, and of that divinity which centres in the cross of Christ. He was a changed character, for he hated that which he had loved, and he now loved that which he had hated. His old manner of cavilling and railing was changed, and he was diligent, in his conferences with Mr. Bilney and others, in his pursuit of truth, and desired the forgiveness of Mr. Stafford, on his death-bed, for his intemperate invectives.

A convert himself, Latimer was now anxious to make others partakers of his joy. He became a public preacher, and a private instructor of the rest of his brethren in the university for the space of three years, conversing at one time with the learned in Latin, and at another with the simple people in his English mother tongue.

There was an Augustine friar, who took occasion upon certain sermons of Mr. Latimer, which he preached about Christmas, 1529, to inveigh against him, because Mr. Latimer, in the said sermons, gave the people certain cards out of the 5th, 6th, and 7th chapters of St. Matthew, in the study of which they might, not only then, but at all other times, occupy their time. For the chief triumph in the cards he selected the heart, as the principal thing with which they should serve God, whereby he quite overthrew all hypocritical and external ceremonies, not tending to the furtherance of God's holy Word and sacraments. For the better attaining hereof, he wished the Scriptures to be in English, in order that the common people might be enabled to learn their duty to God and to their neighbors.

This happened upon the Sunday before Christmas Day; on which day, coming to the church, he entered the pulpit, taking for his text the words of the Gospel aforesaid, "Who art thou?" And, in delivering the cards as above mentioned, he made the heart to be triumph, exhorting and inviting all men thereby to serve the Lord with inward heart and true affection, and not in the outward deeds of the letter only, or in the glittering show of man's traditions, or pardons, pilgrimages, ceremonies, vows, devotions, voluntary works, and works of supererogation, foundations, oblations, and the pope's supremacy. As these sermons were so important in their consequences, we here present the reader with the following beautiful extract from one of them.

EXTRACT FROM A SERMON OF MR. LATIMER, IN CAMBRIDGE, ABOUT THE YEAR 1529.

" '*Tu quis es?*' Which words are as much as to say in English, 'Who art thou?' These be the words of the Pharisees, which were sent by the Jews unto St. John Baptist in the wilderness, to have knowledge of him who he was; which words they spoke unto him of an evil intent, thinking that he would have taken on him to be Christ, and so they would have had him done by their good wills, because they knew that he was more carnal and given to their laws than Christ indeed should be, as they perceived by their old prophecies: and also, because they marvelled much at his great doctrine, preaching, and baptising, they were in doubt whether he was Christ or not; wherefore they said unto him, 'Who art thou?' Then answered St. John, and confessed that he was not Christ.

"Now then, according to the preacher, let every man and woman, of a good and simple mind, contrary to the Pharisees' intent, ask this question, 'Who art thou?' This question must be moved to themselves, on this fashion: 'What art thou of thy only and natural generation between father and mother, when thou camest into the world? What substance, what virtue, what goodness art thou of thyself?' Which question, if thou rehearse oftentimes to thyself, thou shalt well perceive and understand how thou shalt make answer to it, which must be made in this wise: 'I am of myself,' and by myself, coming from my natural father and mother, the child of the anger and indignation of God, the true inheritor of hell, a lump of sin, and working nothing of myself, but all towards hell, except I have better help of another than I have of myself.' Now we may see in what state we enter into this world, that we be of ourselves the true and just inheritors of hell, the children of the ire and indignation of Christ, working all towards hell, whereby we deserve of ourselves perpetual damnation, by the right judgment of God, and the true claim of ourselves: which unthrifty state that we be born unto is come unto us for our own deserts, as proveth well this example following.

"Let it be admitted for the probation of this, that it might please the king's grace now being, to accept into his favour a mean man, of simple degree and birth, because of his own mere motion and fancy: and because the king's grace will more declare his favour unto him, he giveth unto this said man a thousand pounds in lands, to him and his heirs, on this condition, that he shall take upon him to be the chief captain and defender of this town of Calais, and to be true and faithful to him in the custody of the same, against the Frenchmen especially above all other enemies.

"This man taketh on him this charge, promising this fidelity thereunto. It chanceth in process of time, that by the singular acquaintance and frequent familiarity of this captain with the Frenchmen, these Frenchmen give unto the said captain of Calais a great sum of money, so that he will be but content and agreeable that they may enter into the said town of Calais by force of arms. Upon this agreement the Frenchmen do invade the said town of Calais.

"Now the king hearing of this invasion, cometh with a great puissance to defend this his said town, and so by good policy of war overcometh the said Frenchmen, and entereth again into his town of Calais. Then he being desirous to know how these enemies of his came thither, maketh strict search and inquiry by whom this treason was conspired, and found his own captain to be the very author and the beginner of the betraying of it. The king, seeing the great infidelity of this person, dischargeth this man of his office, and taketh from him and his heirs this thousand pounds' possession. Think you not that the king doth use justice unto him, and all his posterity and heirs? Yes truly; the said captain cannot deny himself but that he had true justice, considering how unfaithfully he behaved himself to his prince, contrary to his own fidelity and promise. So likewise it was of our first father Adam: he had given unto him the spirit and science of knowledge, to work all goodness therewith; this said spirit was not given only to him, but unto all his heirs and posterity. He had also delivered him the town of Calais, that is to say, Paradise in earth, the most strong and fairest town in the world, to be in his custody: he, nevertheless, by the instigation of these Frenchmen, that is, the temptation of the fiend, did consent unto their desire, and so he broke his promise and fidelity, the commandment of the everlasting King, his master, in eating of the apple by him prohibited.

"Now then, the King, seeing this great treason in his captain, dispossessed him of the thousand pounds of lands, that is to say, from everlasting life and glory, and all his heirs and posterity: for likewise as he had the spirit of science and knowledge for him and his heirs, so in like manner when he lost the same, his heirs also lost it by him, and in him. So now this example proveth that by our father Adam we had once in him the very inheritance of everlasting joy; and by him and in him again we lost the same.

"And now the world standing in this damnable state, cometh in the occasion of the incarnation of Christ; the Father in heaven perceiving the frail nature of man, that he by himself and of himself could do nothing for himself, by His prudent wisdom sent down the second person in the Trinity, His Son Jesus Christ, to declare unto man his pleasure and commandment: and so at the Father's will Christ took on him human nature, being willing to deliver man out of this miserable way, and was content to suffer cruel passion in shedding his blood for all mankind; and so left behind, for our safeguard, laws and ordinances, to keep us always in the right path unto everlasting life, as the gospels, the sacraments, and the commandments, which if we do keep and observe according to our profession, we shall answer better unto this question ('Who art thou?") than we did before: for before thou didst enter into the sacrament of baptism, thou wert but a natural man, or a natural woman; but after thou takest on thee Christ's religion, thou hast a longer name, for then thou art a Christian man, a Christian woman. Now then, seeing thou art a Christian man, what shall be the answer of this question, 'Who art thou?'

"The answer of this question is, when I ask it unto

myself, I must say that I am a Christian man, a Christian woman, the child of everlasting joy, through the merits of the bitter passion of Christ. This is a joyful answer. Here we may see how much we are bound and indebted unto God, that hath revived us from death to life, and saved us that were damned: which great benefit we cannot well consider, unless we remember what we were of ourselves before we meddled with Him of His laws: and the more we know our feeble nature, and set less by it, the more we shall conceive and know in our hearts what God hath done for us; and the more we know what God hath done for us, the less we shall set by ourselves, and the more we shall love and please God; so that in no condition we shall either know ourselves or God, except we utterly confess ourselves to be mere vileness and corruption. Well, now it is come unto this point, that we are Christian men, Christian women, I pray you, what doth Christ require of a Christian man, or of a Christian woman? Christ requireth nothing else of a Christian man or woman but that they will observe his rule."

To relate the noise and alarm the preaching of these sermons occasioned at Cambridge would require too much time and space.

First came out the prior of Black Friars, named Buckneham, who attempted to prove that it was not expedient for the Scriptures to be in English, lest the ignorant and vulgar sort might be running into some inconvenience.

Mr. Latimer hearing this sermon of Buckneham, came shortly after to the church to answer him. To hear him came a multitude, both of the university and of the town, doctors and other graduates, with great expectation to learn what he could say; among whom also sat Buckneham.

Mr. Latimer, having first recapitulated the arguments of Buckneham, so thoroughly answered the friar's objections that the absurdity of the friar was clear to all men, for the preacher proved plainly that there was so such danger arising from the Scriptures being in English.

But why should we attempt to decipher the names of his adversaries, when swarms of friars and doctors flocked against him on every side, through the whole university? amongst whom was Dr. Watson, Master of Christ's College, whose scholar Latimer had been. In short, almost all the heads of houses were the enemies of this worthy standard-bearer of Christ's Gospel.

At last came Dr. West, Bishop of Ely, who, declaiming against him at Barnwell Abbey, forbad his preaching within the churches of that university any more. Nothwithstanding, the Lord so provided, that Dr. Barnes, prior of the Augustine friars, licensed Mr. Latimer to preach in his church of the Augustines, and he himself preached at St. Edward's Church; whereupon certain articles were gathered out of his sermon, and brought against him by Mr. Tirell, fellow of the King's Hall, and so they were presented by the vice-chancellor to the cardinal.

Mr. Latimer, being thus persecuted by the friars, doctors, and masters of that university, about the year 1529, continued, notwithstanding the malice of these adversaries, preaching in Cambridge for about three years, with the favour of the godly, and even with the admiration of his enemies, who heard him.

Mr. Latimer and Mr. Bilney after this continued in Cambridge for some time, where they conferred together so frequently, that the field wherein they walked was called "The Heretics' Hill."

As their intimacy was much noted by many of the university, so was it productive of many good examples to all who would follow them, both in visiting the prisoners and relieving the needy. The following interesting story will exemplify the benevolence of Latimer. It happened that, in company with Bilney, he went to visit the prisoners in the tower of Cambridge, and, among others, there was a woman who was accused of having killed her own child, which act she distinctly and emphatically denied; wherefore it caused them to search into the whole matter, and at length they discovered that her husband did not love her, and therefore was seeking by every means to compass her destruction. Mr. Latimer, by earnest investigation, conscientiously thought the woman not guilty. Immediately after this, he was called to preach before King Henry VIII at Windsor; and, after his sermon, the king sent for him, and talked familiarly with him; whereupon Mr. Latimer, availing himself of the opportunity, kneeled down, opened the whole matter to the king, and desired her pardon, which the king granted, and gave it to the good intercessor on his return home.

Besides this instance, many other equally benevolent actions were known to have been wrought by this zealous

Christian, insomuch that the enemies of truth soon sought out a means to interrupt the harmony that existed between himself and Mr. Bilney.

Mr. Latimer, having thus laboured in preaching and teaching in Cambridge about three years, was at length cited before the cardinal for heresy, through the instigation of some members of the university, when he was content to subscribe and accede to such articles as they then propounded.

After that he again returned to the university, where, shortly after, by the means of Dr. Butts, the king's physician, a singularly good man, he was placed in the number of those who laboured in the cause of the king's supremacy. On this he went to the court, where he remained a certain time in Dr. Butts's chamber, and preached very often in London. At last, being weary of the court, and having a benefice offered to him by the king, at the suit of the Lord Cromwell and Dr. Butts, he gladly accepted it, and withdrew from the court.

This royal gift was in West Kingston, in Wiltshire, in the diocese of Sarum. Here this good preacher exercised himself with much diligence, teaching his flock and all the country about. In fine, his diligence was so great, his preaching so powerful, the manner of his teaching so zealous, that there also he could not escape enemies. It so happened as he was preaching about the Virgin Mary, and proving all honour belonged to Christ alone, our only Saviour, that certain popish priests being therewith offended, caused him much trouble, drawing out articles and impositions, which they falsely and uncharitably imputed unto him: that he did preach against the Virgin, because he reproved in a sermon the superstitious rudeness of certain blind priests, who taught that she never had any sin, and that she was not saved by Christ.

His chief molesters, besides these country priests, were Dr. Powel, of Salisbury, Dr. Wilson, formerly of Cambridge, Mr. Hubberdin, and Dr. Sherwood—of whom some preached and some wrote against him; insomuch that by their procurement he was cited before Warham, Archbishop of Canterbury, and Stokesley, Bishop of London, January 29, 1531.

Although Mr. Latimer appealed to his own ordinary against this citation, yet notwithstanding that, he was brought to London, before Warham, Archbishop of Canterbury, and the Bishop of London, where he was greatly molested, and detained a long time from his cure, being summoned thrice every week before the said bishops, to vindicate his preaching, and to subscribe to certain articles or propositions. At length, he wrote to the archbishop, partly excusing his infirmity, whereby he could not appear at their commandment, and partly expostulating with them for so detaining him from the performance of his duty.

The bishops required him to subscribe to certain articles, but whether he did so or not remains uncertain. It appears by his letter to the archbishop, that he durst not consent to them; for he says, "I dare not subscribe to these propositions, because I would no ways be accessory to the longer continuance of these popular superstitions, lest I be the author of my own damnation." By the words and the title in Tonstal's register prefixed before the articles, it would appear that he did subscribe. The words of the register are these: "Hugh Latimer, bachelor of divinity, of the University of Cambridge, in a convocation held at Westminster, before the Lord Archbishop of Canterbury, John, Lord Bishop of London, and the rest of the clergy, has acknowledged and made the following confession of his faith, as in these articles, March 21, 1531." If these words are true, it may be inferred that he subscribed. But they ought to be received with great caution, considering the subtlety, artifice, and want of candour that prevailed amongst the Roman party.

After his promotion to the bishopric of Worcester, through the interest of Dr. Butts and the Lord Cromwell, there was one evil willer, and he no mean person, who complained of him to the king on account of his sermons. Latimer gives the particulars of the story, in a sermon before King Edward, as follows:—

"In the king's days that is dead, a great many of us were called together before him, to speak our minds on certain matters. In the end, one kneeleth down and accuseth me of having preached seditious doctrine.

"The king turned to me, and said, 'What say you to that, sir?' Then I kneeled down, and turned first to my accuser, and asked him, 'Sir, what form of preaching would you appoint me in preaching before a king? Would you have me preach nothing as concerning a king in a king's sermon? Have you any commission to appoint me what I shall preach?' Besides this, I asked him divers other questions, and he would make no answer to any of them.

"Then I turned to the king, and submitted myself to his

grace, and said, 'I never thought myself worthy, nor did I ever sue to be a preacher before your grace; but I was called to it, and would be willing (if you mislike me) to give place to my betters; for I grant that there be a great many more worthy of the room than I am. And if it be your grace's pleasure so to allow them for preachers, I could be content to carry their books after them. But if your grace allow me for a preacher, I would desire you to give me leave to discharge my conscience, and thus to frame my doctrine according to my audience. I had been a very blockhead to have preached so at the borders of your realm as I preached before your grace.

"And I thank Almighty God, who hath always been my remedy, that my sayings were well accepted of the king; for, like a gracious lord, he turned into another communication. It is even as the Scripture saith, 'The Lord directeth the king's heart.' Some of my friends came to me with tears in their eyes, and told me they expected I should have been in the Tower the same night."

He continued in his laborious episcopal functions until the passing of the Six Articles. Being then much distressed through the straitness of the times, he felt that he must either sacrifice a good conscience or else forsake his bishopric; accordingly he did the latter. However, he did not altogether escape troubles and labours; for, a little while after he renounced his bishopric, he was much bruised by the fall of a tree; and upon coming up to London for relief, was sent to the Tower, where he was kept a prisoner till King Edward came to the crown.

As the diligence of this man of God never ceased, all the time of King Edward, to profit the Church both publicly and privately, so it is to be observed that the good Spirit of God, who assisted him in preaching the Gospel, did also enable him to foretell those plagues which afterwards ensued. If England ever had a prophet, he seemed to be one. And as regarded himself, he often affirmed that the preaching of the Gospel would cost him his life, for which he was cheerfully prepared; for after the death of King Edward, and not long after Mary had been proclaimed queen, a pursuivant was sent down into the country to arrest him, of whose coming, although Mr. Latimer was duly apprised thereof about six hours before by one John Careless, yet he was so far from endeavouring to escape, that he prepared himself for his journey before the officer arrived at his house.

At this the pursuivant marvelled; when Mr. Latimer said to him, "My friend, you are a welcome messenger unto me. And be it known unto you and to all the world, that I go as willingly to London at this present, as ever I went to any place in the world. I doubt not but that God, as he hath made me worthy to preach his Word before two princes, so will he enable me to witness the same unto the third, either to her comfort or discomfort eternally." When the pursuivant had delivered his letters, he departed, affirming that he was commanded not to wait for him. By this it was manifest that they did not desire his appearance, but rather his departure out of the realm.

When Mr. Latimer came up to London, and entered Smithfield, he merrily said that Smithfield had long groaned for him. He was then brought before the council, where he patiently bore all the mocks and taunts of the scornful papists, and was again sent to the Tower. Assisted by the heavenly grace of Christ, he patiently endured a long imprisonment, notwithstanding the cruel usage of his enemies; yet he showed himself not only patient, but also merry and cheerful, in spite of all their malice against him: yea, such a valiant spirit the Lord gave him, that he was able not only to despise the terror of prisons and torments, but also to laugh to scorn the cruel proceedings of his enemies. It is well known to many what answer he made to the lieutenant when he was in the Tower. For when the lieutenant's man upon a time came to him, the aged father, who had been kept without fire in the frosty winter, and well nigh starved with cold, bade the man tell his master, that if he did not look better after him, perchance he might deceive him.

The lieutenant hearing this, and not knowing what to make of so odd a speech, and fearing that he would make his escape, began to look more strictly to his prisoner, and coming to him, charged him with his words. "Yea, Mr. Lieutenant, so I said," says he, "for I suppose you expect that I should burn; but except you let me have some fire, I am like to deceive your expectation, for I am in danger of starving here with cold."

Mr. Latimer passed a long time in the Tower, with as much patience as a man in his case could do, and thence was carried to Oxford, with Dr. Cranmer, Archbishop of Canterbury, and Dr. Ridley, Bishop of London, there to dispute upon articles sent down from Gardiner, Bishop of Winchester, as before mentioned: which disputations be-

tween them and the university doctors we have already
related. After which Mr. Latimer, with his fellow prisoners, were condemned, and committed again to the prison,
where they continued from the month of April till October,
occupied with brotherly conference, fervent prayer, or
fruitful writing.

Mr. Latimer, by reason of his feebleness, wrote less than
the others during his imprisonment; but in prayer he was
fervent, earnestly sending up to the throne of grace the
following petitions:—

First, That as God had appointed him to be a preacher
of his Word, so also he would give him grace to stand to
his doctrine until his death.

Secondly, That God of his mercy would restore his
Gospel to England once again.

The third was for the preservation of the Lady Elizabeth, whom in his prayer he used to name, desiring God,
even with tears, to make her a comfort to England.

Having thus given the particulars of the life of this
excellent man, we now come to his letters, many of which
were written in Latin, but they are so numerous and so
long, that our limits would not admit of their insertion. As
his sentiments, however, are highly instructive, we shall
present our readers with the following:—

"MR. LATIMER TO MR. MORRICE, CONCERNING
THE ARTICLES WRITTEN, WHICH WERE FALSELY
LAID AGAINST HIM.

"Right worshipful and mine own good master Morrice,
health in Christ Jesus. You would wonder to know how I
have been treated at Bristol, I mean by some of the priests,
who first desired me, welcomed me, made me cheer, heard
what I said, and allowed my saying in all things while I was
with them; when I was gone home to my benefice, perceiving that the people favoured me so greatly, and that the
mayor had appointed me to preach at Easter, privily they
procured an inhibition for all them that had not the
bishop's license, which they knew well enough I had not,
and so craftly defeated master mayor's appointment, pretending they were sorry for it, procuring also certain
preachers to rail against me, as Hubberdin and Powel, with
others, whom when I had brought before the mayor, to
know what they could lay to my charge, wherefore they so
disclaimed against me, they said they spake as they were

informed: however, no man could be brought forth that could stand to anything; so that they had place and time to belie me shamefully, but they had no place or time to lay to my charge when I was present and ready to make them answer.

"OUR LADY WAS A SINNER.

"So they did belie me to have said, when I had said nothing so, but to reprove certain, both priests and beneficed men, which do give so much to our lady, as though she had not been saved by Christ, a whole Saviour, both of her, and all that be or shall be saved: I did reason after this manner—that either she was a sinner or no sinner; if a sinner, then she was delivered from sin by Christ; so that he saved her either by delivering or preserving her from sin, so that without him neither she nor any other could be saved. And to avoid all offence, I showed how it might be answered, both to certain Scriptures, which maketh all generally sinners, and how it might be answered unto Chrysostom and Theophilact, who make her namely and specially a sinner. But all would not serve, their malice was so great; notwithstanding that five hundred honest men can and will bear record. When they cannot reprove that thing that I do say, then will they belie me to say that thing which they can reprove; for they will needs appear to be against me.

"AVE MARIA.

"As for Ave Maria, who can think that I would deny it? I said it was a heavenly greeting or saluting of our blessed lady, wherein the angel Gabriel, sent from the Father of heaven, did annunciate and show unto her the good-will of God towards her, what he would with her, and to what he had chosen her. But I said it was not properly a prayer, as the Pater Noster, which our Saviour Christ himself made for a proper prayer, and bid us to say it for a prayer, not adding that we should say ten or twenty Aves or Marias withal: and I denied not but that we may well say Ave Marias also, but not so that we shall think that the Pater Noster is not good, a whole and perfect prayer, nor cannot be well said without Ave Maria: so that I did not speak against the well saying of it, but against the superstitious saying of it, and of the Pater Noster too; and yet I put a difference betwixt that and that which Christ made to be said for a prayer.

"NO PURGATORY.

"Consider, Mr. Morrice, whether provision for purgatory hath not brought thousands to hell. Debts have not been paid: restitution of evil-gotten lands and goods hath not been made; Christian people (whose necessities we see, to whom whatsoever we do Christ reputeth done to himself, to whom we are bound, under pain of damnation, to do for, as we would be done for ourselves) are neglected and suffered to perish; last wills unfulfilled and broken; God's ordinance set aside; and also for purgatory, foundations have been taken for sufficient satisfaction; so we have trifled away the ordinances of God and restitutions. Thus we have gone to hell with masses, dirges, and ringing of many a bell. And who can pull pilgrimages from idolatry, and purge purgatory from robbery, but he shall be in peril to come in suspicion of heresy with them? And verily the abuse of them cannot be taken away, but great lucre and advantage shall fall away from them, who had rather have profit with abuse, than lack the same with use; and that is the wasp that doth sting them, and maketh them to swell. And if purgatory were purged of all that it hath gotten, by setting aside restitution and robbing of Christ, it would be so poor, that it should not be able to feed so fat and trick up so many idle lubbers."

The zeal which Mr. Latimer felt for the truth impelled him to write a long letter to King Henry VIII the principal object of which was to secure the liberty of reading the Holy Scriptures.

With regard to the memorable actions of this worthy man, among many others this bold enterprise is to be specially noted—the manner of his sending a present to King Henry VIII. It was an old custom derived from the Romans, that, upon the 1st of January, every bishop should present the king with some handsome New Year's gift; some with gold, some with silver, some with a purse of money, or some other thing. Among the rest, Latimer, then Bishop of Worcester, presented to the king a New Testament for his New Year's gift, with a napkin having this posy about it: "Fornicators and adulterers God will judge."

Having given a sketch of the lives of these two eminent men, Ridley and Latimer, to the year 1555, we will relate their last scenes, wherein, like two great characters in a drama, they acted conjointly, till the curtain of death dropped upon them both.

EXAMINATION OF DR. RIDLEY,
IN SEPTEMBER, 1555.

On the last day of September, Dr. Ridley and Mr. Latimer were cited to appear before the Lords Commissioners in the Divinity School at Oxford, at eight o'clock. Dr. Ridley appeared first, and by-and-by Bishop Latimer. But because it was deemed proper to examine them separately, Bishop Latimer was kept back until Dr. Ridley had been interrogated.

The Bishop of Lincoln, in a long oration, exhorted Dr. Ridley to recant, and submit himself to the universal faith of Christ, endeavouring to prove the right of supremacy in the Church of Rome, charging him also with having formerly been favourable to their doctrine, and adducing many other arguments.

When he had concluded, Dr. Ridley desired his patience to suffer him to speak somewhat of the premises, lest the multitude of things might confound his memory; and having received permission, he said—

"I most heartily thank your lordship, as well for your gentleness as for your good and favourable zeal in this learned exhortation, in which I have marked especially three points, by which you sought to persuade me to leave my religion, which I perfectly know to be grounded, not upon man's imaginations and decrees, but upon the infallible truth of Christ's Gospel.

"The first point is this. That the see of Rome, taking its beginning from Peter, upon whom you say Christ hath built his Church, hath in all ages, lineally, from bishop to bishop, been brought to this time.

"Secondly, That even the holy fathers from time to time have confessed the same.

"Thirdly, That in that I was once of the same opinion, and together with you I did acknowledge the same.

"First, as touching the saying of Christ, from whence your lordship gathereth the foundation of the Church upon Peter, truly the place is not to be understood as you take it, as the circumstance of the place will declare. For after Christ had asked his disciples whom men judged him to be, and they answered that some had said he was a prophet,

some Elias, some one thing, some another, then he said,
'Whom say ye that I am?' Then Peter answered, 'I say that
thou art Christ, the Son of God.' To whom Christ answered, 'I say thou art Peter, and upon this stone I will
build my Church;' that is to say Upon this stone, not
meaning Peter himself, as though he would have consti-
tuted a mortal man so frail and brittle a foundation of his
stable and infallible Church: but upon this rock-stone, that
is, this confession of thine, that I am the Son of God, I will
build my Church. For this is the foundation and beginning
of all Christianity, with word, heart, and mind, to confess
that Christ is the Son of God.

"Here you see upon what foundation Christ's Church is
built, not upon the frailty of men, but upon the infallible
Word of God.

"Now as touching the lineal descent of the bishops in the
see of Rome, true it is that the patriarchs of Rome in the
apostles' time, and long after, were great maintainers of
Christ's glory, in which, above all other countries and
regions, there especially was preached the true Gospel, the
sacraments were most duly administered; and as, before
Christ's coming, it was a city so valiant in power and
martial affairs, that all the world was in a manner subject
to it, and after Christ's passion divers of the apostles there
suffered persecution for the Gospel's sake, so after that the
emperors, their hearts being illuminated, received the Gospel, and became Christians, the Gospel there, as well for
the fame of the place, flourished most, whereby the bishops
of that place were had in more reverence and honour, most
esteemed in all councils and assemblies, not because they
acknowledged them to be their head, but because the place
was most reverenced and spoken of, for the great power
and strength of the same. As now here in England, the
Bishop of Lincoln, in sessions and sittings, hath the
pre-eminence of other bishops, not that he is the head and
ruler of them, but for the dignity of the bishopric. Wherefore the doctors in their writings have spoken most reverently of this see of Rome, and in their writings preferred it;
and this is the prerogative which your lordship did rehearse
the ancient doctors to give to the see of Rome.

"In like manner, I cannot nor dare but commend,
reverence, and honour the see of Rome, as long as it
continued in the promotion and setting forth of God's
glory, and in due preaching of the Gospel, as it did many
years after Christ. But after that the bishops of that see,

seeking their own pride, and not God's honour, began to set themselves above kings and emperors, challenging to them the title of God's vicars, the dominion and supremacy over all the world.

"Now where you say I was once of the same religion as you are of, the truth is, I cannot but confess, the same. Yet so was St. Paul a persecutor of Christ. But in that you say I was one of you not long ago, in that I, in doing my message to my lord of Winchester, should desire him to stand stout in that gross opinion of the supper of the Lord, in very deed I was sent, as your lordship said, from the council to my lord of Winchester, to exhort him also to receive the true confession of justification; and because he was very refractory, I said to him, 'What make you so great a matter herein? You see many Anabaptists rise against the sacrament of the altar; I pray you, my lord, be diligent in confounding of them:' for at that time my lord of Winchester and I had to do with two Anabaptists in Kent. In this sense I willed my lord to be stiff in the defence of the sacraments against the detestable errors of Anabaptists, and not in the confirmation of that gross and carnal opinion now maintained.

"In like manner, respecting the sermon which I made at Paul's Cross, you shall understand that there were at St. Paul's, and divers other places, fixed railing bills against the sacrament, terming it 'Jack of the Box,' the 'Sacrament of the Halter,' 'Round Robin,' with such unseemly terms; for which causes I, to rebuke irreverent behaviour of certain evil-disposed persons, preached as reverently of that matter as I might, declaring what estimation and reverence ought to be given to it, what danger ensued the mishandling thereof, affirming in that sacrament to be truly and verily the body and blood of Christ, effectually by grace and spirit; which words the unlearned understanding not, supposed that I had meant of the gross and carnal being which the Romish decrees set forth, that a body having life and motion should be indeed under the shapes of bread and wine."

With that the Bishop of Lincoln, interrupting him, said—

Lincoln.—Mr. Ridley, consider your state, remember your former degrees, spare your body, especially consider your soul, which Christ so dearly bought with his precious blood; do not rashly cast away that which was precious in God's sight; enforce us not to do all that we may do, which is not only to publish you to be none of us, but to cut you off from the Church: we do not, nor can we condemn you to die (as most untruly hath been reported of us), but that is the office of the temporal judges; we only declare you to be not of the Church, and then you must, according to the tenor of them, and pleasure of the rulers, abide their determination, so that we, after we have given you up to the temporal rulers, have no further to do with you. But I trust, Mr. Ridley, we shall not have occasion to do what we may. I trust you will suffer us to rest in that point of our commission, which we most heartily desire, that is, upon recantation and repentance, to receive to reconcile you, and again to join you to the unity of the Church.

Dr. Ridley, notwithstanding frequent interruptions, spake as follows:—

Ridley.—My lord, I acknowledge an unspotted Church of Christ, in which no man can err, without which no man can be saved, which is spread through all the world, that is, the congregation of the faithful; neither do I alligate or bind the same to any one place, but confess the same to be universal; and where Christ's sacraments are duly administered, his Gospel truly preached and followed there doth Christ's Church shine as a city upon a hill, and as a candle in the candlestick: but rather it is such as you that would have the Church of Christ bound to a place, who appoint the same to Rome, that there and nowhere else is the foundation of Christ's Church. But I am fully persuaded that Christ's Church is everywhere founded, in every place where his Gospel is truly received and effectually followed. And in that the church of God is in doubt, I use herein the counsel of Vincentius Lyrinensis, whom I am sure you will allow, who, giving precepts how the catholic Church may be in all schisms and heresies known, writeth in this manner: "When," saith he, "one part is corrupted with heresies, then prefer the whole world before that one part; but if the greatest part be infected, then prefer antiquity." In like manner now, when I perceive the greatest part of Christianity to be infected with the poison of the see of Rome, I repair to the usage of the primitive Church, which I find quite contrary to the pope's decrees: as in that the priest receiveth alone, that it is made unlawful to the laity to receive in both kinds, and such like: wherefore it requireth that I prefer the antiquity of the primitive Church before the novelty of the Romish.

Lincoln.—Mr. Ridley, these faults which you charge the

see of Rome withal are indeed no faults. For, first, it was never forbid the laity, but that they might, if they demanded, receive under both kinds. You know also that Christ, after his resurrection, at the time he went with his apostles to Galilee, opened himself by breaking of bread. So that the Church seemeth to have authority by the Holy Ghost, whom Christ said he would send after his ascension, which should teach the apostles all truth, to have power to alter such points of the Scripture, ever reserving the foundation. But we came not, to reason the matter with you, but we have certain instructions ministered unto us, according to which we must proceed, proposing certain articles, unto which we require your answer directly, either affirmatively or negatively, which articles you shall hear now; and to-morrow, at eight o'clock, in St. Mary's Church, we will require and take your answer, and then according to the same proceed.

THE ARTICLES.

In the name of God, Amen. We, John of Lincoln, James of Gloucester, and John of Bristol, bishops.

1. We do object to thee, Nicholas Ridley, and to thee, Hugh Latimer, jointly and severally, first, that thou, Nicholas Ridley, in this high University of Oxford, in the year 1554, hast affirmed, and openly defended and maintained, and in many other times and places besides, that the true and natural body of Christ, after the consecration of the priest is not really present in the sacrament of the altar.

2. *Item.* That in the year aforesaid thou hast publicly affirmed and defended that in the sacrament of the altar remaineth still the substance of bread and wine.

3. *Item.* That in the said year thou hast openly affirmed, and obstinately maintained, that in the mass is no propitiatory sacrifice for the quick and the dead.

4. *Item.* That in the year, place, and months aforesaid, these the aforesaid assertions solemnly had been condemned, by the scholastical censure of this school, as heretical and contrary to the catholic faith, by Dr. Weston, prolocutor then of the Convocation House, as also by other learned men of both the universities.

5. *Item.* That the premises be true and openly known by public fame, as well to them near hand as also to them in distant places.

After examination upon the above articles, the Bishop of Lincoln concluded in the following words:—

"Mr. Ridley, I am sorry to see such stubbornness in you, that by no means you will be persuaded to acknowledge your errors, and receive the truth: but seeing it is so, because you will not suffer us to persist in the first, we must of necessity proceed to the other part of our commission. Therefore, I pray you, hearken to what I shall say." And forthwith he read the sentence of condemnation, which was written in a long process; the substance of which was, that the said Nicholas Ridley did affirm, maintain, and stubbornly defend certain opinions, assertions, and heresies, contrary to the Word of God, and the received faith of the Church, and could by no means be turned from his heresies. They therefore condemned him as an obstinate heretic, and adjudged him presently, both by word and in deed, to be degraded from the degree of a bishop, from the priesthood, and all the ecclesiastical orders; declaring him, moreover, to be no member of the Church, and therefore they committed him to the secular powers, of them to receive due punishment according to the temporal laws.

THE LAST EXAMINATION OF BISHOP LATIMER BEFORE THE COMMISSIONERS.

Dr. Ridley being committed as a prisoner to the mayor, Mr. Latimer was sent for.

The Bishop of Lincoln began in this manner—

"Mr. Latimer, although yesterday, after we had taken your answers to those articles which we proposed, we might have justly proceeded to judgment against you, especially in that you required the same yet having a good hope of your returning, desiring not your destruction, but rather that you would recant, revoke your errors, and turn to the Catholic Church, we deferred further process till this day; and now, according to the appointments, we have called you before us, to hear whether you are content to revoke your heretical assertions, and submit yourself to the determination of the Church."

Mr. Latimer here interrupted him by saying, "Your lordship doth often repeat the catholic Church, as though I should deny the same. No, my lord, I confess there is a catholic Church, to the determination of which I will stand, but not the church which you call catholic, which ought rather to be termed diabolic."

The notaries took his answer affirmatively. For the second article he referred himself to his answers made before.

After this the Bishop of Lincoln recited the third article, and required a determinate answer.

Latimer.—Christ made one oblation and sacrifice for the sins of the whole world, and that a perfect sacrifice; neither needeth there to be, nor can there be, any other propitiatory sacrifice.

The notaries took his answer affirmatively.

In like manner did he answer to the other articles, not varying from his former answers.

His answers being recorded by the notaries, the Bishop of Lincoln exhorted him to recant, and revoke his errors and false assertions.

Mr. Latimer answered that he neither would nor could deny his master Christ and his verity. The Bishop of Lincoln then desired him to hearken to him. Mr. Latimer accordingly hearkening for some new matter, the Bishop of Lincoln read his condemnation, after which the three bishops brake up their sessions, and dismissed the audience.

The bishop then committed Mr. Latimer to the mayor, saying, "Now he is your prisoner, Mr. Mayor."

And so Dr. Ridley and Mr. Latimer continued in custody till the 16th day of the said month of October.

THE BEHAVIOUR OF DR. RIDLEY
ON THE NIGHT BEFORE HE SUFFERED.

On the night before Ridley suffered, his beard and his legs were washed; and as he sat at supper, at the house of Mr. Irish, his keeper, he invited his hostess, and the rest at the table, to his marriage; "for," said he, "to-morrow I must be married," and he was as merry as ever he had been before. And wishing his sister to be at his marriage, he asked his brother, who was at the table, whether he thought she could find in her heart to be there, to which the latter answered, "Yes, I dare say, with all her heart;" at which he said he was glad to hear of her sincerity. At this discourse Mrs. Irish wept; but Dr. Ridley comforted her, saying, "Oh, Mrs. Irish! you love me not, I see well enough; for in that you weep, it doth appear you will not be at my marriage, neither are content therewith. Indeed, you are not so much my friend as I thought you had been. But quiet yourself; though my breakfast shall be somewhat sharp, yet my supper will be more pleasant."

When they arose, his brother offered to stay all night with him. But he said, "No, no; that you shall not. For I intend, God willing, to go to bed, and to sleep as quietly to-night as ever I did." On this his brother departed, exhorting him to be of good cheer, and to take his cross quietly, for his reward was great in heaven.

MARTYRDOM OF DR. RIDLEY, FORMERLY BISHOP OF LONDON, AND OF MR. LATIMER, FORMERLY BISHOP OF WORCESTER, ON THE 16TH OCTOBER, 1555.

The place for their execution was chosen on the north side of Oxford, in the ditch over against Baliol College; and for fear of any tumult that might arise to hinder the burning of the servants of Christ, the Lord Williams and the householders of the city were commanded by the queen's letters to be prepared to assist if required. When everything was in readiness, the prisoners were brought forth by the mayor and bailiffs.

Dr. Ridley, as he passed towards Bocardo, looked up where Dr. Cranmer lay, hoping to have seen him at the glass window, and spoken to him. Dr. Cranmer was engaged in a disputation with a Spanish friar, Soto, and his fellows, so that he could not see him. But Cranmer looked after them, and devoutly falling upon his knees, prayed to God to strengthen their faith and patience in their last but painful passage. Dr. Ridley then looking back, saw Mr. Latimer coming after, unto whom he said, "Oh, are you there?" "Yea," said Mr. Latimer, "have after, as fast as I can." So he followed a little way off, until they came to the stake. Dr. Ridley, entering the place first, earnestly holding up both his hands, looked towards heaven; then shortly after, seeing Mr. Latimer, with a cheerful look he ran to him and embraced him, saying, "Be of good heart, brother, for God will either assuage the fury of the flame, or else strengthen us to abide it."

He then went to the stake, and, kneeling down, prayed with great fervour, while Mr. Latimer following, kneeled also, and prayed with like earnestness. After this, they arose and conversed together, and, while thus employed, Dr. Smith began his sermon to them upon this text of St.

Paul, in the thirteenth chapter of the First Epistle to the Corinthians: "If I yield my body to the fire to be burnt, and have not charity, I shall gain nothing thereby."

At the conclusion of the sermon, which only lasted a quarter of an hour, Ridley said to Latimer, "Will you answer, or shall I?"

Mr. Latimer said, "Begin you first, I pray you."

"I will," said Dr. Ridley.

He then, with Mr. Latimer, kneeled to my Lord Williams, the Vice-Chancellor of Oxford, and the other commissioners, who sat upon a form, and said, "I beseech you, my lord, even for Christ's sake, that I may speak but two or three words."

And whilst my lord bent his head to the mayor and vice-chancellor, to know whether he might have leave to speak, the bailiffs and Dr. Marshal, the vice-chancellor, ran hastily unto him, and, with their hands stopping his mouth, said, "Mr. Ridley, if you will revoke your erroneous opinions, you shall not only have liberty so to do, but also your life."

"Not otherwise?" said Dr. Ridley.

"No," answered Dr. Marshal; "therefore, if you will not do so, there is no remedy: you must suffer for your deserts."

"Well," said the martyr, "so long as the breath is in my body, I will never deny my Lord Christ and his known truth. God's will be done in me." With that he rose, and said, with a loud voice, "I commit our cause to Almighty God, who will indifferently judge all."

To which Mr. Latimer added his old saying, "Well, there is nothing hid but it shall be opened;" and said he could answer Smith well enough, if he was permitted. They were then commanded to prepare immediately for the stake.

They accordingly obeyed with all meekness. Dr. Ridley gave his gown and tippet to his brother-in-law, Mr. Shipside, who all the time of his imprisonment, although he was not suffered to come to him, lay there, at his own charges, to provide him necessaries, which he sent him by the sergeant in charge. Some other of his apparel he also gave away; the others the bailiffs took.

He likewise made presents of other small things to gentlemen standing by, divers of whom were weeping pitifully. To Sir Henry Lea he gave a new groat; to my Lord Williams' gentleman, some napkins; some nutmegs, some pieces of ginger, his watch dial, and all that he had about him, he gave to those who stood near. Some plucked the points off his hose, and happy was he who could get the least rag for a remembrance of this good man.

Mr. Latimer quietly suffered his keeper to pull off his hose and his other apparel, which was very simple; and being stripped to his shroud, he seemed as comely a person as one could well see.

Then Dr. Ridley, standing as yet in his truss, or trousers, said to his brother, "It were best for me to go in my trouse still."

"No." said Mr. Latimer; "it will put you to more pain."

Whereunto Dr. Ridley said, "Be it, in the name of God," and so unlaced himself. Then, being in his shirt, he held up his hand, and said, "Oh, heavenly Father, I give unto thee most hearty thanks that thou hast called me to be a professor of thee, even unto death. I beseech thee, Lord God, have mercy on this realm of England, and deliver it from all her enemies."

Then the smith took a chain of iron and placed it about both their waists; and as he was knocking in the staple, Dr. Ridley took the chain in his hand, and, looking aside to the smith, said, "Good fellow, knock it in hard, for the flesh will have its course."

Then Dr. Ridley's brother (Shipside) brought him a bag of gunpowder and tied it about his neck. Dr. Ridley asked him what it was. He answered, "Gunpowder."

Then said he, "I will take it to be sent of God, therefore I will receive it. And have you any," said he, "for my brother?" (meaning Mr. Latimer).

"Yea, sir, that I have," said he.

"Then give it him," said he, "in time, lest you come too late."

So his brother went and carried it to Mr. Latimer.

They then brought a lighted faggot, and laid it at Dr. Ridley's feet; upon which Mr. Latimer said, "BE OF GOOD COMFORT, MR. RIDLEY, AND PLAY THE MAN! WE SHALL THIS DAY LIGHT SUCH A CANDLE, BY GOD'S GRACE, IN ENGLAND, AS I TRUST NEVER SHALL BE PUT OUT."

When Dr. Ridley saw the fire flaming up towards him, he cried out, with an amazing loud voice, "Into thy hands, O Lord, I commend my spirit: Lord, receive my spirit!" and continued often to repeat, "Lord, Lord, receive my spirit!"

Mr. Latimer cried as vehemently, "O Father of heaven,

receive my soul!" after which he soon died, seemingly with little pain.

But Dr. Ridley, owing to the bad arrangement of the fire (the faggots being green, and piled too high, so that the flames were kept down by the green wood, and burned fiercely beneath), was put to such exquisite pain, that he desired them, for God's sake, to let the fire come unto him: which his brother-in-law heard, but did not very well understand; so to rid him out of his pain (for which cause he gave attendance), and not well knowing what he did, in his own sorrow, he heaped faggots upon him, so that he quite covered him, which made the fire so vehement beneath, that it burned all Ridley's lower parts before it touched his upper, and made him struggle under the faggots. Ridley, in his agony, often desired the spectators to let the fire come to him, saying, "I cannot burn." Yet in all his torment he did not forget always to call upon God, "Lord, have mercy upon me!" yet intermingling his cry with "Let the fire come unto me, I cannot burn;" in which pains he laboured till one of the bystanders pulled the faggots from above with his bill, and where Ridley saw the fire flame up, he leaned himself to that side. As soon as the fire touched the gunpowder, he was seen to stir no more, but burned on the other side, falling down at Mr. Latimer's feet, his body being divided.

The dreadful sight filled almost every eye with tears, for some pitied their persons, who thought their souls had no need thereof.

The Life and Martyrdom of the Rev. Laurence Saunders, Who Was Burned at Coventry, February 8, 1555.

Notwithstanding the public prohibition of preaching issued in the first reign of Queen Mary, several pious ministers still continued to inculcate the pure doctrine of Christ, not as authorised preachers, but as private pastors of particular flocks. Among these was Laurence Saunders, a man of good parentage. He was educated at Eton, whence, at a proper age, he was elected to King's College, in Cambridge, of which he continued a scholar for three years, and profited in knowledge very much for that time.

In the beginning of King Edward's reign, when true religion was introduced, he resigned his mercantile pursuits, and being much given to study and books, obtained licence and began to preach. He was so liked by the authorities, that they appointed him to be divinity lecturer in the college at Fotheringham, after which he married, and in the connubial state led a blameless life. The college of Fotheringham being dissolved, he was appointed a reader in the minster at Lichfield, where he so conducted himself that his very adversaries bore testimony both to his learning and piety. After a certain space, he departed from Lichfield to a benefice in Leicestershire, called Church Langton, where he taught diligently and kept a liberal house. From thence he was called to take a benefice in the City of London, named Allhallows, in Bread Street.

On Sunday, October 15, Mr. Saunders preached a sermon in his parish, which caused such a commotion, that the Bishop of London sent an officer to arrest him summarily in the afternoon of the same day.

He continued in prison one year and three months, during which time he wrote several letters to Cranmer, Ridley, and Latimer, to his wife, and to others, certifying them both of the public calamity of the time and also of his private afflictions.

THE EXAMINATION OF THE REV. MR. SAUNDERS BEFORE THE QUEEN'S COUNCIL; GARDINER, BISHOP OF WINCHESTER, THE THEN CHANCELLOR, AND OTHER BISHOPS, BEING PRESENT.

In this examination the lord chancellor thus spake:

Lord Chancellor.—It is not unknown that you have been a prisoner for such abominable heresies and false doctrine as have been sown by you; and now it is thought good that mercy be showed to such as seek for it. Wherefore, if now you will show yourself comfortable, and come home again, mercy is ready. We must say that we have fallen in manner all: but now we are risen again, and returned to the Catholic Church; you must rise with us, and come home unto it. Give us forthwith a direct answer.

Saunders.—My lord, and my lords all, may it please your honours to give me leave to answer with deliberation.

Chancellor.—Leave off your painting and pride of speech: for such is the fashion of you all, to please yourselves in your glorious words. Answer, yes or no.

Saunders.—My lord, it is no time for me now to paint. And as for pride, there is no great cause why it should be in me; my learning I confess to be but small; and as for riches or worldly wealth, I have none at all. Notwithstanding, it standeth me in hand to answer your demand circumspectly, considering that one of these two extreme perils is likely to fall upon me, namely, the losing of a good conscience, or the losing of this my body and life. And I tell you truth, I love both life and liberty, if I could enjoy them without the hurt of my conscience.

Chancellor.—Conscience! you have none at all, but pride and arrogancy, dividing yourselves by singularity from the Church.

Saunders.—The Lord is the knower of all men's consciences. And where your lordship layeth to my charge this dividing myself from the Church, I do assure you that I live in the faith wherein I have been brought up since I was fourteen years of age, being taught that the power of the Bishop of Rome is but usurped, with many other abuses springing thereof. Yes, this I have received even at your hands, as a thing agreed upon by the Catholic Church and public authority.

Chancellor.—But have you received, by consent and authority, all your heresies of the blessed sacrament of the altar?

Saunders.—My lord, it is less offence to cut off an arm, hand, or joint of man, than to cut off the head. For the man may live though he lose an arm, hand, or joint; but he cannot without his head. Now you all had agreed to cut off the supremacy of the Bishop of Rome, whom now you will have to be the head of the Church again.

Bishop of London.—And if it please your lordship, I have his hand against the blessed sacrament. How say you to that?

Saunders.—What I have written, that I have written, and further I will not accuse myself. Nothing have you to burden me withal, for breaking of your laws since they were in force.

Chancellor.—Well, you are obstinate, and refuse liberty.

Saunders.—My lord, I may not buy liberty at such a price; but I beseech your honours to be means to the queen's majesty for such a pardon for us, that we may live and keep our consciences unclogged, and we shall live as most obedient subjects. Otherwise, I must say for myself, that by God's grace I will abide the utmost extremity that man may do against me, rather than act against my conscience.

Chancellor.—Ah, sirrah, you will live as you like. The Donatists did desire to live in singularity; but indeed they were not fit to live on earth: no more are you, and that you shall understand within these seven days; therefore, away with him.

Saunders.—Welcome be it, whatsoever the will of God shall be, either life or death. And I tell you truly, I have learned to die. But I exhort you to beware of shedding innocent blood. Truly it will cry. The Spirit of God rest upon you all. Amen.

This is the sum and form of my first examination.

This examination being ended, the officers led him out of the place, and stayed until the rest of his fellow-prisoners were likewise examined, that they might convey them all together to prison. Mr. Saunders, standing among the officers, seeing there a great multitude of people, spoke freely, warning them all of the wrath which they deserved by their falling from Christ to Antichrist; and exhorting them to rise again, and to embrace Christ with stronger faith, to confess him to the end, in defiance of Antichrist, sin, death, and the devil; so should they retain the Lord's blessing.

Having been excommunicated and delivered over to the secular power, he was brought by the sheriffs of London to the Compter, a prisoner in his own parish of Bread Street, whereat he rejoiced greatly, both because he found there a fellow-prisoner, Mr. Cardmaker, with whom he had much comfortable discourse, and because out of prison, as before out of a pulpit, he might have an opportunity of preaching to his parishioners.

On the 4th day of February, Bonner, Bishop of London, came to the prison to degrade him; which, when he had done, Mr. Saunders said to him, "I thank God I am none of your Church."

The day following in the morning, the sheriff of London delivered him to certain of the queen's guard, which were appointed to carry him to the city of Coventry, there to be burned.

On their arrival at Coventry, a poor shoemaker, who used to serve him with shoes, came to him, and said, "Oh, my good master, God strengthen and comfort you." "Good shoemaker," replied he, "I desire thee to pray for me, for I am the most unfit man for this high office that ever was appointed to it; but my gracious God and dear Father is able to make me strong enough." The same night he was put into the common gaol among other prisoners, where he slept little, but spent night in prayer, and instructing others.

The next day, being the 8th of February, he was led to the place of execution in the park, without the city, going in an old gown and a shirt, bare-footed, and oftentimes fell flat on the ground, and prayed. When he was come nigh to the place, the officer in charge of execution said to Mr. Saunders that he was one of them who marred the queen's realm with false doctrine and heresy; wherefore he had deserved death, but yet if he would revoke his heresies, the queen would pardon him; if not, yonder fire was prepared for him. To whom Mr. Saunders answered, "It is not I, nor my fellow-preachers of God's truth, that have hurt the queen's realm; but it is yourself, and such as you are, who have always resisted God's holy word; it is you who mar the queen's realm. I hold no heresies, but the doctrine of God, the blessed Gospel of Christ, that hold I, that believe I, that have I taught, and that will I never revoke."

With that the persecutor cried, "Away with him." Mr. Saunders advanced cheerfully towards the fire, and, falling down on the ground again, prayed earnestly. Rising, he went to the stake, and, embracing it in his arms, kissed it, saying, "Welcome the cross of Christ, welcome everlasting life." He was then fastened to the stake, and, after the application of the fire, soon fell asleep in Jesus.

The Martyrdom of Rawlins White.

Among the more humble persons who suffered martyrdom was Rawlins White, a fisherman, of Cardiff. As regards his religious feelings, it is undoubtedly true that at first he was a great partaker of the superstition which prevailed in the reign of Henry VIII. But, after that God, in his mercy, had caused the light of his Gospel to shine through the government of King Edward VI, Rawlins White began to dislike that which before he had embraced, and to have some good opinion of that to which before, through ignorance, he had been opposed.

Because the good man was unlearned, he knew of no ready way how to satisfy his new desire for the truth. At length he devised the following method of supplying his necessity: he had a little son, whom he sent to school to learn to read English. Now, after the child could read tolerably well, his father, every night after supper, made him read part of the Holy Scripture, and, now and then, some other good book, in which virtuous exercise the old man had such delight, that, as it seemed, he rather practised himself in the study of the Scripture than in his past calling; so that within a few years in the reign of King Edward, through the help of his son and conference with others, he so profited, that he was able not only to resolve his own doubts, but also to admonish others; and therefore, when opportunity presented, he would go from one place to another, visiting such of whose conversion he had a good hope.

When he had continued in this practice about five years, King Edward died, upon whose decease Queen Mary succeeded to the throne, and introduced the reign of persecution, the peril whereof at last pursued this good man so hotly, that he expected every hour to be sent to prison; whereupon many who had received comfort by his instructions began to persuade him to shift for himself, and dispose of his goods for the use of his wife and children.

Notwithstanding all opposition, he continued unmoved in well-doing, till at last he was arrested by the officers of the town as a man suspected of heresy; upon which he was cited before the Bishop of Llandaff, who was then at his house near Chepstow. After divers conflicts with the bishop and his chaplains, Rawlins White was committed to Chepstow Prison. From thence he was removed to the castle of Cardiff, where he continued for a whole year.

At the expiration of a year, the Bishop of Llandaff caused him to be brought from the castle of Cardiff unto his own house near Chepstow; and while he continued there, the bishop endeavoured, by various means, to reduce him to conformity. But when they found their threatenings and their flattering promises ineffectual, the bishop desired him to determine with himself, for he must either recant his opinions or else suffer the rigour of the law, and thereupon he assigned him a fixed day of determination; which day being come, the bishop with his chaplains went into his chapel, with a great number of the neighbours, before them. The bishop began by making a long discourse, declaring that the cause of his being sent for was his being known to hold heretical opinions, and that by his instructions many had been led into error. In conclusion, he exhorted him to consider his own state, and offered him favour if he recanted.

When the bishop had finished, Rawlins boldly replied, "My lord, I thank God I am a Christian man, and I hold no opinions contrary to the Word of God; and if I do, I desire to be reformed out of the Word of God, as a Christian ought to be."

The bishop then told him plainly that he must proceed against him according to law, and condemn him as a heretic.

"Proceed in your law, in God's name," said the fearless Rawlins; "but for a heretic you shall never condemn me while the world stands."

"But," said the bishop to his company, "before we proceed any further with him, let us pray to God that he would send some spark of grace upon him, and it may so chance that God, through our prayers, will here turn his heart." Accordingly, having prayed, the bishop said, "Now, Rawlins, wilt thou revoke thy opinions or not?"

The man of truth replied, "Surely, my lord, Rawlins you left me, Rawlins you find me, and, by God's grace, Rawlins I will continue."

When the bishop perceived that his hypocrisy was without effect, he sharply reproved him, and forthwith made ready to read the sentence; but upon some advice given to him by his chaplains, he thought it best first to say a mass, thinking that by so doing some change would be wrought in Rawlins.

In the meantime, Rawlins betook himself to prayer in a secret place, until the priest came to the consecration of the host, which is a principal part of their idolatry. When Rawlins heard the mass-bell ring, he rose out of his place, and came to the choir door, and there standing awhile, turned himself to the people, speaking these words: "Good people, if there be any brethren amongst you, or at least if there be but one brother amongst you, the same one bear witness at the day of judgment that I bow not to this idol," meaning the host that the priest elevated over his head.

Mass being ended, Rawlins was called again, when the bishop repeated his persuasions; but the blessed man continued so steadfast in his profession, that the prelate found his discourse fruitless, whereupon the bishop caused the definitive sentence to be read. Rawlins was then dismissed and carried to Cardiff, where he was put into the prison of the town, called Cockmarel, a very dark and loathsome dungeon.

Having continued a prisoner there for some time, the head officers of the town, who had the charge of his execution, were determined to burn him, because they would be the sooner rid of him, although they had not the writ of execution, as by law they should have; but by the advice of one H. Lewes, the recorder of the town, they sent to London for the writ above-named, upon the receipt whereof they hastened the execution. The day being at hand whereon the servant of God should crown his faith by martyrdom, he spent the night before in solemn preparation.

On perceiving that his time was near, he sent to his wife, and desired her by the messenger that she should make ready and send him his wedding garment, meaning the shirt in which he should be burned.

The hour of his execution having come, the martyr was brought out of prison. He was accompanied, or rather guarded, with a great number of bills and weapons, which sight when he beheld, "Alas!" said he, "what meaneth all this? By God's grace, I will not run away: with all my heart and mind I give God most hearty thanks that He hath made me worthy to abide all this for His holy name's sake."

He now came to a place where his poor wife and children stood weeping and making great lamentation, the sudden sight of whom so pierced his heart, that the tears trickled down his face. But soon afterwards, as though he were ashamed of this infirmity of his flesh, he began to be, as it were, angry with himself; insomuch that, striking his breast with his hand, he said, "Ah! flesh, hinderest thou me so? Well, I tell thee, do what thou canst, thou shalt not, by God's grace, have the victory."

By this time he approached the stake that had been set up, and was surrounded with some wood for the fire, which, when he beheld, he went forward boldly; but in going towards the stake, he fell down upon his knees, and kissed the ground; and, in rising, a little earth stuck to his nose, when he said, "Earth unto earth, and dust unto dust; thou art my mother, and unto thee I shall return."

Then he went cheerfully, and set his back close to the stake. A smith then came with a great chain of iron, whom when he saw, he cast up his hand, and, with a loud voice, gave God great thanks.

When the smith had fastened him to the stake, the officers began to lay on more wood, with a little straw and reeds, wherein the good old man was no less occupied than the rest; for as far as he could reach his hands, he would pluck the straw and reeds, and lay it about him in places most convenient for his speedy dispatch.

When all things were ready, directly over against the stake, in the face of Rawlins White, there was a stand erected, which a priest mounted and addressed the people, who were numerous, because it was market-day. When Rawlins perceived him, and considered the cause of his coming, he, reaching a little straw unto himself, made two little stays, and set them under his elbows. The priest proceeded with the sermon, wherein he spake of many things touching the authority of the Church of Rome. At last, he came to the sacrament of the altar, when he began to inveigh against Rawlins' opinions, in which harangue he cited the place of Scripture whereby the idolatrous mass is commonly defended. When Rawlins perceived that he went about not only to preach and teach the people false doctrine, but also to confirm it by Scripture, he suddenly started up, and beckoned his hands to the people, saying twice, "Come hither, good people, and hear not a false prophet preaching." Then said he unto the preacher, "Ah, thou wicked hypocrite! dost thou presume to prove thy false doctrine by Scripture?"

Upon this, fearing the effects of his truth upon the people, some that stood by cried out, "Put fire! put fire!" which being done, the straw and reeds cast up a great and sudden flame. While the martyr was being consumed, which was a somewhat long process, he cried with a loud voice, "O Lord, receive my spirit!" until he could not open his mouth. At last, the extremity of the fire was so vehement against his legs, that they were wasted before the rest of his body was hurt, which made his body fall over the chain into the fire sooner than it would have done.

The History and Martyrdom of the Rev. George Marsh, Who Was Burned at West Chester, April 24, 1555.

Mr. Marsh was born in the parish of Deane, in the county of Lancashire, and having received a good education, was brought up by his parents to trade and industry. About the twenty-fifth year of his age he married a young woman of the country, with whom he continued, earning their living upon a farm. His wife dying, he went into the university of Cambridge, where he studied, and became a minister of God's holy word and sacraments, and was for a while curate to the Rev. Laurence Saunders, in which situation he earnestly set forth the true religion, by his godly sermons, to the weakening of false doctrine, as well there and in the parish of Deane, as elsewhere in Lancashire.

At length he was apprehended, and closely imprisoned in

Chester, by George Coates, bishop of that see, where he was kept about the space of four months, not being permitted to have any relief or comfort from his friends. The particulars of his story are recorded by his own pen as follows:—

THE FIRST EXAMINATION OF THE REV. GEORGE MARSH, BEFORE THE EARL OF DERBY AND OTHERS, WRITTEN BY HIMSELF.

"On the Monday before Palm Sunday, which was the 12th of March, it was told me, at my mother's house, that Roger Wrinstone, with other of Mr. Barton's servants, made diligent search for me in Bolton; and when they perceived that I was not there, they gave strict charge to Robert Ward and Robert Marsh to find and bring me to Mr. Barton the day following, with orders to be brought before the Earl of Derby, to be examined in matters of religion.

"I, knowing this by my friends, was diversely affected; my mother and other friends advising me to fly and avoid the peril. To their counsel my weak flesh would gladly have consented, but my spirit did not fully agree, thinking and saying to myself, that if I fled away, it would be said that I did not only fly the country and my nearest and dearest friends, but much rather from Christ's holy word. I, being thus with their counsel and advice, and the thoughts and counsels of my own mind, drawn, as it were, divers ways, went from my mother's house, saying I would come again in the evening.

"In the meantime, I ceased not, by earnest prayer, to seek counsel of God, the giver of all good gifts, and of my friends, whose pious judgments and knowledge I much trusted to.

"I then returned to my mother's house, where several of Mr. Barton's servants had been seeking me; and when they could not find me, they strictly charged my brother and William Marsh to seek me that night, and bring me to Smethehills the next day. They, being so charged, were gone to seek me in Adderton or elsewhere.

"Thus, intending before to have been all night with my mother, but now considering that my tarrying there would disquiet her, I departed and stayed all night with an old friend of mine.

"At my first awakening a person came to me from a faithful friend with letters, who said my friend's advice was that I should in no wise fly, but abide and boldly confess the faith of Jesus Christ. At those words I was so confirmed and established in my conscience, that henceforth I consulted not whether it were better to fly or to remain, but was determined that I would not fly, but go to Mr. Barton, and there present myself, and patiently bear such cross as it should please God to lay upon my shoulders.

"I arose early next morning, and after I had said the English Litany (as my custom was) with other prayers, kneeling by my friend's bed-side, I prepared myself to go toward Smethehills; and, on my way thither, I went into the houses of Henry Widdowes, of my mother-in-law, of Ralph Yeton, and of the wife of Thomas Richardson, desiring them to pray for me, and have me commended to all my friends, and to comfort my mother, and be good to my little children, for, as I supposed, they would see my face no more. I then took leave of them—not without tears shed on both sides, and came to Smethehills about nine o'clock, when I presented myself to Mr. Barton, who showed me a letter from the Earl of Derby, wherein he was commanded to send me with others to Lathum.

"Whereupon he charged my brother and William Marsh to bring and deliver me the next day by ten o'clock before the earl or his council.

"We accordingly went to my mother's, where I, praying, took my leave of her, the wife of Richard Marsh, and both their households, they and I both weeping. The next day we came to Lathum betimes, and remained there till four o'clock in the afternoon.

"Then was I called by Roger Mekinson to my lord and his council.

"After many other questions, my lord commanded me to come to the board, when he gave me pen and ink in my hand, and commanded me to write my answers to the questions respecting the sacrament; accordingly, I wrote as I had answered before; whereat he, being much offended, commanded me to write a more direct answer.

"I then took the pen and wrote that further I knew not; whereat he, being sore grieved, after many threatenings, said I should be put to a shameful death like a traitor, and sometimes giving me fair words if I would turn and be conformable as others were.

"A day or two after, I was sent for to the Vicar of Prescot and the parson of Grapnal. Our conversation was

concerning the mass. Being asked what offended me in it, I
answered the whole offended me; first, because it was in a
strange language, whereby the people were not edified,
contrary to St. Paul's doctrine (I Cor. xiv.); and, secondly,
because of the manifold and intolerable abuses and errors
contained therein, contrary to Christ's priesthood and
sacrifice.

"They demanded in what place thereof; I named several,
which places they went about with gentle and far-sought
interpretations to mitigate, saying those places were understood far otherwise than the words did purport or than I
did take them."

After this Mr. Marsh was sent to Lancaster Castle. Some
weeks later he was removed to Chester, and placed in the
bishop's liberty, where his lordship frequently conferred
with him, and used his utmost endeavours to bring him to
an acknowledgment of the corporeal presence, and, in
short, of all the tenets and practices of the Church of
Rome.

After the Bishop of Chester had taken his pleasure in
punishing his prisoner, and in often reviling him with the
odious name of heretic, he caused him to be brought forth
into a chapel in the cathedral church.

After many vexatious proceedings, at a subsequent interview the bishop took a writing out of his bosom, and began
to read the sentence of condemnation; but when he had
proceeded half through it, the chancellor interrupted him,
and said, "Good my lord, stay, stay: for if you read any
further, it will be too late to call it again." The bishop
accordingly stopped, when his popish priests, and many
other of the ignorant people, called upon Mr. Marsh, with
many earnest words, to recant.

The bishop again asked him whether he would not have
the queen's mercy in time. He answered, he gladly desired
the same, and loved her grace as faithfully as any of them;
but yet he durst not deny his Saviour Christ, lest he should
lose His mercy everlasting, and so win everlasting death.

The bishop then put his spectacles on, and read forward
about five or six lines, when the chancellor, with flattering
words and smiling countenance, again called to the bishop,
and said, "Yet, good my lord, once again stay; for if that
word be spoken, all be past; no relenting will then serve:"
and the bishop said, "I would stay if it would be."

"How sayest thou?" said he; "wilt thou recant?" Many
of the priests again exhorted him to recant and save his

life; to whom he answered, "I would as fain live as you, if in so doing I should not deny my Master, Christ, and then he would deny me before his Father in heaven."

The bishop then read out his sentence unto the end, and afterwards said unto him, "Now I will no more pray for thee than I will for a dog." Mr. Marsh answered, that, notwithstanding that, he would pray for his lordship. After this the bishop delivered him to the sheriffs of the city; when his late keeper, finding he should lose him, said, with tears, "Farewell, good George!" which caused the officers to carry him to a prison at the north gate, where he was very strictly kept until his execution, during which time he had small comfort or relief from any creature.

The day of his martyrdom having arrived, the sheriffs of the city, went to the north gate, and thence brought him forth, with a lock upon his feet.

When he came to the place of execution without the city, near unto Spital-Boughton, one Cawdry, being then a deputy chamberlain of Chester, showed Mr. Marsh a writing under a great seal, saying that it was a pardon for him if he would recant. He answered, forasmuch as it tended to pluck him from God, he would not receive it on that condition.

He now began to address the people, showing the cause of his death, and would have exhorted them to be faithful unto Christ; whereupon one of the sheriffs told him there must be no sermonising now, to whom he said, "Master, I cry you mercy," and then, kneeling down, said his prayers, put off his clothes unto his shirt, and was chained to the post, having a number of fagots under him, and a barrel, with pitch and tar in it, over his head. The fire being unskilfully made, and the wind driving it to and fro, he suffered great agony in his death, which, nevertheless, he bore with Christian patience.

When he had been a long time tormented in the fire without moving, having his flesh so broiled and puffed up, that they who stood before him supposed he had been dead, he suddenly spread abroad his arms, saying, "Father of heaven, have mercy upon me!" and so yielded his spirit into the hands of the Lord.

The Martyrdom of Mr. William Flower.

William Flower, otherwise named Branch, was born at Snow Hill, in Cambridgeshire, at which place he went to school some years, and afterwards to the abbey of Ely, where, after he had remained awhile, he became a professed monk, until the age of twenty-one years, or thereabouts, before which period he was also ordained priest, and celebrated mass. After that, by reason of a visitation and certain injunctions by the authority of Henry VIII, he forsook the house, and, casting from him the monk's habit, assumed the habit of a secular priest, and returned to Snow Hill, and there celebrated mass and taught children for about half a year.

He then went to Ludgate, in Suffolk, where he served as a secular priest about a quarter of a year; from thence he went to Stoniland, where he served as a secular priest also, until the coming out of the six articles, when he departed and went into Gloucestershire, where, after he had abode awhile, he took a wife, according to God's holy ordinance, with whom he ever after faithfully and honestly continued. In Lambeth, near London, he hired a house, where he and his wife dwelt together; however, for the most part he was always abroad, except once or twice in a month when he visited his wife. Being at home once upon Easter Sunday, he went over the water into St. Margaret's Church, at Westminster, when, seeing a priest, named John Cheltam, administering the sacrament of the altar to the people, he was so provoked thereat, that he struck and wounded him upon the head, and also upon the arm and hand, with his wood knife, the priest having at the same time in his hand a chalice, covered with a paten, containing certain consecrated hosts therein.

Being examined before Bishop Bonner, he confessed he had done wrong, and submitted himself willingly to the appointed punishment. Howbeit, touching his belief in the sacrament and the popish ministration thereof, he neither would nor did submit himself.

Being apprehended and confined in the Gatehouse at Westminster, having as many irons as he could bear, he was afterwards summoned before Bishop Bonner, his ordinary (April 19, 1555), where the bishop, after he had sworn him upon a book, ministered articles and interrogatories to him. Previous to this, the following conversation took place between Mr. Flower and Mr. Robert Smith, a fellow-prisoner:—

Smith.—Friend, as I understand that you profess the Gospel, I am bold to come unto you, and, in the way of communication, to demand and learn a truth at your own mouth of certain things by you committed, to the astonishment not only of me, but of others that also profess the truth.

Flower.—I praise God for his great goodness in showing me the light of his holy Word; and I give you hearty thanks for your visitation, in ending, by God's grace, to declare all the truth that you shall demand lawfully of me in all things.

Smith.—Then I desire you to show me the truth of your deed committed on John Cheltam, priest, in the church, as near as you can, that I may hear from your own mouth how it was.

Flower.—I came from my house at Lambeth, over the water, and entering into St. Margaret's Church, and there seeing the people falling down before a most detestable idol, being moved with extreme zeal for my God, whom I saw before my face dishonoured, I drew forth my hanger, and struck the priest which administered the same unto them, whereupon I was immediately apprehended.

Smith—Did you not know the person that you struck, or were you not zealous upon him for any evil will or hatred between you at any time?

Flower—No, verily; I never, to my knowledge, saw the person before, neither had evil will or malice.

Smith.—Do you think that thing to be well done and after the rule of the Gospel?

Flower.—I confess all flesh to be subject to the power of Almighty God, whom he maketh his ministers to do his will and pleasure; not only changing decrees, but also planting zeals to his honour, against all order and respect of flesh and blood.

Smith.—Think you it convenient for me or any other to do the like by your example?

Flower.—No, verily; neither do I know, if it were to do again, whether I could do it again; for I was up very early at St. Paul's Church upon Christ's day in the morning, to have done it in my jealousy; but when I came there I was no more able to do it than now to undo that which is done; and yet now being compelled by the Spirit, not only to come over the water and to enter the church, but being in mind fully content to die for the Lord, I gave over my flesh willingly without all fear, I praise God. Wherefore I cannot teach you to do the like, first, because I know not what is in you; secondly, because the rules of the Gospel command us to suffer with patience all wrongs and injury; yet, nevertheless, if He makes you worthy that hath made me zealous, you shall not be hindered, judged, nor condemned.

Smith.—Are you not assured to have death ministered unto you for the act, and even with extremity?

Flower.—I did, before the deed committed, adjudge my body to die for the same, whereupon I carried about me in writing my opinion of God and the Holy Scriptures, that, if it had pleased God to have given them leave to have killed my body in the church, they might in the said writing have seen my hope, which, I praise God, is laid up safe within my breast, notwithstandinng any death that may be ministered upon my body in this world, being ascertained of everlasting life through Jesus Christ our Lord, and being most heartily sorry for all my offences committed in this flesh, and trusting shortly, through his mercy, to cease from the same.

Smith.—I need not examine or commune with you of the hope that you have any further; for I perceive, God be praised, you are in good state.

And thus Robert Smith departing, left him in the dungeon, and went again to his ward.

Now, to return to the matter of his examination. We showed before that, after his striking the priest, first he was taken to the Gatehouse; then, being examined before Bishop Bonner, he had articles ministered against him, to which the following are his answers:—

WILLIAM FLOWER'S ANSWERS.

"To the first article he answereth and confesseth the same to be true in every part thereof, except that he never consented and agreed in his heart to be a monk.

"The second he confesseth to be true in every part, howbeit he saith that he never did nor yet doth esteem the said order of priesthood according to the order of the said Catholic Church, because he was offended therewith in his conscience.

"To the third article he answereth that he intended to live in holy matrimony, and, not forgetting God, did marry Alice Pulton, and believed that he did according to God's laws; further confessing and believing that all the time when he was professed monk and made priest he did thereby utterly forget God, but that when he did marry Alice Pulton, and, continuing with her, did beget three children, he did remember God.

"To the fourth he answereth and believeth the same to be true in every part thereof.

"To the fifth he confesseth that his conscience, being greatly offended with John Cheltam, priest, for administering the sacrament of the altar to the people at the place and time specified in this article, he did so strike him with his hanger, or wood knife, as well upon his head as upon other parts and places upon his body, which he remembereth not, whereby the blood was shed in the church, as he believeth, having, as he saith, no other cause so to do, but only that his conscience was offended and grieved in that the same priest did so give and administer the said sacrament to the people.

"To the sixth he answereth that whether he be so excommunicated or accursed, as is contained in this article, he referreth himself to the ecclesiastical laws."

After the depositions of certain witnesses were taken, the bishop asked him if he knew any cause why sentence should not be read, and he be pronounced a heretic. Mr. Flower answered, "I have nothing at all to say, for I have already said unto you all that I have to say; and what I have said I will not go from, therefore do what you will." The bishop then proceeded to the sentence, condemning and excommunicating him for a heretic, and after pronouncing him to be degraded, committed him to the secular power. Upon the 24th day of April he was brought to the place of martyrdom, which was in St. Margaret's Churchyard at Westminster, where the offence was committed.

Mr. Cholmley now came to him, desiring him to recant his heresy, whereby he might do good and not be condemned, "Sir," answered the martyr, "I beseech you, for God's sake, to be contented; for what I have said I have said, and I have been of this faith from the beginning, and I trust to the living God he will give me his Holy Spirit so to continue to the end."

After this, his hand, with which he had struck the priest, was held up against the stake, and struck off, his left hand being fastened behind him. When the fire was applied, he cried aloud, "Oh, thou Son of God, have mercy upon me, and receive my soul!" And thus ended his mortal career.

The Martyrdom of Mr. John Cardmaker and Mr. John Warne, May 30, 1555.

Mr. Cardmaker had been an observant friar before the

dissolution of the abbeys; he afterwards married, and in
King Edward's time was appointed a reader in St. Paul's,
where the papists were so enraged against him for his
doctrine's sake, that in his reading they cut and mangled
his gown with their knives. Mr. Cardmaker being apprehended in the beginning of Queen Mary's reign, with Mr.
Barlow, Bishop of Bath, was brought to London and put in
the Fleet Prison, King Edward's laws being yet in force.
But after the sitting of that Parliament, the pope was again
acknowledged as supreme head of the English Church, and
the bishops had also gotten power and authority officially
to exercise their tyranny. These two were brought before
the Bishop of Winchester, the Lord Chancellor, and others
appointed by commission, to examine the faith of such as
were then prisoners; and as unto others before, so now
unto them the chancellor offered the queen's mercy if they
would agree and be conformable.

Mr. Warne being examined upon certain articles on the
23rd of May, answered for the same, confessing the
articles and contents thereof to be true, according as they
were objected in every part, subscribing also the same with
his hand: such strength and fortitude did God's Holy Spirit
work in him, that he stood firmly to the defence of the
doctrine of the Lord Jesus Christ.

The bishop then seeing that, notwithstanding all his fair
promises and terrible threatenings, he could not prevail,
finished this examination with the definitive sentence of
condemnation, and charged the sheriffs of London with
him, under whose custody he remained in Newgate until
the 30th day of May, the day appointed for his execution.
When the solemn hour had arrived, Mr. Warne and Mr.
Cardmaker were conducted to the place where they should
suffer; and having come thither, the sheriffs called Mr.
Cardmaker aside, and talked with him secretly, during
which time Mr. Warne, having prayed, was chained to the
stake, and had wood and reeds arranged about him.

The people who had heard that Mr. Cardmaker was
likely to recant, were much afflicted, thinking that he
would do so at the burning of Mr. Warne. At length Mr.
Cardmaker left the sheriffs, and came towards the stake,
and kneeled down and offered up a long prayer in silence.
His prayer ended, he rose, put off his clothes unto his shirt,
and advanced with a bold courage to the stake, and kissed
it; then taking Mr. Warne by the hand, he heartily comforted him, and cheerfully gave himself to be bound. The

people seeing this done so suddenly, and contrary to their expectation, cried out for joy, as men delivered out of a great doubt, saying, "God be praised! the Lord strengthen thee, Cardmaker! the Lord Jesus receive thy spirit!" And this continued until the executioner set fire to them, and both their souls had passed through the fire to the blessed rest among God's martyrs, to enjoy the crown of victory prepared for the elect warriors of Christ Jesus.

The Proceedings of Bishop Bonner Against John Tooly, Whose Body Being Taken Out of His Grave, Was Given to the Secular Power, and So Burned for a Heretic

There was, about the time that the Spaniards began first to make a stir in England, one John Tooly, a poulterer in London, who conspired with others to rob a Spaniard at St. James's, which was reputed to be a more grievous crime owing to the court's favour to this nation, because of Queen Mary's marriage with King Philip of Spain. Tooly, being found guilty, was sentenced to be hanged.

Being led to the gallows at Charing Cross, while standing upon the cart, he read a certain prayer in a printed book, and two other prayers written in two several papers, desiring the people present to pray for him, and bear him witness that he died a Christian, and that he trusted to be saved only by the merits of Christ's passion and shedding of his blood, and not by any masses, images or saints, which were devised by the Bishop of Rome; and as he and two others, his fellows, who were there hanged with him, did steal and rob for covetousness, so the Bishop of Rome sold his masses from the same motives: "from whose tyranny," continued he, "and all his detestable enormities, from false doctrine and heresy, and from the contempt of thy word and commandment, good Lord, deliver us."

Then he addressed the people, saying, "All you who are true Christians, say with me, Amen;" when immediately three hundred persons and upwards answered, "Amen," thrice.

As soon as the report of this business reached the ears of the priests and prelates, a council was called together, as though it had been a matter of great importance, and it was thought meet that the insult to the pope's holiness should be revenged with fire and fagot. It is probable that Cardinal Pole was no small sharer in this sentence. By this cardinal's orders, the bones of Tooly, were taken up and burned in London, June the 4th.

The Life and Martyrdom of Thomas Haukes.

Thomas Haukes was of the county of Essex, of respectable parents, and brought up from his childhood as a gentleman. His fervent devotion and singular love to true religion rendered him an amiable character.

Haukes, following the fashion of the court, as he grew in years, entered into service with the Earl of Oxford, with whom he remained a long time, being esteemed and loved by all the household, so long as Edward VI lived. But after the king's death all things began to go backward, religion to decay, true piety not only to wax cold, but also to be in danger everywhere, and chiefly in the houses of the great. Haukes, misliking the state of things, and forsaking the nobleman's house, departed thence to his own home, where he might more freely give himself to God, and follow his conscience.

In the meantime, Haukes had a son born, whose baptism was deferred to the third week, because he would not suffer him to be baptized after the papistical ritual. This the adversaries would not suffer, but laying hands upon him, brought him to the Earl of Oxford, there to be reasoned with as unsound in religion, as he seemed to contemn the sacraments of the Church.

The earl, either intending not to trouble himself in such matters, or else feeling himself unequal to contend with him in religious arguments, sent him up to London with a messenger and letters, and put him in the hands of Bonner, Bishop of London, who began to communicate with Mr. Haukes, first asking what induced him to leave his child unchristened so long.

Haukes.—Because we are bound to do nothing contrary to the Word of God.

Bonner.—Why, baptism is commanded by the Word of God.

Haukes.—His institution therein I do not deny.

Bonner.—What deny you, then?

Haukes.—I deny all things invented and devised by man.

Bonner.—What things are those that be devised by man, that you are so offended withal?

Haukes.—Your oil, your cream, your salt, your spittle, your candle, and your conjuring of water.

Bonner.—Ah! sir, you are a right Scripture man, for you will have nothing but the Scripture. There is a great number of your countrymen of your opinion. I perceive you are a stubborn fellow; I must, therefore, go to work another way with you, to win you.

Haukes.—Whatsoever you do, I am ready to suffer it, for I am in your hands to abide it.

Bonner.—Well, you are so; come on your ways, you shall go in, and I will use you Christian-like: you shall have meat and drink, such as I have in my house: but in any wise talk not.

Haukes.—I purpose to talk nothing but the Word of God and truth.

Bonner.—I will have no heresy talked on in my house.

Haukes.—Why, is the truth become heresy? God hath commanded that we should have none other talk in our houses, in our beds, at our meat, and by the way, but all truth.

Bonner.—If you will have my favour, be ruled by my counsel.

Haukes.—Then I trust you will grant me my request.

Bonner.—What is that?

Haukes.—That your doctors and servants give me no occasion: for if they do, I will surely utter my conscience.

"And so thus we departed, and went to dinner, and I dined at the steward's table.

"After dinner, his chaplains and his men began to talk with me. But amongst all others, there was one Darbyshire, Principal of Broadgates, in Oxford, and the bishop's kinsman, who said that I was too curious: 'for ye will have,' said he, 'nothing but your little pretty God's book.'"

Haukes.—And is not that sufficient for my salvation?

Bonner.—Yes; it is sufficient for our salvation, but not for our instruction.

Haukes.—God send me the salvation and you the instruction.

"We then departed until even-song time; and ere even-song was begun, my lord called me into the chapel and said—

Bonner.—The sacrament of the altar you seem to be sound in.

Haukes.—In the sacrament of the altar? Why, sir, I do not know it.

Bonner.—Well, we will make you to know it, and believe in it too, before we have done with you.

Haukes.—No; that shall ye never do.

Bonner.—Yes; a faggot will make you do it.

Haukes.—No; a fig for your faggot! What God thinketh meet to be done, that shall ye do, and more ye shall not do.

Bonner.—Do you not believe that there remaineth in the blessed sacrament of the altar, after the words of consecration be spoken, no more bread, but the very body and blood of Christ?

Haukes.—I do believe as Christ hath taught me.

Bonner.—Why, did not Christ say, "Take, eat; this is my body?"

Haukes.—Christ said so; but therefore it followeth not that the sacrament of the altar is so as you teach, neither did Christ ever teach it so to be.

Bonner.—Why, the Catholic Church taught it so, and they were of Christ's Church.

Haukes.—How prove you it? The apostles never taught it so. Read the Acts, the second and the twentieth. Neither St. Peter nor St. Paul ever taught it, nor insitituted it so.

Bonner.—Ah, sir! you will have no more than the Scripture teacheth, but even as Christ hath left it bare.

Haukes.—He that teacheth me any otherwise, I will not believe him.

Bonner.—Why, then you must eat a lamb, if you will have but Christ's institution only.

Haukes.—Nay, that is not so, for before Christ instituted the sacrament, that ceremony ceased, and then began the sacrament.

Bonner.—Alas! you know not how it began, neither of the institution.

Haukes.—Except you teach me by the Word of God, I will never credit you nor believe you.

"And thus we concluded."

SECOND EXAMINATION OF MR. HAUKES.

"The Bishop of Winchester, then being chancellor, preached that day at St. Paul's Cross, and the Bishop of London said to my keeper, "I think your man will not go to the sermon to-day.'

Haukes.—Yes, my lord; I pray you, let me go, and that which is good I will receive, and the rest I will leave behind me.

"And so I went. And when the sermon was done, I and my keeper came to the bishop's house, and there we remained till dinner was over, when the bishop called for me, and asked me if I was the same man that I was before.

Haukes.—I am no changeling, nor none will be.

Bonner.—You shall find me no changeling neither.

"And so he returned into his chamber, and there he wrote the side of a sheet of paper.

"Then said the bishop's men and his chaplains that my lord commanded me to talk with him. Then they who stood by cried, with a great noise, 'Hang him! burn him! it is a great pity that he lives.'

"With that came the bishop, bringing a letter in his hand, which he had written in my name, and read it unto me after this manner: 'I, Thomas Haukes, do hereby confess and declare before my said ordinary, Edmund, Bishop of London, that the mass is abominable and detestable,and full of all superstition, and also, as concerning the sacrament of the body and blood of Christ, commonly called the sacrament of the altar, that Christ is in no part thereof, but only in heaven.'

"Then he went farther with his writing, and said, 'I, Thomas Haukes, have talked with my said ordinary, and with certain good, godly, and learned men; notwithstanding I stand still in mine opinion.'

Haukes.—Shall I grant you to be good, godly, and learned men, and yet grant myself to stand in a contrary opinion? No; I will not grant you to be good, godly, and learned men.

Bonner.—You will grant that you have talked with us, the other I will put out for your pleasure.

"He then proceeded: 'Here, unto this bill have I set my hand.'

"And then he offered me the bill and his pen, and bade me set my hand to it.

Haukes.—You shall not have my hand to anything of your making or devising.

Bonner.—Wilt thou not set to thy hand? It shall be to thy shame for the denying it.

"And then he called all his doctors, and said he would have every man's hand to it that was in the chamber. And so he had all their hands to it, and said, 'He that will not set his hand to it, I would he were hanged.' And so said all his chaplains.

"Then the bishop thrust me on the breast with great anger, and said he would be even with me and with all such proud knaves in Essex.

Haukes.—You shall do no more than God shall give you leave.

"Then the bishop took the bill and read it again; and when he saw that he could not have my hand to it, then he would have had me to take it into my hand, and to give it him again.

Haukes.—What need that ceremony? Neither shall it come into my hand, heart, or mind.

"Then he wrapt it up, and put it in his bosom, and went away in great anger, and called for his horse, for the same day he rode on his visitation into Essex: and so I went to prison again with my keeper. This was the second time of my examination."

After all these private conferences with Mr. Haukes in the bishop's house, the bishop, seeing no hope of winning him over, was determined to proceed against him after the course of his popish law.

For his adhesion to the faith, Bonner sentenced Haukes to death. On his way thither the godly man lost no opportunity of speaking a word in season for the salvation of his attendants.

When Mr. Haukes was led to the fatal spot, he patiently prepared himself for the fire, and was bound to the stake by a strong chain, cast about his waist. Having promised his friends to show a disregard of pain, he agreed that, God helping him, he would, during his agonies, lift up his hands above his head towards heaven. After the noble man had been some time in the fire, his speech was lost, his skin thoroughly shrivelled, his fingers burnt away to black stumps—yet, mindful of his promise, he suddenly stretched forth his burning hands over his head, and struck; or clapped them three times together; then, sinking down in the fire, he gave up his spirit, June 10th, 1555.

The History of Mr. Thomas Wats.

Thomas Wats was a linendraper, of Billericay, in the county of Essex, in the diocese of London. Before he was apprehended he disposed of his stock-in-trade, bestowing much of his cloth upon the poor; and, being in daily expectation of the virulence of his enemies, he had arranged his concerns, for the sake of his wife and children. On the 26th of April he was apprehended and brought before the Lord Rich and other commissioners, at Chelmsford, and there being accused of not coming to church, was upon the same charge examined before the Lord Rich and others.

When Mr. Wats came before the Lord Rich and the

justices at the sessions at Chelmsford, Lord Rich spoke to him as follows:—

"Wats, you be brought hither, as I understand, because of disobedience to the king and queen's laws. You will not come to the church, you will not hear mass; but have your conventicles a sort of you in corners, contrary to the king and queen's proceeding."

To which Mr. Wats answered, "My lord, if I have offended a law, I am subject to the law."

Justice Brown then answered him, "Wats, I pray thee tell me who has been they schoolmaster to teach thee this religion, or where didst thou first learn it?"

"Forsooth," said Wats, "even of you, sir; you taught it me, and none more than you. For in King Edward's days, in open sessions, you spoke against this religion now used —no preacher more. You then said the mass was abominable, and all their trumpery besides, wishing and earnestly exhorting that none should believe therein, and that our belief should be only in Christ; and you then said that whosoever should bring in any strange nation to rule here, it were treason, and not to be suffered."

Then Mr. Brown said to my Lord Rich, "He belies me, my lord. What a knave is this! He will soon belie me behind my back, when he doth it before my face."

"I dare say he doth so," said my lord.

The commissioners being weary of him, or else, like Gallio, not willing to meddle further in such matters, sent him up to the Bishop of London, with a letter declaring the charges against him.

THE ANSWER OF MR. THOMAS WATS TO THE ARTICLES
BROUGHT AGAINST HIM BY BISHOP BONNER
IN HIS CONSISTORY AT ST. PAUL'S.

To the second article, that he did not believe in the sacraments of the Church, he answered, that he believed in all the sacraments according to Christ's institution, and the catholic Church; but not according to the Bishop of Rome's church; and, further, that he doth not believe now as he had done in times past; for in times past he believed as the Church then believed, but now he doth not so believe; for the Church of Rome had deceived him, and therefore he said he did not believe as the Church of Rome believeth, but as Christ hath taught him; and he further said that he was so taught to believe by the preaching of

Mr. Alvey, and others whose names he remembered not, who did preach the Word of God truly and sincerely.

To the fifth, that the mass is abominable, he replied that he did so believe, and that he will not go one jot from that his belief.

To the sixth, that he neither did, nor yet doth believe, that the priest can absolve him from his sins, he confessed that this was his opinion; howbeit, he denieth not that it is good to ask counsel at the priest's mouth.

To the seventh, that Luther, Wycliffe, and Barnes were good men and martyrs, he said, that he knew not what the opinions of the said persons named in the said article were; and in case the said persons did believe that the body and blood of Christ were really and in very deed in the sacrament of the altar, then that they were not good men. But in case they did believe that the body and blood of Christ was not in the sacrament of the altar really and truly, then he believed that they were good men.

To the eleventh, that he believed and deliberately said that the Church of Rome, in her rites and ceremonies, sacraments, institutions, and traditions, is the synagogue of Satan, and therefore he had assented with John Tooly, hanged of late at Charing Cross, who desired the people to pray to be delivered from the tyranny of the Bishop of Rome, with all his enormities; as much as to say that his authority and doings were tyranny, and had all enormities and iniquities in them: he replied that he believed that the Bishop of Rome is a mortal enemy to Christ and his Church. And as for Tooly, he said he never saw or knew him; but that in case the said Tooly did wish and pray as is contained in the article, then did he likewise wish and consent with him therein. THOMAS WATS.

Thus having answered the articles, the bishop commanded him to appear again in the same place at three o'clock in the afternoon upon the same day; when, after many persuasions to recant, he ordered him to depart, and come again on Saturday, at eight o'clock in the morning. The bishop, however, being absent, Dr. Harpsfield, as his deputy, earnestly exhorted him to deny his opinions. But he being still resolute, as one whose house was built upon a rock, Dr. Harpsfield ordered him to appear there again upon Friday, the 10th day of the same month. Upon this day the bishop sent for him privately into his chamber, but finding all persuasion in vain, Wats was again dismissed

until the 17th of May, and then commanded to appear in
the consistory, when he was condemned, and delivered to
the sheriffs of London, by whom he was sent to Newgate.
He remained here until the 9th of June, when he was taken
to Chelmsford, to Mr. Scott's house, where he ate with Mr.
Haukes and the rest that came down to their burning, and
prayed together both before and after the meal.

After that Mr. Wats retired, and prayed privately. He
then came to his wife and six children, and, having
exhorted them to remain steadfast in the faith, bade them
farewell, kissed them all, and was then carried to the fire.

Being brought to the stake, he kissed it, after which he
thus addressed Lord Rich: "My lord, beware, beware! for
you do against your own conscience herein; and, unless
you repent the Lord will avenge me, for you are the cause
of my death." Then did the martyr resign his soul to Christ
his Saviour.

The History of Mr. John Bland, Preacher and Martyr.

On the 12th of July, John Bland, John Frankesh, Nicholas Sheterden, and Humphrey Middleton, were burned at
Canterbury. Mr. Bland was a man whose whole life was
devoted to the welfare of his fellows, as may be gathered
from the following fact.

After entering the ministry in the Church of God, he
was inflamed with incredible desire to profit his congregation, which may appear by this, that whereas he was twice
cast into Canterbury prison for preaching the Gospel, and
delivered at the intercession of his friends, yet he would
preach again as soon as he was delivered; whereupon,
being apprehended the third time, when his friends again
would have found means to have rescued him, if he would
promise to abstain from preaching, he would not hear of
any such condition, repeating the language of St. Paul—
"Who shall separate us from the love of Christ? shall
tribulation, or anguish, or hunger, or nakedness, or persecution, or the sword?"

ANOTHER SOURCE OF TROUBLE WROUGHT AGAINST
MR. JOHN BLAND, WRITTEN BY HIMSELF.

"Upon Innocents' Day, being the 28th of December,
they had procured the priest of Stodmash to say mass: he
had nigh made an end of matins ere I came; and when he
had ended them, he said to me, 'Mr. Parson, your neigh-

bours have desired me to say matins and mass: I hope you will not be against the queen's proceedings.' 'No,' said I, 'I will offend none of her majesty's laws, God willing.' 'What say you?' quoth he, and made as though he had not heard. Then I spake the same words to him again with a higher voice; but he would not hear, though all the rest in the chancel heard. I spoke so loud the third time, that all the church might hear, That I would not offend the queen's laws; and then he went to mass. And when he was reading the epistle, I beckoned the clerk to me, and said to him, 'I pray you desire the priest, when the gospel is done, to tarry a little; I have something to say to the people; and this the clerk did.

"When, therefore, the priest came down into the stall where he sat, I stood up in the chancel door, and spake to the congregation of the great goodness of God always shown unto his people, unto the time of Christ's coming; and in him and his coming, what benefit they had; and among others I spake of the great and comfortable sacrament of his body and blood. And after I had briefly declared the institution, the promise of life to the good, and damnation to the wicked, I spake of the bread and wine, affirming them to be bread and wine after the consecration, as yonder mass book, saying, 'Holy bread of eternal life, and the cup of perpetual salvation. So that like as our bodily mouths eat the sacramental bread and wine, so doth the mouth of our souls, which is our faith, eat Christ's flesh and blood.' And when I had made an end of that, I spake of the misuse of the sacrament in the mass; so that I judged it in that use no sacrament, and showed how Christ bade us all eat and drink; and in the mass one only eateth and drinketh, and the rest kneel, knock, and worship. And after these things ended, as briefly as I could, I spake of the benefactors of the mass, and began to declare who made the mass, and recited every man's name, and the patch that he put on the mass; but before I had rehearsed them all, the churchwarden and the constable, his son-in-law, violently came upon me, and took my book from me, and pulled me down, and thrust me into the chancel, with an exceeding roar and cry. Some cried, 'Thou heretic!' some, 'Thou traitor!' some, 'Thou rebel!' and when every man had said his pleasure, and the rage was somewhat past, 'Be quiet, good neighbours,' said I, 'and let me speak to you quietly. If I have offended any law, I will make answer before them that are in authority to correct me.'

But they would not hear me, and pulled me, one on this side, and another on that. Then Richard Austen said, 'Peace, masters; no more till mass be done;' and they ceased. He then called to the constable and churchwarden, and bade them put me into a side chapel, and shut the door on me; and there they kept me till mass was ended, when they came into the chapel to me, and searched what I had about me, and found a dagger, and took it from me. Then said Thomas Austen, churchwarden, after many brabblings that they made with me, 'Thou keepest a wife here amongst us, against God's law and the queen's.' 'You lie, goodman Austen,' said I; it is not against God's law, nor, as I suppose, against the queen's.' Thus they brought me out of the church, and without the door they railed on me without pity or mercy; but anon the priest came out of the church, and Ramsey, who of late was clerk, said to him, 'Sir, where dwell you?' And therefore Thomas Austen took him by the arm, and said, 'Come on, sirrah, you are of his opinion,' and took his dagger from him, and said he should go with him. Then they carried me and Ramsey to Canterbury, guarded by eighteen persons."

ANOTHER EXAMINATION OF MR. BLAND.

Baker.—Bland, wherefore were you cast into prison?

Bland.—For an unjust complaint against me.

Baker.—What was the complaint?

Bland.—I told him as truly and as briefly as I could.

Baker.—Let me see thy book. [I gave him a Latin Testament.]

Baker.—Will you go to the church, and obey and follow the queen's proceedings, and do as an honest man should do?

Bland.—I trust in God to do no otherwise but as an honest man ought to do.

Baker.—Will you do as I said?

Bland.—Will it please your mastership to give me leave to ask you a question?

Baker.—Yes.

Bland.—Sir, may a man do anything that his conscience is not satisfied in to be good?

Baker.—Away, away!

"He then threw down the book, and said it was no Testament, and I said it was."

Baker.—Yea, sayest thou so? By St. Mary! and hold thee

there, I will give six faggots to burn thee, ere thou should be unburned. Hence, knave! hence!

"And so we returned into our places again within the bar. And at night, when judgment of felons and all was done, we were called, and the judge ordered the gaoler to deliver us to the ordinary. 'And if,' said the judge, 'they will not be reformed, let them be delivered to us again, and they shall have judgment and execution.' One of our company said, 'My lord, if we be killed at your hands for Christ's sake, we shall live with Him for ever.'"

THE ANSWER OF MR. BLAND AT HIS APPEARANCE BEFORE THE COMMISSARY AND OTHERS, IN THE SPIRITUAL COURT.

Collins.—Mr. Bland, you know that you are presented to us as one suspected of heresy. How say you? Are you contented to conform yourself to the laws of this realm and of the holy Church?

Bland.—I deny that I am justly suspected of heresy.

Collins.—You were brought before Mr. Archdeacon and me, and matter of heresy laid to your charge.

Bland.—That matter was done and said a whole year ago, for I have been in prison this year and more. If you have anything against me by law, I desire that you let me know the law and matter, and I will answer according to the law.

"Then said my lord suffragan, 'But that I am one of the judges, I would rise and stand by thee, and accuse thee to be a sacramentary, and bring witness to prove it; yea, and further, that thou hast called the mass an abominable idol.'

Bland.—You, my lord, never heard me say so; but I heard you once say that, in your conscience, you had abhorred the mass three years.

Collins.—Thou liest; this is but a drift. You had better answer now, else you shall go to prison again, and be called on Monday, and have articles laid to you; and if you answer not them directly, you shall be condemned as a heretic, and that will be worse for you.

Bland.—Sir, I do not now nor will then deny to answer anything that you can lay to my charge by law, wherefore I trust you will let me have the benefit of the law.

Collins.—Well, on Monday, at nine of the clock, you shall see the law and have articles laid unto you.

"Then they espied Mr. Cox, the lawyer, and called him

in and said, 'Here is a lawyer can tell you are bound by law to answer.' And he said as they had said.

"After some conversation, my Lord of Dover cried, 'No more! I command you to hold your peace. Have him away, and bring in another!'

"The following Monday, we were brought to the same place again; but, as before, I demanded what they had to lay to my charge, and to see the law, which they promised before I should see.

"They then brought forth a decretal, a book of the Bishop of Rome's law, to bind me to answer, which my heart abhorred to look upon. The effect was, that the ordinary had authority to examine, and that those whom they so examined must needs answer. But I said that it meant such as were justly suspected, as I was not. And here we had much communication; for I charged them with unjust imprisonment, which they could not avoid."

THE LAST APPEARANCE AND EXAMINATION OF MR. BLAND.

On Monday, the 13th of June, Mr. Bland was brought before the Bishop of Dover, the commissary, and the archdeacon, at Canterbury. Under these a great many were cruelly treated and barbarously slain at Canterbury, amongst whom Mr. Bland was the first. He being brought before the said bishop with his colleagues, viz., John Frankesh, Nicholas Sheterden, Humphrey Middleton, and William Coker, were examined upon various articles. He was asked by the commissary whether he believed that Christ is really in the sacrament, or not. To this he answered that he believed Christ is in the sacrament as he is in all other good bodies, so that he did not think that Christ was really in the sacrament.

He was then ordered to appear on the following Wednesday, and from thence he was deferred again to Monday following, the 20th of June, in the same chapter-house, to hear what further proceedings would be taken in case he would not relent; on which day he appeared as before, and was required to speak his mind plainly on the aforesaid articles, which were again repeated to him.

His answers and confession being taken down, respite was allowed him for a few days to deliberate with himself. And on the 25th day of the same month, he appeared again in the chapter-house, and there boldly withstood the authority of the pope, whereupon he was condemned and committed to the secular power.

The History of John Frankesh, Humphrey Middleton, and Nicholas Sheterden.

Having finished the examination of Mr. Bland, we now proceed with the rest of his fellow-prisoners, who were united with him in the same cause and affliction. Adhering to the truth, they were condemned by the Suffragan of Canterbury, on the 25th of June, the same year. Their examinations need not be dwelt upon, for as the articles ministered against them were the same, so their answers varied little or nothing.

THE EXAMINATION OF MR. SHETERDEN BEFORE THE BISHOP OF WINCHESTER, THEN LORD CHANCELLOR.

"I was called into a chamber before the lord chancellor, the suffragan, and others.

"Then said he, 'I have sent for you because I hear you are indicted for heresy; and being called before the commissioners, you will not answer nor submit yourself.'

"I said, 'I did not refuse to answer; but I did plainly answer that I had been in prison a long time, and reason it was that I should be charged or discharged of that, and not to be examined of articles to hide my wrong imprisonment, neither did I know any indictment against me. If there were any, it could not be just, for I have not been abroad since the law was made.'

"*Win.*—If thou wilt declare thyself to the Church to be a Christian, thou shalt go, and then have a writ of wrong imprisonment.

"*Shet.*—I have no mind to sue now, but require justice: but to make a promise, I will not; and if I offend the law, punish me accordingly. For it might be that my conscience was not persuaded, nor would be, in prison: seeing these things which I have learned were by God's law openly taught and received by the authority of the realm.

"*Win.*—It was not a few that could be your guides in understanding, but the doctors and the whole Church; now, whom wouldst thou believe? either the few or the many?

"*Shet.*—I did not believe for the few or for the many,

but only for him that bringeth the Word, and showed it to me to be so, according to the process thereof.

"So after many words, by which he thought to ensnare me, he came to the Church's faith, and comely order of ceremonies and images. And then I joined to him again with the commandments.

"Win.—That was done that no false things should be made; as the heathen would worship a cat because she killed mice.

"Shet.—It is plain that the law forbids not only such, but even to make an image of God to any manner of likeness.

"Win.—Where find you that?

"Shet.—Forsooth, in the law where God gave them the commandments: for he said, 'Ye saw no shape, but heard a voice only:' and added a reason why, 'lest they should after make images and mar themselves:' so that God would not show his shape, because they should have no image of him who was the true God.

"Win.—You have made a goodly interpretation.

"Shet.—No, it is the text.

"A Bible was then brought. He bade me find it; and so I read it aloud: the place was Deut. iv.

"At last he said that he had sent for me for charity sake to talk with me, but now he would not meddle; and said my wrong imprisonment could not excuse me, but I must clear myself. I said that was easy for me to do, for I had not offended.

"The archdeacon was then called in, and he said that I behaved myself before him with such arrogancy as never was heard: whereas he was minded with such mercy towards me; and many other lies he laid to me, that I was sent home till another time.

THE LAST EXAMINATION, WITH THE CONDEMNATION OF MESSRS. BLAND, FRANKESH, SHETERDEN, AND MIDDLETON.

Now to speak something also of the other martyrs who were examined at the same time, and suffered together with them, namely, Humphrey Middleton, of Ashford, and John Frankesh, vicar of Rolvynden, in the diocese of Kent, above mentioned.

Seven articles being propounded to the persons above named, John Frankesh first answered somewhat doubtfully, desiring further respite to be given him of fourteen days to deliberate with himself, which was granted. Mr. Bland answered flatly and roundly, as before related. Nicholas Sheterden and Humphrey Middleton answered to the first and second articles affirmatively. The third, concerning the Catholic Church, they partially granted. To the fourth, fifth, and sixth, concerning the real presence, and the administrations of the sacrament in the Latin tongue, and in one kind, they utterly refused to answer. Sheterden said he would not answer thereto, before the cause was determined why he was imprisoned, and still remained a prisoner, contrary to the laws of Parliament. Middleton added, moreover, and confessed that he believed in his own God, saying, "Mine is a living God, and no dead god." Thus the above four, upon these answers, were condemned by the Bishop of Dover the 25th day of June, 1555.

And being delivered to the secular power, they were all burnt together at Canterbury, on the 12th of July, at two stakes, but in one fire, where they, in the sight of God and of His holy angels, and of the world, like true soldiers of Jesus Christ, gave faithful testimony to the truth of His holy Gospel.

Mr. Sheterden, a few days before he suffered, wrote an affectionate letter to his wife, two to his mother, wishing her increase of grace and godly wisdom, and two to his brother, Walter Sheterden, expatiating on the true faith and doctrine of Christ. In the last he breathed a manly spirit, worthy of the great cause for which he died. For his brother had informed him that if he would recant, he would bestow a large fortune on him. But this he refused, with the spirit of a Christian hero, confident of the treasures laid up for him in heaven. In the prayer which he offered up to the throne of grace before his death, he evinced consummate meekness, resignation, and a hope in God's mercy.

The Martyrdom of Christopher Waid, Linen-Weaver, of Dartford.

Christopher Waid was condemned for heresy, by Maurice, Bishop of Rochester, and sentenced to be burnt at Dartford, which was his native town. Accordingly, on the morning appointed for his death, a cart was sent early from Dartford with the stake, a load of faggots and tall wood, and a good supply of reeds, that all might be in readiness for the arrival of the martyr. About ten o'clock Christopher Waid and one Margery Polley (a widow who had been previously condemned for heresy) arrived, both riding pinioned, and accompanied by the sheriff, with a large retinue, and many other gentlemen.

When Mrs. Polley saw in the distance the large crowd assembled round the gravel pit where they were to suffer, she said, cheerfully, to Waid, "You may rejoice to see such a company gathered to celebrate your marriage this day."

The procession passed the place, and proceeded down the town, where Mrs. Polley was left until the sheriff returned from Waid's execution. Christopher had his clothes taken off in an inn, where he put on a long white shirt, which was sent for him by his wife, and being again pinioned, he proceeded on foot to the place of execution. When he reached the stake, he put his arms round it and kissed it, he then put his back against it, and stood in a pitch barrel, brought for that purpose; a smith brought a hoop of iron, and fastening two staples under his arms, made him fast to the stake. When he was settled, he lifted up his eyes and hands to heaven, and repeated the last verse of the 86th Psalm—"Show some good upon me, O Lord, that they which hate me may see it, and be ashamed: because thou, Lord, hast helped me, and comforted me." A pulpit had been erected on a little hillock near the stake, which a friar entered with a book in his hand. Immediately Waid espied him, he called earnestly to the people to take heed of the doctrine of the whore of Babylon, and to embrace the Gospel as preached in King Edward's time. While he was thus speaking, the sheriff interrupted him, saying, "Be quiet, Waid, and die patiently." "I am quiet," said he, "I thank God, Mr. Sheriff, and so trust to die." During this time the friar stood still, making as though he was going to speak, but whether astonished at Waid's earnestness, or thinking it hopeless to make the people listen to him, he suddenly came down, and went away to the town. The reeds were then piled about Waid, who arranged them himself, so as to leave an opening for his face, that his voice might be heard. His enemies, perceiving that, kept throwing faggots at his face, but as long as he could he pushed them aside again, though his face was much hurt by the end of one which struck him. When the fire was applied he showed no signs of fear or impatience, but often cried out, "Lord Jesus, receive my soul." At length his voice could no longer be heard, but even after he was dead his hands remained clasped over his head, as if in the act of prayer.

The Apprehension and Martyrdom of Dirick Carver, Brewer of Brighthelmstone, and John Launder, Husbandman, of Godstone, Surrey.

Dirick Carver, of the parish of Brighthelmstone, in the county of Sussex, was burnt at Lewes, on the 22nd of July; and the day following, John Launder, of Godstone, in the county of Surrey, suffered the same fate at Stening. These two men were apprehended about the latter end of October, in the year 1554, by Edward Gage, gentleman, as they were at prayers in the house of Dirick. Gage sent them up to the queen's council, which, after examination, sent them as prisoners to Newgate, there to await the pleasure of Bonner, Bishop of London. They were brought by the keeper of the prison, on the 8th of June, into the bishop's chamber at his house in London; and there, being examined upon divers points of religion, made their several confessions, subscribing them with their own hands. After reading these, the bishop alleged certain other articles against them, and caused them to swear directly their answers thereunto.

After long persuasions and fair exhortations, they were demanded whether they would abide by their answers. Launder said, "I will never go from these answers as long as I live." Carver also confirmed the same, upon which they were commanded to appear again before the bishop in the consistory at St. Paul's, on the 10th of the same month.

On Monday, the 10th of June, Carver and Launder, with some others, were brought by the keeper to the bishop's consistory, where the bishop, first beginning with Carver, caused his confession, with the articles and answers, to be read to him, asking him whether he would abide by the same; to which Dirick answered that he would, "for your doctrine," said he, "is poison and sorcery. If Christ were here, you would put him to a worse death than he was put to before. Your ceremonies in the church are beggary and poison. And further I say that auricular confession is contrary to God's Word."

The bishop seeing his steadfastness, and finding that neither his accustomed flatteries nor his cruel threatenings could move this good man to incline to their idolatry, pronounced his usual blessing, as well upon Dirick as upon John Launder, who, after the like process, manifested the same constancy. They were then both delivered to the sheriffs, and afterwards they were conveyed to the places of execution, and there joyfully gave their bodies to be burned, and their souls into the hands of God, through Jesus Christ.

Dirick was a man whom the Lord had blessed, both with temporal and spiritual treasure; but the former proved no clog to the latter. But there was such havoc of his goods made by the greedy spoilers of that time, that his poor wife and children had little left, save their hope in God.

On Dirick's coming into the town of Lewes to be burned, the people besought God to strengthen him in the faith of Christ. He thanked them, and prayed God to confirm them in the same faith. On his arrival at the sign of the Star, the people gathered round him; and the sheriff said that he had found him a faithful man in all his answers. When he came to the stake, he prayed kneeling upon his knees, while the sheriff made haste to discharge his official duties.

His book was then thrown into the barrel, and, when he had stripped himself, he went into the barrel himself. The faithful martyr then picked up his Testament, and throwing it among the people, spoke as follows:—

"Dear brethren and sisters, witness you all that I am come to seal with my blood Christ's Gospel, because I know that it is true; it is not unknown unto all you, but that it hath been truly preached here in Lewes and in all places of England, and now it is not. And because that I will not here deny God's Gospel and be obedient to man's laws, I am condemned to die. Dear brethren, as many of you as do believe upon the Father, the Son, and the Holy Ghost, unto everlasting life, see you do the works appertaining to the same."

Account of Thomas Iveson, John Aleworth, James Abbes, John Denley, John Newman, and Patrick Packingham.

About the same time, Thomas Iveson, of Godstone, in the county of Surrey, carpenter, was burnt at Chichester. His apprehension, examination, constancy, and condemnation, were in the same form as those of Dirick Carver's and John Launder's.

In the latter end of the month of July, John Aleworth died in prison at the town of Reading, where he was confined for the testimony of the Gospel, whom the Catholic prelates, according to their usual solemnity, excluded from burial.

Among many that endeavoured in these troublesome

days to keep a good conscience, was James Abbes, a young man, who was forced to wander with his brethren from place to place, to avoid apprehension. At length he was caught by the enemy and brought before Dr. Hopkins, Bishop of Norwich, who, examining him respecting his religion, began to threaten and persuade him so strongly, that at last James Abbes was forced into an abjuration.

When he was dismissed, the bishop called him again, and gave him a piece of money. After this Abbes withdrew, but his conscience beginning to prick him, he returned immediately to the bishop, and threw down his money, saying that he repented that he had ever given his consent to their wicked persuasions. Hereupon Dr. Hopkins, with his chaplains, laboured afresh to win him again, but in vain; for he would not yield, but fought manfully in his Master's cause to the end, and endured the torture of the fire, which took place in Bury, the 2nd of August, 1555.

In the midst of this rage of the adversaries against the saints, there was one Edmund Tyrrel, Esq., at that time a justice of the peace within the county of Essex, who, on returning from the burning of some martyrs, met with John Denley, gentleman, and John Newman (both of Maidstone, in Kent), travelling, and going to visit some of their friends in Essex. Full of officious zeal, he apprehended them upon suspicion, searched them, and finding upon them a written confession of their faith, sent them with a letter to the queen's commissioners. The commissioners immediately dispatched them to Bishop Bonner, who, on June 28, caused Denley and Newman, with one Patrick Packingham, to be brought into his chamber, where being examined upon their confessions, they all answered to the same effect. Upon this they were commanded to appear in the bishop's consistory on the 5th of the following month.

ARTICLES OBJECTED BY BISHOP BONNER AGAINST
JOHN DENLEY, JOHN NEWMAN, AND
PATRICK PACKINGHAM, JOINTLY AND SEVERALLY,
THE 28TH OF JUNE, 1555.

First, that the said Denley now is of the diocese of London, and the jurisdiction of the Bishop of London.

Secondly, That he hath not believed, nor doth believe, that there is any catholic Church of Christ here in earth.

Thirdly, That the said Denley hath not believed, nor

doth believe, that this Church of England is any part or member of the said catholic Church.

Fourthly, That he hath believed, and doth believe, that the mass now used in England is full of idolatry and evil, and plain against God's Word, and therefore he hath not heard it, nor will hear it.

Fifthly, That the said Denley hath believed, and doth so believe, that auricular confession now used in this realm of England is not good, but contrary to God's Word.

Sixthly, That absolution, given by the priest on hearing confession, is not good, nor allowable by God's Word.

Seventhly, That the christening of children, as it is now used in the Church of England, is not good, nor allowable by God's Word, but against it: likewise confirming of children, giving of orders, saying of matins and even-song, anointing of sick persons, making of holy bread and holy water, with the rest of the church.

Eighthly, That there are but two sacraments in Christ's catholic Church, namely, that of baptism and the sacrament of the altar.

Ninthly, That forasmuch as Christ is ascended up into heaven, the very body of Christ is not in the sacrament of the altar.

Tenthly, That thou, Patrick Packingham, now being of the age of twenty-one at least, being within the house of the Bishop of London at St. Paul's, and by him brought to the great chapel to hear mass there, the said 23rd day of June, in the year of our Lord 1555, didst unreverently stand in the said chapel, having thy cap on thy head all the time of mass; and didst also refuse to receive holy water and holy bread at the hands of the priest, there contemning and despising the mass.

On the 1st day of July the three prisoners were brought into the consistory in St. Paul's, where Bonner proceeded against them after the usual form, reading first their confessions, articles, and answers, and then tempting them sometimes with fair promises, at other times with threatenings, which indeed were his strongest arguments. In the end, seeing their immovable constancy, upon the 5th of July he condemned them as heretics, and delivered them to the sheriffs of London, as to his executioners. The sheriffs kept them till they were commanded by writ to send them to their several places of suffering; and accordingly Mr.

Denley was conveyed to Uxbridge, where he was burned on the 8th of August.

Such was his experience of the sustaining grace of God, that even in the midst of the flames he sang an entire psalm, which ascended up to heaven mingled with the incense of his own smoking pyre.

Mr. Patrick Packingham suffered at the same town, about the 28th of the said month.

George Tankerfield, Martyr.

George Tankerfield was born in York, but when young he went to London, where he was a cook by trade. He had been a papist in King Edward's reign, but at the age of twenty-seven, Mary being then on the throne, he began to perceive the great cruelty exercised by the Romanists, and to question and abhor their doctrines. Concerning the mass especially he had many doubts, and at length he prayed earnestly that he might be thoroughly persuaded whether it were of God or not. The Lord mercifully heard his cry, and daily he was led to detest more and more his former errors. He then began to read the Testament, and thereby his mind became enlightened with the knowledge of the truth as it is in Jesus, leading him to forsake his former ways, and to confess the change in his religious views. He was so bold in expressing his opinions, that he was soon discovered and betrayed.

He was consequently arrested and brought to Newgate in February, 1555, from whence he was taken for examination before Bishop Bonner, who in his usual manner, questioned him as to his creed. To this Tankerfield answered that he did not believe in auricular confession, declaring he had not confessed for five years to any but God, and that he never again would confess to a priest, as it was contrary to the Bible.

When the bishop began to read his sentence, having first exhorted him to recant, he resisted all persuasion. "I will not," said he, "forsake mine opinions, except you, my lord, can refute them by Scripture; and I care not for your divinity, for you condemn all men, and prove nothing against them." And in reply to Bonner's numerous exhortations, he answered boldly, that the church whereof the pope is supreme head is no part of Christ's catholic Church, and pointing to the bishop, he said to the crowd around him, "Good people, beware of him, and such as he is, for these be the people that deceive you." Bonner then read the sentence of condemnation, and Tankerfield was given up to the secular power. He ended his life with much patience and constancy at St. Albans, on the 26th of August, triumphant in defence of the faith he professed, showing the same steadfastness as that of the first British martyr, Alban, who perished here in the year 287.

AUTHENTIC NOTES CONCERNING
GEORGE TANKERFIELD, AFTER HE WAS CARRIED
TO ST. ALBANS TO SUFFER MARTYRDOM.

Imprimis. He was brought to St. Albans by the high sheriff of Hertfordshire, Edward Brocket, Esq., and Mr. Pulter, of Hitchen, who was under-sheriff.

Item. They put up at the Cross Keys inn, where there was a great concourse of people to see and hear the prisoner; some were sorry to see so pious a man brought to be burned, others praised God for his constancy and perseverance in the truth. Contrariwise, some said it was pity he did stand in such opinions; and others, both old men and women, cried against him; one called him heretic, and said it was a pity that he lived. But Tankerfield spake to them so effectually out of the Word of God, lamenting their ignorance, and protesting unto them his unspotted conscience, that God did mollify their hardened hearts, insomuch that some of them departed out of the chamber weeping.

Item. There came a certain schoolmaster to have communication with him, the day before he was coming to St. Albans, concerning the sacrament of the altar and other points of the popish religion; but as he urged Tankerfield with the authority of the doctors, wresting them after his own will, so, on the other side, Tankerfield answered him mightily by the Scriptures, not wrested after the mind of any man, but being interpreted after the will of the Lord Jesus. So that, as he would not allow such allegations as Tankerfield brought out of the Scriptures without the opinions of the doctors, so, again, Tankerfield would not credit his doctrine to be true, except he would confirm it by the Scriptures. In the end, Tankerfield prayed him that he would not trouble him in such matters, for his conscience was established. He therefore departed from him, wishing him well, and protesting that he meant him no more hurt than his own soul.

Item. When the hour drew on that he should suffer, he desired the wine-drawer that he might have a pint of malmsey and a loaf, that he might eat and drink in remembrance of Christ's death and passion, because he could not have it administered to him by others in such manner as Christ commanded. And then he kneeled down, making his confession unto the Lord with all which were in the chamber with him; and after he had prayed earnestly, and had read the institution of the holy supper by the Lord Jesus, out of the Evangelists and out of St. Paul, he said, "O Lord, thou knowest it, I do not this to derogate authority from any man, or in contempt of those which are thy ministers, but only because I cannot have it administered according to thy Word." And when he had spoken these and such like words, he received it with giving of thanks.

Item. He prayed his host to let him have a good fire in the chamber, which was granted him; and then, he sitting on a form before it, put off his shoes and hose, and stretched out his leg to the flame; and when it had touched his foot, he quickly withdrew his leg, showing the flesh did persuade him one way, and the spirit another. And all this time the sheriffs were at a gentleman's house at dinner, not far from the town, whither also resorted many knights and gentlemen out of the country, because his son was married that day; and until they returned from dinner, the prisoner was left to the care of his host, by whom he was kindly treated; and considering that his time was short, his saying was that "although the day was ever so long, yet at the last it ringeth to evening song."

Item. About two o'clock, when the sheriffs returned from dinner, they brought Mr. Tankerfield out of the inn to the place where he should suffer, which was called Romeland, being a green place near the west end of the abbey church, unto which, when he was come, he kneeled down by the stake that was set up for him; and after he had ended his prayers, he arose, and, with a joyful faith, said that, although he had a sharp dinner, yet he hoped to have a joyful supper in heaven.

Item. While the faggots were set about him, there came a priest and persuaded him to believe in the sacrament of the altar, and he would be saved. But Tankerfield cried, vehemently, "I defy the whore of Babylon! Fie on that abominable idol! Good people, do not believe him.' And then the mayor of the town commanded fire to be set to the heretic, and said, if he had but one load of faggots in the world, he would give them to burn him. Amidst this confusion, there was a certain knight who went unto Tankerfield, and, taking him by the hand, said, "Good brother, be strong in Christ!" This he spake softly. And Tankerfield said, "Oh, sir, I thank you; I am so, I thank God." Then fire was set unto him, and he desired the sheriff and all the people to pray for him; most of them did so. And so, embracing the fire, he called on the name of the Lord Jesus, and was quickly out of pain.

The History of Robert Smith.

Mr. Smith was brought to Newgate on the 5th of November, by John Matthew, a yeoman of the guard, by the command of the council. He had formerly devoted his services to the house of Sir Thomas Smith, Knight, being at the same time Provost of Eton; from thence he was preferred to Windsor, having there in the college a clerkship of ten pounds a year. Of stature he was tall and slender, active about many things, but chiefly delighted in the art of painting, which he practised rather for his amusement than for gain. In religion he was fervent, after he had once tasted the truth, wherein he was much confirmed by the teaching of Mr. Turner, of Windsor, and others. At the accession of Queen Mary, he was deprived of his clerkship by her visitors; and not long after, was apprehended and brought up before Bonner. The following examinations were written with his own hand:—

THE FIRST EXAMINATION OF ROBERT SMITH
BEFORE BISHOP BONNER.

"About nine in the morning, I was, among the rest of my brethren, brought to the bishop's house; and, first of all, I was brought before him into his chamber, where he began as followeth, after he had asked my name:—

"*Bonner.*—How long is it since you confessed to any priest?

"*Smith.*—Never since I had years of discretion. For I never saw it needful, neither commanded by God, to come to show my faults to any of the sinful number whom you call priests.

"*Bonner.*—Thou showest thyself, even at thy first speech, to be a rank heretic, who, being weary of painting, art entered into divinity, and so fallen, through thy departing from thy vocation, into heresy.

"*Smith.*—Although I understand painting, yet, I praise God, I have had little need all my life hitherto to live by it.

"*Bonner.*—How long is it since you received the sacrament of the altar, and what is your opinion in the same?

"*Smith.*—I never received it since I had years of discretion, nor ever will, by God's grace; neither do I esteem it in any point, because it hath not God's ordinance, but rather is set up to mock him withal.

" 'Well,' said Bonner, laughing, 'tell me, how sayest thou of the Church?'

"*Smith.*—I told you whereon the true Church is built, and I affirm it not only in England to be the congregation of God, but also in *omnem terram,* as it is written, 'Their sound is gone forth into all lands,' and this is the afflicted Church, which ye cease not to imprison, slay, and kill. And in Corinth were not all the congregation of God, but only a number of those elect people of God. For neither Paul nor Peter were present at Corinth when they wrote, and yet were they of the Church of God, as many thousands more which also communicate in that Holy Spirit.

"*Bonner.*—What call you catholic, and what call you church?

"*Smith.*—Catholic is universal, and church is a congregation knit together in unity.

"Then, after much talk, it was laid to my charge that my fellow and I spake one thing; for which I praised God, and was sent again to the garden, where, after a while, as I and brother Harwood had been together, came one of my lord's chaplains, that much desired to communicate with me, demanding first if I were a prisoner.

"*Smith.*—I am in this flesh a prisoner, and subject to my master and yours, but I hope yet the Lord's free man through Christ Jesus.

"*Doctor.*—I do much desire to talk to you lovingly, because you are a man I much lament.

"To which I answered, *Sub melle latet venenum.* And, after much ado about his god, I compelled him to say that it must needs enter into the belly, and so fall into the draught.

"*Doctor.*—What derogation was it to Christ when the Jews spit in his face?

"*Smith.*—If the Jews, being his enemies, did spit in his face, and we, being his friends, throw him into the draught, which of us have deserved the greatest damnation? Then, by your argument, he that doth injury to Christ shall have a most plenteous salvation.

"Then the doctor started away, and would have his humanity incomprehensible, making a comparison between the soul of man and the body of Christ, bringing in, to serve his turn, which way Christ came in among his disciples, the doors being shut.

"*Smith.*—Although it be said that when he came the doors were shut, yet have I as much to prove that the doors opened at his coming as you have to prove he came through the door. For that Almighty God who brought the disciples out of prison, which yet, when search was made, was found shut, was able to let Christ in at the door, although it were shut; and yet it maketh not for your purpose, for they saw him, heard him, and felt him, and that you cannot say you do, neither is he in more places than one at the same time.

"At which answer, when he had made many scoffings, he went from me, and we were carried into my lord's hall, where we were baited by the band of servants almost all the day, until our keeper, seeing their rudeness, shut us all up in a handsome chamber, while my lord went into his synagogue to condemn Mr. Denley and John Newman.

"Then they brought my lord mayor up into the chamber, where my lord intended to sup, to hear the matter; and I was the first that was called, where, my lord mayor being set with the bishop and one of the sheriffs, wine was flowing on every side, whilst I stood before them like a mute. But after my lord had well drank, my articles were sent for and read, and he demanded whether I did say as was written.

"*Smith.*—That I have said, I have said; and what I have said, I mean.

"Then my lord rose up and went to the table, where the lord mayor desired me to save my soul. I answered I hoped it was saved through Christ Jesus, desiring him to have pity on his own soul, and remember whose sword he carried.

"I was then carried into the garden, and there abode till the rest of my friends were examined, and then were we sent away to Newgate with many foul farewells, my lord bishop giving the keeper a charge to lay me in limbo.

"Upon Saturday, at eight o'clock, I was brought to his chamber again, and there examined by him as followeth:—

"*Bonner.*—Thou, Robert Smith, sayest that there is no catholic Church here on earth.

"*Smith.*—You have heard me both speak the contrary, and you have writing as a witness of the same.

"*Bonner.*—Well, what sayest thou to auricular confession? Is it not necessary to be used in Christ's Church? and wilt thou not be confessed by the priest?

"*Smith.*—It is not needful to be used in Christ's Church, as I answered yesterday. But if it be needful for your Church, it is to pick men's pockets; and such pickpocket matters is all the whole rabble of your ceremonies, for all that you maintain is but money matters.

"*Bonner.*—If the queen's majesty were of my mind, thou shouldst not come to talk before any man, but shouldst be put in a sack, with a dog in the same, and be thrown into a river.

"At this time Sir John Mordaunt came in, and sat down to hear my examination. Then said my lord, 'How sayest thou, Smith, to the seven sacraments? Believest thou not that they be of God's order, that is to say, the sacrament of—'

"*Smith.*—I believe that in God's Church are but two sacraments; that is to say, the sacrament of regeneration, and the sacrament of the Lord's Supper; and as for the sacrament of the altar and all your sacraments, they may well serve your Church, but God's Church hath nothing to do with them, neither have I anything to do to answer them, nor you to examine me of them.

"*Bonner.*—Why is God's order changed in baptism? In what point do we dissent from the Word of God?

"*Smith.*—First, in hallowing your water; in conjuring of the same; in baptising of children with anointing and spitting in their mouths, mingled with salt, and with many other lewd ceremonies, of which not one point is able to be proved in God's order.

"*Bonner.*—By the mass! this is the most unshamefaced heretic that ever I heard speak.

"*Smith.*—Well sworn, my lord; you keep a good watch.

"*Bonner.*—Well, thou shalt be burnt at a stake in Smithfield, if thou wilt not turn.

"*Smith.*—And you shall burn in hell, if you repent not: but, my lord, to put you out of doubt, because I am weary, I will strain courtesy with you: I perceive you will not with your doctors come unto me, and I am determined not to come unto you, by God's grace. For I have hardened my face against you as hard as brass.

"Then, after many railing sentences, I was sent away.

"On the 12th of July I was with my brethren brought into the consistory, and mine articles read before my lord mayor and sheriffs, with all the assistants: to which I answered.

"My lord proceeded with the rest of my articles, demanding of me if I said not as was written. To which I answered, 'No.' And, turning to my lord mayor, I said, 'I require you, my lord, in God's behalf, unto whom pertaineth your sword and justice, that I may here before your presence answer to these objections that are laid against me, and have probation of the same; and if anything that I have said, or will say, be proved heresy, I shall not only with all my heart forsake the same, and cleave to the truth, but also recant wheresoever you shall assign me, and all this audience shall be witness to the same.

"*Lord Mayor.*—Why, Smith, thou canst not deny but this thou saidst.

"*Smith.*—Yes, my lord, I deny that which he hath written because he hath both added to, and diminished from the same; but what I have spoken I will never deny.

"*Lord Mayor.*—Why, thou speakest against the blessed sacrament of the altar.

"*Smith.*—I denied it to be any sacrament, and I do stand here to make probation of the same; and if my lord or any of his doctors be able to prove either the name or usage of the same, I will recant mine error.

"Then spake my brother Tankerfield, and defended the probation of things which they call heresy. To which the bishop answered—

" 'By my troth, Mr. Speaker, you shall preach at a stake.'

"*Smith.*—Well sworn, my lord, you keep a good watch.

"*Bonner.*—Well, Mr. Controller, I am no saint.

"*Smith.*—No, my lord, nor yet a good bishop. For a bishop, saith St. Paul, should be faultless, and a vessel dedicated unto God; and are you not ashamed to sit in judgment and be a blasphemer, condemning innocents?

"*Bonner.*—Well, Mr. Controller, you are faultless.

"*Smith.*—My lord mayor, I require you, in God's name, that I may have justice. We be here to-day a great many innocents wrongfully accused of heresy. And I require you, if you will not seem to be partial, let me have no more

favour at your hands than the apostle had at the hands of
Festus and Agrippa, who, being heathens and infidels, gave
him leave not only to speak for himself, but also heard the
probation of his cause. This require I at your hands, who,
being a Christian judge, I hope will not deny me that right,
which the heathen have suffered: if you do, then shall all
this audience, yea, and the heathen, speak shame of your
act. For all that do well come to the light, and they that do
evil hate the light.

"At this the lord mayor, hanging down his head, said
nothing; but the bishop told me I should preach at the
stake, and so the sheriff cried with the bishop, Away with
me.

"Thus came I in before them four times, desiring justice,
but could have none: at length my friends required the
same with one voice, but could not have it; so we had
sentence; and then being carried out, were brought in
again, and received it separately. But before the bishop
gave me sentence, he told me, in derision of my brother
Tankerfield, a tale between a gentleman and his cook. To
which I answered, 'My lord, you fill the people's ears with
fantasies and foolish tales, and make a laughing matter at
blood; but if you were a true bishop, you should leave
these railing sentences, and speak the words of God.'

"*Bonner.*—Away with him, away with him.

"I then turned to my fellow-sufferers, and said, 'Well,
good friends, you have seen and heard the great wrong that
we have received this day, and you are all witnesses that
we have desired the probation of our cause by God's book,
and it hath not been granted: but we are condemned, and
our cause not heard. Nevertheless, my lord mayor, forasmuch as you have here exercised God's sword causeless,
and will not hear the right of the poor, I commit my cause
to Almighty God, who will judge all men according to
right, before whom we shall both stand without authority;
and there will I stand in the right, and have judgment, to
your great confusion, except you repent, which the Lord
grant you to do, if it be his will.' And then was I with the
rest of my brethren carried to Newgate."

Thus was this steady martyr condemned on the 12th of
July. While he remained in prison, in the interval between
his sentence and his death, he was very active in exhorting
his fellow-martyrs, and teaching the way of life to those
who were confined for criminal offences, many of whom
he converted to the truth.

He terminated his triumphant career at Uxbridge, on the 8th of August, rejoicing in the cross even in the midst of the flames. While in prison he wrote several letters to his friends, some of which were in verse, a proof that he could not be under any impression of fear at his approaching death.

Martyrdom of Robert Samuel, Minister of Barfold, in Suffolk.

At Cobdock, near Ipswich, in the county of Suffolk, lived a justice of the peace, named Foster, remarkable for his zeal and hatred against the faithful, whom he took every means of persecuting. Among many whom he had troubled was Mr. Samuel, a very faithful preacher of God's Word in King Edward's days. He was minister at Barfold, in Suffolk, where he industriously taught the flock which the Lord had committed to his charge as long as the perils of the time would suffer him to do his duty.

At last, he was removed from the ministry and deprived of his benefice, and although he could not escape persecution, yet would he not give over his care for his flock, but continued to teach them by stealth when he could not openly do so. At last, the papist *delatores* espied him at home with his wife, and brought a word to the officer, who came to the house and beset it with a great company. They captured him in the night, because they durst not do it in the day-time, for fear of trouble and tumult, although Mr. Samuel did not withstand them at all, but meekly yielded himself into their hands. When they had thus caught him, they put him into Ipswich gaol, where he patiently spent his time among his pious brethren so long as he was permitted to continue there. However, not long after, he was carried to Norwich, where Dr. Hopton, bishop of that diocese, and Dr. Dunnings, his chancellor, exercised great cruelty against him. These men were most abhorred instruments of wrath, exceeding all the rest of their class in tormenting the bodies of the martyrs; for although the others were sharp enough in their generation, yet they were satisfied with the imprisonment and death of their victims, and went no farther.

The bishop, therefore, or else his chancellor, thinking that he might as easily prevail with Mr. Samuel as he had done with several before, kept him in a very close prison on his first arrival, where he was chained, bolt-upright to a great post, in such a way, that, standing only on tiptoe, he was fain to support the whole weight of his body thereby.

And to this they added a far more grievous torment, keeping him without meat and drink, whereby he was unmercifully vexed through hunger and thirst, saving that he had every day allowed him two or three mouthfuls of bread, and three spoonfuls of water, rather that he might be reserved to farther torment than that his life might be preserved.

At last, when he was brought forth to be burned, which was but a trifling suffering in comparison with those pains which he had already suffered, there were several that heard him declare what strange things had happened to him during his imprisonment, namely, that after he had been famished with hunger for two or three days together, he fell into a sleep, at which time one clad in white seemed to stand before him, who administered comfort unto him by these words: "Samuel, Samuel, be of good cheer, and take a good heart unto thee; for after this day shalt thou never be either hungry or thirsty:" which came to pass accordingly, for soon after he was burned; and from that time until his martyrdom he felt neither hunger nor thirst.

The History and Martyrdom of Mr. John Philpot.

Mr. Philpot was of a high respectable family, and was born in Hampshire. He was brought up at New College, Oxford, where he studied civil law and other branches of liberal education, particularly that of languages, and became a great proficient in the Hebrew. He was witty, courageous, and zealous, ever careful to adorn his doctrine by his practice, and his learning is fully evinced by what he has left on record.

Desirous of travelling, he went over to Italy, and on his journey from Venice to Padua was brought into no little danger, through a Franciscan friar's accompanying him, who, on arriving at Padua, sought to accuse him of heresy. At length, he returned into England, and availing himself of the greater license permitted in the days of King Edward, had several conflicts with Bishop Gardiner in the city of Winchester.

After that he was made Archdeacon of Winchester, under Dr. Poinet, who succeeded Gardiner in that bishopric, and here he continued during the reign of King Edward, to the great profit of those parts thereabouts. After the decease of that pious prince, his sister Mary succeeded to the crown, and it was her great study to alter convocation of the prelates and learned men to be assembled for the accomplishment of her desire.

In this convocation Mr. Philpot, according to his degree, sustained the cause of the Gospel, with a few others, against the adversary, for which notwithstanding the liberty the house had promised before, he was called to account before the chancellor, who was his ordinary, and by whom he was examined. From thence he was removed to Bishop Bonner and other commissioners, with whom he had divers conflicts and numerous examinations.

One of the memoranda which Mr. Philpot left on record is as follows: "The manner of my being called first before the Bishop of London, the second night of my imprisonment in his coalhouse, where," says the martyr, "I, with my six companions, housed together in straw as cheerfully as others in their beds of down."

THE CONDEMNATION OF JOHN PHILPOT.

In the end, the bishop, seeing his steadfastness in the truth, openly pronounced the sentence of condemnation against him, in the reading whereof, when he came to these words, "And you, an obstinate, pernicious, and impenitent heretic." Mr. Philpot said, "I thank God I am a heretic out of your cursed Church; I am not heretic before God. But God bless you, and give you grace to repent your wicked doings."

Whilst Bonner was about the midst of the sentence, the Bishop of Bath pulled him by the sleeve, and said, "My lord, my lord, know of him first whether he will recant or not." Bonner said, "Oh, let him alone," and so went on with the sentence.

When he had concluded, he delivered him to the sheriffs; and so two officers brought him, through the bishop's house into Paternoster Row, where his servant met him; and, when he saw him, he said, "Ah, dear master!"

"Content thyself," said Mr. Philpot, "I shall do well enough, for thou shalt see me again."

The officers then thrust him away, and took him to Newgate, where they delivered him to the keeper. Then his man strove to go in after his master, and one of the officers said unto him, "Hence, fellow! What wouldst thou have?" And he said, "I would speak with my master." Mr. Philpot then turned about and said to him, "To-morrow thou shalt speak with me."

When the under-keeper understood it to be his servant, he gave him leave to go in with him. And Mr. Philpot and his man were shown into a little chamber on the right hand, and there remained a short time, when Alexander, the chief keeper, came unto him, who said, "Ah! hast thou not done well to bring thyself hither?"

"Well," said Mr. Philpot, "I must be content, for it is God's appointment; and I shall desire you to let me have your gentle favour, for you and I have been of old acquaintance."

"If you will recant," said the keeper, "I will show you any pleasure I can."

"Nay," said Mr. Philpot, 'I will never recant that which I have spoken whilst I have my life, for it is most certain truth; and, in witness hereof, I will seal it with my blood."

Then Alexander said, 'This is the saying of the whole pack of you heretics."

Whereupon he commanded him to be set upon the block, and as many irons to be put upon his legs as he could bear.

Wherefore Mr. Philpot said to his servant, "Go to the sheriff, and show him how I am used, and desire him to be good to me." And so his servant went, and took another person with him.

When they came to the sheriff, and showed him how Mr. Philpot was treated in Newgate, he took his ring from off his finger, and delivered it to the person that came with Mr. Philpot's man, and bade him go unto Alexander the keeper; and commanded him to take off his irons, and to handle him more gently.

And when they returned to Alexander, and delivered their message from the sheriff, he took the ring, and said, "Ah! I perceive that Mr. Sheriff is a bearer with him and all such heretics as he is; therefore, to-morrow I will show it to his betters." Yet at ten o'clock he went in to Mr. Philpot where he lay, and took off his irons.

Upon Tuesday, the 27th of December, while he was at supper, there came a messenger from the sheriffs, and bade Mr. Philpot make ready, for the next day he should suffer and be burned at a stake. Mr. Philpot answered, "I am ready; God grant me strength and a joyful resurrection." And so he went into his chamber, and poured out his spirit unto the Lord God, giving him most hearty thanks that he had counted him worthy to suffer for his truth.

In the morning the sheriffs came, according to order,

about eight o'clock, and calling for him, he most joyfully came down to them. And there his man met him, and said, "Ah! dear master, farewell." His master answered, "Serve God, and he will help thee." So he went with the sheriffs to the place of execution. And when he was entering into Smithfield, the way was foul, and two officers took him up to bear him to the stake. Then he said, merrily, "What! will you make me a pope? I am content to go to my journey's end on foot." But on entering into Smithfield, he kneeled down, and said, "I will pay my vows in thee, O Smithfield!"

On arriving at the place of suffering, he kissed the stake, and said, "Shall I disdain to suffer at this stake, seeing my Redeemer did not refuse to suffer the most vile death upon the cross for me?" And then, with an obedient heart, he repeated the 106th, 107th, and 108th Psalms; and when he had made an end of all his prayers, he said to the officers, "What have you done for me?" And when they severally declared what they had done, he gave them what money he had left.

They then bound him to the stake, and lighted the fire, when the blessed martyr soon resigned his soul into the hands of Him who gave it.

The death of this glorious martyr was the last scene of blood that closed the tragedy of the year 1555.

Martyrdoms in the Reign of Queen Mary, in the Year 1556.
THOMAS WHITTLE'S NARRATION OF HIS TREATMENT
BY THE BISHOP OF LONDON.

"Upon Thursday, which was the 10th of January, the Bishop of London sent for me, Thomas Whittle, minister, out of the porter's lodge, where I had been all night, lying on the earth, on a little low bed, where I had as painful a night of sickness as ever I had. And when I came before him, he talked with me upon many things of the sacrament so grossly, as is not worthy to be rehearsed. And, amongst other things, he asked me if I would have come to mass that morning if he had sent for me. I answered that I would have come to him at his commandment, "but to your mass," said I, "I have small affection." At which answer he was sore displeased, and I said I should be fed with bread and water. And as I followed him through the great hall, he turned back and beat me with his fist, first on the one cheek, and then on the other, as the sign of my beating did many days appear. And then he led me to a little salthouse, where I had neither straw nor bed, but lay two nights on a table, and slept soundly."

After describing his sufferings of conscience, owing to a forced recantation, which he retracted, he concludes as follows:—

"And now, being condemned to die, my conscience and mind, I praise God, are quiet in Christ, and I, by his grace, am very willing and content to give over this body to the death, for the testimony of his truth and pure religion, against Antichrist and all his false religion and doctrine. By me,

THOMAS WHITTLE, Minister."

At the last examination of Mr. Whittle before the bishop, upon the 14th of January, 1556, Bishop Bonner, with others sitting in his consistory, in the afternoon, called him forth by name. Finding him constant, they proceeded in the usual manner to degrade him, and, after having sentenced him, delivered him to the secular power. On the 27th of January, he was brought to the stake in Smithfield, where, in company with his fellow-martyrs, he sealed his confession by his death.

There perished, in company with him at the same time the following: Bartlet Green, John Tudson, John Went, Thomas Browne, Isabel Foster, and Joan Warne, all of whom were burnt at Smithfield, on the 27th of January, 1556.

The Martyrdom of Julius Palmer, John Gwin, and Thomas Askin.

About the 16th of July, Julius Palmer, John Gwin, and Thomas Askin were burnt at Newbury. Palmer was a young man of respectable family, his father having been mayor of Coventry, at which town Julius was born. He was educated at Magdalen College, Oxford, where he became remarkable for the pungency of his wit and his proficiency in disputation. During the reign of Edward, he was a zealous advocate for the Romish Church; and for the hostile disposition he showed to the Protestant teachers, he was expelled from the college. Soon after the accession of Mary, however, he was restored to his living, when, happening to read with attention Calvin's "Institutes," he was convinced of the truth, renounced the errors of popery, openly avowed the Protestant doctrines, and, consequently, became a subject of persecution. In his distress, he applied to his mother for aid; but he got nothing but curses from her for his heresy, as she termed it, telling him that she would give him nothing but faggots wherewith to burn him. In return for this, the follower of Christ blessed her and departed. He was, after this, seized in his bed at Reading, having been betrayed by a friend to whom he had related his story. He was soon brought to trial before Dr. Jeffrey and others. The boldness and force of his arguments hastened his condemnation, and he was committed to the tender mercies of the secular power.

About an hour before he and his fellow-prisoners, Gwin and Askin, went to the place of execution, Palmer, in the presence of many people, comforted his companions with these words: "Brethren," said he, "be of good cheer in the Lord, and faint not. Remember the words of our Saviour Christ, where he saith, 'Happy are you when men revile you and persecute you for righteousness' sake. Rejoice and be glad, for great is your reward in heaven.' 'Fear not them that kill the body, and be not able to touch the soul.' Yea, for coals we shall receive pearls. For God's Holy Spirit certifieth our spirit, that he hath even now prepared for us a sweet supper in heaven for His sake who suffered for us."

When they were come to the place appointed for their suffering, they all three knelt on the ground, and Palmer, with an audible voice, pronounced the 31st Psalm, but the other two made their prayers secretly to Almighty God.

As he spake, a servant of one of the bailiffs struck him in the face with a faggot, so that the blood gushed out. When the fire was kindled and began to take hold upon their bodies, they lifted up their hands towards heaven, and, as though they had felt no pain, cheerfully cried, "Lord Jesus, strengthen us! Lord Jesus, assist us! Lord Jesus, receive our soul." And so they continued calling upon Jesus until they had ended their mortal lives.

Continuation of Martyrdoms Under Queen Mary, in the Year 1557.

Six martyrs were burnt at Canterbury, on the 15th of January; five at Smithfield, on the 12th of April; three at Southwark, in May; seven at Maidstone, on the 18th of June; seven at Cambridge, on the 30th of June; ten at Lewes, on the 22nd of June; and ten at Colchester, on the 2nd of August.

Among these last was Rose Allin, concerning whom we

record the following episode to the glory of God, whose strength is made perfect in weakness.

When Mr. Tyrrel went with his officers to seize Mr. and Mrs. Munt, he found them in bed, and the latter being weak and ill, requested Tyrrel to permit her daughter Rose to fetch her some drink, in order to revive her before she went to prison. This he accordingly granted. Rose, taking a candle and a mug, went to draw the drink. On her return, Tyrrel met her, and bade her advise her parents to return to the Roman Church.

Rose.—"Sir, they have a better instructor than I, for the Holy Ghost doth teach them, I hope, who I trust will not suffer them to err.

Tyrrel.—"Why, art thou still in that mind? Marry, it is time to look upon such heretics indeed.

Rose.—"Sir, with what you call heresy, do I worship my Lord God; I tell you truth.

Tyrrel.—"Then, I perceive, you will burn, gossip, with the rest, for company's sake.

Rose.—"No, sir, not for company's sake, but for Christ's sake, if so I be compelled; and I hope in his mercy, if he call me to it, he will enable me to bear it.

Tyrrel.—(Turning to his company.) "Sirs, this gossip will burn. What do ye think of her?

"Why, truly, sir," said one, "prove her, and you shall see what she will do by-and-by."

On this, Tyrrel, seizing her by the wrist, held her hand over the burning candle until her very sinews cracked asunder.

During this act of cruelty he said often to her, "Why, wretch, wilt thou not cry?" To which she always answered, that she thanked God she had no cause, but rather to rejoice. In the end, when the sinews burst, he thrust her from him with abusive language. But she, quietly suffering his rage for the time, said, "Sir, have you done what you will do?" He said, "Yea; and if thou think not well of it, then mend it."

Rose.—"Mend it! nay, the Lord mend you, and give you repentance, if it be his will. And now, if you think it good, begin at the feet, and burn the head also; for he that set you on work shall pay you your wages one day, I warrant you." And so she went and carried her mother the drink as she was commanded.

On the 17th of September, 1557, four persons were

burnt at Islington—namely, Ralph Allerton, James Austoo, Margery Austoo, and Richard Roth.

In this year, 1558, 39 persons were brought to the stake, and the whole number burnt, during the reign of Mary, amounted to 284; nearly 400 fell a sacrifice on these sad occasions, including those who died by imprisonment and famine. There were burnt 5 bishops, 21 divines, 8 gentlemen, 84 artificers, 100 husbandmen, servants, and labourers, 26 wives, 20 widows, 9 virgins, 2 boys, and 2 infants. 64 more were persecuted for their religion, whereof 7 were whipped, 16 perished in prison, and 12 were buried in dunghills.

The Death of Queen Mary.—The Happy Accession of the Lady Elizabeth to the Throne of England.

On November 17th, 1558, Queen Mary died, being in the forty-third year of her age, after having reigned five years, four months, and eleven days.

The history of her reign proves her excessive bigotry; to this she joined a cruel and vindictive temper, which she endeavoured to confound with a zeal for religion; but when it was not possible to unite them, she plainly showed that she was inclined to cruelty, no less by nature than by zeal. It was her misfortune to be encouraged in this horrid disposition by all persons who approached her. King Philip was naturally morose; Gardiner was one of the most revengeful men living; Bonner was a fury; and the other bishops were chosen from among the most cruel of the clergy. She left to her council the whole conduct of affairs, and gave herself up entirely to the humours of her clergy.

Her half-sister, the Lady Elizabeth, succeeded this bloody queen. Her accession gave infinite joy to the nation in general, but great mortification to the priests and the Romish party, who justly apprehended a new revolution in matters of religion. She passed through London, amid all the joys that a people delivered from the terrors of fire and slavery could express. King Philip proposed marriage to her, but in vain, her answer being that she had espoused her kingdom. She gave orders that all who were imprisoned on account of religion should be set at liberty; upon which a person observing that the four Evangelists were still captives, and that the people longed to see them restored to their liberty, she replied that she would speak to her subjects, in order to know their own minds. A reformation being soon resolved upon, the queen desired that the changes might be so managed as to occasion as little division as possible among her subjects; the final results of which were a new translation of the Scriptures, and the national establishment of the Protestant religion. Queen Elizabeth died in the seventieth year of her age, and the forty-fifth of her reign, on the 24th of March, 1603.

Account of the Discovery of the Gunpowder Treason, in the Year 1605. In the Reign of King James I.

The chief persons concerned in this diabolical plot were Robert Catesby, a gentleman of Norhamptonshire, Thomas Percy, the Earl of Northumberland's cousin, John Grant, Ambrose Rockwood, John and Christopher Wright, Francis Tresham, Guy Fawkes, Sir Everard Digby, Robert and Thomas Winter, Thomas Bates, and Robert Keyes. Some of these consulting together how they might restore the popish religion in England, Percy, one of the most zealous, proposed to kill the king, and offered to perform it himself: to which Catesby answered that if the king were taken off, there were still two young princes and princesses, with the greater part of the nobility and gentry, devoted to the Protestant religion; and unless these were involved in the same fate with the king, they would render their condition rather worse than better, by attempting only his majesty's life. He proposed, therefore, the blowing up the king, queen, and princes, with both the Houses of Lords and Commons, when the king should come to the house to make his speech at the opening of the session. This being approved by the rest as a most glorious undertaking, it was resolved to put it into execution; but some having scruples as to the lawfulness of committing so terrible a slaughter on account of the faith, they agreed, before they proceeded, to ask the opinion of their confessors; whereupon they consulted Henry Garnet, the superior, with Oswald Tesmond and John Gerard, two priests of the Jesuits' order, who applauded the design as just, and even pious, since it was to be executed upon excommunicated heretics, a doctrine formerly taught by Suarez, and approved of by Pope Paul V.

An oath of secrecy was then taken by the conspirators; and mass being celebrated by Gerard, they all took the sacrament, swearing to be faithful, and to promote the plot with all their powers; after which Percy took a house adjoining the House of Lords, from whence they proposed to dig a mine under it, which would contain a sufficient quantity of gunpowder to blow up the whole building. They began to work on their mine about Christmas, 1604. But the Parliament being prorogued, first to February, and then to October, and again to the 5th of November, 1605, they had time enough, or rather too much, to effect their design, though they were obliged to dig through the foundation of a very thick wall. When the conspirators had almost conquered this difficulty, they were surprised to hear a noise and the voices of persons near the place where they were at work, and began to conclude that they were discovered; but sending out Guy Fawkes for intelligence, he brought them word that the voices they had heard were in an adjoining cellar, where coals were exposed to sale; that it was exactly under the House of Lords, and was now on lease. Whereupon Percy went immediately and hired it, putting thirty-six barrels of gunpowder into it, which he had imported from Holland, and covered them with coals and faggots.

The conspirators having thus formed their scheme, and proceeded so far in the execution of it, there remained little more for them to do than to set fire to the train they had laid for blowing up the king, the queen, the prince, the nobility, and the representatives of a great and flourishing people; when, on a sudden, an unaccountable fit of tenderness seized one of the party, who, by endeavouring to rescue a friend, Lord Monteagle, from destruction, discovered the design. The following is a copy of the letter that was sent about ten days before the meeting of Parliament:—

A LETTER TO THE LORD MONTEAGLE.

"My Lord,—

"Out of the love I bear to some of your friends, I have regard to your preservation; therefore would advise you, as you tender your life, to invent some excuse to put off your attendance at this Parliament; for God and man have concurred to punish the wickedness of these times. Think not slightly of this advice, but retire yourself into the country, where you may expect the event in safety; for though there be no appearance of any stir, yet, I say, they shall receive a terrible blow in this Parliament, and shall not see who hurt them. This counsel is not to be contemned, because it may do you good, and can do you no harm, for the danger is past as soon as you have burnt the letter: and I hope God will give you the grace to make good use of it. To whose holy protection I commit you."

His lordship carried the letter, the same evening he received it, to Secretary Cecil, who communicated it to some other members of the Council: but they did not think it of that consequence to make any inquiries about the matter till the king should come from Royston, where he had gone to hunt, and would not return till the last day of October. The next day this letter was shown to his majesty, who, upon perusing it, said he did not think it was to be contemned: to which Cecil answered he was of opinion that it was written either by a fool or a madman. The king, however, ordered all the cellars, and all other places near the Parliament House, to be searched. The Earl of Suffolk, who was then lord chamberlain, and whose proper place it was to see all places prepared for the king's reception, put off the search till the day before the meeting of Parliament, and then, taking Lord Monteagle with him, viewed all the rooms about the Parliament House, and particularly the cellar under the House of Lords, which he found full of wood and coals: and having inquired who it belonged to, was answered, to Mr. Percy, who being a servant of his majesty, and one who made some figure at court, the earl returned, and acquainted the king in what state he found things, without searching further. But the king's suspicion being rather increased than diminished by the report, he ordered all the wood and coals in the cellar, already mentioned, to be removed forthwith; and Sir Thomas Knevet, a justice of peace for Westminster, and gentleman of the privy-chamber, was ordered to see it done, though it was then late at night. This gentleman was so fortunate as to discover the six-and-thirty barrels of powder hidden under the coals; he also found a man standing near the place, booted and spurred, with his cloak on, whom he searched, and found upon him a dark lanthorn and three matches. This person proved to be Guy Fawkes, one of the conspirators, who passed for Percy's man; who, seeing their plot discovered, swore, when he was apprehended, that had he been found within the cellar, he would have blown up himself and them likewise. This discovery being made, the secretary and the lord chamberlain immediately acquainted the king therewith, who was then in bed; and the prisoner, being examined before the Council, was so far from being in any consternation, that he acknowledged the design, took it all upon himself, said his conscience prompted him to it, and would name none of his accomplices; only observing that the devil had betrayed a very good design, and that there was no crime in destroying an heretical king. However, being carried to the Tower the next day, and threatened with the rack, he confessed the conspiracy, and named his accomplices; some of whom were slain, and the remainder arrested and brought to justice.

A Full Account of the Irish Massacre in the Year 1641.

So greatly had the Irish ecclesiastics increased under Charles I by titular Romish archbishops, bishops, and deans, that in the year 1629 it was deemed necessary to forbid the public exercise of the popish rites and ceremonies.

But, notwithstanding this, soon after the Romish clergy erected a new popish university in Dublin. They also proceeded to build monasteries and nunneries in various parts of the kingdom, in which the priests and the chiefs of the Irish held frequent meetings, and from thence used to pass to and fro to France, Spain, Flanders, Lorraine, and Rome, where the plot of 1641 was being hatched by the family of the O'Neils and their followers.

The great design was, that a general insurrection should take place at the same time throughout the kingdom, and that all the Protestants, without exception, should be murdered. The day fixed for this horrid massacre was the 23rd of October, 1641, the feast of Ignatius Loyola, founder of the Jesuits; and the chief conspirators in the principal parts of the kingdom made the necessary preparations for the intended conflict.

The execution of the design was delayed till the approach of winter, that the sending of troops from England might be attended with greater difficulty. Cardinal Richelieu, the French minister, had promised the conspirators a considerable supply of men and money; and many Irish officers had given the strongest assurances that they would heartily concur with their Catholic brethren as soon as the insurrection began.

Now, the day preceding that which was appointed for this horrid transaction had arrived, when, happily for the metropolis of the kingdom, the conspiracy was discovered by one Owen O'Connelly.

The metropolis was thus happily preserved; but the bloody part of the intended tragedy was past prevention.

The conspirators were in arms all over the kingdom early in the morning of the day appointed, and every Protestant that fell in their way was immediately murdered. On the 22nd of October, Sir Phelim O'Neil, upon pretence of paying a visit to Lord Charlemont, first perfidiously seized him in his castle, killed his servants before him, and in a few days murdered his lordship, with some others, in cold blood, as clearly appeared in the trial of Lord M'Guire, who was executed, for high treason, in London, in 1664. The tragedy of blood having begun, it spread all over the country. No age, no sex, no condition were spared. Even the weaker sex themselves, naturally tender to their own sufferings and compassionate to those of others, here emulated their robust companions in the practice of every cruelty. The very children, taught by example and encouraged by the exhortation of their parents, dealt their feeble blows on the dead carcases of the English children.

All the commodious habitations of the planters were laid in ashes or levelled with the ground; and where the wretched owners had shut themselves up in the houses and were preparing for defense, they perished in the flames, together with their wives and families.

The bigoted and merciless papists had no sooner begun to imbrue their hands in blood, than they repeated the horrid tragedy day after day, and the Protestants in all parts of the kingdom fell victims to their fury by deaths of the most unheard-of nature.

The Irish were more strongly instigated to execute the infernal business by the Jesuits, priests, and friars, who, when the day for the execution of the plot was agreed upon, recommended to their hearers diligence in the great design, which, they said, would greatly tend to the prosperity of the kingdom and to the advancement of the Catholic cause. They everywhere declared to the common people that the Protestants were heretics, and ought not to be suffered to live any longer among them, adding, that it was no more sin to kill an Englishman than to kill a dog, and that the relieving or protecting them was a crime of the most unpardonable nature.

Such is the general description of this unparalleled massacre: but we now select a few particulars.

When the papists besieged the town and castle of Longford, and the inhabitants of the latter, who were Protestants, surrendered on condition of being allowed quarter, the besiegers, the instant the townspeople appeared, attacked them in the most unmerciful manner; their priest, as a signal for the rest to begin, first ripped open the belly of the English Protestant minister, after which his followers murdered all the rest, some of whom were hung, others were stabbed or shot, and great numbers knocked on the head with axes provided by the rebels for the purpose.

In the barony of Trelawney, the papists, at the instigation of their friars, compelled above forty English Protestants, some of whom were women and children, to choose the fearful alternative of falling by the sword or of being drowned in the sea. Choosing the latter, they were accordingly forced, by the naked weapons of their inexorable persecutors, into the deep, where, with their children in their arms, they first waded up to their chins, and afterwards sank down and perished together.

There were some of them laid with the centre of their backs on the axletree of a carriage, with their legs resting on the ground on one side, and their arms and head on the other. In this position one of the savages scourged the wretched object on the thighs and legs, while another set on furious dogs, who tore the arms and upper parts of the body to pieces; and in this dreadful manner they were deprived of their existence.

Several were fastened to horses' tails, and the beasts being made by their riders to gallop, the wretched victims were dragged along till they expired. Many were hung on lofty gibbets, and a fire being kindled under them, they finished their lives, partly by hanging, and partly by suffocation. Nor did the more tender sex escape the full share of cruelty that could be devised by their merciless and furious persecutors. Many women, of all ages, were put to deaths of the most cruel nature.

Upwards of 1,000 men, women, and children, were driven, in different companies, to Portendown Bridge, which was broken in the middle, and were there compelled to throw themselves into the water; and such as attempted to reach the shore were knocked on the head.

The inhabitants in Kilmore, which consisted of about 200 families, all fell victims to their rage. Some of them sat in the stocks till they confessed where their money was; after which they were put to death. The whole country was one common scene of butchery, and many thousands perished, in a short time, by sword, famine, fire, water, and every species of cruel death that rage and malice could invent.

They put all the Protestants at Cashel into a loathsome dungeon, where they kept them together for several weeks in the greatest misery. At length they were released, when some of them were barbarously mangled, and left on the highways to perish at leisure; others were hanged, and some were buried in the ground upright, with their heads above the earth.

One man they forced to go to mass, after which they ripped open his body, and left him in that plight. They sawed another asunder, cut the throat of his wife, and after having dashed out the brains of their child, threw it to be devoured by the swine.

It is impossible to conceive the pleasure these monsters took in exercising such cruelty; and to increase the misery of those who fell into their hands, when they butchered them they would say, "Your soul to the devil!" One of these miscreants would come into a house with his hands imbrued in blood, and boast that it was English blood, and that his sword had pricked the white skins of the Protestants even to the hilt.

At a place called Glaslow, a popish priest, with some others, prevailed on forty Protestants to become reconciled to the Church of Rome. They had no sooner done this, than they told them they were in the true faith, and that they would prevent their relapsing and turning heretics, by sending them out of the world, which they did by immediately cutting their throats.

Upwards of thirty Protestants, men, women, and children, in the county of Tipperary, fell into the hands of the papists, who, after stripping them naked, murdered them with stones, poleaxes, swords, and other instruments.

Great numbers in Queen's County were put to the most shocking deaths. Fifty or sixty were placed together in one house, which was set on fire, and they all perished in the flames.

Several were stripped naked, and being fastened to horses by ropes placed round their middles, were dragged through bogs till they expired in the greatest torture.

Several were hung by the feet to tenter-hooks driven into poles, and left till they perished in that wretched posture.

Some were fastened to a tree, having one branch at the top. Over this branch hung one arm, which principally supported the weight of the body; and one of the legs was turned up, and fastened to the trunk, while the other hung straight. In this dreadful and uneasy posture they remained, as long as life lasted, pleasing spectacles to their bloodthirsty persecutors.

Seventeen men were buried alive at Clownes; and an Englishman, his wife, five children, and a servant maid, were all hung together, and their bodies thrown into a ditch.

Many were hung by the arms to branches of trees, with a weight to their feet, and others by the middle, in which postures they were left until they expired.

Others were hung on windmills, and before they were half dead the barbarians cut them in pieces with their swords. Some, both men, women, and children, they cut and hacked in various parts of their bodies, and left them wallowing in their blood to perish where they fell.

No less than 300 Protestants were drowned in one day in the county of Tyrone, and many others were hanged, burned, and otherwise put to death.

The cathedral of Armagh did not escape the fury of these barbarians, it being maliciously set on fire by their leaders, and burnt to the ground. And to extirpate, if possible, the very race of those unhappy Protestants who lived in or near Armagh, the Irish first burnt all their houses, and then gathered together many hundreds of those innocent people, young and old, on pretence of allowing them a guard and safe conduct to Coleraine, when they treacherously fell on them by the way, and inhumanly murdered them all.

Similar barbarities were practised on the wretched Protestants in almost all parts of the kingdom; and when an estimate was afterwards made of the number who were sacrificed to gratify the diabolical cruelty of the papists, it amounted to 150,000.

APPENDIX BY THE EDITOR

The space at our command enables us simply to sketch in outline the history of religious persecution in France, preceding and succeeding the revocation of the Edict of Nantes.

Henry II died on the 2nd of August, 1589, of a wound received from the knife of a Dominican monk, Jacques Clement, and with him the race of Valois, who bear upon their escutcheon the brand of St. Bartholomew, became extinct. Henry IV, King of Navarre, succeeded to the right of the crown in 1589. He belonged to the Reformed or Calvinistic party, but, like thousands, preferring interest to principle, he adopted Romanism shortly after his accession, to secure the allegiance of his Catholic subjects.

Henry had been the champion of truth in opposition to the League of the Guises, but this was rather the result of his political position than of his conscientious faith.

The voice of the faithful counsellor, after the examples of Nathan, John, Ambrose, and Latimer, reached the king's throne, and the expostulations and earnest warnings of Du Plessis Mornay, and of his private secretary, Gabriel D'Amours, bear witness to their fidelity in the hour of their sovereign's treason to conscience and to truth.

Beset with difficulties, and fearing the defection of his Huguenot subjects, the king, with the concurrence of his Prime Minister, Sully, in the month of April, 1598, published at Nantes the famous edict bearing the name of that town, and which guaranteed to the Reformed liberty of worship and the rights of conscience.

On the 14th of May, 1610, Henry IV perished by the knife of Ravaillac, and the Protestants trembled lest the sword of the destroyer should once more be sheathed in their liberties and lives. In the reign of Louis XIII the mutual distrust which both parties felt towards each other broke out into warfare, in which the sacking of the castle of Saumur, the siege of Montauban, and the capture of La Rochelle, are among the most memorable incidents. In vain did the Protestants endeavour to keep those cities of refuge which had been allowed them; the policy and omnipotence of Richelieu despoiled them of their fortresses, though it left them their temples and their liberty of worship. Richelieu laid it down as a maxim of state policy that the Protestants should not aspire to the great offices or emoluments of the state; but under his government they lived for the most part in peace and industry. The Edict of Nantes was respected by the crafty Mazarin, who, caring more for the intrigues of statesmanship than the propagandist orthodoxy of a churchman, saw the advantage of fostering a party in the state who could be relied upon in any domestic or foreign difficulty that might arise. The Protestants, remaining aloof from courts, devoted themselves to commerce and agriculture, and kept themselves free from the commotions of the Fronde. So touched was Louis XIV with these proofs of their fidelity, that on May 21, 1652, he issued a declaration confirming and sanctioning the Edict of Nantes, given by his grandfather, Henry IV.

Louis XIV, on his ascent to the throne, seemed determined to uphold the rights of the Protestants, partly as an act palatable to his own gigantic egotism, partly to thwart the clergy, who had reflected on his morals, and to insult the pope, with whom he had a dispute about the right of asylum; but afterwards, tormented by the terrors of his guilty conscience, he endeavoured to appease the Holy See for his earlier waywardness by a persecution of the most unexampled malignity.

Were it not for the solemnity of the subject, and the unutterable woes which he bequeathed to the French nation, there would be something ludicrous in marking his alternations of zealous or vicious moods, according as the fear of hell or the attractions of his mistresses obtained the greater sway.

Under the lash of conscience he trembled, and sought for a burnt-offering to make his peace with Heaven, but when the paroxysm had subsided, he could laugh both at the terrors of the Church and the groans of the widow, the houseless, and the mutilated, wallowing once more in the pleasures of sin.

The conversion of heretics was his plan for his justification before God, and he hoped that the sums spent upon that object would go to his credit in Heaven's account, and avail for the remission of his sins.

The first glimpse of this project appears to have originated in the king's mind about the year 1669. The king, having been catechised by Bossuet, and being aggrieved with Madame de Montespan, had emancipated himself from her thraldom. During his solitude he reflected on his sins, and thought that he had conceived a masterpiece of wisdom in offering to Heaven the abjuration of multitudes in atonement for his own crimes. But habits could not be laid aside at will; accordingly, a brief period saw him again prostrate at the feet of his mistress, and his project for conversion was forgotten or adjourned.

In 1676, the king growing cold to Madame de Montespan, Bossuet seized on the opportunity, and told him he must relinquish his mistress before he could be admitted to communion. The king was penitent, the lady received her dismissal, and projects of a holy crusade were again suggested to his most Christian Majesty.

The intendants and governors of provinces received orders to organise Catholic missions, and to invite the Protestants to conference and argument. This method was adopted for some time, but with so little success, that the king was obliged to have recourse to other means, and the next in his catalogue of persuasives was the seducing power of gold. If the heretics could not be convinced by arguments, there would be a goodly number whose principles would yield to the blinding bribe. Accordingly, a large portion out of the royal exchequer was devoted to the cause of proselytism, and its administration was entrusted to Pélisson.

The results were at first satisfactory, for in all persuasions there are some fellows of the baser sort; "and some who had earned the crown in one village would do the same in another." Owing to these artifices, the number of conversions was greatly exaggerated in the long lists which the bishops made out of the *nouveaux convertis.*

But as the number of apostates was not unlimited, the venal consciences became at last scarce, and Louis' scruples becoming again clamorous, he began to yearn for new measures to minister peace to his diseased conscience. Meanwhile the tact of Madame de Maintenon was gaining the victory. Her virtues served to whet the king's inclinations, her anxiety for his salvation soothed his fear, and finally her sway over him became absolute, not as his mistress, but, strange to say, as his lawful wife.

The cause of conversion received a mighty impetus, and the demolition of the temples of the Reformed, the abduction of their children, the billeting of soldiers on private families, became now the more deadly supplements to the power of gold.

The refined barbarity of billeting brutal soldiers in the sacred shrine of a virtuous family cannot be over-estimated. But the holy work could at no price be relaxed, for it must not be forgotten, although it is at once a grotesque yet hideous statement, "that the conversion of heretics was the king's proposed means of expiating his own sins, and of securing his own salvation."

The natural result of this employment of soldiers in the work of missions was an exodus of the Protestants, and thousands emigrated, seeking in foreign countries an asylum which their native land would not afford.

On the 18th of October, 1685, the fatal signature was attached to the revocation of the Edict of Nantes.

Historians have generally remarked that from that day the prosperity of Louis declined, and that the king, who in the beginning of his reign was looked upon as fortune's favourite at home and abroad, had to pass under the Caudine Forks, vanquished at Blenheim, Ramillies, and Malplaquet, and to sue for an ignoble peace in the Treaty of Utrecht. Royalty lost its prestige, as the subsequent disasters were attributed to the despotism of one man, a slave to his bigotry or his passions.

Commercially, France was a great sufferer. Vauban tells us that before a year had elapsed France had lost 100,000 inhabitants, sixty millions of money, 9,000 sailors, 12,000 soldiers, and 600 officers. Voltaire states that within three years 50,000 families quitted the kingdom; and Sismondi reckoned that 400,000 established themselves in foreign countries, carrying with them the secret of those arts and manufactures in which France was without a rival. It is concluded that half a million of the most industrious and moral Frenchmen became aliens for conscience sake; and that the number of exiles was prodigious may be gathered from the fact, that in England eleven regiments of French volunteers were formed, and in London alone twenty-two French churches were built within a short time.

The tocsin of Louis XIV sounded during seven years of blood and slaughter. Who can estimate the additional and the unknown victims? Besides the exiles to whom we have just referred, we must sum up those who perished in the dank dungeon; we must number those who were worn out on the convict's bench in the purgatorial galleys; we must take the census of those who perished in desultory conflicts, and in the protracted war of the Camisards in the Cevennes; we must gloss over no single victim of the stake, the scaffold, or the wheel. This is to be our accursed arithmetic, these our bloody statistics, which are to be looked upon as the sequel of the drop of ink which glittered for a moment suspended on the pen of his most Christian Majesty.

It would have been difficult for us to narrate the infinity of legal vexations, not to say aggressive outrages, which harassed the unhappy Protestants even before the overt act of the revocation of the Edict of Nantes; but their cup of misery was now drained to its dregs; their temples were destroyed; their pastors were proscribed, and implacably executed; the penalty for assembling to hear the Word of God and prayer was the galleys for life, imprisonment, torture, death, and hurling the unburied corpse to the dogs and the fowls of the air. Yet such was the tenacity with which the generality of the Protestants adhered to their convictions, that they flocked to hear the Word of God when any secreted pastor gave a rendezvous, albeit the half-breathed "Amen" might be interrupted with the shouts of the murderous dragoons, and wounds or martyrdom be the sequel to the cadence of the hymn.

In this way arose those religious meetings which have procured for the churches the name of "Les Eglises du Desert," and for the pastors that of "Pasteurs du Desert." It is difficult for us to realise the solemn awe which must have invested such meetings, where the worshippers might indeed be said to be worshippers on the confines of eternity. The place often chosen was some deep defile or glen, or some open glade surrounded by woods, whose labyrinths, familiar to the people, would entangle infantry, and be impracticable to cavalry. The videttes were then duly appointed, and upon some neighbouring eminence did the watchers stand, to signal to the band the advent of the king's dragoons. The people for miles would flock to the assembly, and painfully pathetic would be their meeting—numbers of them bereaved of their relatives, and many meeting for the last time. The pastor, himself under the ban of death, would speak with an impassioned pathos to those whose hunger and thirst for the bread of life had drawn them together, at the penalty of confiscation of their goods, the galleys, the wheel, or the scaffold. He himself, hunted like a partridge in the mountains, would bear traces of suffering, danger, and want, and appear a feeble instrument; but his holy themes would cause his soul to burn, and raise him above himself. What fervour would there be in his exhortations, and what pathos in his prayers, when every circumstance stamped a fearful reality upon all they said and did!

It might be supposed that the criminal infatuation and bigotry of Louis had reached its climax, but there was yet an original mode left of laying claim to the eternal obloquy of the human race. Never yet had the world seen its parallel, nor could his crafty advisers even cite a precedent, an argument so valid in courts of law. On March 8, 1715, the king passed an edict, based upon a known falsehood; it was, in short, an embodied legal lie. This was the resolve to consider all the Protestants alike, as having been converted, and to treat them as relapsed, without any distinction whatever. So monstrous was the fiction felt to be, that a large party of Catholics, with Vauban at their head, presented a memorial to the king on the subject. The king's gracious answer to this remonstrance was the decree of death to all who should attempt to escape from the galleys, and the galleys to those who should attempt to leave the kingdom. In this Louis exceeds the Spanish King Philip III in his folly and bigotry, in the extirpation of the Moors from Spain, as also the chiefs of the League, who, if they professedly made war against heresy, allowed their victims to escape at their own will.

But Louis was implacable to them under all conditions: it was martyrdom to stay; it was martyrdom to go: it was confiscation for remaining in France; it was confiscation for leaving France: it was the galleys for tainting his Christian Majesty's soil; but it was the galleys for trying to rid him of the plague: it was death at home, it was death on the frontier; for every place, every clime, every refuge, were alike forbidden to the unhappy Protestant.

Notwithstanding the most rigorous cruelties and the terrible risks, the tide of emigration did not abate. Hundreds disguised themselves as pilgrims, couriers, hunters, herdsmen, and drivers of carts of merchandise. The rich gave fabulous prices to guides to conduct them over the frontier, while the lonely fugitive travelled by night, lurking during the day in the forest or the cavern. Nor did the females refuse to adopt the same method. They dressed in male attire, they dyed their faces, they adopted every imaginable character, disguise, and artifice, to be allowed to escape from their native soil.

The emigrants went forth, carrying with them the versatile talents and refined taste which, when combined with

industry and morality, make the French workman a rival
to be dreaded even by the energetic Anglo-Saxon. Some
went to Brandenburg, where their services were readily
called into exercise in the army, in surgery, in painting, and
in architecture. The trades connected with the manufacture
of hats, gloves, paper, silk, tapestry, glass, and jewellery,
and even agricultural and floral science, all received a
definite impulse in advance.

England received many benefits from this pacific invasion of the rival Gaul. It appears certain that the revocation of the Edict of Nantes scattered some 70,000 French
operatives throughout Great Britain. A great number of
these located themselves in London, in the neighbourhood
of Soho and St. Giles's, and in the untenanted regions of
Spitalfields. The English owe them many obligations, for
they speedily introduced improvements into the manufacture of paper, glass, hats, and a number of other articles.
The refugees bequeathed the art of making the choicest
kinds of brocades, satins, velvets, and linen, while the
branches of horology, cutlery, and practical surgery were
immensely profited by the foreigners' advent. But the
manufacture of silk took the deepest root, and flourished
most vigorously in English soil, so that England, importing
the exotic produce of the silkworm, before long surpassed
in excellence of manufacture those countries where the
animal was indigenous.

In 1691 the royal counsels were leavened with the spirit
of the Jansenists, a party who were opposed to the system
of cruel violence which was so relentlessly advocated by
the Jesuit faction; and Madame de Maintenon, who was
married to the king, and had little to gain by pandering to
his superstitious fears, inclined to a course of mildness
more in unison with the womanly dictates of her heart.
Cardinal de Noailles, a man of noble character and great
ability, ranged himself on the side of the Jansenists, and
thus gave the Protestants the benefit of his protection. But
Père la Chaise, of the Society of Jesus, was keeper of the
king's conscience, and of the portfolio of church promotion, and as such his influence was great.

The History and Martyrdom of Claude Brousson, Pastor of Nismes.

We must now leave our general sketch of the history of
this period, and present our readers with the individual
portrait of one of those apostles who appear at the inter-

vals of centuries, but whom persecution and adverse circumstances to a certain extent throw into relief.

Claude Brousson was born at Nismes, in 1647, and
embracing the legal profession, established himself at Toulouse. So long as it was possible, he was the advocate of the
rights of the Reformed before the tribunal; but the discovery of a "Comité de Resistance," which assembled at his
house, compelled him to escape for his life. The Duke de
Noailles forbad the inhabitants of Nismes, under pain of
death, from receiving the proscribed. Accordingly, Brousson was obliged to wander for two days and nights,
perished and starved, hiding where he could, until he
discovered a way of escape down the great sewer which led
into the Grande Rue. After incredible exertions, he gained
the Cevennes, and having reached Switzerland, settled at
Lausanne. But Brousson's heart was with his people, and
the groanings of the prisoners in the Tour de Constance at
Aigues Mortes, stirred his heart to succour the outcasts of
God's heritage who were languishing without the care of
religion.

Despite the entreaties of his wife, he set out for Languedoc, and amid the fastnesses of the Cevennes, and within
ear-shot of the deadly cannon, he was ordained a minister
of Jesus Christ, by a woollen spinner, named François
Vivens. He assembled his flock by night between two
rocks, lit by a feeble torchlight or the quivering moon-
beam, and descending from his pulpit, would perform all
his ministerial functions. That the perils attending him
were great may be gathered from the fact that the dead
were often obliged to be buried in a hole in a stable, or
even by the side of the couch where they had breathed
their last.

Mr. Borrel, in his life of Brousson, gives a most interesting account, related by an eye-witness, of an assembly
presided over by our martyr, and dispersed by the dragoons:

"Some time before our brothers in the Cevennes had
raised the banner of the holy war, we were told that in
three days the venerable Brousson would hold an assembly
at *des Bergines,* near Vergèze. The place so called was a
large cavern in the eastern slope of a hill covered with
olive trees; the entrance was so small that but one person
could enter at a time, and that only by crawling. The olive
trees seemed to promise us perfect safety, covering with
their thick boughs the place of our retreat. On the morning

of the day fixed, in order not to arouse the suspicions of
the Catholics, some feigned sickness, others ostensibly went
to mass, but at the same time they dug up their psalters,
and also the arms they had succeeded in hiding. The
women trembled; nevertheless, they did not advise any one
not to attend the assembly, for they wished to go themselves, the desire of being united with the brethren enabling
them to brave the danger. It appeared a long day, being
passed in the expectation of a great joy, and the dread of a
great danger. At last the night arrived, and a cold, pene-
trating rain made the weather very gloomy. We stole
stealthily from our dwellings, leaving the old people griev-
ing that they could not follow us, and the mothers praying
for us with deep emotion. I had not reached my eighteenth
year. My sister, and brother, and my father accompanied
me. Upon our way we met the sentinels, who promised to
maintain a good watch. There was already a large assembly
when we arrived; people had come from all parts of the
Vaunage. The people who were engulfed in the deep
trenches made a plaintive whistling, and to lighten these
gloomy places they had several small lanterns. In the
middle of the assembly the venerable Brousson was sitting,
wearing the coarse dress of a peasant. The women had
fastened their black aprons round the chair which served
for a pulpit. The sacramental wine and bread were placed
upon a stone. The service commenced by reading the Bible
and singing a psalm. The preacher took his text from the
memorable words of Jesus in Matt. x. 22—'He that is
faithful unto the end shall be saved.' Wishing to prove that
salvation is only promised unto those who fight without
ceasing the fight of faith, he quoted the example of all the
confessors of ancient and apostolic times. Then he pointed
out the courage of the martyrs of the present day, confounding their judges before the tribunals, moving their
executioners upon the wheel, and receiving in heaven a
crown of life. Then he traced out the miseries of the
cowardly apostates, reserved for eternal fire, and consumed
during this life with agonies of remorse. Oh! what tears of
repentance flowed at this time, what oaths of fidelity were
made! In the midst of sobs the pastor blessed the bread and
the wine for the communion, then we prostrated ourselves
before God, entreating him to pardon and to strengthen us.
All of a sudden a piercing voice cried out, 'The dragoons!
the dragoons! escape! escape! escape without delay!' At
the same moment a discharge of musketry told us that our

last hour was near. What happened in the cavern I cannot tell. We were enveloped in the thickest darkness. The oaths of the soldiers and the cries of the dying confounded us in the frightful tumult. I do not know how I was saved myself. I found my mother half-wild, and at a point of despair. My relations did not come; we watched in vain for them; they never appeared. My father was found lying at the bottom of a precipice, with his skull broken by the fall. My brother received a ball in his breast, and my sister had been taken to the Tower of Constance, with the women who were made prisoners. Fifteen days afterwards, I accompanied my mother to another assembly in the desert."

The assembly thus adjourned *vi et armis* was held elsewhere, and Brousson presided again over its ministrations. But this time the authorities sought his immediate capture, and Baville had ordered the soldiers to take him at all hazards. In the midst of the tumult, however, the intended victim disappeared.

He had slipped into the angle of a rock, where he stood motionless while the dragoons passed him hundreds of times. This failure caused Baville to put a price on his head of 500 livres, and the proclamation was affixed to the doors of all the churches and public places. After this Brousson reached Lausanne, but his apostolic spirit could not rest, and he ministered to the French refugees, traversing the cantons of Vaud, Berne, and Zurich. Whilst in Holland he printed a volume of sermons, entitled "Mystic Manna of the Desert," which he had composed in the forest, and preached to bands of brethren doomed to death.

In September, 1695, Brousson re-entered France. Having crossed the forest of Ardennes, he arrived at Sedan, but was persecuted with such fury, that with difficulty he escaped, disguised as a porter. From thence he reached Normandy, and traversed Flanders and Artois on foot. After a year's pilgrimage through the north of the Loire, he was so hunted, that he was forced to escape into Switzerland in 1696. The peace of Ryswick being concluded, Baville employed his troops in fresh persecutions against the Protestants, and in Languedoc more than 40,000 people became exiles. Cries of misery reached the ears of Brousson, and in 1697 he entered France on his third apostolate. He was detained in Dauphiny during the winter by the snow, but he found there many who heard him with delight, having been for four months without a preacher.

The following spring he entered Vivarais, and went from village to village preaching to multitudes. He then left for the Cevennes, and arrived in the vicinity of Nismes on April 28, 1698. Baville, informed of his return, augmented the price on his head to 200 louis d'ors. The pursuit became still more vigorous, but Brousson boldly entered the town, and posted a petition, signed by himself, to the king. This put the spies on his track, and they surrounded the house in which he had taken refuge. Escape seemed impossible, and he was about to give himself up, when his host made him get into a dry cistern, at the bottom of which there was a hole. Owing to his mistake in delivering a letter to the wrong man, Brousson was arrested at Oloron, and imprisoned at Pau. Being allowed to go out on parole, he had several opportunities of escape, but he remained faithful to his promise, considering his word to be his bond. He was sent to Montpellier the 30th of October, 1698, and was shut up in the citadel, where, five days after, he was brought before Baville. The crimes of which he was accused were treason and conspiracy against the state. These he indignantly repudiated, but confessed that he had preached the Gospel of Christ to sinners. After a short consultation, the judges pronounced the following iniquitous sentence: "Claude Brousson, convicted of rebellion and treason to the laws of the kingdom, is condemned, first, to suffer the question ordinary and extraordinary, then to be broken on the wheel, and finally to be hung after death on the malefactors' gibbet." The victim humbly bowed his head, and began to pray for his judges, and his conduct so touched their hearts, that Baville commuted his sentence, and ordered the executioner not to touch him except on the scaffold. He walked there between two guards of soldiers. Having reached the place of execution, he endeavoured to speak to the multitude, but the rolling of eighteen drums drowned his voice. He was silent, knelt down, joined his hands, raised his eyes towards heaven, and his last words were those of prayer to God; after which he gave himself up to the executioner.

Events Succeeding the Revocation of the Edict of Nantes, Comprising the War of the Camisards and the Sufferings of Some of the Protestant Gallerians.

When the mighty national ruin caused by the revocation of the Edict of Nantes began to be felt, some protests were heard in various parts of the kingdom. The Jansenists

declared the proselytism of the sword, the galleys, and the
scaffold to be a sacrilege against the rights of religion and
conscience, and as such they were arrayed against their
hereditary enemies, the Jesuits, who were the most strenuous advocates of coercive measures. Among individuals
we would mention the names of the Bishops of Grenoble
and Saint Pons, M. de Noailles, Archbishop of Paris, the
Marquis d'Augesseau, the Duke de Beauvilliers, the Marquis de Pompone, Marshal Catinat, Vauban, Racine, Féné-
lon, and even Madame de Maintenon, who had quarrelled
with the king's confessor, the Jesuit La Chaise. But their
efforts only elicited a fresh edict, confirming the fatal one
of October 18th, 1685, abolishing no law of torture, but
merely ordering methods to be taken for the better instruction of heretics.

Among the governors of the provinces who ruled with
fire and sword was Lamoignon de Baville, who had been
for thirty-three years intendant, or, as he was called, King
of Languedoc. He was an apostle of persecution, and
without an emotion could enforce the desolation of a
province, or the massacre of an entire assembly. Nor were
the priesthood unwilling agents of the provincial proconsul,
but often put themselves at the head of the soldiers in the
pursuit of the proscribed heretics. To one of these we must
now draw our attention, as the cruelties he practised were
one of the more immediate causes of the anomalous war of
the Camisards, and the revolt in the Cevennes. Du Chayla
was archpriest and inspector-general of the missionaries of
the Cevennes. In earlier life he had been sent on a mission
to Siam, where he had not only obtained a great insight
into the spirit of persecution, but qualified himself to
become an inventor in the implements of conversion,
having been captured and nearly killed under tortures of
the most horrible description.

He had now a debt of revenge against his race, which he
was determined to repay with interest when opportunity
offered. Half martyred himself, he would martyr others
with tenfold intensity.

The prisoners who unhappily fell into his hands were
subjected to treatment which would be incredible were it
not attested by all the people in the neighbourhood. Sometimes he dragged the hair from their chin and eyebrows
with pincers; sometimes with the same pincers he put
burning coals into their hands, which he closed and pressed
till the fire was extinguished. Often he covered their hands

with cotton steeped in oil or grease, which he lighted, and allowed to burn until the fingers opened or were eaten to the bone by the flames.

The cellars of his palace were turned into dungeons, and crowded with prisoners. To these vaults he could descend at pleasure to behold the sufferings of his victims; and often did he scourge his captives, both young and old, male and female, until he became drenched with their blood. when the various tortures did not succeed to the abbé's satisfaction, he cast them into the stocks.

For twenty years did this atrocious despotism weigh heavily upon the unfortunate people, and those who were able were glad to escape from the country, though at the risk of being caught by the abbé's ecclesiastical videttes, and consigned to his cellars. There were times when the unhappy abbé himself seemed to feel the pangs of agony and fear within himself, as if his conscience were lashing him. He would suddenly be seized with strange shiverings, and falling on his knees, with his hands joined and his head bent, would often remain for hours lost in an abyss of thought, when a cold sweat would stand on his brow. Such was the man who had become an experienced torturer, and anticipating, it may be, his tragic fate, had built his own sepulchre in the church of St. Germain.

Amongst numerous acts of injustice and oppression, we may mention the following. Some persons at Melouze had suspended a dead dog, or wolf, on a cross of stone, erected at a spot bearing the name of "The Cross of Blood" and which was the appointed rendezvous of the Camisard leaders. Above the animal was a rude charcoal tracing, threatening vengeance and death to the wolves who were ravishing the heritage of the Lord. The abbé was informed of the fact, and, indignant at the sacrilege, imposed a severe and public expiation on all the surrounding district, to their great discomfort and irritation. But the following circumstance was the spark which fired the subsequent explosion. In the month of July, 1702, a band of fugitives were collected under the guidance of a muleteer named Massip, who had undertaken to escort them to Geneva. This mournful cavalcade, among whom were several persons highly connected, were making for the left bank of the Rhine, when they fell into an ambuscade of the militia, by whom they were captured and led to the archpriest. Inexorable to all their entreaties and that of their friends, his sentence was short but decisive—"The men and women to torture, the ceps and the galleys; the guide to the gallows." An assembly was held on Sunday, July 23rd, on the mountains of Bougès, when those who laid claim to the gift of prophecy, the chief of whom was Pierre Séguier, incited the audience to attempt their release, crying, "The Lord hath commanded us to take up arms, to deliver our brethren out of captivity, and slay the archpriest of Moloch." Couderc spoke after him to the same effect, and Abraham Mazel, another of the inspired, endorsed the procedure. A rendezvous was appointed, and on the following night fifty persons came together, pledged to the above purpose. Some twenty were armed with guns and pistols, while the rest had only scythes and hatchets. After Séguier had exhorted them and given his benediction to the undertaking, he descended at their head, all of them chanting with one voice a familiar psalm—"those famous hymns of the desert," which often echoed through the wilderness in the tones of prayer, victory, and defeat. On the 14th of July, at ten p.m., Du Chayla was in his palace, surrounded by a few ecclesiastics and soldiers, when his ear caught in the distance the sound of the psalmody of the approaching band. The inmates of the palace, believing it to be a proscribed assembly, were preparing to surprise them, but found themselves unable to quit the castle, which was invested by the besiegers. "The prisoners! the prisoners!" shouted the maddened assailants.

Séguier had now crossed the ditch, and, with the help of a dozen of his comrades, battered at the inside door until it gave way, when the Camisards deployed in the inner court. Above the noise of the strife arose the chant of the psalm, interrupted at last by the abbé's order to fire, when one of the Camisards was killed, and two were wounded. With axe and hammer they attacked the barricade, while others, mounting on the shoulders of their comrades, maintained a plunging fire. Laporte, full of vengeance for the loss of his father, and Séguier, fired by the recollection of his martyed son, led the van. The abbé, in his inner chamber, heard the tumult, and knowing its serious import, gathered round him his household, who knelt around him and received his last absolution. As he pronounced the words the barricades yielded, and the soldiers, pursued by the insurgents, took refuge in a lower hall beneath the chamber of the abbé. Some of the assailants then went in quest of the prisoners, whose cries for help could be heard amid the din of battle. Some of these wretched creatures had been for eight days with their legs jammed in the stocks, and presented a hideous spectacle, with their swollen bodies and broken limbs. The sight of these victims maddened the Camisards, who threw themselves again upon the soldiers. The latter, mounting the stairs, reached the chamber of the abbé, from whence they twice repulsed the insurgents with some loss. Laporte, seeing three men killed and five or six wounded, cried out to his comrades to lay aside their arms, and to set fire to the building. The word was no sooner spoken than carried into execution. In a short time the whole house was on fire, the roof fell in, and the abbé, in his flight, had his shoulder half burnt. Unable longer to resist, he made a cord of the sheets of his bed, which, aided by a valet, he tied to a window looking on the garden, hoping by this means to effect his escape. But in sliding down he fell and broke his thigh; still he dragged himself under the hedge which formed the enclosure of the garden; but the glare of the fire betrayed him to view, and the assailants ran to him, crying, "Let us strangle this persecutor of the children of God!" As soon as he was seized, they reproached him for all his cruelties to the Protestants during the seventeen years he had been inspector of missions in the Cevennes; and added, it was now time that he should expiate his crimes by a death which, however dreadful it might be, could never equal what he deserved. He replied to none of these reproaches, but meekly begged for life with that abject terror which fear of death alone inspires, saying words which were calculated to make an impression on them—"Ah! my friends, if I have eternally lost my soul, do you wish also to lose yours?" This speech, instead of disarming his hearers, was no sooner uttered, than each one hastened to strike him. Each blow was accompanied by "This is for the cruelty you exercised against my father," or "against my mother," or "against my brother," or "against my sister;" "That is for having condemned (such a one) to the galleys;" "This is for condemning (such a one) to death." But as the crimes of which he was accused were too numerous for each to be represented on his body, and as his life ebbed too rapidly from him to be struck so many times, they were at length obliged to put an end to their work. We are told that he received fifty-two wounds, of which twenty-four were mortal.

Such was the first spark which led to the insurrection of the Cevennes, and the extraordinary and romantic war of the Camisards.

The insurgents, headed by Séguier, continued for some time to indulge in unbridled excesses, and to endeavour to compass a general massacre of the priests. When Baville was apprised of these proceedings, he sent a Captain Poul, who succeeded before long in capturing Séguier, and brought him in chains to Florac. The prophet, or fanatic, as he is termed by the other party, manifested a calm bearing before his judges, as was testified by his examiners.

"Your name?"

"Pierre Séguier."

"Why have you been surnamed Esprit?"

"Because the Spirit of God is in me."

"Your dwelling-place?"

"The desert, and soon heaven."

"Ask pardon of the king."

"We have no king but the Eternal."

"Have you no remorse for your crimes?"

"My soul is like a watered garden."

He was condemned to have his hand cut off, and to be burned alive; and on the pyre he triumphed over his sufferings, exclaiming, "Brethren, wait for and hope in God; the desolate Carmel shall rejoice again, and Lebanon shall yet blossom as the rose."

After this the Count de Broglie, supposing the outbreak quelled, dismissed the nobles, and bade the fugitive priests return to their parishes. But the spirit only slumbered for a moment until lit up once more by the long stifled but unconquerable energy of the persecuted. Laporte was the first who took the command of the rebels, calling himself "Colonel of the Children of God," and his camp the "Camp of the Eternal."

Another troop of fanatics was soon formed, under the leadership of Castanet, and another by Roland, whose name figures jointly with that of Cavalier in the annals of the Cevennes for deeds of genius and bravery. He was active and tall in his figure, zealous for the religion of his fathers, and counted it better to perish in battle than to live without temples, pastors, or any of the ministrations of religion.

Another troop was also formed by a young man named Jean Cavalier, who becomes the central figure in the subsequent history of the War of the Cevennes.

The career of this person is indeed remarkable in point of romance and incident, for his innate talent for military tactics and strategy enabled him to maintain his guerilla

warfare in spite of the royal troops, to withstand the
assaults of two marshals of France, and to gain numerous
victories, with a literal handful, over the king's dragoons. If
at last he appeared to be guilty of treachery, allowance
must be made for his self-elation, falling before the wiles
of the tempter, considering that he was but a baker's boy,
and a novice in diplomacy, being at the conclusion of the
war but twenty-three years of age.

On the 22nd of October, 1702, Laporte was betrayed by
treachery, surprised by Captain Poul, and killed at Mont-
leyon; but in the meantime the numbers of insurgents had
increased, and one or two fresh bands, under other leaders,
appeared on the scene, who, infuriated by their long
oppression, retaliated by the murder of the Romish priests,
and the burning of the churches. They held assemblies for
prayer and praise as opportunity offered, which were
generally followed by the capture and matrydom of some
of those present.

All that they did they did at the command of the Spirit,
and often mere children fell into the ecstatic state, and with
the most absolute confidence prescribed a definite line of
conduct. As soon as an oracle had spoken they hastened to
obey; if they were going to attack the enemy, if they were
forming an ambuscade, if they were in flight, if the site of
an assembly was to be chosen, prayer was commanded,
and they fell upon their knees, awaiting some manifestation
of the will of God. Under these inspirations they lost all
fear of death, esteeming the cross of martyrdom a glory;
and even their children waxed valiant in the fight. To their
prophets they attributed their success, and their failures to
their own disobedience. "How," says Elie Marion, "could
we, a small handful, without education, experience, or
military knowledge, have maintained our warfare without
succour from Heaven? Our prophets were our chiefs. They
taught us to receive the first fire of the enemy on our
knees, and to attack them singing psalms." Besides their
prophets, many of their leaders were their ministers, and
Roland, Castanet, and Cavalier performed all the sacred
functions for their respective bands. The assemblies were
generally held without the time or place being fixed,
sometimes in a cavern, a valley, or a wood, but when
possible secret intelligence was conveyed to all in the
neighbourhood, when crowds flocked to hear the Word of
God. The service consisted of the reading the Word of
God, singing psalms, public prayer, sermons, all of which

were often interrupted by ecstatic manifestations on the
part of those who felt themselves inspired by the Holy
Spirit. They had public prayer three times a day; their
motley band, armed with guns, swords, pikes, or scythes,
fell upon the foe singing a psalm, and after the action knelt
down on the field of battle to return thanks to God. In
order to provision themselves, which was a matter of
difficulty, besides what they took from the Catholics, they
received contributions of various articles—cheese, butter,
bread, soup—from the Protestants at a fixed rendezvous,
when supplies were meted out by the chiefs to their bands
with the utmost order and exactitude. But when the resources of the country had been drained, or their supplies
cut off by the vigilance of the royal troops, they had to
betake themselves to other expedients. They accordingly
formed magazines in the recesses of the desert, in the
depths of the woods, and in caverns, where they stored the
wheat and other provisions which they might have procured by foraging; but it often happened that they had to
endure long and enforced fasts. The supply of shoes was a
matter of much difficulty, and especially the supply of
powder and ball. But industry and enterprise overcame all
obstacles. They collected all the saltpetre they could, which
they boiled in caldrons; the forests gave a plentiful supply
of willows, of which they made charcoal, and ground it up
by force of labour. After mixing the materials, they dried
the powder in the sun, and then storing it in barrels or
sacks, sent it by trusty agents to different secret deposi-
tories, in remote or almost inaccessible places. The lead
was taken from houses, churches, and windows, but this
not sufficing, they smelted all the pewter vessels they could
seize, of which they made bullets, the wounds of which
were more deadly than those of lead. They made use of
their caverns as hospitals for the wounded, and all the
medical and surgical skill that was to be found among
them was generally consecrated to the relief of the
sufferers. But we cannot follow this paradoxical war into
its details; suffice it to say that Roland and Cavalier, with a
handful of men, held their own from November, 1702, to
April, 1704, notwithstanding the opposition of three field
marshals of France, and all the resources of the Grand
Monarque Louis XIV. Often did Cavalier gain brilliant
victories, as at Cauvi, Vagnas, Lussan, Nages, Aubais; and
often were whole regiments of the king's dragoons cut to
pieces in some well-concerted ambuscade. Besides the rec-

ord of ordinary warfare, various tragic events stand out in bloody relief in the chronicles of the time, and in connection with one of those the name of Marshal Montrevel is steeped with obloquy. On Palm Sunday two or three hundred old men, women, and children, from the city of Nismes, were gathered for prayer at the house of one Mercier, the proprietor of a mill near the gate of Cannes. Their psalm discovered their retreat, and the lieutenant of police informed the marshal of the fact. Rising from table, and heated with wine, he put himself at the head of a battalion, and invested the mill. The soldiers broke in upon the hapless multitude, but the marshal, impatient at the slow progress of the sword, ordered the mill to be fired. A universal cry rose to heaven, the victims tried to escape, but, bloody and wounded, and black with smoke, or seared with the fire, they were driven back by the bayonets of the soldiers, to complete the hecatomb. The tumult was heard even in the cathedral, where the congregation was seized with a panic, fearing that it was an attack of the Camisards, until the bishop, Fléchier, apprised of the true cause, calmed his audience, and concluded the vesper chant. Every single person perished in this diabolical massacre.

Labaume, Fléchier, and even Madame de Maintenon had to become apologists for this fiendish slaughter. Two other monstrous outrages on human nature were likewise the work of the same Marshal Montrevel. The first was the literal depopulation of certain proscribed parishes in the Cevennes, and the deportation of all their inhabitants. But the marshal had conceived a still nobler idea; this was nothing less than the devastation of the high Cevennes by fire, so that not a shred of food or shelter might be left for the unhappy Protestant. Four hundred and sixty-six towns, villages, and hamlets, inhabited by 19,500 persons, were absolutely destroyed.

The futility of Montrevel's reign of terror to suppress the rebellion having been proved, Marshal Villars was appointed as his successor, who sought to effect his purpose through pacific overtures and the blinding arts of flattery. He commenced negotiations with Cavalier, and an interview was arranged between them, in which the baker's boy and the plenipotentiary of Louis XIV discussed, upon terms of equality, a truce and the demands of the insurgents for the rights of conscience. Cavalier entered Nismes like a conqueror, and was hailed by the people as their deliverer. "Had the king himself been there," says St.

Simon, "a greater concourse could not have been gathered together." His interview with Villars, the conqueror of Fredlingen, accompanied by Baville, the intendant of Languedoc, and Sandricourt, the governor of Nismes, took place on the 16th of May, 1704, in the "Jardin des Récolets," near that exquisite relic of antiquity, the "Maison Carrée." He appears, however, to have succumbed to the tempter, and to have conceded some of the vital points for which his brethren had risen up in arms. Roland rejected with contempt the proffered terms, and determined to carry on the war, notwithstanding the defection of Cavalier. But disaster attended him. He was betrayed, and slain; Ravanel was defeated; Catinat, Castanet, Joani, Salomon, and Elie retreated to Geneva; whereupon Marshal Villars, considering the insurrection virtually concluded, left Languedoc. Cavalier afterwards came to England, and was appointed governor of Jersey. He died at an advanced age at Chelsea Hospital.

Having thus given a brief outline of this period of French history, we revert to the records of individual faith, and allude to some of those noble martyrs who wore out years, or even a lifetime, at the purgatorial galleys.

The Baron de Salgas was a nobleman of the house of Pelet, one of the most ancient in France. He was born a Protestant, but combining somewhat of the traits of Nicodemus and Demas, veiled his convictions from motives of worldly policy and self-interest. Castanet, one of the leaders of the Camisards, considering this conduct of the baron to be inconsistent with the fearlessness of Christian integrity, determined to force him from his neutrality, and to compromise him by the overt act of assisting at one of their religious assemblies. Accordingly, on Sunday, the 2nd of February, 1703, he put himself at the head of eighty armed men, and marched to the Château of Salgas, where the baron lived. De Salgas, taken by surprise, was obliged to place himself at the disposal of the band, who, treating him to a certain extent as a prisoner, placed him in the centre of the troop, and marched to Vebron, where an assembly had been arranged. Worship commenced; they read, prayed, sang, and preached, and at its conclusion the baron was informed that he might return when he pleased. It appears that he remained afterwards two hours with Castanet and his troops, probably to take measures to prevent his castle being burnt, as some half-dozen others in the neighbourhood had been during the preceding week.

But in thinking of his property he forgot himself, for by this imprudence he had furnished Montrevel with a pretext for his arrest. He, however, informed the intendant of the violence to which he had been subjected, and was advised to be more discreet and guarded for the future.

De Salgas was present, not long after, at a meeting of the nobles which Marshal Montrevel had summoned, and on being presented to him, the latter observed that the Camisards must be friends of his, since they had conducted him to their assembly and sent him away scatheless. The baron felt the keen satire which lurked in the remark, but replied, "This was fortunate for me, sir, but you must not on that account think less of my zeal for his majesty's service." Some conversation ensued, and the marshal, embracing him on both cheeks, promised to be more friendly to him than his late compulsory entertainers. Although the baron urgently placed his services at Montrevel's disposal, they were not accepted, but he was ordered to repair to his château, and not to leave his domains without orders. Not long after this, Montrevel summoned the baron to appear at Nismes, with which order the latter, fearing the perils of the route, hesitated to comply. The marshal accordingly marked his victim. One day, as the baron was going out hunting, he saw a detachment of from 700 to 800 men approach his château. Thinking they had lost their way to Vebron, he went to meet them with kind inquiries and the offer of refreshment. An officer of his acquaintance, by name Prefosse, was at the head of the squadron. De Salgas embraced him, and pressed him to accept of his hospitality. The latter at first seemed inclined to refuse, but at last allowed himself to be overcome, and entered the castle. The déjeuner was served, and Prefosse executed his mission of arresting the baron with all the grace and delicacy possible. He was conducted to St. Hippolyte, and on his entrance into the citadel the governor took from him his purse, containing 186 louis d'ors, and returned him ten for his own use. In a day or two, Montrevel and Baville entered St. Hippolyte, and the latter repaired to the citadel to hear the process.

"I appeared eighteen times before him," says the baron, in his manuscript memoirs, "and was confronted with twenty-eight witnesses, who altogether did not advance enough to secure the whipping of a school-boy, and the greatest charge they brought against me was the voluntarily remaining two hours with Castanet and his troop."

Every effort was made to procure evidence to condemn the unhappy baron, and he would doubtless have lost his head, but for the good disposition of some of the officials. Judgment was given at Alais, on the 27th of June, by the intendant Baville, assisted by certain counsellors from Nismes. Salgas was condemned "to the galleys for life, to serve his majesty as a convict; he and his posterity were degraded from their rank and titles; his goods were all confiscated, and his château of Rousses was to be razed to its foundations." On hearing the sentence the baron trembled and turned pale; a chain, weighing 30 lbs., was fastened round his neck, and it was a most piteous sight to see his children clinging to him until he was dragged from their embraces, so that many in the crowd, though they were Roman Catholics, felt one throb of the common humanity, and could not resist shedding tears at so heartrending a tragedy.

Such was the sentence of the king's court—such the justice of Louis XIV—such the clemency shown to this most venial act. On hearing the sentence a gentleman exclaimed, "O French nobility! your heart must be changed if you think such treatment preferable to death. O God! into what contempt and ignominy have we fallen!" The baron was convicted of no other crime, and although they subjected him to the torture, ordinary and extraordinary, he pleaded guilty to nothing else but having been present at the assembly at Vebron, and having voluntarily remained two hours with Castanet and his troops. Despite the iron despotism which coerced the expression of opinions, public feeling was sorely grieved at this case, and the noble birth of Baron de Salgas, his age, his family, and his large estates, excited the greatest sympathy on behalf of the unhappy sufferer. On the galley the baron occupied the third place on his bench of rowers, which was one of the least fatiguing, for the old man had not strength to row; he, however, went through one cruise. His resignation, his meek patience, his charity, made him an example of suffering affliction, and his companions in tribulation glorified God in him. Thus did he earn a crown of martyrdom brighter than earth's proudest heraldry, and more honourable than titles bequeathed by an ancestral line of kings.

After fourteen years of suffering, through the powerful interest of some friends, coupled with the death of the arch-persecutor, Louis XIV, the baron obtained his freedom. The solicitations of Queen Anne had proved ineffectual; but, after that princess's death, the Duchess de la Force interested the Princess of Wales, afterwards Queen of England, in his favour, and she wrote the most pressing letters to the Dowager Duchess of Orleans, the Regent's mother, who, in her turn, never ceased entreating her son to loose the chains of the illustrious slave. At length she procured his release. The baron received the news on the 26th of October, 1716. On obtaining his freedom he joined his wife at Geneva, where he died, August 14th, 1717.

Several of the baron's tenants were involved in their master's ruin. Among others two were condemned, the one to the wheel, the other to the gallows, at Meade, as accomplices to the massacre of Fraissinet. The first, Jacques Pointier, of Rousses, was visited in prison by Louvreleuil. After his sentence had been read, the priest was going up to him, but he cried out with horror, "Away from me! you are a Satan to me; leave me." The priest replied that he had only come to strengthen him in the agonies of death. "I have no need of you. It is not in man that I ought to put confidence in my troubles, but in God alone." Then raising his eyes to heaven, he said, "It is to thee alone, O Saviour of the world, to whom I have recourse. Look upon me with pity in this day of sorrow. Thou hast not commanded me to seek any other minister; but thou hast said to me, and to all thy faithful children, 'Come unto me, all ye that are heavy laden, and I will give you rest.' At this time, then, oh, merciful Christ, Son of David, show thy great mercy towards me." When he had finished, the priest wished to speak, but he again interrupted him, and raising his eyes to heaven, repeated a psalm. Louvreleuil listened almost an hour, and then rose to go, saying that if he could do nothing for his spiritual welfare, he would with pleasure discharge his last commissions on behalf of his family. On hearing this, Pointier's manner changed. "You remember," he replied, "that our Lord said, 'Whatsoever ye do unto the least of these my brethren, ye do it unto me.' I believe that you will perform your promise. Therefore will you please write what I will dictate." Louvreleuil immediately did as he was asked. Pointier, after giving his blessing to his wife and children, and commending them to God, mentioned several people to whom he had lent money without security, and begged them to repay the debts to his widow, or else to Louvreleuil; he then added a request to one of his friends to give several bushels of wheat to the poor. He

then signed the document as well as he could, with his
hands tied, and perished.

The Martyrdom of Sieur Boeton.

About the same time another insurrectionary effort on
behalf of liberty broke out in the department of Rouergue,
and was headed by a native of Saint Laurent d'Aigouses,
named Boëton. He had been an officer in the army, and
risen to the rank of captain through prodigies of valour;
but his military career had been cut short by the revocation
of the Edict of Nantes. He put himself in communication
with the Camisards, and an arrangement was made for
their mutual co-operation. A day was named, and a place
of meeting fixed; but the imprudent zeal of Catinat, one of
the Camisard leaders, led to the discovery of the plot.
Catinat and his followers were attacked by the military,
and obliged to retreat. Boëton, not having been informed
of his reverse, presented himself with one hundred men at
the place appointed, but finding no one there, retreated to
the mountains, whither he was pursued, and obliged to
capitulate. An amnesty was offered, and in this way an
insurrection was crushed, which, in conjunction with that
of the Camisards, might have involved the most serious
issues, and occasioned the utmost alarm to the province
and to the court. At the same time the Marquis of
Guiscard was agitating for a general rising in the whole of
France, which was groaning under an Egyptian bondage,
and crushed under an incubus of taxation, which had
prepared multitudes for any desperate effort to rid them of
their miseries; but mishaps attended all the subordinate
plans, the co-operation of Labourlie, Jonquet, and the
English fleet off the coast was not successfully concerted,
and the whole plot, like that of Theudas, came to nought.
In April, 1705, further efforts were made for the same
purpose, and Ravanel, Catinat, Vilas, Elie, Jonquet, and
others met at the house of Boëton, situated between
Nismes and Montpellier. Boëton, doubted not that the time
had come for rebuilding the Protestant temples, whilst his
zeal was inflamed from the personal injuries he had received, from having been some time in irons. But the
conspiracy was discovered, when at the point of execution,
and the leaders arrested. Boëton's house was invested by a
regiment of fusiliers, commanded by Baron De St. Chattes,
who was related to him by marriage, and he was conducted

in triumph to Nismes, and afterwards transferred to the citadel at Montpellier. On his way there he met his wife and his son, who came from Montpellier to intercede on his behalf. Nothing could be more touching than this interview; the last adieus of the loving couple, and the advice which the father gave the son, were tenderly pathetic. The day following his arrival at Montpellier he was condemned to be broken on the wheel, after undergoing the torture. His calm courage never deserted him, and De Baville, who witnessed its first application, expecting to receive his confession, seemed more irritated than the sufferer, and forgot himself so far as to outrage the very instincts of human nature by striking the martyr on the face.

The scaffold for his execution was erected on the esplanade, where the wheel was also prepared for its victim. Boëton was taken there in a cart, amid the sounds of drums which were intended to drown his voice, and to prevent his words of exhortation reaching the bystanders. About half-way to the esplanade was a shop, to which one of his friends had fled, whom Boëton addressed as follows: "Why do you fly from me? Is it because I wear the livery of Jesus Christ? Why do you weep when He graciously calls upon me, unworthy as I am, to seal with my blood my defence of His cause?" These adieus were abridged by the officials, and without a murmur Boëton went forward to death. When he perceived the scaffold, he raised his hands towards heaven, and cried out in rapturous tones, "Courage, my soul! I see the place of thy triumph, and thou wilt soon enter heaven free from these weary fetters.

He was assisted to mount the scaffold, as his legs were powerless to support him, owing to the torture he had undergone. On reaching the top he stretched himself on the St. Andrew's cross. The attendant tied him with cords to every point of the machine, and then retired. The executioner advanced in his turn, holding in his hand a square bar of iron, an inch and a half wide, three feet long, and rounded at one end. At the sight of him Boëton began to chant a psalm, which he interrupted by a slight cry. The executioner had just broken the bone of his right leg; but soon he resumed his hymn of praise, and continued it without stopping, although, one by one, the thigh, the other leg, the other thigh, and both arms were dislocated. Then the executioner took this shapeless, mutilated body, which still breathed love to God, and lifting it from the cross, placed it on the wheel, first bending the broken thighs under the body, so that the heels touched the back of the head. During all these horrors, Boëton's voice never ceased to be lifted up in praise to God. Perhaps never had an execution produced such an effect on the witnesses, and the last scene of the tragedy was therefore hastened. Baville ordered the executioner to finish the work, and he was about to give a deadly blow on the chest, when an archer who was near said that the Huguenot must not die so soon, as he had not suffered enough. At these atrocious words the victim raised his head, and said, "My friend, you think I am in pain, and you are not mistaken: I do suffer; but He who is with me, and for whom I suffer, gives me strength to bear my agony with joy." But De Baville's orders were renewed, and the executioner once more drew near. Seeing his last hour was come, Boëton exclaimed, "My dear brothers, let my death strengthen you in the belief of the Gospel, and be my faithful witnesses that I die in the faith of Christ and of His holy apostles." Scarcely had he uttered these last words, when the iron bar fell on his chest; a few accents of prayer were still heard, when the head fell back, and the martyr ceased to breathe.

The History of Jean Fabre.

We pass over a considerable lapse of time, to dwell briefly on an incident worthy to be recorded. The religious assemblies continued to be proscribed with the utmost rigour of the law, and those who were apprehended were still liable to the most severe penalties.

At one held on the 1st of January, 1756, several citizens from the town of Nismes were arrested, among whom was Jean Fabre. He was seventy-eight years of age; but neither age nor character availed aught, and he was condemned to the galleys. He had a son who was young and strong, and who, on the dispersion of the assembly, had made good his escape. On hearing of the apprehension of his father, he boldly presented himself to the commander of the troops, and implored him, with tears in his eyes, to take him as a ransom for his father, which request he obtained only after prolonged and earnest entreaties. The Duc de Mirepoix sent the son to the galleys at Toulon, allowing him to bear the brand of crime, and to be confounded with the criminal offscourings of society. For seven weary years did the son wear the chain of a slave, and languish out a miserable existence at the felon's oar.

The above touching incident was embodied in a drama called "L'Honnête Criminel;" and such was the effect which the piece had in its representation, that it did more than anything else to touch the public conscience to a sense of outraged humanity, and to procure the release of the filial hostage.

Memorial of the Two Last Protestant Gallerians.

We append here a memorial relative to the cases of the two last Prostestants who were imprisoned at the galleys, and released in 1775, in consequence of a petition to the king, Louis XVI.

"TO THE KING.

"SIRE,—Two unfortunate old men, one more than seventy, and one more than sixty years of age, in chains for thirty years, on account of their religion, throw themselves at your majesty's feet, imploring you to grant them the liberty of which they have been so long deprived; which grace they merit by their long expiation of the fault committed, by their old age, which renders them incapable of working at the galleys, where they were condemned for life, and by their behaviour hitherto, behaviour which has edified all the officials, and especially MM. the naval commissioners, who will not refuse their testimony on behalf of the prisoners. Already Antoine Riaille and Paul Achard, both of them of the diocese of Die, and both condemned, in 1745, to the galleys for life, on account of their faith, by the Parliament of Grenoble, have seen the fetters broken off all the Protestants suffering with them for the like cause. Not more guilty, shall these two men alone languish under the weight of their misery? Shall not thirty years' suffering and punishment be a sufficient expiation to the penal laws? Sire, may your great soul be touched with compassion towards them, so that while France is glorying in her king, these unfortunate men may bless him in the bosom of their families. These families will bless you, sire; all the kingdom will applaud the clemency of your majesty; and those who were estranged by the severity of the ancient penal laws will congratulate themselves on being Frenchmen; they will dread displeasing so good and just a monarch."

At the same time the defender of the Protestant gallerians wrote a note to the keeper of the seals, ending with

these words: "And you, monsigneur, who were always just
and good, on looking back to the day when you will have
obtained the pardon of these two old men, the last victims
at present of error, of this kind at least, and of the rigour
of the laws, will rejoice in having made use of your
position, and will feel the delight of being noble in power
and goodness."

These multiplied petitions were not fruitless. "My prayer
for the two confessors at the galleys," writes Gébelin later,
"has been received in the most gracious manner, and I hear
they will be liberated at a fixed and not distant time. I had
appended to my petition a notice of all that had been
suffered in 1745, the year in which these two brave
Israelites were condemned. It made a great sensation;
people could scarcely credit such horrors. It is to be hoped
no more such examples will be ever seen."

We will conclude our notice of French martyrology by a
brief description of the Tower of Constance, a place
mournfully prominent in the persecuting annals of the
eighteenth century. The Tower of Constance, at Aigues
Mortes, was a circular building, eighty-seven feet in height.
The interior consisted of two rooms or halls, the one above
the other. The lower received light and air through a hole
in the floor of the upper, which in its turn was lit through
an aperture situated at the central point of the vault, which
allowed the cold wind and the rain to penetrate inside. The
poor captives spent a miserable day, seated on the circular
stone seat which ran round the building. At night they lay
upon damp straw, hearing in the distance the beating of the
surge and the whistling of the wind over the lagoons in the
vicinity of the sea. In 1764 there were fourteen prisoners
incarcerated there. One of them, Marie Béraud, over eighty
years of age, and blind for a long time, had been a prisoner
thirty-seven years. Marie Rey and Naviliad had been
separated from their children twenty-seven years, and
Anne Guissart had been incarcerated for more than thirty
years; but the most touching case of all was that of Marie
Durand, who, for the crime of being the sister of a pastor,
was imprisoned at the age of fifteen, and languished in this
frightful den for thirty-eight years! She had corresponded
with Paul Rabaut, and she gives many melancholy details of
prison life. After repeated protests on the part of Paul
Rabaut, the Prince de Beauveau determined to inspect the
prisoners, and was accompanied by his nephew, Chevalier

Boufflers, who has left the following account of the scene:—

"No language can describe the effect of a spectacle to which our eyes were unaccustomed; it was at once hideous and affecting, and disgust increased its horror. We saw a large round hall, deprived of air and light; fourteen women languished there in misery and in tears. The commandant could scarcely contain his emotion; and doubtless, for the first time, these unhappy beings perceived compassion on a human countenance. I see them still. At this sudden appearance they fell at our feet, bathed them with tears, attempted to speak, but found only sighs; and at length, emboldened by consolations, related to us all at once their common sufferings. Alas! all their crime was that they were educated in the religion of Henry IV. The youngest of these martyrs was nearly fifty years of age. She was only eight when they seized her, as she was going to the sermon with her mother, and her punishment had not yet terminated."

We cannot dwell on the subsequent outbreaks at Nismes in 1815-16, which, in their vile atrocities, were quite equal to the precedents of history.

An Account of John Bunyan, Who Was Imprisoned Twelve Years in Bedford Gaol for Conscience' Sake.

John Bunyan was born in 1628, and was the son of an itinerant tinker. His father, from the character of his profession, was not able to pay much attention to the education of his boy; thus John was often left to follow his own inclinations while his father was absent from the village of Elstow. Being talented, active, and high-spirited, with no one to control him or direct his energies in the right way, he soon became the dread and plague of the village, always discovering new plans of mischief, and never failing in energy to carry them out. About the age of nine he began to have very extraordinary and startling dreams, some of such a solemn character that he never forgot them. They did not, however, reform his character, as he went on from bad to worse, until the age of seventeen, when he enlisted in the army, and astonished even the wicked with the surpassing vileness of his language and conduct. A great blessing was, however, in store for him; for he succeeded in securing the affections of a pious young woman, whom he married. But he still followed his evil ways, much to the grief of his wife, who, striving earnestly to reform him, succeeded at last, and saw her husband changed into a humble Christian. The wife died soon after this, without living to see how her husband was able to labour and suffer for the sake of the Saviour, to whom she had led him. The wonderful change in John naturally astonished all who had formerly known him, and many came to him to inquire about the religion he now followed. In this way he gradually became a preacher, and determined to give up all his talents and energies to spreading the religion of Jesus.

Another name besides that of Bunyan sheds lustre on the town of Bedford, and, curiously enough, is identified with the same locality. A few miles in its environs is the village of Cardington, where the trees still flourish planted in 1672 by John Howard, the philanthropist, an Englishman unsurpassed in the triumphs of benevolence. When high sheriff of this county, in 1773, his attention was, from what came under his official notice, first turned to the subject of prisons, and Bedford gaol became the starting-point in what Burke beautifully calls his "circumnavigation of charity." If it be no exaggeration to say that through Howard this prison exercised a real influence on the temporal interests of thousands, or at least of Europe, it is equally true that some years previously it materially contributed to the spiritual improvement of the human race. It contained a man who was capable of entertaining himself in a dungeon with scenes more beautiful than any that could be found in the whole compass of Nature. His mind was his kingdom, and the stony limits which held captive his body could not enthral his spirit. In this place John Bunyan lingered for twelve years. He sang praises to God, and composed that wondrous allegory, which, from its genius and piety, has become a text-book among Christians of every tongue. Two minds in that century possessed the imaginative faculty to an eminent degree. One of those minds produced 'Paradise Lost,' the other 'The Pilgrim's Progress.' "

Having gone through the experimental conviction of sin, he became, when converted, a truly earnest man, and his labours among the people bore witness to this fact. His zeal sometimes brought about a collision with the authorities; and even under the rule of Cromwell he was in danger of imprisonment—a disaster, however, which did not befall him until the Restoration. He is supposed to have been the first victim for conscience' sake. On the 12th of November,

1660, he had arranged to meet a small congregation, in a house at Samsell, in Bedfordshire, but before the time appointed he was informed that a warrant had been issued for his seizure. The danger did not cause him to swerve from what he believed to be the path of duty. He was accordingly arrested at the meeting, but not before he had uttered the following words: "You see we are prevented of our opportunity to hear the Word of God, and are likely to suffer for the same; but be not discouraged: it is a mercy to suffer for so good a cause. We might have been apprehended as thieves or murderers, but, blessed by God, it is not so. We suffer as Christians for well-doing; and better be the persecuted than the persecutors." After being taken before a magistrate, he was committed for trial at the next sessions, when he was indicted for "devilishly and perniciously refraining from coming to church, to hear Divine service; and for being an upholder of conventicles, to the great disturbance of the good subjects of this kingdom, and in contradiction to the laws of the king." On this charge he was convicted, and sentenced to imprisonment, with an intimation that if he did not conform within a given time, he should be banished out of England. In prison he suffered much, for it was very damp—so damp, that Bunyan said it was enough to "make the moss grow upon his eyebrows."

Had Bunyan promised not to preach, he would have been set at liberty, but he thought it was his duty to suffer for Christ's sake, and "he endured as seeing him who is invisible." But the counsels of his enemies, were turned into foolishness, for he converted his prison into a pulpit, whence his voice might "go out through all the earth, and his words unto the end of the world." During this imprisonment he wrote that wondrous book of which it may safely be affirmed that no other book except the Bible has been translated into so many languages, passed through so many editions, commanded so many millions of readers, or been useful to the spiritual welfare of such multitudes.

Bunyan had no library to refer to while he was writing: his Bible and an old Concordance were the only books he had; and he was reduced to such a state of poverty, owing to his long imprisonment, that his blind daughter used to knit stay-laces, her father, "the immortal tinker," tagged them, and the poor wife (for he had married a second time) used to sell them in the streets.

We see in history how often events similar in their

outlines repeat themselves, and synchronise. In 1668, when
Bunyan was in Bedford gaol, William Penn was a prisoner
for conscience' sake, and from forth the Tower of London
issues another work, "No Cross, No Crown," prolific of
good to multitudes.

Bunyan's death was worthy of his life. While lodging
with his friend, Mr. Strudwick, a grocer, he was summoned
into the country, to effect a reconciliation between a father
and a son. He complied with the summons, and happily
effected his object. On returning to London, on horseback,
he was drenched with rain, before arriving at his lodgings.
This exposure resulted in a fever, under which he sank,
and died at the sign of the "Star," Snow Hill, the residence
of his friend, on the 31st August, 1688, in the 81st year of
his age, the author of more than sixty works. He was
buried in Bunhill Fields, London, in September, 1688.

An Account of the Sufferings of George Penn in the Spanish Inquisition.

George Penn, the admiral's eldest brother, having married a Catholic lady of Antwerp, settled in the south of
Spain, as a merchant, residing chiefly at Seville, Cadiz,
Malaga, and San Lucar. As an English Protestant, his
conduct was scrutinised with jealous closeness by the
officers of the Holy Inquisition; but he cautiously abstained
from giving ground for offence, particularly in regard to
the religious prejudices of the country in which he lived, so
that malice itself was foiled in the attempt to draw him into
the snare. But as he grew rich, with years of industry and
success, the Church, eagerly covetous of his wealth, became impatient of his blameless life, and seized him on its
own secret warrant. When the familiars of the Holy Office
broke into his house at San Lucar, they commenced their
proceedings by casting him out, body and soul, from the
Christian Church and the fold of God. They seized his
money and furniture, his plate and pictures, his wearing
apparel and his wife's jewels, his stock of merchandise, his
books, papers, and accounts, and every other particle of
property, down to the nail in the wall.

His wife was carried off he knew not whither; he himself
was dragged to Seville, where he was cast into a loathsome
dungeon, only eight feet in diameter, and as dark as the
grave, in this living tomb he was left with a loaf of bread
and a jug of water. For seven days no one came near him;
and then the gaoler simply brought another loaf and

another jug of water, and disappeared. This course was continued for three years, during which time he was worn to a skeleton. No one was allowed to visit him in his cell, no letter or message was suffered to be sent out.

At the end of the first month of his confinement there was a break in the horrible monotony of his life. The silent and masked familiars of the office came into his cell, took him by the arms, stripped him naked, and tied him fast to the iron bars of his dungeon door; when one of them, armed with a powerful whip made of knotted cords, dealt out fifty merciless lashes. Every month this flogging was repeated, the new stripes crossing and tearing up the former wounds, until his body was one huge festering sore; and all this time he was unable to learn the name or nature of the crimes laid, truly or falsely, to his charge. Three years having elapsed without provoking self-accusation, the prisoner was brought into the trial-chamber, and, in the presence of seven judges, was accused of various crimes and heresies—particularly with having tried to seduce his wife from the Catholic faith. He pleaded not guilty; but, instead of producing witnesses to prove his alleged crimes, the judges ordered him to be tortured in their presence, until he confessed the truth of what was charged against him. For a while his strength and resolution defied the agonies of the rack; but his tormentors persevered, and at the end of four hours of excruciating and accumulating torments, he gave way, and offered to confess anything they wished. Not satisfied with a confession which, by the usages of Spain, gave up his whole property to the Holy Office, the judges put him to the rack again, and, by still more refined and delicate tortures, forced from him a terrible oath that he would live and die a Catholic, and would defend that form of faith, at the risk of his life, against every enemy, on pain of being burnt to death, if found recalcitrant. He was then cut down from the rack, placed on a hurdle, and conveyed to his former dungeon.

As soon as he was sufficiently recovered from his wounds to walk, he was taken to the great cathedral of Seville, in solemn procession, accompanied by the seven judges, their households, by several hundred priests and friars, and by a vast multitude of people, and, in the presence of the congregation, was exposed as a signal instance of the great mercy of the Holy Inquisition. His wife was taken from him, and forcibly married to a good Catholic; the whole of his estate, amounting, in plate, furniture, jewels, goods, and merchandise, to £12,000, was confiscated; the money found in his hands belonging to other parties was seized; and he was finally commanded to quit the country in three months, on pain of death.

The last injunction only added insult to injury; for the judges well knew that, having seized his estate, the moment he left the cathedral he would be arrested for debts which he had no means of discharging. The very same day he was thrust into a common gaol, with little or no hope of ever obtaining a second release.

The exhibition in the cathedral being public, several English residents in Seville were present; and the intelligence of his brother's position soon reached the young admiral on his station in the Channel. His measures were prompt and characteristic. Instead of appealing to Cromwell, and setting the dilatory diplomacy of London and Madrid at work to procure his release, he seized in one of his prizes a Spanish nobleman, Juan de Urbino, then on his way to Flanders, where he held the post of secretary to the Government, stripped him naked, like a common prisoner, and treated him with many indignities. This act, indefensible in itself, spoke home to the Spanish sovereign, and George Penn was soon released, and sent back to England.

The death of Cromwell prevented any reparation being made for his losses and sufferings; but when the Restoration was effected, King Charles appointed him his envoy at the court of Spain, with a view to his proper reinstatement in the opinion of his old friends in Seville and San Lucar, and to add weight to his claim for damages in body and estates. This act of substantial justice, however, came too late. His aged flesh had been torn, his limbs dislocated and ill-set, his body starved for more than three years on bread and water; and he died in London only a few weeks after receiving the royal appointment, leaving his claims as a legacy to the admiral and his family.

William Penn

The great William Penn, the founder of the state of Pennsylvania, and himself a minor martyr for conscience' sake, was George Penn's nephew. He was born in London, 14th October, 1644. Owing to his views on religion at different periods of his life, he underwent much persecution. During his seven months' imprisonment in the Tower, in 1668, he wrote his best work, "No Cross No Crown." He was twice imprisoned in Newgate, and once in the

Fleet, so that he had lodged in prisons as well as in palaces. In 1696 Penn made the acquaintance of the Czar of Russia, and vainly endeavoured to convert him to Quakerism. Peter the Great was at this time in England, working in the dockyard at Deptford as a common carpenter and shipwright. Mr. Penn received the grant of Pennsylvania from the English Crown, in discharge of a debt of £16,000, due to his father, the admiral; but at the close of his life, when encompassed with difficulties, he mortgaged his province to the Crown for the sum of £6,800, a transaction which he did not live to see completed. During his stay in America many were the peaceful triumphs of the founder of Pennsylvania—in the establishment of twenty townships, with their civil organisation, and in many conferences with the Indians, with nineteen tribes of whom a friendly relationship was cemented by treaties. Besides the moral glory attaching to his pacific government, the memory of Penn may further be honoured as the champion of the slave, and the pioneer of American emancipation. It was under his legislature that it was resolved that buying and selling men was contrary to the spirit of the Gospel, and Penn obtained the admission of slaves to places of worship, and set on foot measures for ameliorating their condition, and affording them moral instruction. He died at Ruscombe, in Berkshire, July 30th, 1718.

The History of John Williams, Missionary, Who Was Martyred at Erromanga, November 20th, 1839.

John Williams was born of respectable but obscure parents, and rose from the humbler classes, which have furnished many bright ornaments to the Church of Christ. Thomas Cranfield, the tailor; John Pounds, the cobbler, the originator of ragged schools; Harland Page, the joiner; Roger Miller, the copper-plate printer; William Reeves, the coach-builder; Leonard Dober, the potter; Alexander Patterson, the ploughman; Sarah Martin, the dressmaker, were all missionaries in the Lord's vineyard, and, though humble, have left streaks of light behind them, by having during their lives turned many to righteousness. Of this holy brotherhood was John Williams, the apprentice of an ironmonger. It was in the year 1814 that John Williams was awakened to spiritual life, by the ministry of the Rev. Timothy East, of Birmingham. From that moment the Gospel wrought a mighty change in his whole nature, so

that, feeling the powers of the world to come, he became a
new creature. He immediately became a teacher in a
Sunday-school. As his knowledge increased, so did his zeal,
and though his heart yearned over the masses of practical
heathens in England, yet the claims of those who had never
heard the name of Jesus, or of the Gospel of salvation,
were paramount in his heart. He accordingly offered himself to the London Missionary Society, and was sent to the
South Seas. Mr. Williams sailed for Polynesia on the 17th
of November, 1816, in the ship *Harriet,* and was accompanied by his wife, a truly pious and excellent woman. On
the 16th of November, 1817, they reached Tahiti; and in
June, 1818, Mr. Williams selected the island of Raiatea as
the head-quarters of his future labours.

Mr. Williams, having with incredible industry mastered
the Tahitian language, at Eimeo, in the space of ten
months, preached three times a week at Raiatea from the
commencement of his sojourn in that island. The following
were the two main principles which animated Mr. Williams, namely—that kindness is the key to the heart, and
that the arts of civilisation, though they need not precede,
should most emphatically accompany the Gospel. "The
missionary," said he, "does not go to barbarise himself, but
to elevate the heathen; not to sink himself to their standard, but to raise them to his." Accordingly he selected a
site on Raiatea, and commenced building, and his mechani-
cal genius and inventive talent were brought into full
exercise. The native house consisted of but one apartment,
covered with a thatched roof, open at the sides and
carpeted with dirty grass, and on this the family were all
huddled together for every purpose. Mr. Williams was
anxious that his dwelling should embody the ideas of
refinement, civilisation, and progress, and be a stimulus to
native emulation. His house was accordingly sixty feet by
thirty, and consisted of three front and four back rooms.
Its framework was wood, plastered inside with coral lime,
which was afterwards coloured. A garden, with pathways
and flower-beds, was laid out and planted, while a poultry
farm was soon stocked with its additions to domestic
comfort. In a letter, dated September 5th, 1819, to the
Directors of the Society, Mr. Williams reports his progress:
—"When we came to this place there were only two native
habitations, and it was difficult to walk along the beach for
the bushes. But the former wilderness is now an open,
clear, and pleasant place, with a range of houses extending

nearly two miles along the sea beach, in which reside about a thousand of the natives. We earnestly desire to see the moral wilderness present the same improved appearance. The king, who, we are happy to say, is one of the most consistent characters, resides very near us. He is a very constant attendant both at the chapel and the schools. He will probably be one of the first whom we shall baptise in the islands. We are happy in being able to state that his behaviour is circumspect, and that he is very active in suppressing crime. We are glad to be able to inform you that many have built themselves very neat little houses, and are now living in them with their wives and families. The king, through seeing ours, and by our advice, has had a house erected near us. It contains four rooms, wattled, and plastered inside and out, and floored. He is the first native on these islands that ever had such a house; but many others are now following his example. . . . Thus while teaching them the things which belong to their eternal peace, we do not forget their temporal improvement, and desire to remember the connection between being 'fervent in spirit,' and 'diligent in business.' "

Such was the spirit of the man who was an apostle at once of Christianity and civilisation. He was a pastor, a preacher, an instructor of the people in the way of godliness, and also a builder, a shipwright, a weaver, a planter, a smith, and a mason; but all he had and all he did was devoted to Christ, and to the furtherance of the Gospel.

We have not space to narrate the manifold triumphs of the Gospel in the various groups of the South Sea Islands, or the adventures of this champion of the cross. He was killed on the 20th of November, 1839, at the island of Erromanga, one of the New Hebrides, whither he had gone to introduce the Gospel. The details connected with his martyrdom will be best gathered from the interesting account of it given by Mr. Cunningham, who was standing by his side, and narrowly escaped with his own life. After describing their landing, he proceeds:—

"Mr. Williams called for a few pieces of print, which he divided in small pieces, to throw around him. Mr. Harris said he wished to have a stroll inland, which was not objected to, and he walked on, followed by a party of the natives. Mr. Williams and I followed, directing our course up the side of the brook. The looks and manners of the savages I much distrusted, and remarked to Mr. Williams that probably we had to dread the revenge of the natives, in consequence of their former quarrel with strangers, wherein perhaps some of their friends had been killed. Mr. Williams, I think, did not return me an answer, being engaged at the instant repeating the Samoan numerals to a crowd of boys, one of whom was repeating them after him. I was also trying to get the names of a few things around us, and walked onward. Finding a few shells lying on the bank, I picked them up. On noticing they were of a species unknown to me, I was in the act of putting them into my pocket, when I heard a yell, and instantly Mr. Harrris rushed out of the bushes about twenty yards before me. I instantly perceived it was run or die. I shouted to Mr. Williams to run (he being as far behind me as Mr. Harris was in advance,) and I sprang forward through the natives that were on the banks of the brook, who all gave way. I looked round, and saw Mr. Harris fall in the brook, and the water dash over him, a number of savages beating him with clubs. Mr. Williams did not run at the instant I called to him, till we heard a shell blow; it was an instant, but too much to lose. I again called to Mr. Williams to run, and sprang forward for the boat, which was out of sight; it was round a point of bush. Mr. Williams, instead of making for the boat, ran directly down the beach into the water, and a savage after him. At the instant I sighted the boat I heard a yell behind me, and looking round, found a savage close after me with a club. I stooped, and picking up a stone, struck him so as to stop his further pursuit. The men in the boat had, on seeing Mr. Williams and me running, given the alarm to Captain Morgan, who was on the beach at the time. He and I jumped into the boat; at the same instant several stones were thrown at the boat. Mr. Williams ran into deep water, and the savage close after him. On entering the water he fell forward, but did not attempt to swim, when he received several blows from the club of the native on the arms and over the head. He twice dashed his head under water to avoid the club, with which the savage stood over him, ready to strike the instant he arose. I threw two stones from the boat, which for a moment averted the progress of the other native, who was a few paces behind; but it was only for an instant. The two rushed on our friend and beat his head, and soon several others joined them. I saw a whole handful of arrows stuck into his body. Though every exertion was used to get up the boat to his assistance, and though only about eighty yards distant, before we got half the distance our friend was dead, and about a dozen savages were dragging the body on the beach, beating it in the most furious manner. Several arrows were shot at us, and one, passing under the arm of one of the men, went through the lining and entered the timber. This alarmed the men, who remonstrated, as, having no fire-arms to frighten the savages away, it would be madness to approach them, as Mr. Williams was now dead. To this Captain Morgan reluctantly assented, and pulled off out of reach of the arrows, where we lay for an instant to consider what we should do, when it was proposed that we should, if possible, bring up the brig, now about two miles distant, and, under cover of two guns which she carried, land, and, if possible, obtain the bodies, which the natives had left on the beach, having stripped off the clothes. We hastened on board, and beat up for the fatal spot. We could still perceive the white body lying on the beach, and the natives had all left it, which gave us hope of being able to rescue the remains of our friend from the ferocious cannibals. Our two guns were loaded, and one fired, in hopes that the savages might be alarmed and fly to a distance; several were still seen on a distant part of the beach. Shot we had none, but the sailors collected pieces of iron to use if necessary. Our hopes were soon destroyed, for a crowd of natives ran down the beach and carried away the body, when we were within a mile of the spot. In grief we turned our backs and stood from the fatal shores. We had all lost a friend, and one we loved, for the love he bore to all, and the sincerity with which he conveyed the tidings of peace to the benighted heathen, by whose cruel hands he had now fallen."

An Account of the Persecutions of the Christians in the Island of Madagascar.

Madagascar is a large island in the Indian Ocean. Its area is greater than that of Great Britain and Ireland, and its population is estimated at about five millions.

One of the most important events in the history of Madagascar was the treaty between Sir Robert Farquhar and King Radama. Radama's reign was one of great prosperity to the island. Having been educated in Great Britain, he abolished infanticide, suppressed the slave trade, discouraged the belief in witchcraft, formed a regular army on the European model, and, with a force of 30,000 men, reduced the whole island to one monarchy. Nor was he ignorant of the important part which roads

and methods of communication play in the work of civilisation. Agents of the London Missionary Society reached
Madagascar in 1818, and received a most cordial welcome
from this enlightened monarch. They reduced its language
to writing, arranged its grammar, translated the Holy
Scriptures; and in the space of ten years 15,000 natives
could read, and a large number write, while multitudes
were converted to Christianity. As in the South Seas, so
likewise here, Christianity, true to herself, gave blessings
for this world as well as for the next, and agriculture,
trades, and commerce received a beneficial impetus.
Numbers of youths were trained as carpenters, tanners,
curriers, builders, shoemakers, and in other branches of
handicraft, and initiated in the art of working the
metals. Unfortunately, when a brilliant success appeared
about to crown the monarch's projects, he was poisoned by
his queen in July, 1828. A reaction was inaugurated, the
schools were closed, the old *régime* reinstated, and the idol
keepers once more obtained their pernicious sway over the
heathen masses. In 1835 it was enacted that no Malagasy
should profess Christianity, and the missionaries and the
foreign artisans were ejected from the island. On their
departure, many who were suspected of being Christians
had to pass through the ordeal of drinking the tanjena, or
poison water, and the following year several others were
punished by fine, imprisonment, and perpetual slavery.

The first Christian martyr suffered in 1837, and later
more than a hundred martyrs were added to the Church
triumphant. The missionaries were expelled in 1836, but
they left behind them the oracles of God, which they had
translated into the native language, and whose words were
hidden in the hearts of many. The history of Christianity in
this island is remarkable, as affording an instance of the
self-reliant energy of the Word of God, for after the
withdrawal of the missionaries in 1836, it was the portion
of the Word of God secretly circulated that maintained
spiritual life in the island, much to the astonishment and
joy of the missionaries when they visited it in 1853. After
the exile of the teachers various persecutions broke out.
The usual subtlety and invention of malice were called into
exercise, and every form of violence was enlisted to crush
the truth. Yet the same simple faith which triumphed in
the dungeons of the Inquisition, in the fires of Smithfield,
and in the galleys of France, was victorious in this remote
latitude. The converts wandered about in deserts and caves

of the earth, until, in 1842, sixteen of them were arrested while endeavouring to effect their escape from the island, and nine of them were put to death in the capital. General attention was thus drawn to the subject of the Christian religion. In 1846 the Crown Prince renounced heathenism, and was baptised, and proved himself a faithful protector. His conversion greatly angered the queen mother, who regarded him as the victim of witchcraft, and vented her wrath in the violent persecution of 1849, when more than 2,000 persons were mulcted in some form or other, and many put to death. We subjoin some details, extracted from the work of the Rev. William Ellis, who visited Madagascar in 1853, 1854, and 1856:—

"The authorities in Madagascar, who sought, by torture and death, to extinguish the Christian faith, by whatever motives they may have been actuated, only imitated the Diocletians of the early ages, and the Alvas, the Medicis, and the Marys of more recent times, and with corresponding results in the invincible constancy of those who fell, and the subsequent fruits of the imperishable seed which was scattered in the martyrs' blood. Deeply affecting were the details which I received of the sorrows and the consolations of the sufferers; of their conduct in the hour of peril, as well as on the day of impeachment and of trial; with the noble testimony which they bore, when brought before judges and rulers, for His name's sake. The following exact and verbatim statements refer to the severe persecution in the year 1849, and will make their own appeal to every heart. They are offered without apprehension, as those to whom they refer have passed into a world where 'the fury of the oppressor' and the cruelty of the persecutor can never enter:—

"On the 14th of March, 1849, the officer before whom the Christians were examined, said—'Do you pray to the sun, or the moon, or the earth?'

"R——answered, 'I do not pray to these, for the hand of God made them.'

" 'Do you pray to the twelve mountains that are sacred?'

"R——answered, 'I do not pray to them, for they are mountains.'

"R——.—'I do not pray to them, for the hand of man made them.'

" 'Do you pray to the ancestors of the sovereigns?'

"R——.—'Kings and rulers are given by God that ᵥ should serve and obey them, and render them hoᵣ

Nevertheless, they are only men like ourselves. When we pray, we pray to God alone.'

" 'You make distinct and observe the Sabbath-day.'

"R——.—'That is the day of the great God; for in six days the Lord made all his works. But God rested on the seventh, and he caused it to be holy; and I rest or keep sacred that day.'

"And in similar manner answered all the Christians. And when a man who had kept aloof saw that one, a woman, did not deny God, and remembered that to deny God was followed with compunction, he went and spoke as the others had done. And when these brethren and sisters were bound, the husband of one of them, who had heard their confession, came and said to them, 'Be not afraid, for it is well if for that you die.' He was a soldier from a distance, and not of the number of the accused. Then he was examined, and as he made the same avowal, they bound him also. And they removed these ten brethren and sisters, and made their bands hard or tight, and confined them each in a separate house. The writers of the journal add, 'And at one o'clock at night we met together and prayed.' On the 22nd of March, when one had said, 'Jehovah is God alone, and above every name that is named, and Jesus Christ is also God,' the people cried out, mocking. And to another the officer said, 'Rabodampoimerina (the sacred name of our queen) is our God, but not your God.' He answered, 'The God who made me is my God; but Rabo-doa is my queen or sovereign.' And when he refused other answer, they said, 'Perhaps he is an idiot, or a lunatic.' He answered, 'I am not an idiot, and have not lost my understanding.' Then there was a commotion and buzz among the people, saying, 'Take him away.' And they took him to prison.

"And before it was light, on the following day, the people assembled at A——y. Then they took the eighteen brethren that chose God and to inherit life, and to become his sons and his daughters, and they bound their hands and feet, and tied each of them to a pole, wrapped in mats, and placed them with the other prisoners. And of these united brethren and sisters, ten were from Vonizongo. And when the ——ers, and troops, and judges arrived, they read over ——s of each class of prisoners, and then placed them —elves, and stationed around them soldiers with —d spears; and the sentences were then delivered, some to fine and confiscation, others to slavery, others to prison and chains, some to flogging, and eighteen to death—four to be burned, and fourteen to be hurled from the rocky precipice, and afterwards burned to ashes.

"And the eighteen appointed to die, as they sat on the ground, surrounded by the soldiers, sang this hymn.—

> 'When I shall die, and leave my friends,
>   When they shall weep for me,
> When departed has my life,
>   Then I shall be happy.'

"And when the sentences were all pronounced, and the officer was about to return to the chief authorities, the four sentenced to be burned requested him to ask that they might be killed first, and then burned; but they were burned alive. When the officer was gone, they took those eighteen away to put them to death. The fourteen they tied by their hands and their feet to long poles, and carried on men's shoulders. And these brethren prayed and spoke to the people as they were being carried along. And some who beheld them said that their faces were like the faces of angels. And when they came to the top of Nampaminarina, they cast them down, and their bodies were afterwards dragged to the other end of the capital, to be burned with the bodies of those who were burned alive.

"And as they took the four that were to be burned alive to the place of execution, these Christians sang a hymn, beginning, 'When our hearts are troubled,' each verse ending with 'Then remember us.' Thus they sang on the road. And when they came to Faravohitra, there they burned them, fixed between split spars. And there was a rainbow in the heavens at the time, close to the place of burning. Then they sang:—

> 'There is a blessed land,
>   Making most happy;
> Never shall the rest depart,
>   Nor cause of trouble come.'

That was the hymn they sang after they were in the fire. Then they prayed, saying, 'O Lord, receive our spirits, for thy love to us has caused this to come to us; and lay not this sin to their charge.' Thus they prayed as long as they had any life. Then they died; but softly, gently: indeed, gently was the going forth of their life.

The following are some of the recent details, gathered from the latest sources of information:

Persecution commenced again within ten months after Mr. Ellis's departure from the island. A new punishment was invented during this persecution, and one of a peculiarly painful nature. Large iron bars were made, with ponderous rings attached, weighing fifty pounds each. These rings were fastened round the necks of the victims, and five or six coupled to each bar. Similar instruments of torture were used for the feet, the ankle rings weighing about seven and a half pounds. Fifty-seven Christian men and women were fastened in this manner, and sent away to different parts of the island where the fever was prevalent, in order that the chains and the fever might aggravate their sufferings. The chains were not removed until after death, and often one of a gang would die, and his dead body remain fastened to the bar with the living survivors. Many died within twelve months, others lingered for years. At the Anniversary Meeting of the London Missionary Society, Mr. Ellis exhibited a bar and ring which one man had worn for four years and four months. He saw some of the sufferers, who, though emaciated, scarred, and wounded, were happy in Jesus, and rejoicing that they were thought worthy to suffer for his name. In the same persecution 250 Christians were sold into slavery, eight were poisoned, and several of the most distinguished and intelligent converts were stoned.

An Account of the Imprisonment of Dr. Judson, in Ava, in the Year 1826.

Adoniram Judson, the well-known missionary to Burma, was born at Malden, in Massachusetts, and at an early age gave promise of unusual abilities. In his sixteenth year he entered Providence College, where his course was marked by an honourable and conscientious career. It was in 1809 that he became the subject of deep religious impressions, and in February, 1810, he resolved to devote his energies to the fulfilment of Christ's last command, of preaching the Gospel to every creature. In 1810 he came to England, when he was captured and imprisoned by the French. On his release he had an interview with the Directors of the London Missionary Society, after which he returned to the United States, and was appointed a missionary by the American Board of Foreign Missions. On February 19th, 1812, Mr. and Mrs. Judson embarked for Calcutta, but as the East India Company was both theoretically and practically opposed to every effort for the evangelisation of India, they were ordered to leave the country and return to America. After suffering much from the intolerance of the Company, he managed to reach the Isle of France, on May 7th, 1813. The opportunities for transit being few, they were obliged to return to Madras. Being again within the jurisdiction of the Company, their case was reported to the Governor-General, and they would have been obliged to return to England, had they not found a vessel going to Rangoon. We cannot recount in detail the efforts of this noble man, of his intercourse with the Burmese Emperor, and his visits to Ava. Owing to the war between the English and Burmese, he was suspected and imprisoned; some account of which, selected from the graphic narrative of Mrs. Judson to her brother, as recorded by Dr. Wayland, will command the sympathy of every reader, and possess a charm which could never be imparted to any narrative re-written or condensed by a foreign pen. :—

"Rangoon, May 26, 1826.

"On the 8th of June, just as we were preparing for dinner, in rushed an officer, holding a black book, with a dozen Burmans, accompanied by one whom we knew to be an executioner. 'Where is the teacher?' was the first inquiry. Mr. Judson presented himself. 'You are called by the king,' said the officer—a form of speech always used when about to arrest a criminal. The man instantly seized Mr. Judson, threw him on the floor, and produced the small cord, the instrument of torture. I caught hold of his arm; 'Stay,' said I, 'I will give you money.' 'Take her too,' said the officer; 'she also is a foreigner.' Mr. Judson, with an imploring look, begged they would let me remain till further orders. The scene was now shocking beyond description. The whole neighbourhood had collected; the masons at work on the brick house threw down their tools and ran; the little Burman children were screaming and crying; the Bengalee servants stood in amazement at the indignities offered their master; and the hardened executioner, with a kind of hellish joy, drew tight the cords, bound Mr. Judson fast, and dragged him off I knew not whither. In vain I begged and entreated him to take the silver and loosen the ropes, for he spurned my offer, and immediately departed. I gave the money, however, to

Moung Ing, to follow after, and make some further attempt to mitigate the torture of Mr. Judson; but instead of succeeding, when a few rods from the house, the unfeeling wretches again threw their prisoner on the ground, and drew the cords still tighter, so as almost to prevent respiration. The officer and his gang proceeded to the court-house, where the governor of the city and officers were collected, one of whom read the order of the king to commit Mr. Judson to the death-prison, into which he was soon hurled, the door closed, and Moung Ing saw him no more. What a night was now before me! I retired into my room, and endeavoured to obtain consolation from committing my case to God, and imploring fortitude and strength to suffer whatever awaited me. The next morning I sent Moung Ing to ascertain the situation of your brother, and give him food, if still living. He soon returned, with the intelligence that Mr. Judson and all the white foreigners were confined in the *death-prison,* with three pair of iron fetters each, and fastened to a long pole, to prevent their moving! The point of my anguish now was, that I was a prisoner myself, and could make no effort for the release of the missionaries. . . .

"During these seven months the continual extortions and oppressions to which your brother and the other white prisoners were subject is indescribable. Sometimes sums of money were demanded, sometimes pieces of cloth and handkerchiefs; at other times an order would be issued that the white foreigners should not speak to each other, or have any communication with their friends without. Then, again, the servants were forbidden to carry in their food without an extra fee. Sometimes for days and days together I could not go into the prison till after dark, when I had two miles to walk in returning to the house. Oh! how many, many times have I returned from that dreary prison at nine o'clock at night, solitary, and worn out with fatigue and anxiety, and thrown myself down in that same rocking-chair which you and Deacon L—— provided for me in Boston, and endeavoured to invent some new scheme for the release of the prisoners!

"The situation of the prisoners was now most distressing. There were above a hundred prisoners shut up in one room, without a breath of air, excepting from the cracks in the boards. I sometimes obtained permission to go to the door for five minutes, when my heart sickened at the wretchedness exhibited. The white prisoners, from incessant perspiration and loss of appetite, looked more like the dead than the living. I made daily applications to the governor, offering him money, which he refused; and all that I gained was permission for the foreigners to eat their food outside, and this continued but a short time."

The noble-hearted Mrs. Judson has left on record a bright example of female heroism and womanly devotedness. By perseverance she gained access to the prisoners in Ava; for seven months did she live near them in a bamboo hut, erected within the enclosure of the prison, where, amidst everything to appal, she gave birth to a daughter. When the prisoners were treated with greater severity, and her bamboo hut torn down, she was still a constant intercessor with the governor of the prison; and when the captives were suddenly removed to Oung-pen-la, where death appeared certain, accompanied by her child, she followed, at all hazards, in a wretched cart, and found shelter in a filthy hut, where, for six months, she endured the worst discomfort of body, and the most exquisite mental tortures of suspense and fear. With the success of the English army came deliverance, and Sir Archibald Campbell ordered the liberation of all the captives.

A Brief Account of the Karen Converts in Burma.

The Karens are a people inhabiting a wild region of Burma and occupying the mountain ranges south of the Irriwadi. They were an artless, inoffensive race, but, like most uncivilised nations, addicted to drunkenness and other degrading habits. But, in one point of view, they offered a good field for the introduction of the Gospel, as they were unfettered with religious prejudices, and rejected with scorn the idolatry of the Burman and the Hindoo.

The Gospel was introduced among them through the labours of Mr. Boardman, a brother in spirit and in calling to the missionary Judson. The first Karen convert was a poor slave, by name Ko-thah-by-u, who had been brought to Christ through the instrumentality of Dr. Judson. Such success was granted to his unwearied labours, that the slave and criminal obtained the lofty title of the Apostle of the Karens; so truly does real Christianity beautify and exalt what it touches. The man had been conspicuous for his wickedness even among his heathen brethren; he had been a robber and a murderer, but he became a "new creature," and was unwearied in the blessed work of preaching the Gospel to his benighted countrymen. He was the first Karen Christian in 1828, and in 1840 1,270 were officially

reported to be members of Christian churches in Pegu, and
as many as 1,000 in Burma Proper. There are now in the
provinces of Tenasserim and Pegu 100,000 Karens rejoicing in the liberty of truth, who thirty years ago were
ignorant of the name of Christ.

The Church of Burma has had its martyrs. One of the
native pastors and forty members of his flock were seized
by the authorities, and after being hooked together, were
flogged and imprisoned. Several old men were promised
release, on paying a fine of 130 rupees; but when the
money was paid, they were again put in irons. The pastor
was next brought forth for torture. He was flogged, and
afterwards squeezed between bamboos—a mode of punishment peculiar to India, and threatened with death if he did
not pay a ransom of 170 rupees. "I have no silver, my
lord," replied the prisoner. "Give his ransom, and take
your leader; if not, we will slaughter him," said the officer
to some converts who were present. The demand was
complied with, but the promise of liberty was not fulfilled,
and the martyr was sent back to his prison. He remained
there two days, when the judge came again, and scornfully
said, "If your God is almighty, bid him take you out of
these hooks." "If the eternal God does not now save me
from your hands, he will save me eternally in the world to
come," was the firm reply. "How do you know that?"
demanded the judge. "God's holy book tells me so, and it is
true." Furious at the calmness of his victim, the judge had
him severely flogged and sent back to his cell. Three days
afterwards he was again brought out, and the judge said,
"Your God, you tell me, can save you; read his book
before me now." "Though I read, you will not believe me,
but persecute me still; but the eternal God, my Judge and
your Judge, the Lord Jesus Christ, he will save me."
"Command him, then, to save you from my hands now."
exclaimed the infuriated judge. The pastor was beaten with
a cudgel thirty times, and sent back to prison. The magistrate urged the judge to kill him, promising him a viss of
silver if he would do so. "I dare not kill him," said the
judge; he nevertheless took the money. In a few days the
magistrate again desired their death, offering fifty rupees
more. At length the judge promised to oblige him, if the
magistrate would marry his son to the judge's daughter.
This arrangement being satisfactorily concluded, the martyr was brought forth; his tormentors commenced their
cruelty by administering three frightful scourgings. "If

because I worship God you torture me, kill me at once. I entreat you," said the martyr. He was then beaten sixty times; after this torture he was crucified and shot.

An Account of the Death of Captain Allen Gardiner.

We rank this noble-hearted man as one worthy of a place among the list of our heroes, from his disinterested zeal and catholic benevolence, and as a martyr in spirit, not to say in deed, though he perished not by the hand of man. After an unsuccessful attempt to carry the Gospel into Southern Africa, and into that portion of Chili inhabited by the Araucanian Indians, Captain Gardiner's attention was directed to the more southerly part of the American Continent, comprising Patagonia and the Fuegian Archipelago. His first effort, in conjunction with Mr. Hunt, was made in 1845, at Gregory Bay, from which, however, he was expelled by the intrigues of the Romish priests at Port Famine. Unweary in well doing, he returned to England, and organised another missionary party, consisting of Mr. Joseph Erwin, carpenter, and four seamen. On arriving at Staten Island, he found that the strength of the currents rendered the boat which he had brought with him useless; accordingly, having arranged with the master of the ship, he proceeded to Tierra Del Fuego. They made Picton Island, and landed at Banner Cove in March, 1848. Their residence here was found to be impossible, not so much from any direct hostility on the part of the Fuegians, as from the inveterate thievish habits of the natives, which necessitated a constant watch over all the stores on land or sea. Finding this second effort abortive, Captain Gardiner returned to England in the *Clymene*, to carry out another plan, which appeared more hopeful. His idea was, that a couple of large decked boats, which could move about in the waters of the Archipelago, would secure the safety of the mission, and exempt it from the marauding islanders. After two years' exertions, he raised the requisite funds, and had two large boats built at Liverpool. They were three-quarter decked, and of about five tons burden; and each carried with her a small dingy. This third and last effort was made in September, 1850, when the dauntless leader, accompanied by Mr. R. Williams, surgeon, and Mr. J. Maidment, as catechists, Mr. Joseph Erwin, and three Cornish fisherman (Badcock, Bryant and Pearce), left Liverpool in the barque *Ocean Queen*. Captain Gardiner hoped to be able to maintain himself on Picton Island, by

six months' stores which he took with him, by the capture
of fish, fowl, and game on the spot, by monthly communications with the Falkland Islands, and by occasional supplies from England. His calculations were, however, in
God's wisdom, destined to disappointment, in one of those
mysterious providences which assure us that it is the glory
of God to conceal a matter. Their stores would have amply
lasted them for six months, and even for nine, had they
found the additional resources in the place which they had
anticipated. Unhappily, at first they could find no fish; and
when the fishing season arrived, their small boats were
sunk, their large boats were too shattered to use, and their
net was lost. They could not procure a sufficient supply of
game and fowl, owing to the want of powder. No attempt
was spared to send out stores, but difficulties beset the
accomplishment of the plan, so that it was found impossible to convey them, and the melancholy result was that
Captain Gardiner and his party perished from starvation.

The details connected with this mysterious tragedy will
be best gathered from Captain Morshead's official dispatch
to the Admiralty.

"H.M.S. Portland, at Valparaiso, February 21, 1852.

"SIR,—Enclosed is Captain Morshead's report of the
death by starvation of Commander A. Gardiner, and the
whole of the party sent out by the Patagonian Missionary
Society, in September, 1850, to Picton Island, the southern
extremity of America.

"Their lordships will deeply deplore the fate of these
devoted missionaries; but this lesson of experience will
have its effect. The earnest application of sanguine minds
for the propagation of Christianity must, in a climate like
Cape Horn, first consider the locality where existence can
be ensured. I have desired Captain Morshead to carefully
pack the remnants that he has collected, and they will be
forwarded to the Admiralty, by the *Daphne.*

FAIRFAX MORESBY,
"Rear-Admiral, and Commander-in-Chief.
"The Secretary of the Admiralty."

"H.M.S. Dido, at sea, latitude 55.58 South;
longitude 66.0 West.
"January 22, 1852, Cape Horn, West, 30 miles.

"SIR,—In compliance with orders from the Lords Commissioners of the Admiralty, dated October 25, 1851, directing me to ascertain the fate of Captain Gardiner and his missionary party, in Terra del Fuego, on my way to the Pacific, it is my melancholy duty to report, for their lordships' information, that the whole party have perished by starvation. . . .

"The following day, January 20th, was devoted to scouring the coast and the adjacent inlet; and after many hours of fruitless search, without a sign of the party, and when on the point of giving them up, some writing was seen on a rock across a river, which we instantly made for, and found written—'Go to Spaniard Harbour.' On another rock adjoining we read—'You will find us in Spaniard Harbour.' On a third piece of rock we read—'Dig below,' which we instantly did, but found only a broken bottle, without any paper or directions. On searching one of the numerous wigwams in the neighbourhood, we read on one of their poles, 'A bottle under this pole,' but we could not find it, although we sent for shovels and crowbars, and dug deep and carefully for it; but it was evident, from some fragments of stores found on the spot, that the mission had rested here.

"Accordingly, the next morning, January 21, I sailed early for Spanish Harbour, and entered it on the same evening at seven o'clock. Our notice was first attracted by a boat lying on the beach, about one mile and a half inside of Cape Kinnaird. I instantly sent Lieutenant Pigott, and Mr. Roberts, the master, to reconnoitre and return immediately, as I was anxious to get the ship to sea again, in safety for the night. They returned shortly, bringing some books and papers, having discovered the bodies of Captain Gardiner and Mr. Maidment, unburied.

"From the papers found, Mr. Maidment was dead on the 4th of September; and Captain Gardiner could not possibly have survived the 6th of September, 1851. On one of the papers found was written, legibly, but without date—'If you will walk along the beach for a mile and a half, you will find us in the other boat, hauled up in the mouth of a river at the head of the harbour, on the south side. Delay not, we are starving.' At this sad intelligence it was impossible to leave that night, although the weather looked very threatening; neither the aneroid barometer nor sympiesometer being very unfavourable, I held on for the night.

"I landed early the next morning (January 22), and visited the spot where Captain Gardiner and his comrade were lying, and then went to the head of the harbour with Lieutenant Gaussen, Mr. Roberts, and Mr. Evan Evans, the surgeon. We found there the wreck of a boat, with part of her gear and stores, with quantities of clothing, and the remains of two bodies, which I concluded to be Mr. Williams (surgeon), and John Pearce (fisherman), as the papers clearly show the deaths and burial of all the rest of the mission party.

"The two boats were thus about a mile and a half apart. Near the one where Captain Gardiner was lying was a large cavern, called by him 'Pioneer Cavern,' where they kept their stores and occasionally slept; and in that cavern Mr. Maidment's body was found.

"Among Captain Gardiner's papers, which I will notice presently, I extract the following:—'Mr. Maidment was so exhausted yesterday, that he did not rise from his bed till noon, and I have not seen him since.' Again, on the 4th of September, alluding to Mr. Maidment, he writes:—'It was a merciful providence he left the boat, as I could not have removed his body.' Captain Gardiner's body was lying beside the boat, which apparently he had left, and being too weak to climb into it again, had died by the side of it. We were directed to the cavern by a hand painted on the rocks, with Psalm lxii. 5—8 under it.

"Their remains were collected together and buried close to this spot, and the funeral service read by Lieutenant Underwood; a small inscription was placed on the rock, near his own tent; the colours of the boats and ship struck half-mast, and three volleys of musketry, were the only tribute of respect I could pay to this lofty-minded man and his devoted companions, who have perished in the cause of the Gospel for the want of timely supplies; and before noon the *Dido* was proceeding safely on her voyage.

"In looking over the papers found in the cavern, I am enabled to trace out the wanderings and many of the sufferings which beset the party up to the time of their unhappy end:—

"February 28.—Mr. Williams is unwell in the boat, and Captain Gardiner removes to a tent to make more room.

"In the beginning of April another of the party (J. Bryant) gets the scurvy; and the disease gaining on the others, they become enfeebled in consequence.

"April 23.—They have provisions enough to last for two

months, but some are very low; and a fox pilfering from
them, they kill him by putting a piece of pork opposite the
muzzle of a gun attached by a string to the trigger; and as
they can only issue pork three times a week, they dine off
this fox, and salt the remainder; altogether, they appear to
have been very frugal with their supplies. I find a notice of
five large fish caught, and an account of the number of
ducks shot, as their powder having been left on board the
ship, and a flask and a half being all they have, they keep
it for emergencies.

"May 12.—Is a note of the biscuit being short, and
altogether, as they have not supplies for more than three
weeks, all (but the sick) go on short allowance.

"May 19.—The preserved meat is out, and Mr. Williams
appears to be failing.

"June 11.—J. Erwin and another of the party take the
scurvy, and misfortune seems hovering around them. Their
fishing-net is swept away, and J. Badcock dies on the 28th
of June, and is buried on a bank under the trees at Cook's
River. After performing the last offices, they retire to their
boat for prayers.

"July 22.—They were reduced to living on mussels, and
feel the want of food, and sometimes the craving of hunger
is distressing to them. Captain Gardiner writes:—'After
living on mussels for a fortnight, I was compelled to give
them up, and my food is now mussel broth and the soft
part of limpets.'

"July 28.—Captain Gardiner writes of the party in the
other boat:—'They are all extremely weak and helpless;
even the garden seeds used for broth are now all out.'

"August 14.—Captain Gardiner takes to his bed, but a
rock weed is discovered, which they boil down to a jelly,
and find nourishment from.

"August 23.—Joseph Erwin dies.

"August 26.—J. Bryant dies, and Mr. Maidment buries
them both in one grave.

"John Pearce, the remaining boatman, is cast down at
the loss of his comrades, and wandering in his mind, but
Mr. Williams is somewhat better.

"September 3.—Maidment has never recruited from that
day of bodily and mental exertion. The remaining remarks
I transcribe literally, and they must speak for themselves.

"'Thursday, September 4.—There is now no room to
doubt that my dear fellow-labourer has ceased from his

earthly toils, and joined the company of the redeemed in
the presence of the Lord whom he served so faithfully;
under these circumstances, it was a merciful providence
that he left the boat, as I could not have removed the body.
He left a little peppermint-water which he had mixed, and
it has been a great comfort to me, but there was no other
drink; fearing I might suffer from thirst, I prayed the Lord
would strengthen me to procure some. He graciously
answered my petition, and yesterday I was enabled to get
out, and scoop up a sufficient supply from some that
trickled down at the stern of the boat, by means of one of
my india-rubber overshoes. What combined mercies am I
receiving at the hands of my heavenly Father; blessed be
His holy name!

" 'Friday, September 5.—Great and marvellous are the
loving-kindnesses of my gracious God unto me. He has
preserved me hitherto, and for four days, although without
bodily food, without any feelings of hunger or thirst.'

"These last remarks are not written so plainly as the
previous day's, and I concluded that they were the last; but
I find another paper, dated September 6, addressed to Mr.
Williams, and written in pencil, the whole being very
indistinct, and some parts quite obliterated, but the following appears to be the correct reading:—

" 'My dear Mr. Williams,—The Lord has seen fit to call
home another of our little company. Our dear departed
brother (Maidment) left the boat on Tuesday, and has not
since returned—doubtless he is in the presence of his
Redeemer, whom he served so faithfully. Yet a little while,
and through grace we may join that blessed throng, to sing
the praises of Christ throughout eternity. I neither hunger
nor thirst, though five days without food! Marvellous
lovingkindness to me, a sinner!

" 'Your affectionate brother in Christ,

" 'ALLEN F. GARDINER.

" 'September 6, 1851.'

"From the above extracts I must therefore conclude that
the two bodies found at Cook's River were those of Mr.
Williams and J. Pearce; and, considering their weak state,
it is unreasonable to suppose they could have survived
Captain Gardiner, who could scarcely have lived over the
6th of September, 1851.

'W. H. MORSHEAD, Captain.

"Rear-Admiral Moresby, C.B."

An Account of the Imprisonment of Manuel Matamoros at Granada, in 1862.

In August, 1860, a young man in Granada, who was being educated for the priesthood, was suspected of Protestantism, and considering himself in danger, fled to Gibraltar.

José Alhama, a hatter of Granada, was suspected of aiding his flight. He was suddenly arrested, his house searched, and himself carried off to a dungeon—his wife and family being left wholly unprovided for. Among the letters found in Alhama's house were some from Don Manuel Matamoros, of Barcelona, the son of a Lieutenant-colonel in the Spanish artillery, and who was himself for some time in the army. Matamoros resigned his commission in the army, principally in consequence of a statement made in the confessional by an officer in his company, who was a convert; but having sent the little tract "Andrew Dunn" to his mother, she insisted upon his recantation, and he consequently confessed to the regimental chaplain, who gave Matamoros much serious annoyance, and obliged him to leave the service. After quitting the army, he was engaged as a missionary, and was pursuing his work at Barcelona, when a telegraphic order was dispatched for his arrest. He was arrested in his bed early on the morning of October 9th, 1860, and on being taken before a magistrate, was asked, "Do you profess the Catholic Apostolic Roman faith? and if not, what?" He answered, "My religion is that of Jesus Christ. My rule of faith is the Holy Bible, which, without a word altered, curtailed, or added, is the basis of my belief. The Roman Catholic Church not being based upon these principles, I do not believe in her dogmas, and still less do I obey her in practice."

He was immediately hurried off to prison, kept for eight days in "terrible solitary confinement," from which he was "only relieved to be confined with criminals." After having been kept for many weeks at Barcelona, he was removed to Granada, and put into the same prison with Alhama. There Sir Robert Peel visited them, and his kind exertions secured to them for a time better treatment. Subsequently, however, they were treated with increased rigour.

In December, 1861, Matamoros and Alhama were sentenced to seven years of penal servitude at the galleys, and Trigo to four years of the same, for propagating Protestant principles.

In September, 1862, another trial took place, and on the

4th of October the following sentence was pronounced:—
"José Alhama to nine years' imprisonment, and Manuel
Matamoros to eight years' imprisonment; and both are for
ever prevented from following the profession of teacher,
interdicted from all political offices and rights during the
term of their sentence, and condemned to pay a quarter of
the expenses each."

Efforts were made to obtain their release. In December,
1860, a deputation of the Protestant Alliance, Evangelical
Alliance, and other gentlemen, to the number of eighty,
including Lord Stratford de Redcliffe, and several members
of Parliament, waited on Earl Russell. Large meetings were
addressed by Sir Robert Peel in London, at Bristol and
Liverpool, in their behalf; and General Alexander went to
Madrid to intercede with the Spanish Government. They
were afterwards set at liberty, but condemned to exile.

The Massacre of Protestants at Barletta, in 1866.

The following is the account given in the daily journals
of the outrage at Barletta, bearing the ominous heading—

"ITALY—THE MASSACRE OF PROTESTANTS.

"Florence, March 27.

"We have bad news from the south. The pleasant,
thriving city of Barletta, famous in history for the brilliant
feat of Italian arms, so graphically recorded in M. d'Azeg-
lio's romance of 'Ettore Fieramosca,' has just been the
scene of a most ferocious outburst of Christian Thuggism.
That religious fanaticism should have produced such deplorable results in the heart of the nineteenth century,
appears absolutely incredible. Unhappily, there is no doubt
about the facts, which are as follow:—For about two years
a small Protestant society has existed in Barletta. Beginning
with two or three individuals, this body had, little by little,
swelled to forty members, who managed to support a little
school and a chapel, in which officiated a pastor named
Gaetano Giannini, a native, I believe, of Florence. The
existence of this modest Evangelical community was a
thorn in the flesh to the priests of the Romish faith, who
naturally traced this alarming spread of heresy to the
introduction of the pestilential Sardinian statute. So far
nothing can be said. Prayers were offered up in the
churches for the conversion of these benighted brethren,

who probably returned the compliment at their own Sunday services. Even this was a polite attention for which both parties might be reciprocally grateful. But so idyllic a state of things was doomed to be abruptly terminated, by the arrival of three *quaresimalisti*, or Lenten preachers dispatched to the rescue of the faith, which appeared to be somewhat on the wane in Barletta. These ecclesiastical firebrands (the names of two of them are Fathers Postiglione and Trentadue) lost no time in denouncing the hideous wickedness of which the folks of Barletta had been guilty, in tolerating the presence of these God-forsaken heretics. And it was hinted, that as the benign influence of prayer had proved ineffectual in the present case, a good oaken cudgel might be advantageously substituted as a means of orthodox persuasion. This pious exhortation was renewed with additional unction on St. Joseph's Day, and the congregations, brimful of Divine zeal, rushed out of the churches with fiendish yells of 'Death to the Protestants!' 'Death to the damned!' 'Hurrah for Jesus Christ!' 'Down with the heretics!' 'Long live the Church!' 'Long live Victor Emmanuel!' In fact, all kinds of cries were raised, any shout and any weapon being good for the occasion. The houses of the Protestants were sacked, *the occupants thrown out of the windows or hacked to pieces*, and the mutilated victims, some dead, some dying, *burned in the street*, an immense fire having been kindled for the purpose. The women were roused to a pitch of indescribable fury, stabbing and stoning many of the hapless martyrs.

"For two hours the rioters had it all their own way, and, as the Protestant minister had taken refuge in the house of the prefect, the place was besieged by the mob, the officials were put to flight, and all the furniture was thrown out of the windows. The under prefect received a blow on the head from a stone, and a delegate of police, who by some mistake was supposed to be the pastor Giannini, received such ill usage, that he died on the following day. In the course of time order was restored, and 400 soldiers are now quartered in the city. As many as seventy-five persons have been arrested, including four priests, a Capuchin, and six or seven women. The prisoners have been removed to Trani, not without a vigorous attempt to rescue them. But the rioters were kept under, and fortunately without bloodshed.

"Thirteen lives have been lost in this lamentable affair, which appears to have been no accidental circumstance, but to have had its origin in certain general measures concerted at Rome for the purpose of maintaining an agitation among the ignorant classes, the ultimate object being evidently to produce a state of things by which the Emperor of the French may be induced to postpone the withdrawal of his troops from Rome."

Thus have we erected our tribute to the memory of many of the noble army of martyrs; but man's praise is temporal, and is bounded by the resurrection-day. The Lord's praise endureth for ever.

Urbanus, Menidemus, and Theodorus, with eighty other orthodox clergymen in the neighbourhood of Constantinople, petitioned the emperor to relieve them from the oppressions and cruelties of the Arians. But the tyrant, instead of redressing their grievances, ordered them all to be embarked in a ship, and the vessel to be set on fire. This infernal order being executed, they perished in the flames.

BOOKS YOU'VE ALWAYS WANTED TO OWN
Complete and Unabridged

CHRISTY by Catherine Marshall   **1.25**
The adventures of a high-spirited young girl of nineteen who was determined to teach in the Appalachians in early 1900. Romance, mystery and suspense fill her year in the mountain community.

THE CROSS AND THE SWITCHBLADE by David Wilkerson
     with John and Elizabeth Sherrill   **75¢**
The fantastic but true story of what happened when a small town minister accepted God's leading and fearlessly faced teen-age crime on the streets and slums of New York City.

GOD'S SMUGGLER by Brother Andrew with John and
     Elizabeth Sherrill   **75¢**
The true life story of an irrepressible Dutch missionary who carries contraband Bibles past armed border guards to people behind the Iron Curtain.

Three fascinating historical novels by Eugenia Price:

LIGHTHOUSE   The story of James Gould's big, impossible dream to build a lighthouse.   **1.25**

NEW MOON RISING   The story of the Gould family during the period preceding the Civil War.   **95¢**

THE BELOVED INVADER   The remarkable story of Anson Dodge and his two loves, Ellen and Anna.   **95¢**

TIME TO RUN, adapted from the screenplay by Allan Sloane   **1.50**
The book version of the smashing movie success. A moving, timely story which penetrates some of the problems contemporary families face.

MAN, HAVE I GOT PROBLEMS by David Wilkerson   **95¢**
Workable solutions to life's difficult problems—drug addiction, juvenile delinquency, divorce, alcoholism, homosexuality, etc., from a man who is dedicated to helping people in trouble.

ORDER FROM YOUR BOOKSTORE

If your bookstore does not stock these books, order from
SPIRE BOOKS
Box 150, Old Tappan, New Jersey 07675
Please send me the books indicated. Enclosed is my payment plus 15¢ mailing charge on first book ordered, 10¢ each additional book.

Name_____

Address_____

City_____State_____Zip_____

_____ Amount enclosed _____Cash _____Check _____Money order (No c.o.d.'s)

S-1

BOOKS YOU'LL USE AGAIN AND AGAIN
Complete and Unabridged